HUSSERL'S POSITION IN THE SCHOOL OF BRENTANO

PHAENOMENOLOGICA
SERIES FOUNDED BY H.L. VAN BREDA, AND PUBLISHED
UNDER THE AUSPICES OF THE HUSSERL-ARCHIVES

150

ROBIN D. ROLLINGER

HUSSERL'S POSITION IN

THE SCHOOL OF BRENTANO

Editorial Board:
Director: R. Bernet (Husserl-Archief, Leuven) Secretary: J. Taminiaux (Centre d'études phénoménologiques, Louvain-la-Neuve) Members: S. IJsseling (Husserl-Archief, Leuven), H. Leonardy (Centre d'études phénoménologiques, Louvain-la-Neuve), U. Melle (Husserl-Archief, Leuven), B. Stevens (Centre d'études phénoménologiques, Louvain-la-Neuve)
Advisory Board:
R. Bernasconi (Memphis State University), D. Carr (Emory University, Atlanta), E.S. Casey (State University of New York at Stony Brook), R. Cobb-Stevens (Boston College), J.F. Courtine (Archives-Husserl, Paris), F. Dastur (Université de Paris XII), K. Düsing (Husserl-Archiv, Köln), J. Hart (Indiana University, Bloomington), K. Held (Bergische Universität Wuppertal), D. Janicaud (Université de Nice), K.E. Kaehler (Husserl-Archiv, Köln), D. Lohmar (Husserl-Archiv, Köln), W.R. McKenna (Miami University, Oxford, USA), J.N. Mohanty (Temple University, Philadelphia), E.W. Orth (Universität Trier), B. Rang (Husserl-Archiv, Freiburg i.Br.), P. Ricœur (Paris), K. Schuhmann (University of Utrecht), C. Sini (Università degli Studi di Milano), R. Sokolowski (Catholic University of America, Washington D.C.), E. Ströker (Universität Köln), B. Waldenfels (Ruhr-Universität, Bochum)

ROBIN D. ROLLINGER
Freiburg University,
Freiburg i. Br., Germany

HUSSERL'S POSITION IN THE SCHOOL OF BRENTANO

KLUWER ACADEMIC PUBLISHERS
DORDRECHT / BOSTON / LONDON

A C.I.P. Catalogue record for this book is available from the Library of Congress.

ISBN 0-7923-5684-5

Published by Kluwer Academic Publishers,
P.O. Box 17, 3300 AA Dordrecht, The Netherlands.

Sold and distributed in North, Central and South America
by Kluwer Academic Publishers,
101 Philip Drive, Norwell, MA 02061, U.S.A.

In all other countries, sold and distributed
by Kluwer Academic Publishers,
P.O. Box 322, 3300 AH Dordrecht, The Netherlands.

Printed on acid-free paper

All Rights Reserved
© 1999 Kluwer Academic Publishers
No part of the material protected by this copyright notice may be reproduced or
utilized in any form or by any means, electronic or mechanical,
including photocopying, recording or by any information storage and
retrieval system, without written permission from the copyright owner

Printed in the Netherlands.

For *Sadie*

CONTENTS

PREFACE xi

INTRODUCTION 1

CHAPTER ONE: HUSSERL AND BRENTANO 13
   1. Franz Brentano (1838-1917) 13
   2. Husserl as a Pupil of Brentano 15
   3. Relevant Doctrines of Brentano 21
      3.1. Descriptive Psychology 23
      3.2. Distinguishing Features of Psychical Phenomena 25
         3.2.1. Presentations as Founding Acts 25
         3.2.2. Intentional Reference 26
         3.2.3. Inner Perception 27
      3.3. Classification of Psychical Phenomena 33
         3.3.1. Presentations 34
         3.3.2. Judgments 36
         3.3.3. Phenomena of Love and Hate 40
      3.4. Ontology 43
   4. Relevant Doctrines of Husserl 44
      4.1. Pure Logic 45
      4.2. Methodological Innovation 48
      4.3. Intentional Reference 50
      4.4. Presentations as Founding acts 52
      4.5. Perception 56
         4.5.1. Inner Perception 56
         4.5.2. Categorial Perception 58
         4.5.3. Perception and Time-Consciousness 59
         4.5.4. Perception of Things 59
      4.6. Parts and Wholes 62
      4.7. Value 63
   5. Concluding Remarks 67

CONTENTS

CHAPTER TWO: HUSSERL AND BOLZANO 69
   1. The Brentanist Reception of Bolzano 69
   2. Bolzano on the Objects of Logic 74
   3. Husserl on the Objects of Logic 79
   4. Concluding Remarks 82

CHAPTER THREE: HUSSERL AND STUMPF 83
   1. Stumpf as a Pupil of Brentano 83
   2. Husserl as a Pupil of Stumpf 86
   3. Intentional Reference 89
       3.1. The Immanence of States of Affairs and Other Objects 89
       3.2. Apprehension of Contents and Objects 93
       3.3. Indeterminacy 99
   4. Parts and Wholes 100
       4.1. *Über den Ursprung der Raumvorstellung* 102
       4.2. *Tonpsychologie* 106
       4.3. *Philosophie der Arithmetik* 107
       4.4. *Logische Untersuchungen* 110
   5. Stumpf's Critique of *Ideen* I 114
   6. Concluding Remarks 122

CHAPTER FOUR: HUSSERL AND KERRY 125
   1. Remarks on Kerry and the Psychological Method 126
   2. Relevant Doctrines in Kerry's Work 129
   3. Husserl's Reaction to Kerry 133
   4. Concluding Remarks 136

CHAPTER FIVE: HUSSERL AND TWARDOWSKI 139
   1. Twardowski on Content and Object 140
   2. Husserl on Twardowski's Theory of Meaning 145
   3. Husserl on Intentional Objects 147
   4. Concluding Remarks 152

CHAPTER SIX: HUSSERL AND MEINONG 155
   1. *Hume-Studien* (1877/82) 159
       1.1. Indirect Presentations 160
       1.2. Causation 162

1.3. Identity	164
2. *Zur Psychologie der Komplexionen und Relationen* (1891)	166
3. *Beiträge zur Theorie der psychischen Analyse* (1894)	167
3.1. Analysis, Founded Contents, and Relations	168
3.2. The Temporal Principle of Extension	172
4. *Psychologisch-ethische Untersuchungen zur Werth-Theorie* (1894)	175
5. *Über Gegenstände höherer Ordnung und deren Verhältnis zur inneren Wahrnehmung* (1899)	178
5.1. Founding	179
5.2. Temporally Distributed Objects and Perception	183
6. *Über Annahmen* (1902)	186
6.1. The Argument from Convictionless Negation	188
6.2. The Argument from Linguistic Considerations	190
6.3. The Argument from the Grasp of Formal Validity	194
6.4. Objectives and Meanings	196
6.5. Conclusion	199
7. *Über Gegenstandstheorie* (1904)	199
7.1. Comparison with the *Logischen Untersuchungen*	200
7.2. The Principle of Independence	203
8. *Über die Stellung der Gegenstandstheorie im System der Wissenschaften* (1907)	206
9. Concluding Remarks	207
CHAPTER SEVEN: HUSSERL AND MARTY	209
1. Intentional Reference	211
1.1. Marty's Early Immanentism	211
1.2. Idea-Dependent Similarity	217
1.3. Husserl's Alternative	223
2. Existence	226
2.1. The Concept of Existence and its Origin	226
2.2. The Real and the Non-Real	229
2.3. Double Judgments and Positing Names	234
3. Meaning	236
3.1. Meaning and Manifestation	237
3.2. Meaninglessness	238
4. Value	240
5. Concluding Remarks	243

CONCLUSION 245

APPENDIX ONE: "Intentional Objects" by Edmund Husserl 251

APPENDIX TWO: "Syllabus for Psychology" by Carl Stumpf 285

APPENDIX THREE: "Syllabus for Logic" by Carl Stumpf 311

BIBLIOGRAPHY 339

INDEX OF NAMES 361

PREFACE

An attempt is made in the following to determine Husserl's position vis-à-vis a number of philosophers who have not received nearly as much attention from posterity as he has. There are nevertheless sound reasons for devoting a study to their relation with Husserl. These reasons are stated in the introduction. Here it may be said that, while this study is primarily concerned with matters in the history of philosophy, its results will hopefully be of some interest to contemporary philosophers who are occupied with a wide range of issues, such as intentionality, non-existent objects, the ontological status of the objects of logic and mathematics, the relation between linguistic expressions and acts of consciousness, and many others too numerous to mention here.

In a work which relies on as many sources as this one there is always a temptation to use abbreviations in order to save space. Yet, the reader all too easily loses track of these and must time and again look up what they stand for. In order to avoid this, I have only used abbreviations for three sources which are drawn upon throughout the study. Whenever a volume from the collected works of Husserl (*Husserliana*) is referred to, it is cited as "Hua". Roman numerals are used to indicate the relevant volumes and Arabic numerals to indicate the relevant pages. The recently published critical edition of his correspondence, *Edmund Husserl. Briefwechsel*, edited by Karl and Elisabeth Schuhmann (Dordrecht: Kluwer, 1994), is cited as *Briefwechsel*. Again, Roman and Arabic numerals are used for volume and page numbers respectively. Finally, the chronicle of Husserl's life by Karl Schuhmann (The Hague: Martin Nijhoff, 1977) is referred to by its main title, *Husserl-Chronik*. Pages are indicated by Arabic numbers. All other writings are normally cited in footnotes according to the customary procedure.

Many of the sources for this study are taken from unpublished materials, namely from the Husserl Archives in Louvain. They are cited by those signatures (e.g., K II 4) according to which they are classified in the Archives. Wherever the signature is followed by a slash, the Arabic numeral(s) to the right of the slash indicates the page(s) of the cited manuscript.

Unpublished materials which are relevant to this study are often quoted at length. The English translation of them is quoted in the text, whereas the original German is quoted in the footnotes. This practice is also adopted with regard to materials which have been published, but are now out of print or very difficult to obtain. Though the titles of German texts are given with their original spelling, I have modernized the spelling of passages quoted from them. Wherever I quote from easily obtainable German texts, e.g., the collected works of Husserl or his correspondence, the English translation will suffice. Unless otherwise indicated, translations here are my own.

This work could not have been completed without the help of many whom I should like to acknowledge here. As already indicated, I have relied to an unusually great extent on unpublished materials. I thank Professor Samuel IJsseling, former director of the Husserl-Archives in Louvain, for kindly allowing me to use them. Thanks also to the staff members at the Archives who have helped me to determine the correct transcription of certain words and phrases from Husserl's Gabelsberger stenography. Professor Ullrich Melle and Mr. Steven Spileers have been particularly helpful in this regard.

In the course of writing I have discussed Husserl and the school of Brentano with various scholars, some of whom have read an earlier version of my work in its entirety or parts thereof. Their many comments, questions, and criticisms have certainly prompted me to meet a much higher standard than the one I would have otherwise met. Among such scholars I would like to mention the following with the utmost gratitude: Liliana Albertazzi, Wilhelm Baumgartner, Reinhard Fabian, Denis Fisette, Rudolf Haller, Dale Jacquette, Johannes Marek, Roberto Poli, Barry Smith, and Richard Tieszen. If I have forgotten anyone, I apologize. Above all, I thank Professor Karl Schuhmann, without whom this project would never have been realized and whose outstanding devotion to scholarship and many extraordinary accomplishments therein provide me, as well as many others, with the finest example that anyone could ever hope for.

R.D. Rollinger

INTRODUCTION

While the phenomenological movement is certainly one of the most significant philosophical currents of the twentieth century,[1] it is nonetheless only natural to raise the question whether phenomenology involves any definite link with science or any aspiration to philosophize scientifically. It is in fact not uncommon to associate it with existentialism or with one of the explicitly anti-scientific tendencies which prevail nowadays. Historically speaking, such associations are quite understandable. There are, after all, *prima facie* compelling reasons to see Edmund Husserl, indisputably the central figure of the phenomenological movement, as one of the main forces behind contemporary anti-scientific philosophy. Most notably, he was the one responsible for advancing the career of Martin Heidegger, who inspires much of the philosophy of this kind in certain academic circles and beyond.

In recent years, however, there has been a growing respect for Husserl among the more scientifically inclined philosophers in the analytic tradition.[2] Moreover, when we turn to what Husserl himself has to say about phenomenology, we see that he insists on "its by no means extravagant claim to have opened up for the very first time and started down the path on which all conceivable problems of philosophy must be formulated and solved in a manner true to their origins, working soberly in the spirit of rigorous scientific procedure" (Hua V, 138). This ambition to philosophize scientifically stems from the profound and enduring impression made by the lectures of Franz Brentano, for these lectures convinced Dr. Husserl, the young mathematician, "that philosophy, too, is a field of serious work, that it, too, can and consequently also must be treated in the spirit of the most rigorous science" (Hua XXV, 305).

Husserl was certainly not the only one to be so deeply affected by the lectures of Brentano. There were many others, some of them very prominent and influential, who had the same mentor. The legacy of Brentano, which includes the direct impact on his

---

[1]For a historical overview of this movement, see Herbert Spiegelberg, *The Phenomenological Movement* (Dordrecht: Kluwer, 1982).

[2]See, for instance, David Bell, *Husserl* (London: Routledge, 1990); Barry Smith and David Woodruff Smith (eds.), *The Cambridge Companion to Husserl* (Cambridge: Cambridge University, 1995); Leila Haaparanta (ed.), *Mind, Meaning and Mathematics: Philosophical Views of Husserl and Frege* (Dordrecht: Kluwer, 1994); Richard Cobb-Stevens, *Husserl and Analytic Philosophy* (Dordrecht: Kluwer, 1990).

students, but which also extends beyond that, is indeed something that historians of philosophy have only begun to explore.[1] Given the influence of Brentano on Husserl and others, the question naturally arises how Husserl's philosophical orientation stands vis-à-vis that of each of these others. Since they often share with Husserl an ambition to philosophize scientifically and also a philosophical development which not only begins with, but often departs from, Brentanian doctrines, it is worthwhile to inquire whether Husserl's departure from these doctrines is in fact as radical and indeed more in step with the spirit of science as he sometimes claims. In this regard the parallels and contrasts which are to be found in the development of his thought with those of other pupils of Brentano should be examined. The purpose of the present study is to investigate these matters in considerable detail.

Besides Husserl, the list of students of Brentano also includes the names of Carl Stumpf (1848-1936), Benno Kerry (1858-1889),[2] Kasimir Twardowski (1866-1938), Alexius Meinong (1853-1920), Alois Höfler (1853-1922), Anton Marty (1847-1914), Christian von Ehrenfels (1859-1932), and Thomas Masaryk (1850-1937). To be sure, if different philosophers have a mentor in common, this is not a sufficient reason to speak of them as belonging to the same school. One may here think of the case of Hermann Lotze, who certainly had influence through his lectures and publications, though there was never anything that could properly be called "the school of Lotze".[3] But all of the pupils of Brentano, or "Brentanists", under consideration here, at least in the early stages of their career, did in fact share a philosophical orientation which they inherited from their mentor. They were moreover fully aware of this common legacy. To this extent, it is justifiable to speak of the school of Brentano.

Before discussing this orientation, it should be pointed out that there are indeed very large gaps in the literature on Husserl's position in the school of Brentano. This is already to be seen from the fact that most literature on Husserl focuses on his later philosophy, whereas a study of his relations to Brentano and his fellow Brentanists

---

[1] See Barry Smith, *Austrian Philosophy: The Legacy of Franz Brentano* (Chicago: Open Court, 1994). See also the literature cited there.

[2] The name of Kerry might here be somewhat baffling, for he is all but unknown. Nonetheless, as will become clear in Chapter Four, there are good reasons for regarding him as a Brentanist and treating his relation to Husserl.

[3] See Georg Misch's extensive introduction to his edition of Hermann Lotze, *Logik. Drei Bücher vom Denken, vom Untersuchen und vom Erkennen* (Leipzig: Felix Meiner, 1912).

must rather draw primarily upon his earlier work.[1] Though the relation between Husserl and Brentano has received some attention,[2] it still has not been discussed as fully as the material requires. The present study, however, is first and foremost concerned with Husserl's relation with other pupils of Brentano. A full treatment of the Husserl-Brentano relation should rather be left for a lengthy study in itself.

As far as studies regarding Husserl's relations with other pupils of Brentano are concerned, only the relation with Twardowski and the one with Masaryk have been treated rather thoroughly.[3] The present study will nonetheless contain a discussion of the former relation, for this is absolutely crucial to understanding Husserl's position in the school of Brentano. There is however no chapter on Husserl and Masaryk, for the *philosophical* links between these two are rather insignificant, in spite of the impact which Masaryk had on Husserl in biographical terms. Moreover, the relation between Husserl and Meinong has by no means been neglected,[4] but it has not yet been discussed as fully as the material demands. As regards Husserl's relations with Stumpf, Kerry, and Marty, these have only been touched upon as peripheral matters.[5] These

---

[1] Some of the studies in which there is an exceptional focus on Husserl's early work are the following: Dallas Willard, *Logic and the Objectivity of Knowledge: A Study in Husserl's Early Philosophy* (Athens Ohio: Ohio University, 1984); Karl Schuhmann, "Intentionalität und intentionaler Gegenstand beim frühen Husserl", *Phänomenologische Forschungen* 24/25 (1991): 46-75; Karl Schuhmann, "Husserls doppelter Vorstellungsbegriff: Die Texte von 1893", *Brentano Studien* 3 (1990/91): 119-136.

[2] See Maria Brück, *Über das Verhältnis Edmund Husserls zu Franz Brentano, vornehmlich mit Rücksicht auf Brentanos Psychologie* (Würzburg: Triltsch, 1933); Dieter Münch, *Intention und Zeichen. Untersuchung zu Franz Brentanos und zu Edmund Husserls Frühwerk* (Frankfurt: Suhrkamp, 1993); R.D. Rollinger, "Husserl and Brentano on Imagination", *Archiv für Geschichte der Philosophie* 75 (1993): 195-210; Herman, Philipse, "The Concept of Intentionality: Husserl's Development from the Brentano Period to the Logical Investigations", *Philosophy Research Archives* 12 (1986/87): 13-33.

[3] Karl Schuhmann, "Husserl and Masaryk", in J. Novak (ed.), *On Masaryk*. (Amsterdam: Rodopi, 1988), pp. 129-156; Karl Schuhmann, "Husserl and Twardowski", in F. Conglione et al. (eds.), *Polish Scientific Philosophy: The Lvov-Warsaw School* (Amsterdam: Rodopi, 1993), pp. 41-58; Jens Cavallin, *Content and Object: Husserl, Twardowski and Psychologism* (Dordrecht: Kluwer, 1997).

[4] Hans Schermann, *Meinong und Husserl. Eine vergleichende Studie* (Louvain: unpublished dissertation, 1970); Hans Schermann, "Husserls II. logische Untersuchung und Meinongs Hume-Studien I", in Rudolf Haller (ed.), *Jenseits von Sein und Nichtsein* (Graz: Akademische Druck- und Verlagsanstalt, 1972); J.N. Findlay, "Meinong the Phenomenologist", *Revue Internationale de la Philosophie* 27 (1973): 161-177; R.D. Rollinger, *Meinong and Husserl on Abstraction and Universals: From Hume Studies I to Logical Investigations II* (Amsterdam: Rodopi, 1993).

[5] This goes for much of the literature which has already been mentioned. For some interesting remarks on these relations one may also consult the name index in Elmar Holenstein, *Phänomenologie der Assoziation. Zur Struktur und Funktion eines Grundprinzips der passiven Genesis bei E. Husserl* (The Hague: Martinus Nijhoff, 1972).

relations will however be discussed as central themes in the present study.

The only above-mentioned Brentanists whose relation with Husserl will not be explored here in special chapters are Masaryk (for reasons already mentioned), Höfler, and von Ehrenfels. Since Höfler followed lectures of Brentano in Vienna and was clearly influenced by them (but more so by Meinong), he can correctly be included among the Brentanists. Still, there is no entire chapter in this study concerning his relation with Husserl because there is simply not enough material to justify such a lengthy treatment of this topic. In spite of claims to the contrary,[1] von Ehrenfels can be regarded as a pupil of Brentano. Like Höfler, he was also very much influenced by Meinong, but he also differs from Höfler insofar as he stayed on good terms with Brentano. Though his philosophical work moreover is to a large extent very Brentanian in character, there will nonetheless be no special chapter in this study on the relation between him and Husserl because there is, once more, not enough material to justify such a treatment.

Now concerning the common philosophical orientation among the Brentanists, it may first of all be pointed out that this consists not only in the conviction that philosophy is to be done scientifically, but also in the conception of scientific philosophy as a discipline which is primarily occupied with psychological matters. In this light it is significant that Brentano's only major philosophical publication bore the title *Psychologie vom empirischen Standpunkte*.[2] A brief list of titles of publications of some of the aforementioned Brentanists also makes clear how prominent psychological considerations were in their work.

Stumpf,
Über den psychologischen Ursprung der Raumvorstellung (1873)
Tonpsychologie (1883/90)

Marty,
Über subjectlose Sätze und das Verhältnis der Grammatik zu Logik und Psychologie (1884/94-95)

---

[1] Reinhard Fabian, "Leben und Wirken von Christian v. Ehrenfels. Ein Beitrag zur intellektuellen Biographie", in Reinhard Fabian (ed.), *Christian von Ehrenfels. Leben und Werk* (Amsterdam: Rodopi, 1986), p. 7.

[2] This work was originally published (Duncker & Humblot: Leipzig, 1874) as the first volume of a more lengthy project which was never realized. It will be the pages from this original edition which will be cited in this study wherever no volume number is mentioned. Wherever *Psychologie vom empirischen Standpunkt* II is referred to, the second volume of the edition by Oskar Kraus (Leipzig: Felix Meiner, 1925), which includes material that had not been published in the 1874 edition, is meant.

von Ehrenfels,
Über Fühlen und Wollen. Eine psychologische Studie (1887)

Meinong,
Zur Psychologie der Komplexionen und Relationen (1891)
Psychologisch-ethische Untersuchungen zur Werth-Theorie (1894)

Twardowski,
Zur Lehre vom Inhalt und Gegenstand der Vorstellungen. Eine psychologische Untersuchung (1894)

This concern with psychological matters is of course a feature which the school of Brentano shared with other philosophical movements in the nineteenth century. One of these movements is to be found in the associationist psychology which James Mill and his son, John Stuart Mill, took up from David Hume. Another movement of this kind is to be found in the psycho-physiology which was pioneered by Gustav Fechner and E.H. Weber and later worked out experimentally by Wilhelm Wundt.[1] But in Brentano's *Psychologie vom empirischen Standpunkte*, published in the same year in which Wundt's *Grundzüge der physiologischen Psychologie* first appeared, we find an approach in psychology which clearly differs from both the associationist and the psycho-physiological ones. Unlike any of the other psychologically oriented philosophical movements, the central notion in Brentano's psychology was one taken from the Aristotelian tradition and ultimately from Aristotle himself, namely the notion of intentionality or, to keep closer to the original terminology, intentional reference.[2] A

---

[1] Mention should here be made also of the psychologistic logics which appeared in the late nineteenth century, the most outstanding example being Sigwart's two-volume *Logik* which first appeared in 1873/78. Of course, the psychological orientation was not shared by all the philosophical schools of the time, for much of the Neo-Kantian movement was emphatically anti-psychologistic. Nowadays one might want to add Frege to the list of anti-psychologistic philosophers of the late nineteenth century and indeed as the most important one, but at the time he did not generate anything like a philosophical movement. Moreover, the range of problems which he treated was much more narrow in scope than the ones treated in some of the psychologistic movements, including the Brentano School, and also in the Neo-Kantian movement. In these schools there are attempts to deal with the entire range of philosophical problems handed down to them by tradition.

[2] Any suggestion here of intention in the sense of *purpose* should be avoided here, but one must also be careful not to associate this notion too closely with reference from a purely *linguistic* standpoint. Though the term "intentionality" is often used nowadays, following Husserl, this is not the term which Brentano used. The term "intentional reference" (*intentionale Beziehung*) is used here, as found in *Vom Ursprung sittlicher Erkenntnis* (Leipzig: Duncker & Humblot, 1889), p. 14, although the terms "intentional inexistence of an

desire, for instance, is to be regarded as a psychical phenomenon because it intentionally refers to the desired object, but an act of imagining a unicorn likewise intentionally refers to a unicorn and is therefore a psychical phenomenon as well. All the psychological investigations in the school of Brentano set out from this notion and then branch out into wide-ranging inquiries in logic, aesthetics, ethics, metaphysics, ontology, and semantics.

While it is no longer in vogue to conduct philosophical investigations in the name of psychology, this does not mean that the Brentanian approach to philosophical problems is simply a museum piece. As it turns out, many of the problems which Brentano and his pupils regarded as "psychological" are nowadays relegated to "philosophy of mind", "phenomenology", or some other discipline with an appropriately fashionable label. The theme of intentional reference is indeed still a focal issue within a wide range of philosophical endeavors, although the relevant investigations which grew out of the school of Brentano are often unjustly ignored.[1]

Husserl is of course famous for his theory of intentional reference and often receives considerable attention in this regard, though it is less often acknowledged that this theory, as it is found in the *Logische Untersuchungen* (1900/01), is at least partly a result from critical confrontations with other Brentanist theories of intentional reference. As regards writings later than the *Logische Untersuchungen*, however, Husserl is very outspoken in his denial that his theory of intentional reference is a *psychological* theory. Thus, if we accept the preliminary characterization of the school of Brentano in terms of its psychological orientation and its emphasis on intentional reference, it may appear that Husserl does not properly belong to this school. If, however, we consider the titles of some of Husserl's early publications, we see that

---

object" (*intentionale Inexistenz eines Gegenstandes*), "reference to a content" (*Beziehung auf einen Inhalt*), "direction towards an object" (*Richtung auf ein Objekt*), and "immanent objectivity" (*immanente Gegenständlichkeit*) were used in *Psychologie vom empirischen Standpunkte* (Leipzig: Duncker & Humblot 1874), p. 115. The question whether the object of intentional reference is somehow contained in the relevant psychical phenomenon, allowing us to speak of intentional inexistence, is an issue to be discussed in the following chapters.

The link with Aristotle is made in footnotes to both of the passages referred to here. In *Psychologie vom empirischen Standpunkte* (p. 115 f., n) Brentano says, "Already Aristotle has spoken of this psychical inherence. In his books on the soul he says that what is sensed qua sensed is in the sensing entity, that the sense receives the sensed without the matter, that what is thought is in the thinking intellect". Here there is of course a definite suggestion of inexistence. In *Vom Ursprung sittlicher Erkenntnis* (p. 51), however, he maintains that the "first seeds" of intentional reference can be found in *Metaphysics*, 1021 a 29, where it is said: "that which is measurable or knowable or thinkable is called relative because something else is related to it". The suggestion of the inexistence of the object is not to be found in this passage.

[1] See, for example, John R. Searle's influential book, *Intentionality: An Essay in the Philosophy of Mind* (Cambridge: Cambridge University, 1983).

they also explicitly indicate an occupation with psychological matters.

Über den Begriff der Zahl. Psychologische Analysen (1887)
Philosophie der Arithmetik. Psychologische und logische Untersuchung (1891)
Psychologische Studien zur elementaren Logik (1894)

The psychology that is found in these works is moreover one in which intentional reference is a central theme.

It can also be added here that the last of the works just mentioned, already written in 1893, is very much in the spirit of Brentano as regards its concern with elementary logic, for one of the lectures of Brentano which Husserl had followed in Vienna (WS 1884/85) was entitled *Elementare Logik und die in ihr nötige Reform.*

Prior to 1894 Husserl was without a doubt a whole-hearted disciple of Brentano. This is also confirmed by the fact that during this period Husserl diligently studied the notes which he had taken from lectures of Brentano and also notes from additional lectures of Brentano which had been copied from other students. It is of course our habit nowadays to view Husserl as a highly original philosopher who blazed his own trail. In view of this habit one cannot emphasize enough what a thoroughly orthodox Brentanist he was. His earliest philosophical intention, as far as the content of his work at that time indicates, was by no means to produce a new philosophical system, but rather to do little more than to work out the Brentanian philosophy of mathematics, i.e., to develop one of the specialized branches of what he believed to be an already well established scientific philosophy.[1] His contributions to elementary logic may of course have been less specialized, but they were hardly unorthodox as far as Brentano was concerned.

If now we turn to the *Logische Untersuchungen*, the fact that the title does not indicate a psychological orientation need not as such be taken as a sign of a divergence from the teachings of Brentano. But when we take into account that the first volume of this work, *Prolegomena zur reinen Logik*, is an attempt to establish the thesis that the tasks of logic cannot be fulfilled without a "pure logic" which is free of all psychology, it is only natural to have doubts whether Husserl at this stage is still a Brentanist.

Doubts about whether he is are soon assuaged, at least to some extent, when it is observed that the *Prolegomena* are followed by a second volume entitled *Untersuchung zur Phänomenologie und Theorie der Erkenntnis*, which largely consists of what Husserl calls "phenomenology" or, using a Brentanian label, "descriptive psychology"

---

[1] This has already to some extent been confirmed by David Bell, "A Brentanian Philosophy of Arithmetic", *Brentano Studien* 2 (1989): 139-144.

(Hua XIX/1, 24). Once again, intentional reference is the central theme in this descriptive psychology. It is therefore no surprise that as late as 1914 Husserl says that he regards it "as the finest fruit of my *Logische Untersuchungen* that one is now finally beginning to do justice to this extraordinary thinker [i.e., Brentano]" (Hua XXVIII, 460). As far as the *Prolegomena* are concerned, it will be seen that the pure logic which Husserl defends there is comparable to a philosophical project of at least one other Brentanist, namely Meinong's theory of objects. Thus, even the turn away from psychology, though alien to Brentano himself, has its parallel within the *school* of Brentano.

It may of course be pointed out that already in 1903 Husserl retracted the characterization of phenomenology as psychology (Hua XXII, 206 f.). Again, in a letter to Theodor Lipps (January 1904) Husserl maintains that there is a "slight nuance" which divides phenomenology and psychology into "fundamentally different ways of reflection" (*Briefwechsel* II, 124). The refusal to characterize phenomenology as psychology, even as *descriptive* psychology, is moreover emphatically stated in the second edition of the *Logische Untersuchungen* (Hua XIX/1, 23) and is repeated throughout Husserl's subsequent lectures and writings. But it should also be noted that the investigations which are found in the second volume of the *Logische Untersuchungen* were meant only as a "first series" (Hua XIX/1, 3), thus to be followed by a second series. This second series, which was left in manuscript, was taken up into his 1904 lectures (during the summer semester and therefore months later than the above-mentioned letter to Lipps) on the *Hauptstücke der deskriptiven Psychologie der Erkenntnis*.[1] Hence, it turns out that even in the very early twentieth century psychology was not definitively demoted by Husserl to a philosophically insignificant discipline. Where he does decisively depart from his earlier psychological orientation is in the 1906/07 lectures on logic and epistemology, for in these lectures he begins to speak of a phenomenological reduction as the distinguishing methodological feature of phenomenology in contrast with descriptive psychology (Hua XXIV, 201 ff.). In 1907

---

[1] These lectures were again held in the winter semester of 1904/05 under the title *Hauptstücke aus der Phänomenologie und Theorie der Erkenntnis*. The topics were perception, attention, imagination, and time-consciousness. The part on time-consciousness was edited by Edith Stein in 1917 and published in 1928 under the ostensive editorship of Martin Heidegger, and is now to be found in Hua X. The part on imagination is to be found in Hua XXIII, which also includes the original text of 1898 that had been intended for the *Logische Untersuchungen*. One may of course ask to what extent this change in title is significant. In R.D. Rollinger, "Husserl and Brentano on Imagination" it has been argued that no methodological innovations are to be found in the *Hauptstück* on imagination. In the one on time-consciousness Husserl does in fact maintain "that Brentano is not aware of the principal importance of strictly separating psychological and phenomenological matters" (Hua X, 401). In spite of this charge, however, and also in spite of Husserl's critique of Brentano's theory of time-consciousness, it is not made clear how the failure to make the "strict separation" in question leads to error.

this methodological feature is given even more emphasis throughout the seven lectures published under the title *Die Idee der Phänomenologie* (Hua II). It must be kept in mind, to be sure, that the phenomenological reduction and the concomitant distinction between phenomenology and psychology gradually came to prominence in Husserl's thinking. While this makes it difficult to pinpoint precisely when he left the school of Brentano, it should be sufficient to say here that he did not do so until some years after the publication of the *Logische Untersuchungen*.

Given both the psychological orientation in Husserl's early work and the emphasis on intentional reference in this work, it will be permissible for us to regard his philosophical views during this time in the context of the school of Brentano. Though the *Logische Untersuchungen* will here be the focus, as far as Husserl's position in this school is concerned, his earlier works will also naturally receive a good deal of attention. Only in exceptional cases, however, will there be any consideration of his later work, especially the philosophy which he conducted in the name of the "phenomenological reduction" or "transcendental phenomenology".[1] Since Husserl's early work is usually viewed in the context of this transcendental phase, the present study is therefore meant to provide a relatively fresh perspective on this work. The examination of it in the context of his relation to other Brentanists will hopefully contribute to a new evaluation thereof, for their cool reception of it (in contrast to the enthusiasm of Husserl himself, his younger disciples, and certain contemporary scholars) suggests that it is best evaluated with considerable caution and sobriety.

---

[1] While it may accordingly be said that we are primarily concerned here with Husserl's pre-transcendental philosophy, this does not mean that the division of his philosophical development into a pre-transcendental and transcendental phase is the only one worth using. If it is used, the latter phase should certainly be sub-divided in some way since Husserl's thinking by no means remained static during the very long span of time (about thirty years) which this phase encompasses. It is also clear that that the pre-transcendental phase, which lasted almost twenty years, can be sub-divided into an orthodox Brentanist period and a Platonist period (inspired by Lotze and Bolzano).

Another convenient and recommendable way of dividing up the development of Husserl's philosophy is by identifying three phases which correspond to his three successive academic affiliations. Accordingly, we may speak of the Halle period (1887-1901), the Göttingen period (1901-1916), and the Freiburg period (1916-1938), as first suggested by Eugen Fink in his preface to "Entwurf einer 'Vorrede' zu den *Logischen Untersuchungen*", *Tijdschrift voor Philosophie* 1 (1939): 106-133, 319-339, and elaborated on by Walter Biemel, "Die entscheidenden Phasen der Entfaltung von Husserls Philosophie", *Zeitschrift für philosophische Forschung* 13 (1959): 187-213. One may also wish to divide the Freiburg phase into the teaching period (1916-1928) and the period of retirement (1928-1938). In light of either the threefold or fourfold division the present study is for the most part - though not exclusively - restricted to the Halle period. While the development of Husserl's philosophy is discussed according to the fourfold division by J.N. Mohanty in "The Development of Husserl's Thought" (*The Cambridge Companion to Husserl*, pp. 45-77), this commentator wrongly ascribes the *Logische Untersuchungen* to the Göttingen period (pp. 53-56). This work was however written during the years at Halle and even appeared in its entirety before Husserl left for Göttingen.

If the transcendental phase accordingly recedes into the background of the present study, this must not however be considered as an understatement of Husserl's philosophical accomplishments and therefore as a bias in favor of the other Brentanists. For Husserl reached the verdict that the *Logische Untersuchungen* were already a decisive breakthrough (Hua XVIII, 8; Hua VII, 230) which left his contemporaries, including the entire school of Brentano, toiling in the rear (Hua VI, 237). In short, if his high estimation of his philosophical achievement is correct, then this should become apparent within the framework of the present study which will thus have implications for an evaluation of Husserl's later writings. This is not to say that the *Logische Untersuchungen* and other early writings of Husserl should not or will not be treated for their own merits. The point is rather that the chapters which follow need not be regarded as irrelevant to the evaluation of his later work as well, as confirmed by the hints at such an evaluation (and indeed sometimes very strong ones) which are given from time to time.

Before I begin discussing Husserl's relation to other Brentanists, it will be necessary to consider the relevant historical background. The first chapter will fulfill part of this task by providing an overview of the descriptive psychology which Husserl and other Brentanists learned from Brentano. Husserl's own descriptive psychology in the *Logische Untersuchungen* will be discussed in the same chapter, particularly with a focus on parallels and contrasts with doctrines of his mentor. While the first chapter will thus shed some light on the Husserl-Brentano relation as such, this relation will not be examined exhaustively.

Not all of the issues which Husserl discussed with other Brentanists arise from a consideration of Brentano's philosophy alone. Besides Brentano himself, the most outstanding influence on the school of Brentano was Bernard Bolzano. According to Husserl, Bolzano was indeed one of the chief inspirations behind his concept of pure logic (*Briefwechsel* I, 39). In the second chapter I shall accordingly discuss the doctrines of Bolzano which were influential in this regard. The same chapter will contain a consideration of Husserl's pure logic in connection with the relevant Bolzanian doctrines. The discussion of these doctrines will moreover prove pertinent to the examination of other philosophical positions in the school of Brentano.

As regards the succeeding chapters, their order is not completely arbitrary. The chapter on Husserl and Stumpf precedes the others, because Stumpf was Husserl's second mentor in philosophy.[1] The fourth chapter concerns Husserl's relation with

---

[1] I add "in philosophy" here, for Husserl had one other important scientific mentor, namely the mathematician Carl Weierstrass. During Husserl's studies in Berlin (1878-1881) he followed Weierstrass' lectures. Though his dissertation on variation calculus was completed in Vienna under Leo Königsberger in 1882, he nevertheless returned to Berlin in the summer semester of 1883 to work with Weierstrass. Even late in

Kerry, for the focus here will be on Husserl's very first writings. The fifth chapter is a discussion of Husserl's relation to Twardowski, because the concept of intentionality which Husserl formulated in the *Logische Untersuchungen*, and which underpins much of his later work, was initially formulated in his critical exchange with Twardowski, primarily in his 1894 paper on intentional objects. While the succeeding chapters, on Husserl's relation to Meinong and Marty respectively, might be read independently of each other, the understanding of them will certainly be enhanced by reading the first five chapters.

Though Husserl's *Logische Untersuchungen* will, as already mentioned, receive considerable attention throughout this study, it should be pointed out that material from his *Nachlass* cannot be neglected here. During his life he published only a small amount in comparison to what he actually wrote. In many cases, moreover, a look into the writings which had been left unpublished gives us considerable insight into what he actually thought on this or that topic. Though much of the material from his *Nachlass* has appeared posthumously, there is much of it which still awaits publication. In this study I have drawn upon both posthumously published and unpublished writings of Husserl, wherever these have proved themselves to be relevant to the topics under consideration. In some cases the annotations which Husserl wrote in his copies of works by his fellow Brentanists will be quoted and discussed, for these, too, sometimes give us insight into Husserl's position in the school of Brentano. Often I had no choice but to transcribe unpublished materials from Husserl's Gabelsberger stenography, which is particularly difficult to decipher in his early writings.

This study includes three translations as appendices. The first of these is a translation of Husserl's "Intentionale Gegenstände", a text which was written in 1894 in response to Twardowski. Though it has already been translated elsewhere,[1] the earlier translation was made from the text which had been published in Hua XXII, 303-348. This edition of the text, however, is not the definitive one, for a new edition which contains various improvements has recently appeared.[2] The translation in Appendix One is made from this recent edition of "Intentionale Gegenstände". In the second and third appendices I have translated Stumpf's still unpublished "syllabi" (*Diktate*) for psychology and logic which are found in Husserl's literary remains and were of great

---

Husserl's career he paid tribute to Weierstrass as a significant mentor (*Husserl-Chronik*, 6-9, 11, 345).

[1]Edmund Husserl, *Early Writings in the Philosophy of Logic and Arithmetic*, translated by Dallas Willard (Dordrecht: Kluwer, 1994), pp. 345-387.

[2]Karl Schuhmann, "Husserls Abhandlung 'Intentionale Gegenstände'. Edition der ursprünglichen Druckfassung", *Brentano Studien* 3 (1990/91): 137-176. The numerals in brackets in Appendix One indicate the page numbers of this edition. All footnotes in italics are the translator's.

interest to him during his years as a Brentanist. These syllabi, which are written out in complete sentences, were the bases for Stumpf's lectures on the subjects in question. Given the fact that Brentano himself published so little of his philosophical work, they give us a rare look into the orthodox views which were espoused in his school in the late nineteenth century. A reading of them, moreover, will especially enhance the understanding of the Brentanian philosophy which forms the background of much of Husserl's early thought.

CHAPTER ONE

HUSSERL AND BRENTANO

While the definitive influence which Brentano had on Husserl certainly calls for a thorough-going study of the relation between them, the present chapter will be concerned with this relation only insofar as it is relevant to Husserl's relation to other Brentanists. The discussion here is nonetheless a rather lengthy one, since it provides the indispensable background for subsequent chapters. Besides some biographical information about Brentano and Husserl as his pupil, some of the doctrines which Husserl learned from Brentano and Husserl's development of alternative views will be discussed. The opposing views in question will moreover be ones which are espoused in the *Logische Untersuchungen* or closely related texts.

1. FRANZ BRENTANO (1838-1917)[1]

On 16 January 1838 Franz Brentano was born in Marienberg, a small city near Boppard on the Rhine. In the same year his family moved to Aschaffenburg where Brentano was to grow up. His uncle and aunt, Clemens Brentano and Bettina von Arnim, have a secure place in the history of German literature. His father, Christian Brentano, was a writer whose fame was restricted to the Catholic world of his day. Moreover, his brother Lujo Brentano was to become a distinguished economist.

Brentano began his studies in Berlin under the Aristotelian Trendelenburg. From Berlin he went to Munich and from Munich to Tübingen where he took his doctorate in 1862. As a student Brentano saw the philosophy of Aristotle as a viable alternative to both German idealism and the scepticism about philosophy in general which had prevailed since the decay of German idealism (i.e., since the middle of the nineteenth century). His doctorate thesis (1862), *Von der mannigfachen Bedeutung des Seienden nach Aristoteles*, was therefore concerned with a topic from Aristotelian metaphysics. Not only was Aristotelianism viewed as an antidote against the current scepticism

---

[1]The biographical information here is drawn from the following sources: Oskar Kraus, *Franz Brentano. Zur Kenntnis seines Lebens und seiner Lehre* (Munich: Oskar Beck, 1919), which includes memoires of both Stumpf and Husserl; the *Selbstdarstellung* of Stumpf in Raymund Schmidt (ed.), *Die Philosophie der Gegenwart in Selbstdarstellungen* (Leipzig: Felix Meiner, 1924), pp. 24-61; Alfred Kastil, *Die Philosophie Franz Brentanos. Eine Einführung in seine Lehre* (Bern: A. Franke, 1951), pp. 7-24.

about philosophy, but it was also seen by Brentano as preferable to the neo-Kantianism which began to come into vogue during the 1860's and continued to attract adherents well into the twentieth century.

In 1864 Brentano was ordained priest and within two years did his habilitation in Würzburg with another work on Aristotle, namely *Die Psychologie des Aristoteles, insbesondere seine Lehre vom Nous Poietikos*.[1] One of the theses defended in his habilitation was the claim: "The true method of philosophy is none other than that of the natural sciences".[2] This conception of philosophy - with its separation (in accordance with the model of natural science) of descriptive from genetic investigations and Brentano's concomitant scorn for the speculations of his German predecessors (including Kant as well as Fichte, Schelling, and Hegel) - is an enduring characteristic of Brentanism.[3] It is therefore not surprising that it was normal for pupils of Brentano, including Husserl, to begin their careers with a profound bias against Kant and especially against post-Kantian idealism.[4]

Brentano became a professor at Würzburg in 1872. But since 1870 he already had very profound doubts about the Catholic faith. While the proclamation of papal infallibility in this year certainly encouraged Brentano's doubts, they were not limited to this doctrine. In 1873 he resigned his professorship and formally left both the priesthood and the Catholic church in general. Though Brentano by and large rejected the so-called mysteries of faith, he never abandoned theism or his belief in immortality. He also found value in meditation as practiced among Catholics.

In 1874, the year after his resignation from Würzburg, he published *Psychologie vom empirischen Standpunkte* and began as a professor in Vienna. His opposition to German idealism suited the Austrian guidelines for education very well. Though his being an ex-priest did not ultimately prevent him from becoming a professor in Vienna, his career was interrupted by his marriage in 1880 to Ida von Lieben. He resigned his

---

[1] This work was published in 1867 (Mainz am Rhein: Kirchheim).

[2] Quoted in Barry Smith, *Austrian Philosophy*, p. 31.

[3] See, for instance, Franz Brentano, *Wahrheit und Evidenz*, ed. Oskar Kraus (Leipzig: Felix Meiner, 1930): "I consider the entire Kantian philosophy as an aberration which has led to yet greater errors and eventually to total philosophical chaos. I do of course believe that I have learned from Kant, not what he wanted to teach me, however, but rather above all how seductive for the philosophizing masses and how deceptive is the fame which the history of philosophy has attached to names."

[4] See Iso Kern, *Husserl und Kant. Eine Untersuchung über Husserls Verhältnis zu Kant und zum Neukantianismus* (The Hague: Martinus Nijhoff, 1964), pp. 8 ff. In Husserl's very first lecture, an introduction to epistemology and metaphysics (WS 1887/88), he speaks of the "dark mist of the idealist or, better, mystical pseudo-philosophy which at first attached itself to Kant" (Hua XXI, 220).

professorship in the same year, but continued to lecture in Vienna for some time as a *Privatdozent*. As in Würzburg, his lectures were very widely and enthusiastically attended. But due to the loss of his professorship his influence was limited, primarily because he was not a member of the faculty and therefore could not direct dissertations or participate in the acceptance or rejection of habilitation theses. For this reason, and also because Brentano published very little in his lifetime, his influence was restricted primarily to the impact which he had through lectures and personal contact. This influence was nevertheless a very deep and lasting one for many of his students.

After the death of his first wife in 1894 and his resignation from his lectureship in 1895, Brentano moved from place to place and eventually settled down in Florence. In 1897 he got married once again, this time to Emilie Rueprecht. He continued to live in Florence, afflicted by poor eyesight and ultimately blindness, until he moved once again, in the wake of World War I, in 1915 to Zürich, where he died in 1917. Though he had no affiliation with a university and published very little during the last two decades of his life, he nevertheless dictated manuscripts in great abundance throughout this period. Many of these, as well as much of Brentano's correspondence and, most importantly, the notes which he used for lectures, still await publication.

2. HUSSERL AS A PUPIL OF BRENTANO

In 1876 Husserl began his studies at the University of Leipzig. Though he attended lectures by Wilhelm Wundt in philosophy, his main interests were in astronomy and mathematics. At Wundt's lectures, however, he sat next to Masaryk, who was to become a close friend and mentor in Leipzig and in later years. Masaryk was nine years older than Husserl and more at home in philosophy, for he had come to Leipzig from Vienna, where he had been a disciple of Brentano. As the young Husserl was struggling with Wundt's lectures on modern philosophy, his friend helped him in this area and, more importantly, urged him to go to Vienna (where Masaryk himself wanted to do his habilitation) in order to attend the lectures of Brentano.[1] Since Husserl's interests turned more and more towards mathematics, however, he did not follow Masaryk's recommendation.

In 1878 Husserl moved to Berlin where he was to study mathematics under Carl Weierstrass for three years. There he also attended lectures of another philosopher, namely Friedrich Paulsen, who made a greater impression on him than did Wundt in

---

[1]Karl Schuhmann, "Malvine Husserls 'Skizze eines Lebensbildes von E. Husserl'", *Husserl Studies* 5 (1988): 111. See also Schuhmann, "Husserl and Masaryk", p. 137 n.

Leipzig, but Husserl still had every intention to pursue a career in mathematics and was interested in philosophy only as a part of his general education. The same applies to Husserl's fellow student and friend Carl Runge who, together with Husserl, attended lectures of both Paulsen and Weierstrass, but later became a distinguished mathematician. In 1881 Husserl, as an Austrian, decided that he could be more successful in this career in Austria and therefore went to Vienna (*Briefwechsel* III, 500), where he finally received his doctorate in mathematics in January 1883. Masaryk in the meantime had been in Vienna since 1877 and *Privatdozent* there since 1879. As Husserl worked on his dissertation in mathematics, he stayed in close contact with Masaryk. Though it is highly probable that the figure of Brentano loomed in their conversations at this time, there is no definite indication that Husserl attended lectures of Brentano then.

Husserl's minor study in Vienna was philosophy, for which he was examined by Robert Zimmermann and Theodor Vogt. But he still did not give up his hope of becoming a mathematician. While it is unclear why he did not try to fulfill this hope in Vienna after receiving his doctorate, his return to Berlin in 1883, where he assisted Weierstrass, was no doubt ultimately meant to serve the purpose of a habilitation there. Since Weierstrass fell ill and could therefore not help him in this regard, his prospects in Berlin looked bleak.

After a year of military service (chosen perhaps as an occasion for reflection) Husserl resumed his studies in Vienna in the winter semester of 1884/85, but this time he did not follow lectures in mathematics. Instead, he began attending lectures of Brentano with great enthusiasm. Though his later account of the matter leads us to think that he initially attended these lectures "out of mere curiosity" (Hua XXV, 305), it appears that he had been intending to shift from mathematics, in which a career no longer looked promising, to philosophy. Since Brentano had been on the horizons since Husserl's initial contact with Masaryk, it was only natural for Husserl to go to Brentano as a guide in philosophy. Moreover, the fact that Husserl had purchased books on probability and statistics in 1884 (*Husserl-Chronik*, 12) indicates that he was under the influence of Masaryk in this year, for these were not only favorite themes of Masaryk, whose habilitation thesis was on the statistics of suicide, but ones which Masaryk and Husserl had discussed in their correspondence (*Briefwechsel* I, 101 ff.). It must however be conceded that Husserl was in addition curious about Brentano. What made him so curious, according to his own account, was the public attention which Brentano received from both friends and enemies in Vienna. It was surely interesting to see the talk of the town for himself.

Within a couple of years Husserl was called "a new star" in Brentano's circle.[1] The following lectures and seminars of Brentano were attended by Husserl:

WS 1884/85:
Practical Philosophy
Elementary Logic and Necessary Reform in It
Seminar on Hume's *Enquiry concerning Human Understanding*

SS 1885:
Elementary Logic
Seminar on Hume's *Enquiry concerning the Principles of Morals*

WS 1885/86:
Practical Philosophy
Seminar on Helmholtz' *Die Tatsachen in der Wahrnehmung*
Selected Questions in Psychology and Aesthetics

Husserl relates that the above-mentioned lectures were primarily occupied with problems in "descriptive psychology" and briefly describes their content as follows (Hua XXV, 307 f.):

In the lectures on elementary logic [WS 1884/85] it was a particularly detailed treatment and obviously creative re-shaping that he gave to the descriptive psychology of the continua with a thorough-going consideration of Bolzano's *Paradoxien des Unendlichen*. He also treated the distinctions of 'intuitive and unintuitive', 'clear and unclear', 'distinct and indistinct', 'authentic and inauthentic' presentations, and in the following summer [1885] he made the attempt of a radical investigation of all descriptive moments which lie behind the traditional distinctions of judgment and exhibitable in the immanent essence of judgment itself. Immediately afterwards he was intensively occupied (and as a theme in a special course of lectures [WS 1885/86][...]) with descriptive problems of imagination, and especially with the relation of phantasy presentation and perceptual presentation. These lectures were especially inspiring, for they showed the problems in the flow of investigation, while lectures such as those on practical philosophy (or also on logic and metaphysics, of which I could use concise notes), in spite of the critical-dialectical exposition, had - in a certain sense - a dogmatic character. That is to say, they made and were supposed to make the impression of firmly obtained truths and definitive theories.

Husserl also relates that he and other students would go to Brentano's home after seminars and have dinner with him. On these occasions the philosophical discussions, often pursuing the theme of the seminar, were extensive and lively. In the summer of

---

[1] It is Christian von Ehrenfels who called Husserl this in a letter (26 February 1886) to Meinong. See Reinhard Fabian, "Leben und Wirken von Christian von Ehrenfels. Ein Beitrag zur intellektuellen Biographie", *Christian von Ehrenfels. Leben und Werk*, p. 17.

1886 Husserl also went on a holiday with Brentano to St. Gilgen, where Brentano and his wife painted a portrait of Husserl, which was later sent to Husserl's bride, Malvine Steinschneider (but later destroyed in the bombing of Antwerp in 1940).[1] At that time Husserl also did his first philosophical work on continua, a theme familiar from Brentano's 1884/85 lectures on elementary logic. There is also a very strong indication that Husserl met Anton Marty on this holiday, for Brentano says in a letter to Stumpf (13 August 1886) that Marty, who had to go away to be with his sick mother, is to *return* to St. Gilgen.[2] Thus Husserl had penetrated into the inner sanctum of the school of Brentano.

Since Brentano was only a *Privatdozent* when Husserl was following his lectures, he could not be of much assistance for a habilitation in Vienna. Thus, Brentano recommended Husserl to his erstwhile pupil Carl Stumpf and thus Husserl went to Halle where he completed his habilitation thesis, *Über den Begriff der Zahl* (reprinted in Hua XII, pp. 289-339), in 1887. Though this work was printed, it never appeared in the book shops. But it appears "almost verbatim" as part of Husserl's *Philosophie der Arithmetik* (reprinted in Hua XII, 1-283), which was published in 1891 and dedicated to "my teacher Franz Brentano with intimate gratitude" (Hua XII, 3). Though Brentano thanked Husserl for this dedication upon receiving a copy of the work from the author (*Briefwechsel* I, 6) and then again some thirteen years later (*Briefwechsel* I, 19), having forgotten that he had done so before, he obviously never read the work, as evinced by the fact that the pages of his copy had never been cut. It must not be inferred from this, however, that Brentano had a low opinion of Husserl as a philosopher, for in a letter to Stumpf (21 December 1887) Brentano says of Husserl's habilitation thesis that there are too many demands on him "to enter into these remote questions".[3] Husserl's work on the philosophy of mathematics was therefore regarded as too peripheral to be of considerable interest to Brentano.

According to Husserl, he and Brentano corresponded very little (Hua XXV, 313). He explains that, while he was developing his own views, he hesitated to confront his mentor with these, for Brentano was often displeased when pupils departed from orthodoxy. While the correspondence between them is more extensive than we might think from Husserl's remark, it would have no doubt been not only more voluminous, but

---

[1]See Herbert Spiegelberg, *The Context of the Phenomenological Movement* (The Hague: Martinus Nijhoff, 1981), pp. 119-122.

[2]Franz Brentano, *Briefe an Carl Stumpf 1867-1917*, edited by Peter Goller and Gerhard Oberkofler (Graz: Akademische Druck- und Verlagsanstalt, 1989), p. 83.

[3]Brentano, *Briefe an Carl Stumpf 1867-1917*, p. 91.

also more interesting, philosophically speaking, had Brentano only been more tolerant of dissent from his pupils.

The divergence from Brentanian doctrines is not to be found in the *Philosophie der Arithmetik*, but rather in the *Logische Untersuchungen*. This work had been in preparation for at least the second half of the 1890's. When it was finally published in 1900 (first volume) and 1901 (second volume), Brentano's eyesight was very poor and subsequently only deteriorated. Given his reliance on others to read aloud or on hearsay, he could hardly devote as much time to the study of this work as required by its bulk alone, not to mention the difficulty of its arguments. But he and Husserl exchanged letters (*Briefwechsel* I, 24-40) regarding Husserl's attack on psychologism in the first volume of the *Logische Untersuchungen*. The central point in their disagreement on this matter seems to concern whether truth is to be ascribed to acts of judging or to objects which are neither physical nor psychical. This disagreement will be discussed more thoroughly below. It will also be seen, however, that the *Logische Untersuchungen* involve more divergences from Brentanian doctrines than what Husserl and Brentano discussed in their correspondence with each other.

In March 1907 Husserl visited Brentano in Florence. Both of them described this visit. It is instructive to contrast their respective descriptions. Husserl reports as follows (Hua XXV, 314):

These days I recall only with the greatest emotion. How it moved me when he, who was almost blind, explained from the balcony the incomparable view of Florence and the landscape or guided me and my wife into the two villas where Galileo once lived. [...] In these days it seemed to me as if the decades since my studies in Vienna had become an impotent dream. Once again I felt like a timid beginner in comparison to him, the excellent and intellectually powerful one. I preferred listening to him rather than speaking myself. [...] But once he wanted himself to listen and received a report, without interrupting me with objections, about the sense of the phenomenological manner of investigation and, in conjunction with this, my earlier struggle against psychologism. No agreement was reached.

In a letter to Hugo Bergmann the same visit is described by Brentano as follows:

He [Husserl] overwhelmed me with assurances of gratitude and veneration, and I would do him an injustice if I believed this to be mere flattery. He also said that he always assures people that I do not really belong among the proponents of psychologism. Apparently he believes that this exonerates me from a dreadful suspicion. The presence of his wife and the distraction due to the many interesting things which Florence offers on the first visit prevented an exhaustive exchange of views. But I did get to hear a few grotesque claims. A more thorough-going discussion might have caused him to forgo them, given Husserl's apparent good will to take criticisms into account.[1]

---

[1]Brentano, "Briefe Franz Brentanos an Hugo Bergmann", edited by Hugo Bergmann, *Philosophy and Phenomenological Research* 7 (1946/47): 93: "Er überschüttete mich mit Beteuerungen seiner Dankbarkeit und Verehrung, und ich würde ihm Unrecht tun, an blosse Schmeichelreden zu glauben. Auch sagte er, dass

20   CHAPTER ONE

There is certainly no inconsistency in these reports as far as the objective facts are concerned, but there is a very definite contrast between the emotional states which are conveyed in them. While Husserl expresses himself in very warm, perhaps even sentimental tones, Brentano's report is full of disappointment about the failure to discuss philosophical matters successfully. It is also clear that a successful discussion in this regard, as far as he was concerned, could only have meant Husserl's recanting of heresy.

It must however be added that, while Husserl may not have been insincere in his expressions of gratitude and veneration, it would not be unjust to accuse him of a certain amount of insincerity in the above-mentioned exoneration of Brentano from the charge of psychologism, for it turns out that he had told Paul Natorp on 21 January 1897 that his work in progress, i.e., the *Logische Untersuchungen* and more particularly the first volume, was "directed against the subjectivist-psychologizing logic of our time (thus against the standpoint which I advocated earlier as a pupil of Brentano)" (*Briefwechsel* V, 43).[1] Husserl's admission to having been a proponent of psychologism was moreover not kept as a secret between him and Natorp, for it is expressed again in the preface to the second edition of the *Logische Untersuchungen*: "As far as the candid critique which I have made of psychologistic logic and epistemology, I may remind you of the quotation from Goethe: 'One opposes nothing more stringently than errors which have just been sworn off'" (Hua XVIII, 7). While this passage involves no mention of Brentano, it certainly implies that he, too, had been a proponent of psychologism, for Husserl's early philosophical thinking, as already pointed out, was hardly anything more than an attempt to apply orthodox Brentanism to the philosophy

---

er immer den Leuten versichere, ich gehöre nicht wahrhaft den Psychologisten, womit er, scheint's, von einem schauderhaften Verdacht mich zu reinigen glaubt. Die Anwesenheit seiner Frau und die Zerstreuung durch das viele Interessante, was Florenz beim erstmaligen Besuch bietet, verhinderten eine erschöpfende Aussprache. Einige groteske Behauptungen bekam ich aber zu hören. Bei dem guten Willen, den Husserl zu haben scheint, einem kritischen Wort Rechnung zu tragen, hätte vielleicht eine eingehendere Erörterung ihn davon abstehen lassen."

[1] In the 1907 visit Husserl made Brentano aware of Johannes Daubert, who was responsible for spreading enthusiasm for Husserl's phenomenology among his fellow students in Munich, many of whom went to Göttingen to learn more from Husserl himself. In the same year Brentano went to Munich to visit his brother and, while he was there, called upon Daubert to visit him on two occasions. According to a letter from Brentano to Bergmann (30 July 1907), Daubert was asked various questions. "In the answers", Brentano continues, "there seemed to be an unmistakable desire to soften the differences as much as possible. The term 'proponent of psychologism' was allegedly meant very innocently. It was thus allegedly not applicable to us [In den Antworten schien ein Wunsch, die Differenzen möglichst zu mildern, unverkennbar. Der Terminus 'Psychologist' wurde sehr unschuldig gedeutet. Er würde so auf uns keine Anwendung haben"] ("Briefe Franz Brentanos an Hugo Bergmann", p. 96). Daubert's report of his visits to Brentano in Munich (*Briefwechsel* II, 54 f.) contains no mention at all of an attempt on his part to soften the differences between Husserl's side (including Daubert himself) and Brentano's.

of mathematics and then, with only slight adjustments, to so-called elementary logic. It will be further argued below that Husserl's arguments against psychologism cannot withstand an interpretation that would allow us to regard them as compatible with Brentano's approach to logic.

The 1907 meeting in Florence was the last encounter between Husserl and Brentano. As both of them indicate, it had resulted in no agreement. Nor was an agreement reached in later years, though they continued to correspond. While Husserl was convinced that Brentano was a mere precursor of phenomenology, Brentano was convinced that the novelties in this phenomenology were merely "grotesque". By the end of this chapter the contrast between what Husserl learned from Brentano and what he espoused in the *Logische Untersuchungen* and related writings will hopefully be seen.

3. RELEVANT DOCTRINES OF BRENTANO

Brentano's philosophical views naturally underwent considerable development from his Würzburg period to his death in 1917. The views which interest us here are of course the ones from the Vienna period, especially from the time during which Husserl followed his lectures. It is in this regard most regrettable that we cannot draw upon Husserl's own notes from these lectures, for the notes in question and also other ones which he or his wife had copied from other pupils have unfortunately been lost.[1] Published material is moreover often of rather limited value, for Brentano published so little, and especially so little of philosophical importance, in his lifetime. The most important publication is of course *Psychologie vom empirischen Standpunkte*, but it must be kept in mind that this had been written just before Brentano came to Vienna, a decade before Husserl began attending his lectures.[2] Some of the notes which Husserl

---

[1] As regards copies of notes from others, it will be indicated which ones are still to be found in Husserl's literary remains. In a letter to Brentano (29 December 1889) he reports his usage of notes on logic which had been copied by Ernst Böck (Husserl writes "Beck") (*Briefwechsel* I, 5). The notes from Böck and, no doubt, from others, together with Husserl's own were donated by him in 1935 to the Brentano Archives in Prague. Stumpf also handed over notes to this establishment, as indicated in *Philosophia* 2 (1937): 404. But the Brentano Archives did not survive the German invasion of Czechoslovakia in 1938. While Brentano's manuscripts, which had also naturally been kept there, were taken out of the country by Georg Katkov and are still extant, the above-mentioned lecture notes were left behind. They have been lost ever since.

[2] Another inadequacy of the mentioned work is that is it incomplete. It is of course not a full-fledged philosophical text, for psychology, as Brentano conceives it, can at best provide only the basis for the other philosophical disciplines. What was published of the work in question consists of only one volume (consisting in turn of two "books"), which is moreover not even complete as a psychology, for in the preface Brentano indicates that it is to be followed by "a book which investigates in particular the peculiarities and laws of presentations, another one which investigates those of judgments, and again another which

collected or copied (or had his wife copy) from others, however, are still for one reason or another to be found in his *Nachlass*. These prove to be of some value for our purposes here.

Among lecture notes of the kind just mentioned are the following: 1) A copy (stenographic, in Husserl's own hand) of notes which Franz Hillebrand had taken from Brentano's 1883 lecture on selected psychological questions (Q 9), 2) notes in an unidentifiable hand from Brentano's 1883/84 lectures on metaphysics (Q 8), and 3) Husserl's copy (in his wife's hand) of notes which Hans Schmidkunz had taken from Brentano's 1888 lectures on descriptive psychology, though only a fragment of this copy is extant (Q 10). While all these notes are taken from lectures either shortly before or after Husserl's tutelage under Brentano, their closeness to this period makes it permissible for us to use them as sources. Moreover, we may be assured that the views which are conveyed in them are at least ones actually familiar to Husserl.[1]

---

investigates those of emotions and the will. The last book, finally, is to treat the connection of our psychical organism with our physical one, and there we shall also concern ourselves with the question whether a continued existence of psychical life after the decay of the body is conceivable" (*Psychologie vom empirischen Standpunkte*, p. v). Thus, even if we disregard the fact that the work in question is a limited philosophical undertaking, it was originally meant to be a rather ambitious one, far more ambitious than anything which would be called "psychology" nowadays. While the considerations of the mind-body problem and immortality are not particularly relevant to the present study, it would benefit immensely from the projected extensive and detailed treatments of the different classes of psychical phenomena. What Brentano has to say on these topics in the only published volume is of course only a preliminary sketch.

In 1889 Brentano "dares to hope" that his descriptive psychology will soon be published in its entirety (*Vom Ursprung sittlicher Erkenntnis*, p. vi). This new work is meant to consist of "essential continued developments of my own views advocated in *Psychologie vom empirischen Standpunkte*", but he again failed to realize the publication of the descriptive-psychological investigations. While his lectures covered a wide range of philosophical topics and not only attracted many students, but also inspired them in certain outstanding cases to become notable philosophers and scientists, Brentano's failure to publish the results from these lectures is no doubt one of the reasons why he does not receive all the attention he deserves.

[1] A letter (c. May 1891) confirms the fact that, after Husserl left Vienna, he by no means disregarded further developments in Brentano's philosophical views. Here Brentano expresses to Husserl the hope of a forthcoming opportunity to discuss "the advancement of my psychognostic investigations, about which you ask with so much interest" (*Briefwechsel* I, 6). The investigations which Brentano refers to here were presented in lectures held in 1890/91. The term "Psychognosie" is used in these lectures as a synonym for "descriptive psychology". They have been published in a volume, edited by Roderick M. Chisholm and Wilhelm Baumgartner, entitled *Deskriptive Psychologie* (Hamburg: Felix Meiner, 1982). These lectures will also be referred to here.

3.1. Descriptive Psychology

All of the material under consideration here is concerned in one way or another with psychological matters. This is no surprise, given what has already been said about Brentano's general philosophical orientation. All of the practical philosophical disciplines, namely logic,[1] ethics, and aesthetics, draw their fundamental concepts from psychology. Logic, for example, is the doctrine of correct judgment. Since judgments for Brentano are psychical phenomena of a certain type, the theory of judgment which is the basis for logic can only come from psychology. Though ethics and aesthetics are based on theories of psychical phenomena of other sorts, these theories are no less psychological than the theory of judgment which is used in logic. Besides these practical branches of philosophy and besides psychology itself as a theoretical discipline, philosophy also includes metaphysics. Since this theoretical discipline involves defences against scepticism and thereby occupies itself with the evidence (*Evidenz*) attached to acts of judgment of different types, psychical phenomena also fall within the purview of its concerns.

The psychology which Brentano advocates as the central philosophical discipline is *empirical*. That is to say, all of its concepts are drawn from our experience (or perception) of psychical phenomena. The controversial notion of a soul which somehow lies behind these phenomena plays no initial role in this psychology. It is rather most convenient to begin with a "psychology without the soul".[2] The phenomena which are

---

[1] It is no doubt peculiar to some of us nowadays to see logic classified among the practical philosophical disciplines, but it must be kept in mind that traditionally logic has been regarded as an art (an *organon*). In the German speaking world of the nineteenth century it became particularly fashionable to refer to logic as a *Kunstlehre*. The practice which is to be enhanced by logic, according to this conception, is of course our activity of thinking. By using logic we can think *correctly*. The increased formalization of logic in the twentieth century has of course opened up areas of logical investigation which are far removed from any concern with enhancing our ability to think correctly. The same can be observed in other areas in mathematics where applications are yet to be found, if indeed they ever will be found.

[2] *Psychologie vom empirischen Standpunkte*, p. 13. The expression *Psychologie ohne Seele* is taken from Friedrich Albert Lange, *Geschichte des Materialismus* (1st ed.), p. 465. Since the late sixteenth century, when the term *psychologia* came into vogue, it was used, as its etymology suggests, to designate a discipline whose subject-matter is the soul. It is therefore understandable that Lange proposed something rather shocking under the above heading. It may however be argued that there had already been a psychology without the soul beginning at least as far back as Hume. As far as Brentano is concerned, he wishes only to *begin* with such a psychology. Cf. Q 9/1: "What is meant by 'psychology'? Some say the science of the soul. [...] Another definition runs: psychology is the science of psychical phenomena. What is thought of here as 'phenomenon' is however not something opposed to that which truly is; rather, a psychical occurrence. [...] We prefer to subscribe to the second definition, not as if we regarded the first as false, but rather because we leave the matter undecided for the time being [Was versteht man unter Psychologie? Die einen sagen, sie sei die Wissenschaft von der Seele. [...] Eine andere Definition lautet: die Psychologie sei

thus given for Brentano's initial psychological investigations are occurrences or "acts" of judging, feeling, and so forth.

It is naturally to be expected for psychology to fix this concept of psychical phenomena more precisely by identifying characteristics which do not belong to other phenomena, namely physical ones such as colors, sounds, odors, etc. Before we discuss Brentano's attempt to identify such characteristics, something additional must be said about the psychology which for him makes up the central psychological discipline. We have already said that this psychology is to be empirical, but it must be added that this psychology is also to be *descriptive*. Such a psychology, in contrast with a "genetic" psychology, has the following task: "To give clarity about what inner experience immediately shows, hence not a genesis of facts, but first and foremost a description of the subject-matter. This part is not psycho-physiological, but purely psychological. We must in advance know how the facts look: and this is shown by an inner glance into the psychical".[1] Genetic psychology is, by contrast, concerned with the causes of psychical phenomena and is in large measure psycho-physiological. It is important to note that Brentano, far from forbidding genetic psychology, maintains that descriptive psychology is prior, just as descriptive sciences are generally prior to genetic ones (e.g., as anatomy is prior to physiology, or as geography is prior to geology).

Two remarks about descriptive psychology will prove relevant here. First of all, one way in which this discipline differs from genetic psychology is in its exactness.[2] While inexact disciplines (e.g., meteorology) can tell us that certain general laws obtain "more or less", exact disciplines (e.g., mathematics and mechanics) can state certain laws without exception. Secondly, while various methods (e.g., deduction and induction) are to be used in descriptive psychology, Brentano says the following of the specialist of this discipline: "Wherever the necessity or impossibility of the union of certain elements becomes clear from the concepts themselves, he must intuitively grasp these general laws".[3] While Brentano is not clear here about specific examples of such

---

die Wissenschaft von den psychischen Phänomenen. Unter 'Phänomen' denkt man hier aber nicht einen Gegensatz zum wahrhaft Seienden; vielmehr ein psychisches Ereignis. [...] Wir schliessen uns lieber der zweiten Definition an, nicht als ob wir die erste für falsch hielten, sondern weil wir es einstweilen ganz dahingestellt sein lassen]."

[1] Q 10/4: "Klarheit darüber zu geben, was die innere Erfahrung unmittelbar zeigt; also nicht eine Genesis der Tatsachen, sondern zunächst erst Beschreibung des Gebietes. Dieser Teil ist nicht psychophysiologisch, sondern rein psychologisch. Vorweg müssen wir wissen, wie die Tatsachen aussehen: und dies zeigt ein innerer Blick ins Psychische."

[2] *Deskriptive Psychologie*, pp. 3 f.

[3] *Ibid.*, p. 73.

intuitively graspable laws, the ways in which he distinguishes psychical phenomena from physical ones may suffice for this purpose. Before discussing these, it may be noted that the aspect of descriptive psychology just mentioned is comparable to Husserl's celebrated "eidetic intuition". While there is no doubt a similarity here, stress must be laid on the fact that the intuition which Brentano has in mind does not involve an ontological commitment to a realm of essences. In this regard it is emphatically distinct from eidetic intuition as conceived by Husserl.

3.2. Distinguishing Features of Psychical Phenomena

Though Brentano thinks that the notion of psychical phenomena is sufficiently clear from examples,[1] in *Psychologie vom empirischen Standpunkte* he attempts to identify a number of features which distinguish them from physical phenomena. Three of these are important for us here. As indicated by the relevant section headings from the work just mentioned, these are stated as follows:

Psychical phenomena are presentations or have presentations as their foundations.
Characteristic for psychical phenomena is the reference to an object.
Psychical phenomena can be perceived only through inner consciousness; for physical ones only outer perception is possible.[2]

Each of these statements will now be discussed in some detail.

3.2.1. Presentations as Founding Acts

"As we used the word 'presenting'", says Brentano, "'being presented' is equivalent to 'appearing'".[3] It is important to note here, however, that appearing is thus understood in a very broad sense. If I merely imagine an object, this object appears to me and is therefore presented. In this sense the appearing object need not be perceived, nor even exist in reality. Besides presentations, two other main classes of psychical phenomena are identified by Brentano, namely judgments and acts of love or hate. If one of these

---

[1] *Psychologie vom empirischen Standpunkte*, pp. 102 f.

[2] The sections under consideration are the headings of § 3, § 5, and § 6 of Book II, Chapter One (*ibid.*, pp. 104-111, 115-120). The section headings are stated in the table of contents (*ibid.*, p. x). The second statement here is marked in Husserl's copy of the work in question.

[3] Ibid., p. 106. This passage is marked in margin by Husserl. He also underlines the last word.

latter phenomena occurs, a presentation is nonetheless the foundation for the phenomenon in question. If, for instance, I wish to hear a piece of music (and I am thus engaged in an act of love), I must present this piece of music to myself, otherwise I would not know what to wish. Another important claim which Brentano makes about presentations concerns their peculiar association with *names*. "If I hear and understand a name," he says, "I present to myself that which it designates; and in general it is the goal of names to summon up presentations".[1]

The thesis that every psychical phenomenon which is not itself a presentation is based on a presentation turns out to be a troubling matter for Husserl. We shall see that he upholds this thesis, but only by adopting the notion of a presentation that differs from Brentano's understanding of this notion.

3.2.2. Intentional Reference

The claim that psychical phenomena characteristically refer to an object is likewise a matter of exegesis and dispute among the Brentanists. As this thesis is stated in *Psychologie vom empirischen Standpunkte*, this "intentional reference" is also called "intentional inexistence".[2] The object of reference is said to exist in the phenomenon which refers to it and is accordingly called "immanent object" or "content".[3] We shall see that Husserl revises Brentano's notion of intentional reference in two different ways. First of all, he allows for certain lived experiences (*Erlebnisse*) which have no intentional reference. Secondly, he leaves no doubt about whether the object of reference is to be understood as something existing in the act which refers to it, for he emphatically allows for cases where the object is not in any way contained in the act. We shall see that the resulting conception of intentional reference is upheld against other Brentanists, most notably against Stumpf, Twardowski, and early Marty, who still prefer to say that in some sense the object of an act is contained in the act.

The difficulties in understanding intentional reference are already manifest in a footnote in *Psychologie vom empirischen Standpunkt*.[4] Here Brentano gives credit to Aristotle as the philosopher who introduced this notion by maintaining that in sensation

---

[1] *Ibid.*, pp. 261 f. This passage is partly underlined by Husserl.

[2] *Ibid.*, p. 115.

[3] *Deskriptive Psychologie*, p. 22.

[4] *Psychologie vom empirischen Standpunkte*, pp. 115 f. n.

and thought the form of the object is received without its matter by the sensing and thinking entity. From this remark it seems clear that, strictly and properly speaking, the object is, at least as far as its form is concerned, contained in the relevant psychical act. This has recently been emphasized "against the grain of a seemingly unshakeable tendency to twist Brentano's words at this point".[1] In the very same footnote, however, Brentano warns us against confusing inexistence with existence "in the proper sense" (*im eigentlichen Sinn*) and points out a number of cases in the history of philosophy, e.g., Anselm's ontological argument, where precisely such confusion has led to grave errors. It is therefore Brentano himself who twists his own words. The tension which is thus apparent in his doctrine of inexistence ("immanentism", as we shall call it) therefore gives way to two different tendencies in his school. There is, on the one hand, Twardowski, who wishes to stress that only in a modified sense does the object exist in the act which refers to it. On the other hand, we shall see that Stumpf and the early Marty give every impression that the immanence of the object in the act is to be understood in the proper sense. In either case, as we shall see, Husserl recommends that we forgo speaking of inexistence altogether and therefore attacks the immanentism of the three Brentanists just mentioned.

3.2.3. Inner Perception

The third of the above cited statements may seem tautologous, since the notions of inner and outer perception, as Brentano uses them, seem to be characterized precisely in terms of their objects. Accordingly, inner perception is *by definition* the perception of psychical phenomena, while outer perception is *by definition* the perception of physical phenomena. But Brentano gives the thesis in question a deeper significance by attributing to inner perception "that immediate, infallible evidence which belongs to it alone among all cognition of experiential objects".[2] This high epistemological evaluation of inner perception was of such importance to Brentano that in his 1883/84 lectures on metaphysics he replied to no less than thirteen objections against it. We shall soon consider certain refinements which are introduced into his theory of inner perception by replying to some of these objections.

Outer perception, according to Brentano, is not only fallible, but it is "strictly

---

[1] Barry Smith, *Austrian Philosophy*, p. 42.

[2] *Psychologie vom empirischen Standpunkte*, p. 119.

speaking, not a perception".[1] What is meant here is that the physical phenomenon which is accepted in outer perception, e.g., the color which appears in sight or the sound which appears in hearing, does not exist in reality. What exists in reality, as natural science teaches us, is rather waves of light which cause sensations of color or vibrations of air which cause sensations of sound. Nonetheless, we blindly and instinctively accept physical phenomena as if they existed in reality. We are however justified in regarding them only as *signs* of the physical things which are crucial to the hypotheses of natural science.

All psychical phenomena, according to Brentano, are perceived. Thus, he opposes all attempts to defend the thesis of an "unconscious consciousness" (*unbewusstes Bewusstsein*).[2] One of the most threatening considerations in favor of an unconscious consciousness is to be found in the infinite regress argument. According to this argument, the denial of an unconscious consciousness implies an infinite regress of inner perceptions. If a given psychical phenomenon is perceived, then the perception thereof is an additional psychical phenomenon, and so on into infinity.[3] Brentano attempts to circumvent this infinite regress by distinguishing between primary and secondary objects of consciousness.[4] While he concedes that the primary object requires a distinct psychical phenomenon in order to be perceived, he maintains that this is not the case with the secondary object. Each psychical phenomenon, on his view, is the secondary object of itself. The perception of such a phenomenon is therefore not an *additional*

---

[1]*Ibid.*

[2]While this term seems intrinsically contradictory, Brentano points out that it is not (*ibid.*, p. 133). The term "consciousness" here stands for any act such as perceiving, imagining, etc., whereas "conscious" here means at least "presented" or at most "perceived". An unconscious consciousness is accordingly any psychical act which is not itself presented by anyone, not even by the "subject" of this act. The notion here is accordingly no more contradictory than that of an unseen seeing.

[3]Cf. Herbart, *Psychologie als Wissenschaft, neu gegründet auf Erfahrung, Metaphysik und Mathematik*, in *Sämtliche Werke. In chronologischer Reihenfolge* V (Langesalze: Hermann Beyer & Söhne, 1890), p. 192: "However much the outer data had to be inwardly apprehended, and all apprehensions are to be attributed to the facts of consciousness, it can still by no means be claimed *that the apprehending itself is again inwardly perceived* - no more than it can be claimed that this perceiving of the apprehending has in turn become the object of a higher perception - which would go on into infinity! [Wiewohl nun auch die äusseren Begebenheiten innerlich mussten aufgefasst werden, und alle innere Auffassungen zu den Tatsachen des Bewusstseins zu rechnen sind: so kann man doch keineswegs behaupten, *dass das Auffassen selbst wiederum innerlich wahrgenommen sei*, ebensowenig, als dass dieses Wahrnehmen des Auffassens abermals Gegenstand einer höheren Wahrnehmung geworden sei, - welches ins Unendliche laufen würde!]" While Brentano opposes this argument, it may noted that Herbart speaks of inner perception and is apparently the one from whom Brentano borrowed this term. The first edition of work just cited by Herbart (Unzer: Königsberg, 1824/25), incidentally, was in Husserl's possession

[4]*Psychologie vom empirischen Standpunkte*, pp. 166 ff.

psychical phenomenon, but rather an internal feature of the phenomenon in question.

One of the restrictions which Brentano makes on inner perception concerns its inability to grasp temporally extended phenomena, e.g., changes and motions.[1] This is not to say that he regards outer perception as superior in this respect. He even rejects Aristotle's classification of rest and motion, which are of course temporally extended, as *koina aisthèta* (i.e., as perceivable by more than one sense, as shape can be both felt and seen).[2] In the 1883 lectures he says the following on this topic:

> No sensation presents as past or future that which is sensed. As no past or future stimulus produces a sensory presentation, that which is presented in the sensory presentation is also explicitly presented as present. What I present as past or future is a matter of phantasy presentation. While all this is correct, it is also correct to say that no presentation of locomotion or rest, and likewise of other sorts of change and permanence, can belong to a sensory presentation. It is accordingly incorrect when we say that we see someone going or standing, or that we hear a melody. [...] Of something past and future the sensory presentation knows nothing at all. The entire time-presentation we owe to the imagination: Motion and rest are therefore not *koina aisthèta*.[3]

While this refusal to allow for the *outer* perception of temporally extended phenomena may be acceptable to modern philosophers, some of them nonetheless wish to allow for the accessibility of such phenomena to *inner* perception. Kant and his followers, for instance, maintain that time is the form of inner sense.

In reply to such philosophers Brentano says the following in his 1883/84 lectures on metaphysics.

> It must be denied that inner perception shows us time. Memory and expectation show us time. But in fact we see something only as present, but not as past or future. A motion without before or after, however, is

---

[1] The theory of time-consciousness to be exposited in the text is only the second one Brentano adopted, of course the one which Husserl learned in Vienna, but which was also abandoned in 1895 for another. This third one was later replaced by a fourth one. See Oskar Kraus, "Zur Phänomenognosie des Zeitbewusstseins. Aus dem Briefwechsels Franz Brentanos mit Anton Marty, nebst einem Vorlesungsbruchstück über Brentanos Zeitlehre aus dem Jahre 1895, nebst Einleitung und Anmerkungen veröffentlicht", *Archiv für die gesamte Psychologie* 75 (1930): 1-22.

[2] *De Anima* 418 a 17 f., 425 a 13 f.

[3] Q 9/41-42: "Keine Empfindung stellt das Empfundene als vergangen oder zukünftig vor. Wie kein vergangener oder zukünftiger physischer Reiz eine Empfindungsvorstellung hervorruft, so ist auch das, was in der Empfindungsvorstellung vorgestellt wird, nur als gegenwärtig vorgestellt. Was ich als vergangen oder zukünftig vorstelle, das ist Sache der Phantasievorstellung. Wenn nun aber das Ganze richtig ist, so ist es auch richtig, dass keine Vorstellung von örtlicher Bewegung oder Ruhe, und ebenso von anderen Arten von Wechsel oder Bestand, einer Empfindungsvorstellung als solcher angehören kann. Somit ist es nicht richtig, wenn wir sagen, dass wir jemanden gehen oder stehen sehen. Oder dass wir eine Melodie hören. [...] Von einem Vergangenen und Zukünftigen weiss die Empfindungsvorstellung gar nichts. Die ganze Zeitvorstellung verdanken wir der Phantasie: Bewegung und Ruhe sind also keine *koina aisthèta*."

impossible. Memory conveys the before and after. One never sees something move. The same goes for inner perception too. If one believes that one inwardly perceives an increase or decrease in anger, one deceives oneself. Memory alone shows time. It may be subject to deception, but inner perception cannot be.[1]

It may be somewhat baffling that in the passage just cited Brentano ascribes the concept of time at first to memory and expectation, then to "memory alone". What he has in mind here, however, is that memory is the *primary source* for the concept of time. Every presentation, according to him, is followed immediately by a memory of the presented object. This process is called "original association". While we arrive at the concept of the past in this way, the concept of the future is reached only by analogy, by "reversing the direction", as it were (see Stumpf's syllabus for psychology, § 25, in Appendix Two).

Before proceeding further in the exposition of Brentano's theory of time-consciousness, it is worthwhile to stress that, as counter-intuitive as it is to deny the perceivability of temporally extended objects, the problem at hand demands that we say something counter-intuitive. If we say that temporally extended objects can be perceived, then we must also say that the present itself is extended or that part of the past or even the future is perceivable. The thesis that the present is temporally extended, adopted in the school of Wundt and also by William James, is not without difficulties, as evinced by the peculiar investigations of its adherents regarding just how long the perceivable present endures.[2] Moreover, it had already been argued by Augustine that the present must be punctual, since any stretch of time can be divided into parts, only one of which (if any) can be present. If this thesis is rejected and we also wish to insist on the perceivability of temporally extended objects, then there is no other choice but to say that part of the past or the future is perceivable. Both Meinong and Husserl were inclined to say this, assimilating the memory of the immediate past as much as possible to perception. Whatever the advantages of such a position may be, it too is certainly counter-intuitive.

Let us now resume the exposition of Brentano's theory of time-consciousness. We might recall that he makes the distinction between determining and modifying terms (adjectives or predicates). While a *rich* person is certainly a person, a *dead* person is

---

[1] Q 8/121-122: "Es muss geleugnet werden, dass die innere Wahrnehmung uns die Zeit zeigt. Das Gedächtnis und die Erwartung zeigen uns die Zeit. Aber in der Tat sehen wir etwas nur als gegenwärtig, aber nicht als vergangen oder zukünftig. Eine Bewegung ohne vor oder nach ist aber nicht möglich. Das Gedächtnis vermittelt das Vor- und Nachher. Man sieht nie etwas sich bewegen. Ähnliches gilt auch von der inneren Wahrnehmung. Wenn man innerlich wahrzunehmen glaubt, dass der Zorn zu- oder abnehme, so täuscht man sich. Das Gedächtnis allein zeigt die Zeit. Dieses mag der Täuschung unterworfen sein, nicht aber die innere Wahrnehmung."

[2] See James, *Principles of Psychology* I (New York: Henry Holt, 1890), pp. 605-642.

not a person. This distinction comes into play in his theory of time-consciousness. The terms "past" and "future" (like "fictitious" or "dead"), according to him, are modifying terms. A sound which is past or future, for instance, is not (i.e., no longer or not yet) a sound. The term "present", however, turns out to be neither determining nor modifying.[1] It is not modifying, for a present sound is most assuredly a sound. It is not determining, for a present sound is nothing more than a sound. Nothing is added to the concept of a sound by designating it as present.

The conviction that temporally extended phenomena cannot be inwardly perceived has at least one important effect on the results of Brentano's descriptive psychology, namely in connection with his doctrine of the unity of consciousness.[2] He maintains that various psychical phenomena, e.g., acts of seeing and hearing, can be perceived together and to this extent the unity of consciousness is indeed an irreducible and primitive fact of psychical life. While some of us would be more ambitious and claim that there is in addition a "stream of consciousness" (as James says), i.e., a temporally extended unity, Brentano does not venture to say this. The unity which he claims is limited to only simultaneously given phenomena.

Another way in which inner perception is limited, according to Brentano, is to be found in our inability to *observe* our own psychical states.[3] Observation (*Beobachtung*), as he uses the term, involves making the object under consideration the focus of attention. It is indeed the confusion between inner *perception* and inner *observation* which has led some to deny the possibility of the former, whereas the distinction between them allows us to see that it is only the latter which is impossible. If, for instance, we try to observe our anger while we are actually angry, the anger vanishes. Nevertheless, as long as we make no such attempt and as long as our anger does not subside for any other reason, we know by inner perception that we are indeed angry.

Insofar as it is denied that inner observation is possible and that temporally extended phenomena are not available to inner perception, rather strict limits are put on the role of inner perception in descriptive psychology. It is therefore understandable why Brentano maintains that an indispensable methodological supplement is to be found "through the consideration of earlier psychical states in *memory*".[4] It must however be admitted that memory is fallible. To the extent that descriptive psychology

---

[1] *Deskriptive Psychologie*, p. 94. The class of terms which neither modify nor determine had already been discussed by Marty, in "Über subjectlose Sätze" (1896): 33 f., under the heading *aorista*.

[2] *Psychologie vom empirischen Standpunkte*, pp. 204-232.

[3] *Ibid.*, pp. 35 ff.

[4] *Ibid.*, p. 42.

must rely on memory, it is likewise fallible.

This must indeed be stressed, for Brentano himself fails to stress it, often giving the impression that psychology is epistemically superior to other sciences. The fallibility of descriptive psychology must not however be regarded as a reason to forgo investigations in this area, no more than the failure to reply to radically sceptical arguments against natural science or mathematics justifies us in forgoing investigations in these areas. However infallible some restricted cognition might be, e.g., a single momentary inner perception or a single *a priori* grasp of this or that truth, it is, after all, difficult to see how an entire science could be declared "infallible". It would nonetheless be lunacy to abandon scientific inquiry for this reason. We simply have to live with the fact there is a middle ground between total infallibility and total ignorance. If descriptive psychology is a science, it is by no means exceptional in belonging to this middle ground.

Before leaving this discussion of inner perception, one final refinement in Brentano's conception thereof should be considered. This refinement comes into play in his reply to one of the objections treated in the 1883/84 lecture on metaphysics. The objection in question concerns whether the pain which is felt in a phantom limb is a case where inner perception is deceptive. Brentano replies:

Here there is obviously a deception, but one of outer rather than inner perception. But pain, sadness is, after all, perceived by inner perception? Of course! Pain, to be sure, in one sense, but not in another sense. Thus someone says of an ugly tone: The tone is a pain to me, i.e., it is a tone to whose presentation there is connected a pain; it is unpleasant to present the tone. The tone is a physical, not a psychical phenomenon. But the pain which is connected to the tone is certainly an object of inner perception. [...] Connected to the presentation of the sensory quality is pleasure or displeasure; but language has linked pleasure or displeasure with the quality itself. In the case of the feeling of pain it is therefore outer perception which is deceptive when one believes that a pain is felt in one's foot. One is deceived about sensory quality. (It is already made clear that quality and feeling are actually different by the fact that in the case of the most diverse qualities the feeling of pleasure or displeasure is nonetheless always more or less the same.) The error at stake here is one in localization. Hence, only that faculty can err which localizes, and the same with regard to those appearances which are localized; but only outer appearances show localization, while the inner ones never show localization. Inner perceptions have no extension, after all. Therefore an error in localization can only be assigned to outer perception. What is false is therefore only the appearance of the quality in the foot; this is however a matter of outer perception.[1]

---

[1] Q 8/114-117: "Hier liegt offenbar eine Täuschung vor, aber nicht der innern, sondern der äussern Wahrnehmung. Aber Schmerz, Traurigkeit wird ja durch innere Wahrnehmung wahrgenommen? Ja! Wohl Schmerz in einem Sinne, aber nicht in dem andern Sinne. So sagt jemand von einem garstigen Tone: Der Ton ist mir ein Schmerz, d.h. das ist ein Ton, an dessen Vorstellung sich Schmerz knüpft, es ist unangenehm, den Ton vorzustellen. Der Ton ist ein physisches, kein psychisches Phänomen. Aber der Schmerz, der sich an den Ton knüpft, ist allerdings Sache der innern Wahrnehmung. [...] An die Vorstellung der sinnlichen Qualität knüpft sich die Lust oder die Unlust; aber die Sprache hat Lust oder Unlust mit der Qualität selbst verbunden. Bei dem Schmerzgefühl täuscht also die äussere Wahrnehmung, wenn man glaubt, man spüre einen Schmerz im Fusse. Man täuscht sich über sinnliche Qualität. (Dass Qualität und

The implications of this reply are far-reaching, for it would not only be the case that the so-called pain in the phantom limb is in fact an outwardly perceived quality to which a feeling of pain is attached, but also all the localized phenomena which we normally call "feelings" are likewise outwardly perceived qualities.[1] One's own body and all of its outermost and innermost parts can only be an object of outer perception. The claim that all localized phenomena are the objects of outer perception alone, however, is especially relevant to us here, for we shall see that some of the doubts which Husserl has about inner perception are the ones which Brentano dismisses in the passage just cited.

3.3. Classification of Psychical Phenomena

Now that we have considered how Brentano proposes to distinguish psychical phenomena from physical ones, we can turn to other relevant doctrines of his. One of these doctrines which was stated in *Psychologie vom empirischen Standpunkte*, and still upheld as late as 1911,[2] is his classification of psychical phenomena into presentations,

---

Gefühl wirklich verschieden sind, geht schon daraus hervor, dass bei den verschiedensten Qualitäten das Gefühl der Lust oder Unlust doch immer so ziemlich dasselbe ist.) Es handelt sich hier um einen Irrtum in der Lokalisation. Also kann nur die Fähigkeit irren, welche lokalisiert, und ebenso bei Beziehung jener Erscheinungen, welche lokalisiert sind; aber nur die äussern Erscheinungen zeigen Lokalisation, die innern zeigen nie Lokalisation. Die innern Wahrnehmungen haben eben keine Ausdehnung. Also kann ein Irrtum in der Lokalisation nur der äussern Wahrnehmung zufallen. Falsch ist also nur das Auftreten der Qualität im Fusse; das ist aber Sache der äussern Wahrnehmung."

[1] Given this analysis, one may wish to know just what the qualities in question are. They will of course differ from case to case. When I burn my hand, the quality to which the pain in the proper sense is attached is obviously heat. When my hand gets stuck by a pin, the relevant quality is sharpness. These however are easy cases. What is the relevant quality, for instance, when I have a headache? Is there one here for which we simply have no name? Or is this a counter-example which shows that Brentano's conception of pain and pleasure is unacceptable? If it does, then perhaps this weakness is indeed a reason why one could be inclined to adopt Husserl's conception of pains and pleasures of the kind under consideration here as involving non-intentional elements. We shall nonetheless see that Husserl fails to confront Brentano adequately on this matter.

[2] In this year Book II of *Psychologie vom empirischen Standpunkte* was republished under the title *Von der Klassifikation der psychischen Phänomene*. This is of course the part in which Brentano argues in favor of his threefold classification of psychical phenomena.

judgments, and acts of love or hate.[1] This classification was a challenge to the prevailing Kantian classification of psychical phenomena into thinking, feeling, and willing. While it would take us much too far afield to examine Brentano's critique of this and other attempts to classify psychical phenomena,[2] it may be pointed out that his classification allows him to account for the threefold division of practical philosophy into logic, ethics, and aesthetics.[3] As already mentioned, logic is meant to guide us in making judgments. Aesthetics and ethics, on the other hand, therefore have the task of guiding our acts of presentation and acts of love and hate respectively. The three "transcendentals" of scholasticism, namely the true, the beautiful, and the good, are moreover construed as the ideals of the practical philosophical disciplines. Logic aims at the true, while aesthetics and ethics are respectively concerned with reaching the beautiful and the good.

3.3.1. *Presentations*

Let us now look at some of the claims which Brentano makes regarding each class of psychical phenomena. Besides the already-discussed claim that presentations are the founding acts, various sorts of presentations are identified by Brentano. This has of course already been mentioned above in Husserl's description of the lectures which he attended in Vienna. In the 1883 lectures on selected psychological questions, however, we find only a distinction between sensory and abstract presentations. While a sensory

---

[1] Brentano gives credit to Descartes for having first offered this classification (*Vom Ursprung sittlicher Erkenntnis*, pp. 14 f.). Thus he quotes (*ibid.*, pp. 51 f.) the following passage from the "Third Meditation": "Some of my thoughts are as it were the images of things, and it is only in these cases that the term 'idea' is strictly appropriate - for example, when I think of a man, or a chimera, or the sky, or an angel, or God. Other thoughts have various additional forms: thus when I will, or am afraid, or affirm, or deny, there is always a particular thing which I take as the object of my thought, but my thought includes something more than the likeness of the thing. Some thoughts in this category are called volitions or emotions, while others are called judgements" (translated by John Cottingham et al., in *The Philosophical Writings of Descartes* II [Cambridge: Cambridge University, 1984], 25 f.). Brentano takes "thoughts" (*cogitationes*) as equivalent with "psychical acts". While Descartes however apparently classifies emotions and volitions together with judgments, Brentano insists, contrary to Windelband and also contrary to the impression which Descartes gives elsewhere, that judgments, on the Cartesian view, are not volitions (*Vom Ursprung sittlicher Erkenntnis*, pp. 52 ff.). Brentano has difficulties with another one of Descartes' claims, also put forward in the "Third Meditation", namely that evidence belongs to ideas. As will be seen below, Brentano insists that only judgments can be evident. While he also allows for the *analogue* of evidence in the case of phenomena of love and hate, presentations are not given credit for having evidence in the proper sense or by analogy.

[2] *Psychologie vom empirischen Standpunkte*, pp. 233 ff.

[3] *Ibid.*, pp. 340 ff.

presentation is a sensation or the founding presentation of an inner perception, an abstract presentation is, "in relation to this, a simplification of the presentations".[1] This distinction, however, made it difficult for Brentano to find a place for phantasy presentations. In this light he came to regard presentations as differing in their degrees of authenticity (*Eigentlichkeit*). The extreme case of authenticity is that of intuitions (*Anschauungen*), i.e., sensory presentations in the sense already indicated. While the extreme case of inauthentic presentations is for him to be found in contradictory concepts such as "round square", he allows for presentations which lie between the two extremes. Among these are phantasy presentations, which only approximate intuitions.[2]

Brentano advocates an empiricism which can be elucidated only in connection with his theory of presentations.[3] According to this empiricism, abstract presentations (i.e., concepts) are in all cases derived from concrete ones (i.e., intuitions). By no means is this an empiricism in which it is claimed that *sensations* are the origins of all concepts, for concepts such as "willing" and "inferring":

stem from intuitions of psychical content [i.e., inner intuitions]. This is where the concepts "purpose, "cause" (we notice, for instance, a causal connection between our belief in the premises and our belief in the conclusion), "impossibility" and "necessity" (we obtain them from judgments which affirm or reject something not simply assertorically, but rather - as one likes to express oneself - apodictically) and many others which some moderns, having failed in fathoming their true origin, wanted to regard as categories given from the outset.[4]

This is an empiricism in the Lockean sense, not to be confused with other varieties of empiricism, most notably the kind advocated by Mill, according to which all general judgments can only be legitimized through induction.

It is in this light that we must construe Brentano's rather extreme pronouncements in favor of experience as the foundation of science, as found at the beginning of his

---

[1] Q 9/31: "... im Verhältnis dazu eine Vereinfachung der Vorstellungen." A third class of presentations which, according to Brentano, is sometimes added to this list is that of *a priori* presentations, i.e., innate ideas à la Descartes and Leibniz or Kantian categories. As we shall see, however, he is clearly in favor of the Lockean theory, according to which there are no such ideas.

[2] For a fuller discussion of these matters, see R.D. Rollinger, "Husserl and Brentano on Imagination".

[3] Brentano's empiricism has rightly been emphasized by Rudolf Haller, "Franz Brentano, ein Philosoph des Empirismus", *Brentano Studien* 1 (1988): 19-30. As regards the compatibility between this empiricism and the allowance for *a priori* cognitions, see Johann C. Marek, "Psychognosie - Geognosie: Apriorisches und Empirisches in der desriptiven Psychologie Brentanos", *Brentano Studien* 2 (1989): 53-62.

[4] *Vom Ursprung sittlicher Erkenntnis*, p. 51.

1887 lecture on descriptive psychology:[1]

Our science or in any case the essentially most proximate parts are based on experience as its foundation. Due to the fact that the middle ages did not sufficiently take it as the foundation, they remained unsuccessful in their efforts; they did not however have contempt for experience, but failed to take possession of it. Contempt began with Hegel. Today that statement [in favor of experience as the foundation of science] is more unshakeable than ever.

Since all concepts are derived from experience, science cannot afford to despise experience. We shall see that in the *Logische Untersuchungen* Husserl put forward criticisms of empiricism. When it comes time to discuss these criticisms, we shall consider whether these are effective against Brentano.

3.3.2. Judgments

Now let us discuss Brentano's theory of judgments. These are of course regarded as phenomena which are founded on presentations. One way in which it might be suggested that they are thus founded is in terms of their complexity. That is to say, it might be thought that every judgment is no more than a combination of presentations. While this view had been advocated by many of Brentano's predecessors, especially Kant,[2] he himself altogether rejects it. A mere combination of presentations, according to him, is itself a presentation, albeit a complex one, and not a judgment. The combination of the presentation of green and that of a tree, for instance, may yield the presentation of a green tree, but this presentation is by no means equivalent to the judgment that a tree is green or that a green tree exists. This judgment is brought about if, in addition to presenting the green tree, this object or, more precisely, *its existence* is also accepted. The judgment that the green tree does not exist, moreover, is brought about when the existence of the presented object in question is rejected.

---

[1] Q 10/1: "Unsere Wissenschaft oder doch die wesentlich nächsten Teile ruhen auf der Erfahrung als Grundlage. Weil das Mittelalter sie nicht genug zur Grundlage nahm, blieb es in seinen Versuchen unglücklich; verachtet hat man sie aber nicht, nur eben nicht besessen. Jenes kam erst mit Hegel. Heute steht jener Satz fester als je."

[2] See, for instance, *Prolegomena zu einer jeden künftigen Metaphysik*, edited by Karl Vorländer (Leipzig: Felix Meiner, 1920), § 22, p. 63: "The union of presentations in a consciousness is a judgment". This is not just a casual remark, for it goes together with Kant's division of judgments into synthetic and analytic. A synthetic judgment is one whose predicate adds something to the subject, whereas the predicate of an analytic judgment is already contained in the subject. In either case the judgment has a subject-predicate form. The presentations which are allegedly combined in a judgment are of course the subject-presentation and predicate-presentation.

All judgments are accordingly characterized as existential, their underlying presentations being called their "matter" and their affirmative or negative character being called their "quality". The traditional distinction between existential and categorical (predicative) judgments is therefore not accepted by Brentano. Judgments which are explicitly stated as categorical, he insists, can always be reformulated in accordance with his conception. On this point he feels compelled to meet the challenge posed by John Stuart Mill, who maintained that such a judgment as "the centaur is a fiction of the poets" is a case where something is predicated of a subject whose existence is not affirmed.[1] According to Brentano, however, this judgment can be conveyed by saying: "There is a poetic fiction which conceives a human upper body with the torso of a horse united into one living being".[2] It is therefore a certain *fiction* which is accepted in the case cited by Mill. Moreover, when the centaur is characterized as something made up (*fingiert*) by the poets, Brentano is quick to point out that this "being made up" has a modifying effect, just as "dead" does when we speak of a dead human being.[3] As we are by no means committed to the conclusion that a certain human being exists when we say that this human being is dead (and thus that there *is* a dead human being), we are likewise not committed to positing the existence of a centaur when we judge that it *is* a fiction of the poets (and thus that there is a fiction of the sort already described).

Brentano saw great implications for logic in his theory of judgment. This can be seen in his attempt to construe all universal judgments as negative and all particular judgments as affirmative. The universal judgment in its traditional formulation, e.g., "all human beings are mortal", may appear to be affirmative, but when it is reformulated as Brentano prescribes, i.e., "there is no human being which is not mortal", it turns out to be negative. Thus, it becomes clear that the particular judgment that some human beings are mortal must not be inferred from the universal one under consideration. Likewise, the universal judgment "no plants are animals" is construed as "there is no plant which is an animal" and therefore as such does not imply that some plants are not animals.

The alleged relevance of the descriptive psychology of judgment to logic is especially important here in view of the fact that Husserl argues at length that logic as a practical discipline cannot be founded on psychology alone, but also on a pure logic which concerns itself with propositions as ideal objects and not with acts of judging.

---

[1] *A System of Logic*, I.4.1.

[2] *Psychologie vom empirischen Standpunkte* I, p. 287 n.

[3] *Ibid.*, p. 288.

While these ideal objects become the primary bearers of truth and falsity for Husserl, Brentano adhered to the view that truth and falsity are primarily ascribable to acts of judging.[1] To be sure, it is acknowledged by Brentano that truth and falsity are *equivocally* ascribable to various objects, including things such as money, friends, and of course the linguistic expressions (declarative sentences) which manifest acts of judging. But in all these cases we may identify *judgments* which are the relevant bearers of truth or falsity in the strict and proper sense. The application of these predicates beyond the sphere of judgment, in other words, is always derived from its application in this sphere. Someone is a true friend, for instance, only insofar as the judgment that this person is a friend is true.

Given Brentano's conception of logic as the doctrine of correct judgment and his insistence that this practical discipline is derived from the psychology of judgment, the question arises as to how he understands the laws of logic. If these were laws about judgments, then they would apparently have to do with limitations on the judgments we can make. The law of contradiction, for instance, would tell us "that the appearance of any positive mode of consciousness cannot occur without excluding a correlative negative mode; and that the negative mode cannot occur without excluding the correlative positive mode".[2] Accordingly it would be impossible for an affirmation and the corresponding negation to occur simultaneously in the same consciousness. Such a formulation of the law of contradiction and of the laws of logic is however not the one accepted by Brentano. He points out that there are, after all, philosophers such as Hegel and (to a more limited extent) Trendelenburg (Brentano's own mentor) who deny the law of contradiction and are indeed eager to point out concrete examples where contradictions obtain.[3] The belief in these alleged examples, a belief which Brentano regards as sincerely held by its advocates, would be impossible if this law were construed in accordance with the above-cited conception. How, then, should this law and other laws of logic be conceived? We shall come back to this point in our discussion of Husserl's critique of psychologism.

As only judgments can be true or false, they are also the only psychical phenomena which can be evident or blind. The contrast can be clarified by comparing inner and outer perceptions, both of which belong to the class of judgments rather than presenta-

---

[1] Brentano, *Wahrheit und Evidenz*, ed. Oskar Kraus (Leipzig: Felix Meiner, 1930), p. 6.

[2] John Stuart Mill, *An Examination of Sir William Hamilton's Philosophy and of the Principal Philosophical Questions discussed in his Writings* (London, 1878), p. 491. Here Mill expresses his agreement with Herbert Spencer. The same passage is cited by Husserl (Hua XVIII, 90), who says that it is an "oversight when Spencer appeals to the law of the excluded middle rather than the law of contradiction".

[3] Q 8/159 f.

tions.[1] As already pointed out, Brentano regards the objects of outer perceptions as not actually existent at all. Since these judgments are accordingly false, they are obviously blind. Only by instinct do we affirm the objects of our sensations. Other blind judgments, however, are habitual rather than instinctive. Many of the prejudices which we learn from early childhood on are blind judgments of the habitual kind. Inner perceptions, however, are clear-cut cases where we affirm the object with evidence. This is not to say that Brentano regards these as the only instances of evident judgments, for he also maintains that in axioms we can likewise judge with evidence and indeed with the same immediacy whereby we cognize through inner perception. By drawing inferences, moreover, we can also judge evidently, but in this case the resulting judgments are *mediately* evident. It is important to note that Brentano explicitly rejects the view that evidence of any kind at all is not to be identified with a feeling of compulsion or one of intensity, or indeed with a feeling of any kind, contrary to what Hume and some nineteenth century philosophers (e.g., Sigwart) have maintained.

It is nonetheless obvious that Brentano's theory of evidence has much in common with British empiricism, above all in his stress on inner perceptions as assertoric judgments with immediate evidence and the cognition of axioms as apodictic judgments with immediate evidence. Between British empiricism and Brentano there was of course Kant. Among Brentano's contemporaries, as already indicated, there was a rather prevalent Neo-Kantian movement which could not simply be ignored. Since the distinction between two types of judgment *a priori*, namely analytic and synthetic ones, was a major innovation which Kant had introduced and was by no means forgotten in the nineteenth century, Brentano had to come to grips with this distinction. As is well known, judgments are characterized by Kant as *a priori* insofar as they are both universal and necessary. The analytic ones, however, are distinguished from the synthetic ones in two different ways. They are said to be the judgments in which the predicates are included in the subjects, but they are also said to be the ones whose denial would defy the law of contradiction. Synthetic judgments, on the other hand, may be characterized negatively: either as those judgments whose predicates are not included in the subject or as those whose denial would indeed be false, but certainly not contradictory. The most controversial Kantian thesis regarding these matters had been for a long time the assertion that there are indeed judgments which are both synthetic and *a priori*. On Kant's view, these are to be found in arithmetic and geometry, but also in the foundations of the natural sciences.

The question which concerns us now is how Brentano stands on this matter. It is of

---

[1] *Psychologie vom empirischen Standpunkte* I, pp. 276 ff. *Vom Ursprung sittlicher Erkenntnis*, pp. 75 f.

course clear that the characterization of analytic judgments as ones in which the predicates are included in the subjects cannot be suitable to him, for he maintains that the alleged subject-predicate form of judgments is only a linguistic dressing, to be replaced by the logically correct existential form. Of course, he does maintain that there are some judgments, e.g., "AB is A" (or better: "AB which is not A does not exist"), which are true insofar as their denial would defy the law of contradiction. The crucial question is accordingly whether he maintains that all the judgments which are both universally and necessarily true are analytic in the sense just indicated. In the 1883/84 lecture on metaphysics he maintains emphatically that they are and accordingly denies the Kantian thesis that there are synthetic *a priori* judgments.

Without entering into details about his criticisms of various peculiarities in Kant's attempt to support this thesis, it should be pointed out that he especially attacks Kant's denial that analytic judgments are "informative" ones (*Erweiterungsurteile*). Here Brentano maintains that we can speak of informative judgments in two different senses. "The judgment 'A is A' brings, to be sure, no new concept; the presentation is not enriched. It is however another matter whether or not knowledge is enriched. A alone contains no judgment. If, however, we say 'A is A', knowledge is nonetheless enriched when one progresses from the concept to the judgment".[1] By failing to appreciate this sense in which analytic judgments are informative, it is only natural that they have not been assigned an important role in science.

Brentano's denial that there are synthetic *a priori* judgments has been discussed here because, as will be seen later, Husserl diverges from his mentor in this regard. We shall also see that this divergence met with great disapproval from Stumpf.

3.3.3. Phenomena of Love and Hate

We now turn to a discussion of the third class of psychical phenomena, namely acts of love and hate. While Kant and his followers distinguished feeling and willing as two distinct classes, Brentano insists that they belong to the same class. Their belonging together is confirmed not only by inner perception,[2] but also by the consideration of series such as the following one: "sadness - longing for the missed good - hope that it will become ours - desire to obtain it - courage to undertake the effort - decision to

---

[1] Q 8/207: "Das Urteil A ist A bringt zwar keinen neuen Begriff, die Vorstellung wird nicht bereichert. Etwas anderes ist aber, ob nicht die Erkenntnis bereichert wird. A allein enthält kein Urteil. Wenn wir aber sagen, A ist A, so ist doch die Erkenntnis bereichert, wenn man vom Begriffe zum Urteile fortschreitet."

[2] *Psychologie vom empirischen Standpunkte*, p. 307.

perform the deed".[1] While an instance of what is ordinarily called "feeling" lies at one extreme and an instance of what is ordinarily called "willing" lies at the other extreme, each phenomenon differs from the adjacent one only by degree and not by a specific difference. Doubts may arise, however, if we compare the series in question with a series of gradually varied colors. We may, for instance, consider a surface which is colored red on one side, yellow on the other, and orange in the middle. The shift from one color to the next may moreover be a gradual one, and yet we would still be inclined to say that yellow and red differ in species. Such considerations give rise to misgivings about Brentano's conception of loving and hating as a class which includes both feelings and volitions. His appeals to inner perception on the matter are of course as convincing as appeals to inner perception generally are. That is to say, whoever is not already convinced is not likely to be impressed by such appeals.

In order to make a convincing case for the alleged unity of feelings and volitions in one class (distinct from the other two classes), it is of course necessary for Brentano to identify a common feature of these phenomena. This is found in a feature which they have as an *analogue* to judgments. This is explained as follows by Brentano:

As the general nature of judgment consists in the acceptance or rejection of a fact, the general character of the sphere under our consideration now, according to the testimony of inner experience, also consists in a certain accepting or rejecting - not in the same sense, but in an analogous one. If something can be a content of a judgment insofar as it is acceptable as true or rejectable as false, it can become a content of a phenomenon of the third class insofar as it is agreeable as good (in the broadest sense of the word) or disagreeable as bad. At stake in this case is the value or disvalue of an object, as truth and falsity are at stake in the former case.[2]

This analogy between psychical phenomena of the third class and those of the second (judgments), according to Brentano, allows us to speak of correctness and incorrectness of psychical phenomena of the former type.

In addition he maintains that the analogy in question allows us to characterize some, though certainly not all, psychical phenomena as evident. If it is asked whether knowledge, for instance, should be loved (as it is by all human beings, according to Aristotle) or not, the enjoyment of knowledge, says Brentano:

is an enjoyment of that higher form which is the analogue of evidence in the realm of judgment. In our species it is universal; if, however, there would be another species which, as it had different preferences regarding contents of sensation, loved error as such and hated insight, we certainly would not say, as we would in the other case [concerning their different preferences regarding contents of sensations]: that is a matter of taste, *de gustibus non est disputandum*; no, we would decisively declare here that such loving and

---

[1] *Ibid.*, p. 308.

[2] *Ibid.*, p. 312. Husserl marks this passage in the margin.

hating is fundamentally wrong, that the species hates what is indubitably good and loves what is indubitably bad in itself.[1]

Since our love of knowledge bears the analogue of evidence as well as that of correctness, an ethical relativism or scepticism (whether such a position involves construing good and bad as relative from one individual to another or construing them as relative from one species to another) is emphatically dismissed by Brentano.

As long as inner perception remains the only ground for claiming the analogy between judgments and phenomena of love and hate, the opposition to relativism and scepticism in ethics is, as in all cases where inner perception is the final court of appeal, unlikely to persuade relativists and sceptics. While no one may doubt that phenomena of the latter kind are analogous to judgments insofar loving is in some sense an accepting and hating in some sense a rejecting, we may still ask whether loving and hating are analogous to affirming and denying, i.e., judging, in *all other* respects. Brentano later concedes that the analogy is incomplete, for he says, "There is in the realm of judgment a true and a false. Between them, however, there is no middle ground, no more than there is between being and non-being, according to the well known law of the excluded middle. But there is for the realm of love not only a 'good' or 'bad', but also a 'better' and 'less good', 'worse' and 'less bad'". Not only this, but there seems to be another difference between the two "realms", namely that sometimes it is neither correct nor incorrect to love. Such cases are already mentioned by Brentano when he cites the maxim: *de gustibus non est disputandum*. What every opponent of ethical scepticism and relativism must keep in mind is that this maxim does indeed sometimes apply, that there are, in other words, matters of mere taste. If a person prefers, say, one flavor of ice cream over another, or if some other species enjoys certain odors or flavors which are repulsive to us, without there being any apparent biological function of this enjoyment, it is counter-intuitive to say that the act of love in either of these cases is correct or incorrect. While the sceptics and the relativists wish to regard *all* cases of loving or hating as matters of mere taste, it would be wrong to oppose them by denying the existence of such matters altogether. Insofar as Brentano is prepared to allow for them, he admits that the analogy between judgments and phenomena of love and hate does not apply in all respects. But where does this analogy stop? We shall return to this question in our discussion of Marty's views.

---

[1] *Vom Ursprung sittlicher Erkenntnis*, p. 21.

3.4. Ontology[1]

Finally, a few words about Brentano's early ontology. This is of course important to us here, for Brentano found Husserl's *Logische Untersuchungen* objectionable precisely on ontological grounds. He saw this work as containing an affirmation of universals, sentences-in-themselves and other *Undinge*. It must be kept in mind, however, that this criticism in large part stems from Brentano's reism, i.e., his view that only *realia* can exist and can indeed be thought. During the period under consideration here, however, he was far more tolerant of *irrealia*. This is made clear in *Vom Ursprung sittlicher Erkenntnis*, where he criticizes Christoph Sigwart's claim that existence is equivalent to perceivability as follows: "Now everyone sees at once that this concept of existence is too narrow, as it could well be claimed, for instance, that there is much that is imperceivable, such as a past and a future, an empty space and any lack, a possibility, an impossibility, and so forth and so on".[2] We shall see below that Husserl nonetheless departs from this doctrine of *irrealia* as imperceivables, for he allows for both the perceivability and the non-reality of certain objects.

Perhaps the most important influence which Brentano had on Husserl's ontology was through the theory of parts and wholes. While a more thorough-going discussion of this topic will be found in the chapter on Husserl and Stumpf, it should be mentioned here that for Brentano various types of parts of a whole can be distinguished. The right and left halves of a red surface, for instance, are called "physical parts" of the surface, whereas the color red and the extension of the surface are called "metaphysical parts". Besides physical and metaphysical parts, logical parts may be distinguished. Color, for instance, is a logical part of red and, quite generally, genera are parts of species (and species parts of individuals). Finally, collective parts are to be found in any collection, as soldiers make up the collective parts of an army.

---

[1] When I speak of ontology *simpliciter* I mean the inquiry which can, as Quine says, "be put in three Anglo-Saxon monosyllables: 'What is there?'" (*From a Logical Point of View: Logico-Philosophical Essays* [New York: Harper & Row, 1961], p. 1). In the chapter on Husserl and Stumpf we shall speak of *formal* ontology and *material* ontologies, concerned with *what objects are* and not *whether they are* and therefore consisting of inquiries which are quite different from ontology *simpliciter*.

[2] *Vom Ursprung sittlicher Erkenntnis*, p. 62. The distinction which comes into play here is equivalent to the one, which had already been discussed by Marty in "Über subjectlose Sätze" (1884): 171 ff., between existence and reality.

4. RELEVANT DOCTRINES OF HUSSERL

As already stressed in the introduction, in Husserl's early work we find a focus on psychological matters. The basic psychological concepts, especially that of intentional reference, are moreover clearly taken from Brentano. Both the habilitation thesis of 1887 and the first volume of *Philosophie der Arithmetik* (1891) are written by a wholeheartedly orthodox Brentanist. A shift, however, began to occur a few years after the publication of the latter work. While an attempt was made to write a second volume, none of the texts which thus resulted (Hua XII, 340-429; Hua XXI, 3-215, 252-261) proved satisfactory. In 1893 a new project was taken up, namely a philosophy of space (Hua XXI, 262-311), which was again to be worked out along the lines of Brentanian philosophy, but the outlines and sketches for this project likewise came to nothing.

After Husserl abandoned it, he became more and more concerned with logic instead of the more restricted area of arithmetic and geometry. This shift was only natural, since he had learned from Lotze and Leibniz that the discipline which we normally call "mathematics" is but a specialized branch of logic.[1] The epistemological and ontological problems which Husserl had already explored in the philosophy of mathematics from the standpoint of Brentano, as far as Husserl was concerned, were by no means abandoned in his new focus on logic. Moreover, as already mentioned, the concern with "elementary logic" was inherited from Brentano. But the transition which took place in Husserl's thinking cannot merely be construed as a broadening of interests, for already in his *Psychologische Studien zur elementaren Logik* (1894) and in a more extensive text of 1893, which has been published posthumously (Hua XXII, 269-302), he distinguished between representations and intuitions. While this distinction does not at first look like a serious challenge to Brentanian psychology, Husserl claims that acts of the two types in question are called "presentations" in "totally different" senses (Hua XXII, 283).[2] Such an equivocation (Hua XXII, 119) would indeed pose a serious threat to the threefold division of psychical acts according

---

[1] Here we confront the Leibnizian notion of a *mathesis universalis* which again and again meets with approval from Husserl (Hua XVIII, 222 ff.; Hua III/1, 22 n, 23, 26, 32 f., 218, 307; Hua XVII, 15, 20, 53, 78, 84 f., 96, 104 f., 107, 113, 143 f., 146, 148, 159, 182, 198, 211; Hua VI, 45, 47, 75, 95). As far as Lotze is concerned, see Hua XVIII, 171, where Husserl cites this philosopher's *Logik*, § 18, p. 34 and § 112, 138. The impact of this conception of mathematics in relation to logic, as it was taken up by Frege and again by Russell, is of course well known. Since there is nowadays so much zeal about finding connections between Husserl and Frege, it might be tempting to view Husserl's acceptance of the same conception as an instance of the influence of Frege on him. In view of all indications from Husserl himself, however, the only conclusion admissible is that the influence in question comes from Leibniz and Lotze.

[2] For a discussion of Husserl's double concept of a presentation, as this is adopted in the texts just mentioned, see Karl Schuhmann, "Husserls doppelter Vorstellungsbegriff".

to the orthodox Brentanian position. It will be seen that, while this alleged equivocation is no longer asserted in the *Logische Untersuchungen*, it is nonetheless maintained by Husserl in the latter work that there are indeed other equivocations in the term "presentation" which call for revisions in Brentano's thesis that every psychical phenomenon which is not itself a presentation is founded on a presentation.

In 1894 Husserl showed himself to have drifted even farther from Brentano, insofar as the essay on intentional objects which he wrote in that year exhibits a definite influence of Bolzano. The usage of the concept of *objective* presentations is already unparalleled in the orthodox Brentanian position. That is to say, while Brentano spoke of presentations in a strictly psychological sense, these are only the subjective ones for Bolzano and not the objective ones. Of greater importance, however, is the fact that Husserl decides more in favor of Bolzano on the problem which arises when the Bolzanian notion of objectless presentations, e.g., "golden mountain" or "round square", is contrasted with the Brentanian thesis that *each and every* psychical phenomenon, including *each and every presentation*, refers to an object. The latter thesis is affirmed by Husserl only in an improper sense. Accordingly, he maintains that, strictly and properly speaking, there are indeed objectless presentations. In this way he feels no need at all to construe intentional reference as inexistence, for one is naturally compelled to adopt this conception of intentional reference precisely in those cases where the presentation turns out to be objectless. There will be more about this in the chapter on Husserl and Twardowski.

4.1. Pure Logic

Perhaps the most dramatic departure from orthodoxy occurred in 1896, however, when Husserl lectured on logic and attacked the claim that logic is a practical discipline whose only theoretical foundation is to be found in psychology. His alternative to this "psychologism",[1] was to be found in the notion of a "pure logic", which has "sentences in themselves" and other non-psychical objects as its subject matter. The basic argument of this lecture was again presented in the first volume of the *Logische Untersuchungen*, the *Prolegomena zur reinen Logik*. Though Brentano's name occurs only once in the entire volume (Hua XVIII, 48), Husserl's arguments cannot be construed so

---

[1]This view was accepted by Husserl in the early 1890's. In a text which was written circa 1893 he says the following about logic: "As far as theoretical parts of logic are concerned, it is nothing but a re-arrangement of the psychology of judgment, guided by certain ends. The logician is interested in precisely anything which opens up an understanding of cognitive processes only insofar as this understanding serves him as a means to the end of the advancement of cognition" (Hua XXI, 263).

as to exonerate his mentor - in spite of his efforts to do so when they met in Florence (and also in spite of Daubert's efforts in Munich).[1] This conclusion is unavoidable in light of at least two considerations regarding the very substance of Husserl's argument in the *Prolegomena*.

First of all, crucial to Husserl's attack against psychologism is his conception of objective sentences (or propositions) as the proper bearers of truth. Psychologism, on the contrary, involves the claim that psychical phenomena, namely judgments, are the proper bearers of truth. Moreover, Husserl argues explicitly that the ascription of truth to judgments alone ends in relativism. Since Brentano is committed to the view that truth is to be ascribed only to judgments, Husserl's position in the *Prolegomena* entails that Brentano succumbs to psychologism and consequently to relativism.

In this regard one may consider Husserl's attack on Sigwart, who maintains that truth and falsity are properties of judgments. "The judgment which expresses the law of gravity", says Husserl, "would not have been true [on Sigwart's view] prior to Newton. And thus, to be precise, it would have been, properly speaking, contradictory and altogether false" (Hua XVIII, 134). The very same argument would apply to Brentano's view of truth as well as Sigwart's, although Brentano is certainly for the most part no friend of Sigwart. In this connection it should be pointed out that Brentano insists: "If judgments alone are true, the predicate 'not true' - but by no means the predicate 'false' - belongs to everything which is not a judgment".[2] A desk or a chair, for instance, is not true, but neither of these objects should for this reason be called "false". It is surprising that Husserl loses sight of this point in the above-cited attack on Sigwart and equates "not true" with "false".[3] If, however, this oversight is eliminated, the strength of Husserl's argument in favor of propositions as the proper bearers of truth becomes highly questionable. Moreover, if we consider the fact that Husserl conceives propositions as timeless, it is doubtful whether this conception will allow him to say that a given proposition *was* true *before* the corresponding judgment came into being. For this would introduce a temporal aspect into the notion of propositions. In this regard it would be better to characterize them as *eternal* rather

---

[1] The fact that Brentano himself still regarded himself as under attack is made clear from his discussion in *Psychologie* II, pp. 179-182.

[2] *Vom Ursprung sittlicher Erkenntnis*, p. 70.

[3] See Sigwart's reply in the third edition of *Logik* I (Tübingen: J.C.B. Mohr [Paul Siebeck], 1904), pp. 23 f. Cf. Gerardus Heymans, *Die Gesetze und Elemente des wissenschaftlichen Denkens* (Leipzig: Johan Ambrosius Barth, 1905. See also Moritz Schlick, *Philosophische Logik*, edited by Bernd Philippi (Frankfurt a.M.: Suhrkamp, 1986), pp. 44 f.

than timeless,[1] assuming of course that there would be any need to posit them in the first place.

There is a second reason why Husserl's arguments in the *Prolegomena* should not be construed in such a way that Brentano would be exonerated from the charge of psychologism. If they were construed in this way, it would follow that the basic argument put forward in the *Prolegomena* is based on a false dilemma. According to this argument, a pure logic is to be accepted precisely *because* psychologism is fundamentally flawed, leaving us with no third option. If, however, those who clearly reject a pure logic, such as Brentano, can be exonerated from the charge of psychologism, it would follow that there is a third alternative which is left out of consideration in the *Prolegomena*.

While Brentano cannot be exonerated from this charge, it may further be asked whether Husserl's arguments against psychologism effectively show the Brentanian conception of logic to be unacceptable. It is doubtful that they do. The psychology which Husserl regards as an inadequate theoretical foundation of logic is clearly a genetic psychology, whereas the one which is the foundation of logic for Brentano is clearly descriptive. Particularly regarding Husserl's argument for a pure logic in connection with the formulation of the laws of logic, we may doubt whether this argument is effective against Brentano. The formulations which he attacks all concern limitations on our capacity to judge (Hua XVIII, 88-109). The law of contradiction, according to such a formulation, says that an affirmation and a corresponding denial cannot occur simultaneously in one consciousness. The laws of logic are not construed in this manner by Brentano. It is clear from his correspondence with Husserl that these laws rather concern the truth and falsity of judgments and have nothing at all to do with restrictions on what judgments can or will occur. According to Brentano's formulation of law of contradiction: "whoever affirms and denies one and the same thing (explicitly or implicitly), in other words, whoever contradicts himself, thinks absurdly" (*Briefwechsel* I, 32). While Husserl wishes to say that this law applies first and foremost to propositions rather than judgments, it is difficult to see any reason why his position is preferable. As we have already seen, in his attack on Sigwart he fails to show that *truth* belongs to propositions rather than judgments. In Husserl's discussion of the laws of logic in the *Prolegomena* there is only a passing consideration of them in connection with judgments, as conceived by Brentano (who is of course not mentioned), only to say: "It is evident that yes and no are mutually exclusively in a *correct* judgment, but this is also to express a statement which is equivalent with the

---

[1] It is therefore wrong, at least in the present connection, to say, "Platonism becomes much more palatable when one keeps in mind that 'timeless' does not mean 'eternal'", as D. Føllesdal says in "Noema and Meaning in Husserl", *Philosophy and Phenomenological Research* 1, Suppl. (1990): 271.

logical one and by no means a psychological one" (Hua XVIII, 97). Even if it is however granted that the statement of the kind under consideration is not a psychological one (though it seems arbitrary on Husserl's part to say this), the question arises whether logical laws can be interpreted in this manner and thereby avoid the tendency to posit timeless objects.

Before closing this discussion of Husserl's conception of logic in contrast with Brentano's, we must consider whether Husserl's arguments in the *Prolegomena* against empiricism (Hua XVIII, 94 f.), which he closely associates with psychologism, are in any way effective against Brentano's empiricism. These arguments are launched against two types of empiricism. Against *extreme* empiricism (represented by John Stuart Mill), according to which all general knowledge is inductively derived, Husserl argues that it cannot account for the principles of induction. Since these are of course to be formulated as no less general than the conclusions which are reached by induction, they could be justified only by induction. Such an empiricism is accordingly circular or even absurd.[1] Against moderate empiricism (represented by David Hume), "which attempts to hold on to the sphere of logic and mathematics [...] as *a priori* justified and only gives up the sciences of fact in an empiricist manner" (Hua XVIII, 95), Husserl argues that the principles at work in these sciences are still left unaccounted for, except in a purely psychological way, e.g., by appeal to the association of ideas. Here we must recall how Brentano's empiricism is to be understood as the doctrine that the concepts which are used in science, as indeed all genuine concepts, must have their *origin* in experience. The extreme and the moderate versions of empiricism which Husserl attacks, however, are concerned with the justification of judgments and not with the origin of concepts. Brentano's empiricism, i.e., Lockean empiricism, is therefore apparently immune to these attacks.[2]

4.2. Methodological Innovation

We have thus seen that in the *Logische Untersuchungen* Husserl rather ineffectively rejects the psychological orientation of his mentor, at least insofar as this is relevant to the concerns of *logic* as a purely theoretical discipline. If, however, we take into

---

[1] It should however be noted that Mill himself tries to remedy this situation by his appeal to the uniform course of nature. Thus Husserl's criticism is of limited effectiveness against Mill.

[2] It is therefore ironic that Heidegger says, "Thanks to E. Husserl we have again not only understood the sense of all genuine philosophical 'empirical observation', but also learned to use the tool necessary for it" (*Sein und Zeit*, p. 50 n.).

consideration Husserl's later claim to have discovered a whole new method (the phenomenological reduction) and thereby to have opened up a whole new area (transcendental consciousness) for investigation - an area which is moreover far more relevant to the concerns of philosophy than the sphere of psychical phenomena is - it turns out that he ultimately rejected Brentano's psychological orientation far more radically than what is suggested by the *Prolegomena*. This is sharply indicated in the following passage from a manuscript from 1927 (see *Husserl-Chronik*, 323 f.):

The *phenomenological reduction* is at first needed as a fully conscious exposure of the purely psychical sphere. Also needed, however, is the epoche regarding all methodical pre-convictions about how a sphere of 'facts' is to be treated scientifically, i.e., regarding the manner of description, classification, and the like. [...] One may not, like Brentano, regard descriptive psychology from the outset as an analogue of descriptive natural science, in which already prejudices are contained which conflict with the peculiar essence of the psychical.[1]

As late as 1905, however, Husserl still has plenty of praise for Brentano's methodological orientation. Thus, in his lectures on the theory of judgment from that year, he says of his mentor: "Methodically his psychology is admirable. He begins as one must begin, with pure descriptions".[2] To be sure, Husserl at this time is very critical of certain results of Brentano's descriptive psychology. But these divergences can be ascribed to an alternative descriptive psychology, not to an entirely new discipline. We shall now look at these divergences, without concerning ourselves with the "small nuance" which allegedly makes the difference between phenomenology and descriptive psychology. The evaluation of the transcendental project from the standpoint of a rather orthodox Brentanist will be discussed in the chapter on Husserl and Stumpf.

---

[1] A VI 26/143: "Es bedarf zunächst der phänomenologischen Reduktion als vollbewusster Herausstellung der reinen psychischen Sphäre. Es bedarf aber auch der Epoche hinsichtlich aller methodischen Vorüberzeugungen darüber, wie eine Sphäre von 'Tatsachen' wissenschaftlich zu behandeln sei, also hinsichtlich der Art der Begründung, der Klassifikation u.dgl. [...] Man darf nicht wie Brentano die deskriptive Psychologie von vornherein als ein Analogon der deskriptiven Naturwissenschaft ansehen, worin schon Vorurteile beschlossen sind, die dem Eigenwesen des Psychischen widerstreiten."

[2] F I 27/3a: "Methodisch ist seine Psychologie bewundernswürdig. Er beginnt, wie begonnen werden muss, mit reinen Deskriptionen".

4.3. Intentional Reference

Regarding Brentano's ways of describing the consciousness of objects, namely in terms of an act's intentional reference to these objects or in terms of the intentional existence of the objects in the act, there are two "misinterpretations" which Husserl warns against in the *Logische Untersuchungen* (Hua XIX/1, 385):

> first, that what is under consideration here is a concrete action of consciousness or the ego performed on the 'consciously' given thing, at least a relation between the two which is to be found descriptively in every act; *secondly*, that what is under consideration is a concrete relation of two things, act and intentional object, both of which can be found in consciousness in the same way, something like a real containment of a psychical content in other ones.[1]

That these are misinterpretations to be avoided is shown more particularly by the cases in which the object in question is one that does not even exist. If, for instance, one presents the god Jupiter, then there does not obtain a relation between two things, between the act of presenting and the god Jupiter. Nor is Jupiter something which exists in consciousness. "He is of course also not *extra mentem*, he is not at all" (Hua XIX/1, 387).

As already indicated, Brentano's conception of intentional reference can be interpreted in two ways, depending on whether "inexistence" is taken in the proper or the modified sense. If it is taken in the former sense we may speak of strong immanentism, whereas weak immanentism is the view that the object of an act exists in the act in a modified sense and, properly speaking, does not exist at all. In the chapter on Husserl and Twardowski we shall examine Husserl's attack on *weak* immanentism. Here we may briefly consider his rejection of *strong* immanentism as this is found in

---

[1] The term "relation" in the passage cited in the text is a translation of the term *Verhältnis*, as used in the first edition of the *Logische Untersuchungen*. While Brentano speaks of an "intentional reference to something" (*intentionale Beziehung zu etwas*) (*Vom Ursprung sittlicher Erkenntnis*, p. 14), the second edition warns us against thinking "that what is under consideration is a real process or a real referring which takes place between consciousness or ego and the 'consciously given' thing [dass es sich um einen realen Vorgang oder ein reales sich Beziehen handle, das sich zwischen dem Bewusstsein oder Ich und der 'bewussten' Sache abspiele]" (Hua XIX/1, 385). This warning is accordingly more specifically directed against Brentano than in the first edition. It is of course obvious why Husserl does not prefer to speak of the direction towards an object. Here we find the suggestion of movement, which is just as erroneous as the suggestion of containment. It is accordingly clear why the term "intentionality" (*Intentionalität*) makes its appearance already in the first edition of the *Logische Untersuchungen* (Hua XIX/1, 401, 515) and is of course the preferred term in later works. Only one confusion is thereby left (especially in English), namely that what is at stake here is something *essentially* teleological in character, as when we ordinarily speak of someone's intention to do this or that.

the 1894 text on intentional objects (see Appendix One).[1] First of all, it may be observed that immanentism of any kind is tempting because it allows us to say that there is an object of intentional reference even in those cases where there is clearly no object in actuality. While the presentation which is associated with expressions such as "Jupiter" has no object in actuality, we nonetheless present *something* in this case, namely a particular immanent object. But now consider this view in connection with contradictory expressions, such as "round square". Husserl points out that the acceptance of immanent objects in cases of this kind would require a revision of the law of contradiction. While many since Aristotle had thought that contradictory objects of any kind do not exist, strong immanentism would compel us to say that this law only holds good for objects outside the mind.[2] Thus, if for no other reason but to uphold the law of contradiction, and accordingly the laws of logic in general, strong immanentism must be rejected.

While Husserl prefers not to speak of intentional inexistence, he nonetheless makes the consciousness *of objects*, which is also called "acts" or "intentional experiences", a central theme of his descriptive psychology. However, he diverges from Brentano further in that he does not regard acts as the exclusive subject-matter of psychology. Besides these there are also various contents, such as sensations and phantasms, which must not as such be construed as instances of the consciousness *of* this or that object. These contents may however be part of acts, insofar as they are "apprehended" (*aufgefasst*), "interpreted" (*gedeutet*), or "apperceived" (*apperzipiert*), and are accordingly often called "contents of apprehension" (*Auffassungsinhalte*), although they will for the most part be called "phenomenological contents" in this study.[3] It will be seen below, especially in the chapter on Husserl and Marty, that this aspect of Husserl's descriptive psychology is objectionable.

Here we may briefly consider its implications with respect to the Brentanian thesis that intentional reference is one of the peculiar characteristics of psychical phenomena and indeed the most important one. If Husserl is right, there are psychical phenomena which do *not* have this characteristic. Nevertheless, he maintains that an entity (*Wesen*)

---

[1] One of the criticisms which can legitimately be raised against this text is that the distinction between strong and weak immanentism is hardly, if at all, made by Husserl. Nonetheless, once we make this distinction for ourselves, it is possible to sort out arguments in the text under consideration which apply to one form of immanentism or the other.

[2] "Intentionale Gegenstände" (Schuhmann's edition), p. 147.

[3] Husserl also, especially in the sixth "Logical Investigation", uses the term "representatives" (*Representanten*) in reference to phenomenological contents. This term is however best avoided perhaps even more than "contents of apprehension".

which consisted only of phenomenological contents should never be called a psychical entity (Hua XIX/1, 378 f.). It might therefore be said that the phenomenological contents are not properly "psychical" until they are apprehended and thereby integrated with an intentional phenomenon. A psychical phenomenon could thus be characterized as *either* an intentional one *or* part of an intentional one. In this way the thesis that psychical phenomena (or acts of consciousness) cannot exist without intentional reference can still in some sense be maintained,[1] though the problem still remains regarding the status of this thesis in view of presentations such as "round square" and "golden mountain". Husserl's approach to this problem will be discussed in the chapter on his relation with Twardowski.

4.4. Presentations as Founding Acts

In Husserl's theory of consciousness an attempt is made to defend the Brentanian thesis that presentations are the founding acts, but the resulting understanding of the notion of presentations clearly diverges from the corresponding notion in Brentano's descriptive psychology. This divergence is based on Husserl's reflections regarding matter and quality. These terms, which Brentano had used in his theory of judgment, are borrowed by Husserl, but they are given a meaning which extends to acts of *all* sorts. In this regard the following passage from Husserl's 1905 lecture on judgment may be cited:

For various reasons I have had to find fault with these doctrines from which I started as a pupil of Brentano. What was very difficult for me was the distinction between quality and matter, which is obviously necessary on the one hand and obviously dubious on the other. It is on the one hand, I say, necessary: it must contain a proper sense; in a certain proper sense we can and must still distinguish in the judgment, as in all acts, between quality and matter. [...] Towards one and the same object there can be directed heterogeneous acts - let us say differently qualified acts: judgments, wishes, volitions, etc. And again, acts of the same kind can be directed towards different objects. For phenomenological reflection, as for purely immanent psychology, the direction towards the object is something which must be settled in the act itself. In the act itself lies the

---

[1] It has been maintained in Herman Philipse, "The Concept of Intentionality: Husserl's Development from the Brentano Period to the *Logical Investigations*", that Husserl's conception of perception as the apprehension of sensations has a much stronger bearing on the thesis under discussion, namely insofar as this conception implies that intentional reference is a relation after all, i.e., a relation between the act of perceiving and "a trangible entity which has a certain existence even if we discover that the object of which we thought that it appeared as this phenomenon does not exist at all" (*ibid.*, p. 305). This so-called entity or phenomenon is moreover identified with the noema which Husserl thematizes in *Ideen* I. If this interpretation is correct, then the act of imagining, which involves the apprehension of phenomenological contents no less than perception does, also requires such an entity. There is however no textual support in the *Logische Untersuchungen* for attributing the view in question to Husserl as regards either perception or imagination.

consciousness of the object; the reference to such and such an object is something immanent in the act itself. If we use the term "matter" for that moment of the act which gives direction to the relevant object, then every act, and thus also every judgment, is shown to be a complex of quality and matter. The same matter can be combined with different qualities. If it is combined with an affirmation, then the affirmation refers to the object; if combined with a wishing, then the object is wished for, and so forth.[1]

Two acts are accordingly equal as regards their matter insofar as they are directed towards the same object, equal as regards their quality insofar as they are both acts of judging, both acts of wishing, etc. The judgment that there is intelligent life on Mars is equal in *matter* to the wish for there to be intelligent life on Mars, while the judgment that 2 x 2 = 4 is equal in *quality* to the judgment that Ibsen is the father of modern realism in drama (Hua XIX/1, 426).

It is however important to note here that the fact that differently qualified acts are directed at one and the same object is not alone a sufficient condition to regard these acts as equal in matter (Hua XIX/1, 428 f.). These acts must also be directed at the object in question "in the same way" - this phrase being understood as something altogether distinct from the variation of quality. When we speak of equiangular triangles the objects to which we refer are precisely the same as those which are meant by the name "equilateral triangles". Yet, we do not mean these objects in the same way. Accordingly, the acts of meaning them are different as regards their matter, in spite of the fact that their objects are the same.

While Husserl identifies a certain moment of the act as the one which determines its direction to an object, the only concept which he finds in Brentano's descriptive

---

[1] F I 27/73a: "An diesen Lehren, von denen ich als Schüler Brentanos ausgegangen bin, habe ich aus verschiedenen Gründen Anstoss nehmen müssen. Was mir nicht geringe Schwierigkeit machte, war die einerseits offenbar notwendige und andererseits offenbar bedenkliche Unterscheidung zwischen Qualität und Materie. Sie ist einerseits, sage ich, notwendig: ein guter Sinn muss in ihr stehen, in einem gewissen guten Sinne können und müssen wir doch beim Urteil sowie bei allen Akten zwischen Qualität und Materie scheiden. [...] Auf eine und dieselbe Gegenständlichkeit können sich verschiedenartige, sagen wir verschieden qualifizierte Akte richten, Urteile, Wünsche, Wollungen u.s.w. Und wieder können sich Akte derselben Art auf verschiedene Gegenständlichkeiten richten. Für die phänomenologische Betrachtung sowie für die rein immanente Psychologie ist die Richtung auf Gegenständlichkeit etwas, das im Akte selbst zum Austrag kommen muss. Im Akte selbst liegt das Bewusstsein vom Gegenständlichen, das sich auf das und das Gegenständliche Beziehen ist etwas dem Akte selbst Immanentes. Bezeichnen wir dasjenige Moment des Aktes, das Richtung auf die betreffende Gegenständlichkeit gibt, als Materie, so stellt sich jeder Akt und damit auch jedes Urteil als Komplexion zwischen Qualität und Materie dar. Dieselbe Materie kann sich mit verschiedenen Qualitäten komplizieren. Kompliziert sie sich mit einem Anerkennen, dann bezieht sich das Anerkennen auf die Gegenständlichkeit, kompliziert sie sich mit einem Wünschen, dann ist die Gegenständlichkeit erwünscht u.s.w." In the margin next to this passage Husserl points out that the "combined parts" (*komplizierte Teile*) under discussion here, i.e., the matter and quality of a given act, "are only absract moments [*sind nur abstrakte Momente*]". That is to say, it is impossible for one of them to exist in separation from the other. In this regard, as Husserl rightly observes, it misleading to speaking of a "complexion" (*Komplexion*) here.

psychology as a means to account for this direction is the concept of a presentation (Hua XIX/1, 443 ff.). Two different judgments, on Brentano's view, can be directed towards one and the same object insofar as they are founded on equivalent presentations. In this case, however, Husserl finds it impossible for Brentano to account for the fact that one presentation can have an object which is totally different from the other presentation. It will not help, he insists, to say that different presentations can have different objects and to leave it at that, for the direction towards an object is itself immanent in the act, in this case a presentation. We are accordingly left with no other choice but to say that each presentation has a moment which gives it direction and another which qualifies it as a presentation, and not as a judgment, a wish, etc.

If one thus wishes to avoid construing the presentation itself as the matter, an attempt might be made to regard presentations in another sense as the founding acts. In this sense presentations are to be found in "all cases of mere presentation through imagination, in which the appearing object is meant neither as being nor as not-being and there are no other acts with regard to this; or also cases in which we understand an expression, perhaps a declarative sentence, without deciding to believe or disbelieve" (Hua XIX/1, 444). While Husserl certainly has no doubt that such "mere presentations" occur, he insists that they are not the foundation of all acts. Most importantly, they are not the foundation for acts of perceiving. In this regard Husserl considers an act which is, as far as one knows, a perception and is followed by an exactly corresponding mere presentation (Hua XIX/1, 459). In a wax museum one may see a charming young lady waving and may then realize that what was before one's eyes was only a wax figure. The mere presentation which thus remains, namely the presentation of the young lady, is by no means a substrate of the previous "perception". Rather, the whole quality of the act has changed, while the matter has remained the same. This example is meant to show that *mere presentations* are not the foundations of perceptions. It is accordingly not as if there had first been a mere presentation *plus* the alleged perceptual judgment and then the latter was subsequently subtracted.

Another way in which presentations may be understood would be as *nominal* acts in contrast with *propositional* acts (Hua XIX/1, 476 ff.). Such a view is already suggested by Brentano's claim, already mentioned, that the expressions with which presentations are correlated are *names*. Propositional acts, according to Husserl, are directed at states of affairs in a "two-rayed" manner. If a state of affairs is meant in a "one-rayed" manner, the act in question is a nominal act. The difference here can be made clear by an example. If someone judges that it has finally rained, the act is a propositional act. If, however, someone judges that the fact that it has finally rained pleases the farmers, the part of the act which is indicated by "the fact that it has finally rained" is a nominal act. As a complete sentence in the one case is transformed into a name in the other case, the propositional act is transformed into a nominal act. But this distinction between nominal and propositional acts, according to Husserl, is a distinction in *matter*. Since acts are properly differentiated in terms of *quality*, presentations in the claim under discussion (that every act is either a presentation or founded on a presentation) are not to be understood as nominal acts.

The difference between nominal and propositional acts is regarded by Husserl purely as a difference in matter, because he insists on a distinction between positing and non-positing nominal acts or "names". He asks us to consider such names as "Prince Heinrich", "the statue of Roland in the market place", "the postman rushing by" and says: "Whoever uses these names in true speech and in the normal sense 'knows' that Prince Heinrich is an actual person and no creature of fiction, that there is a statue of Roland in the market place, that the postman is rushing by" (Hua XIX/1, 482). As regards a non-positing name Husserl asks us to consider the subject term in the sentence "a triangle with two right angles does not exist" (Hua XIX/1, 483). Moreover, if we consider acts which are not as such correlated with names (as we usually understand this term, i.e., linguistic expressions of a certain type), but are still nominal as opposed to propositional, then positing nominal acts are to be found in perception, memory, expectation, whereas the acts of mere imagination, e.g., the one directed at the young lady in the wax musem after the illusion has been exposed, are examples of non-positing nominal acts. For every positing nominal act a corresponding non-positing one is obviously possible. But if we ask what the two acts have in common, e.g., the act directed at the young lady in the wax museum before the illusion is exposed as compared to the subsequent act, the only thing which is left over, Husserl insists, is the matter. Positing and non-positing nominal acts are therefore not to be included into two classes which both belong to the qualitative genus "nominal act", for there can be no such genus.

Husserl is therefore not willing to claim that every psychical act is either a presentation or founded on a presentation if "presentation" here is synonymous with "nominal act". He subscribes to this claim only if objectifying acts (*objektivierende Akte*) are meant by "presentations" (Hua XIX/1, 496 ff.). Such acts are those which are either positing ones with non-positing counterparts or vice-versa. If I judge that it is raining, this act has a non-positing counterpart, namely in the act of understanding this judgment without assenting to it. Wishing as such, on the other hand, is a non-positing act which has no positing counterpart and is therefore not a presentation in the Husserlian sense. As Husserl understands the claim that non-presentational acts are founded on presentations, it does in fact come into conflict with Brentano's understanding of it. For judgments and perceptions, according to Husserl, are classified among the ultimately founding acts. In this regard we may consider once again the above example of seeing the wax figure. While one is "perceiving" the young lady, there is no underlying presentation which is later uncovered, as it were, when the illusion is exposed. The presentation of the young lady which then results is simply a phantasy presentation, an act with a new quality, but with the same matter as the preceding act. Both the preceding act (the "perception") and the resulting mere presentation are presentations.

4.5. Perception

Before we close this discussion of Husserl's views in the *Logische Untersuchungen*, considered in contrast with (or as reactions to) Brentano, it will be helpful to take into account the theory of perception in this work. Besides the differences already indicated, namely that a *perception* for Husserl is not founded on a presentation as it is for Brentano and may include parts (e.g., sensations) which have no intrinsic intentional reference, there are additional other differences which arise. In these other cases, too, Husserl was fully aware of taking a path which diverged from his mentor's.

4.5.1. Inner Perception

The first of these divergent views is to be found in Husserl's treatment of the distinction between inner and outer perception. As we recall, this distinction for Brentano goes together with the distinction between psychical and physical phenomena; while the former are inwardly perceived, the latter are outwardly perceived. We may further remember that there is an important difference in evidence between the two types of perception; while inner perception is "infallible" and "immediate", outer perception can at best provide us with signs which indicate what the things in the external world are like. Strictly and properly speaking, outer perception is not perception at all. We should also keep in mind that for Brentano there is no unconscious consciousness and that all psychical phenomena are accordingly perceived.

As regards Brentano's denial of an unconscious consciousness, Husserl accepts the infinite regress argument which Brentano attempts to refute by distinguishing between the primary and the secondary direction of consciousness (Hua XIX/1, 366 f.). This distinction is quickly dismissed by Husserl as an "artificial theory" which can be avoided "as long as the necessity of an assumption of the continuous action of inner perception cannot be empirically demonstrated" (Hua XIX/1, 367). Here Husserl sees clearly that such a demonstration would indeed have to be empirical, for as Brentano himself already insists, there is nothing absurd in the very notion of an unconscious consciousness. It is also right of Husserl to observe implicitly that the demonstration is not to be found in Brentano's treatment of inner perception. The distinction between the primary and the secondary direction of consciousness is used only to show that there is nothing absurd in the denial of an unconscious consciousness. Even if he succeeds in showing this, it does not follow that there actually is an unconscious consciousness. We are of course nowadays familiar with all sorts of extravagant theories which have been generated from this notion which Brentano found so objectionable. But Husserl's affirmation of the infinite regress argument should not be construed as an open invitation to these theories as scientifically acceptable.

As regards the alleged infallibility of inner perception, Husserl says "that most perceptions of psychical states cannot be evident since they are perceived with a bodily location" (Hua XIX/2, 761). Here he points out instances such as the feeling of pain in a tooth. We have seen that Brentano proposes to overcome this objection by saying that the pain or the pleasure which is allegedly localized is in fact only a sensory quality, to which a pain or pleasure, properly speaking, is attached. If, for instance, there is pain in my tooth, a certain quality is outwardly perceived in my tooth and, in addition, I have a feeling of pain *about* this quality. Whether such a reply is acceptable, it must be pointed out that Husserl does not effectively deal with it. To be sure, he admits that there occurs in the cases of the kind under consideration an outer perception as well as an inner one. But he adds that this is to no avail. He would be right in saying this if it were claimed that the pain in the tooth, the "toothache" as we say, were perceived by both inner and outer perception together. This is however not what Brentano claims. We must distinguish between two *senses* of the word "pain", according to him, and regard the pain in one sense (the quality) as the object of outer perception and the pain in the other sense (the pain proper) as an object of inner perception. This distinction does not come into consideration in Husserl's discussion of the matter in question.

While Husserl thus rejects Brentano's views that every psychical phenomenon is inwardly perceived and that inner perception is in all cases infallible, it must be kept in mind that Husserl does not reject the notion of inner perception altogether as did Comte. Not only does he find it perfectly acceptable to say that some experiences (*Erlebnisse*) are inwardly perceived, but he also maintains that some of these are adequately perceived whereas outer perceptions are never adequate. That is to say, sometimes an inner perception is one "which ascribes to its objects nothing which is not itself intuitively presented in the perceptual experience itself and cohesively given" (Hua XIX/1, 365). In light of this high epistemological assessment of inner perception in contrast with outer perception, it would be very wrong to see Husserl's divergence from Brentano on this topic to be comparable to certain extreme anti-Cartesian tendencies which are to be found among certain twentieth century philosophers, such as Wittgenstein, Ryle, and Strawson.

4.5.2. Categorial Perception

Another way in which Husserl's theory of perception differs from his mentor's is to be found in the concept of categorial perception. In Husserl's copy of Brentano's *Vom Ursprung sittlicher Erkenntnis*, in the margin next to the passage where it is claimed that perceivability cannot be the same as existence since the non-real exists and yet cannot be perceived (p. 62), it is written "categorial perception!"[1] Thus, Husserl maintains that non-real objects can in fact be perceived. The perception of them is called "categorial perception" and is contrasted with "sensory" or "straightforward perception" (Hua XIX/1, 670 ff.). One can see not only a piece of white paper, but also that a piece of paper *is* white. While the white paper is an object of straightforward perception, the addition of "is" makes the perception a categorial one. Among the objects which are categorially perceivable, according to Husserl, are not only states of affairs, such as the object called "that the paper is white", but also general objects or "specific singularities". Whenever the white of a piece of paper, for instance, is seen as an *example* of white in general, the general object called "white" or "whiteness" is categorially perceived.

Even if the notion of categorial perception is acceptable, we should nonetheless be on guard against using it in connection with Brentano's list of non-real objects. Some the objects in question, to be sure, can be construed as states of affairs and therefore as categorially perceivable. A possibility, for instance, may be regarded as the state of affairs that such and such is possible, as indeed an impossibility can be regarded as the state of affairs that such and such is impossible. Brentano's list of non-real objects however includes the past and the future. Can these be perceived at all? Even if the notion of perception can be stretched to include the memory of the immediate past, so-

---

[1] "Kategoriale Wahrnehmung!" While it is difficult to date Husserl's reading of *Vom Ursprung sittlicher Erkenntnis* with precision, the remark in question must have been made almost a decade after the publication of this work or perhaps later. We are of course familiar with the notion of categorial perception from the sixth "Logical Investigation", where Husserl maintains that categorial perception (or intuition) includes the fulfilling acts whereby we grasp general objects. Though he remarks that a term such as "general intuition" is one "which of course to many will not sound better than wooden iron" (Hua XIX/2, 690), in one of the unpublished texts which was written in September 1898 and originally intended for the *Logische Untersuchungen* Husserl bluntly says: "Perceived concepts belong together in one class with wooden iron [Wahrgenommene Begriffe gehören in Eine Klasse mit dem hölzernen Eisen]" (K I 64/5). The full-blown notion of categorial perception is accordingly one which Husserl came upon rather late during the writing of the *Logische Untersuchungen*.

called "primary memory" (*primäres Gedächtnis,* also called "retention" in Husserl's later jargon), most of the past is not accessible to perception in this broad sense.

4.5.3. Perception and Time-Consciousness

These remarks lead us to a consideration of Husserl's celebrated theory of time-consciousness are in order, for this theory is indeed in large measure concerned with answering the question whether temporally extended objects, e.g., melodies, are *perceivable*. As we have seen, Brentano had embraced the rather unattractive alternative of denying their perceivability. Husserl subjects this view and the concomitant theory of original association to an extensive critique (Hua X, 10-19). Since the present study is primarily concerned with Husserl's relation with his fellow Brentanists, it would take us too far afield here to discuss this critique. It is sufficient to say that for Husserl temporally extended objects are at least in *some sense* perceivable, namely in the sense already indicated. That is to say, the perception of the present always involves primary memory in which the just-past (*eben vergangen*) is given firsthand. The difference between primary memory, as Husserl conceives of it, and original association in the Brentanian sense is that the former has the same epistemic value as the perception of the present. Husserl's approach to time-consciousness has much in common with the one which Meinong had already taken in 1899. For this reason Husserl took it upon himself in 1905 to set his views on the matter apart from those of Meinong. More about this in the chapter on Husserl and Meinong.

4.5.4. Perception of Things

When we speak of perceiving, it is normally *outer* perception which we have in mind. Moreover, the objects which we outwardly perceive are, more often than not, *things* such as tables and chairs, plants and animals. Yet, we may recall that Brentano was reluctant to say that we can perceive anything besides our present acts of consciousness. To be sure, he tells us that some of our presentations are sensations, which moreover are the basis for judgments in which physical phenomena are accepted. But he also regards such the judgments in question as blind and the phenomen in question, e.g., colors and sounds, as very different from the things which exist outside of consciousness, i.e., the things which are indispensable to the hypotheses of natural science, such as light-waves and sound-vibrations. What we find missing in Brentano's account of outer perception is an account of the colored, extended, shaped, warm (or cold) thing which is allegedly already perceived before natural science does its work. Husserl, by contrast, gave a good deal of attention to the concept of a thing in this sense. The following passage from his 1898 manuscript on perception (originally intended for publication in the *Logische Untersuchungen*) may be quoted in this regard:

The perceived things are not the things in themselves. Everyone who executes an outer perception perceives in it an outer thing. When the philosopher disparages outer perception as deception and, no matter how and with what right, posits an underlying thing beneath the appearing thing, then outer perception is not transformed for him into a new percpetion, namely one of things in themselves; rather, perception loses altogether the perceptual character [...] and there is linked to the on-going perceptual presentation the coneptual thought that something existing in itself corresponds in such and such a way to the appearing and still only appearant object. This thing in itself, which is to be thought of only conceptually, is of no concern at all to psychology of sensation and perception; it is not a possible object of perception, even if such peception be presumptive (i.e., deceptive here).[1]

Thus Husserl maintains that outer perception cannot be described unless it is construed as an act directed at things in the ordinary sense and not at the things posited in natural science, which can be grasped only through conceptual thought, if indeed they are grasped at all. The conception of outer perception first and foremost as "thing-perception" (*Dingwahrnehmung*) is the basis for Husserl's analysis of perception in the text from which the above-cited passage is taken. This conception is again taken up in his 1904/05 *Hauptstück* on perception and further elaborated on in his 1907 lecture on thing and space (Hua XVI) and indeed throughout the rest of his philosophical career.

---

[1] K I 66/24 f.: "Die wahrgenommenen Dinge sind nicht die Dinge an sich. Jedermann, der eine äussere Wahrnehmung vollzieht, nimmt in ihr ein äusseres Ding wahr. Wenn der Philosoph die äussere Wahrnehmung zur Täuschung herabwürdigt und dem erscheinenden Ding, gleichgiltig wie und mit welchem Recht, ein darunterliegendes Ding an sich supponiert, so wandelt sich ihm die äussere Wahrnehmung nicht in eine neue Wahrnehmung, nämlich in eine solche von Dingen an sich um; sondern die Wahrnehmung verliert ganz und gar den Wahrnehmungscharakter (die Wahrnehmung geht über <in> die Falschnehmung) und an die fortdauernde Wahrnehmungsvorstellung knüpft sich der begriffliche Gedanke an, dass dem erscheinenden und doch nur scheinbaren Gegenstand in der oder jener Weise ein gewisses an sich seiendes Etwas korrespondiere. Mit diesem nur begrifflich zu denkenden Ding an sich hat es die Psychologie der Empfindung und Wahrnehmung in keiner Weise zu tun, es ist kein möglicher Gegenstand auch nur vermeintlicher (d.h. hier täuschender) Wahrnehmung".

This passage and many other parts of the manuscript are written in the hand of Husserl's wife. Though Husserl later scratched out some words and added new ones in stenography, the passage has been quoted in its original 1898 state.

Omitted from the translation is the sentence in parentheses where the term *Falschnehmung* is used. This term as such is difficult to translated and all the more so given the contrast with *Wahrnehmung*. Here it should nonetheless be noted that Brentano had characterized outer perception as *Falschnehmung* in the sense of belonging among false judgments. Accordingly, the passage in question is clearly directed at Brentano, though he is not mentioned by name.

While the resulting analyses are marred by the view that outer perception takes place via the apprehension of sensations, the notion of a thing in the pre-scientific sense is clearly missing from Brentano's descriptive psychology.

In this connection it is interesting to note what Husserl in his final work, *Die Krisis der europäischen Wissenschaften und die transzendentale Phänomenologie*, has to say about the innovation of the *Logishe Untersuchung* (Hua VI, 237):

> Their innovative character lies [...] in the subjectively directed investigations (primarily the fifth and sixth ones of the second volume of 1901) in which for the first time the *cogitata qua cogitata* as essential moments of every conscious process, as it is given in genuine inner experience, come into their own and immediately dominate the whole method of intentional analysis. Thus "evidence" (this rigid logical idol) is made a problem there for the first time, liberated from the preference of scientific evidence and expanded to general original self-giving. Genuine intentional synthesis is discovered in the synthesis of several acts into one act [...].

The notion of synthesis which is featured in the sixth "Logical Investigation" in a general way (and, according to Husserl, was never appreciated by Brentano and the other Brentanists) had already been used throughout the 1898 text on perception. The perception of a thing is considered to be a synthesis insofar as the thing is regarded as an identical object which appears now from one perspective, now from another. Though we may have misgivings about Husserl's attempt to ascribe this synthetic character to all evidence, including that which is appropriate in logic and mathematics, the ascription of it to outer perception is perhaps one of Husserl's greatest contributions to descriptive psychology. It is of course to be noted most emphatically that the conception of thing-perception had already been formulated in 1898 and is therefore by no means a result of the transcendental turn.

The notion of synthesis, more particularly the synthesis of identity through perception, is obviously to be appreciated in the context of the above-discussed theory of time-consciousness. Both the perception of temporally extended objects and that of things requires primary memory as much as perception in the narrower sense, i.e., in the sense of being limited to the present moment if indeed this notion is permissible. The things we perceive, after all, are regarded as identical across time. Yet, if we recall Brentano's highly plausible claim that a past tone is not a tone since "past" and "future" are modifying terms, the notion of identity across time may be called into question. How can the house which I now perceive be identitical with something that I perceived yesterday? Must we not say that a past house is not a house and cannot as such be identical with a present house? If we must say this, however, Husserl's conception of thing-perception is not without difficulties. The identity of a thing across time, it seems, is at best identity in a modified sense. If so, it must be asked where identity in the strict and proper sense obtains. Until this question and no doubt many others regarding identity are answered, Husserl's theory of perception is still in need of further development.

4.6. Parts and Wholes

In the notion of categorial perception we encounter the epistemological side of that Platonistic tendency which Brentano found so objectionable in Husserl's *Logische Untersuchungen*. It is important to note here, furthermore, that the specific singularities in Husserl's ontology are *not* regarded as parts of the objects which instantiate them. Color, for instance, is not regarded as part of red. Whatever Husserl drew from Brentano's theory of parts and wholes, it is clear that his Platonism comes into conflict with Brentano's notion of logical parts. This conflict is made clear in the following text (perhaps from October 1895, as indicated in *Husserl-Chronik*, 45):

Brentano conceives the relation of logical genus and species as a part-relation. He does so with a view to certain cases where we believe that we intuitively find the logical part actually "in" the whole. However, in other cases (e.g., 1000 is a finite number), where we have a cognition of the relation, we do not find the alleged part in the whole, at least not as an explicit part.

One could also object that we speak of a part and whole only where precisely a plurality of parts are linked to a unity, which is not the case here. To me there seems to be here a mere derivation of the concepts of part and whole, by a rather remote analogy, as we speak, for instance, of inclusion and exclusion in the case of sentences, though there is no composition, no actual being-contained.[1]

While Brentano's notion of logical parts is thus abandoned in favor of a more Platonistic position, it will nonetheless be seen below that other aspects of Brentano's theory of parts and wholes, especially as this theory was conveyed by Stumpf, survives in Husserl's ontology.

---

[1] A III 1/56 b: "Brentano fasst das Verhältnis von logischer Gattung und Art als Teilverhältnis. Er tut es mit Rücksicht auf gewisse Fälle, wo wir anschaulich wirklich 'im' Ganzen den logischen Teil zu finden glauben. Indessen in anderen Fällen (z.B. 1000 ist eine endliche Zahl), wo wir eine Erkenntnis des Verhältnisses haben, finden wir den angeblichen Teil nicht im Ganzen, wenigstens nicht als expliziten Teil.

"Man möchte auch einwenden, dass wir von einem Teil und Ganzen nur sprechen, wo eben eine Mehrheit von Teilen zu einer Einheit verknüpft sind, was hier nicht der Fall ist. Mir scheint hier eine blosse Übertragung der Begriffe von Teil und Ganzem vorzuliegen, nach ziemlich entfernter Analogie, ähnlich wie wir z.B. bei Sätzen von Einschluss und Ausschluss sprechen, ohne dass eine Zusammensetzung, ein wirkliches Enthalten-sein vorläge."

4.7. Value

Another aspect of Brentano's philosophy which endures to a significant degree in Husserl's is to be found in the latter's ethics and value theory. We have already seen that the crucial point in Brentano's ethics is the alleged analogy between acts of judging on the one hand and acts of feeling and willing on the other. Accordingly acts of the latter kind, which are of course the acts which are relevant to ethics, have their analogues of truth and falsity, in some cases even their analogues of evidence. Even in *Ideen* I, where Husserl is far beyond the psychological orientation which is characteristic of the school of Brentano, he nonetheless maintains: "'Theoretical' or 'doxological' truth, or evidence, has its parallel in 'axiological and practical truth, or evidence', though the 'truths' of the latter title come to expression and cognition in doxological truths, namely in specifically logical (apophantic) ones" (Hua III/1, 321). In a footnote to this passage he cites Brentano's *Vom Ursprung sittlicher Erkenntnis* as the inspiration behind this view concerning truth and evidence in ethical matters.[1] In fact, as far as Husserl's lectures on value theory and ethics can be traced back,[2] the same position, which is essentially taken over from his mentor, is adopted as the antidote against ethical scepticism and relativism. In later lectures Brentano is upheld as the founder of the notion of a formal axiology, which Husserl regards as essential to a properly philosophical treatment of values (Hua XXVIII, 70-101). Whether the formal treatment of matters of value comes to anything may of course be distinguished from the question whether or how ethical scepticism and relativism are to be opposed. It has been argued above that Brentano's attempt to oppose them rests on a rather dubious analogy. Insofar as Husserl draws on the same analogy, this is to be regarded as a weakness in his value theory too.

Unfortunately there are only fragments left from Husserl's early lectures on ethics and value theory. In the following previously unpublished text which Husserl may have used for lecture material as early as 1902 and had perhaps written earlier than 1900,[3] Husserl notes some points of difference between him and Brentano:

Points of difference vis-à-vis Brentano.
It is correct to say that the concept of the good in the broadest sense is a unitary one and not one, as Aristotle taught, merely by analogy. But corresponding to the various types of activities in the realm of the third class [i.e., phenomena of loving and hating] it is nonetheless, once again, a varied one. What evokes

---

[1] Husserl erroneously refers to the work in question as *Vom Ursprung der sittlichen Erkenntnis*.

[2] See the editor's introduction in Hua XXVIII, especially pp. xvi ff.

[3] See the editorial remarks of Ulrich Melle in Hua XXVIII, 518 f.

in us a correctly characterized pleasure is not good in the same sense as what we will with a correctly characterized willing. And this is the basis for the distinction between the good as understood in ethics and the good as understood in aesthetics.

Ethics uses "good" in the sense of "morally good", i.e., that which is to be willed with a correctly characterized will. Here only the character of the volitional act decides about good and bad. Indeed, to use that analogy with the realm of judgment which has guided it [ethics] so excellently in its discoveries, we would for the sake of precision have to declare only the volitional act in the primary and proper sense as good and bad, that which is willed, however, only in the same derived sense as that which is affirmed is declared "true" (at first evidently true).

Against the declaration that only the will is good, there arises an obvious objection. We call the emotions of every kind, not only volitional acts, morally objectionable or morally good. Enjoyment of the good - enjoyment of the suffering of others, base desire, etc. offer examples at random. Yet this objection is solved upon exact consideration. Not directly, but only mediately does the predicate "morally good" and "morally bad" belong to these acts, namely insofar as they determine our will. Ethics puts forward only norms for our action. Emotions of any kind can now be motives for our will. Since now a willing which is directed at a good in the broadest sense appears thus itself as correctly characterized, the good of any kind is to be regarded also as good in the narrower sense of the morally good. But in any case the reference to the value-giving act changes. And therefore the difference would have to be stressed. Likewise, we must fight the bad of every kind, for it is morally objectionable, the will which is directed towards it is characterized as incorrect. (The character "as incorrect" must be affirmed as a positive character! Unless there is a correctly characterized counter-willing.) And is especially to be fought, since immoral motives are strengthened for the future. The specific differences within the third class make it possible for several cases to arise with regard to the relations of acts among each other.

A correctly characterized love of any kind is a correctly characterizing motive for a love of any kind. Every pleasure, every wish, every hope, every desire, every willing, which is directed at a good is therefore eo ipso good. A correctly characterized love of any kind is effective for a hate of any kind as an incorrectly characterizing motive. The displeasure, the aversion with respect to a good is incorrect. Likewise, correctly characterized hate: a love directed at this incorrect. Correctly characterized hate: a hate directed at this correct.

In aesthetics the concept of the beautiful plays an analogous role. The beautiful is that the presentation of which evokes a correctly characterized pleasure. Again, the pleasure would properly be called "beautiful", but linguistic usage is definitively against this. We call the object of pleasure which we conceive as the reason (cause) thereof "beautiful". This concept of the beautiful is the starting point of aesthetics, as the concept of the morally good is the one of ethics. I say only "starting point", for aesthetics and ethics are arts. And they are not only concerned with the decision whether something is beautiful and good, but rather they are meant to give rules as well for the realization of it. Indeed, still more. They are concerned with the realization of the best and most beautiful. As logic falls into logic of testing and logic of discovery, the same would be true of those two disciplines, of course with the distinction: in the realm of the third class there are differences in value and gradations which are missing in the realm of the second class [judgments]. And thus what is at stake in the aesthetic decision is not merely whether there is a correctly characterized pleasure linked to a work at all and justifiably so, but whether this occurs to an especially high degree. "The best among the things attainable". Thus there takes place here a weighing. There is, to be sure, no decision about this in the realm of aesthetics. The number of means for reaching a given goal is nothing offered and surveyable while deciding. Things are different in the realm of the will. Deliberation extends to the limited number of reachable and available moments and thus one can require that the best should be chosen in accordance with the circumstances of the case.

One more thing: Ethics, I said, is also concerned with the realization of the morally good. It does this as a moral doctrine of education. It teaches the motives, which can work detrimentally and those which work favorably, those which are suited for advancing the morally good and those suited for impeding it. And it, too, relies in this respect on experience and draws therefrom the moments whereby moral ideals can be characterized.[1]

---

[1] F I 20/96 f.: "Differenzpunkte gegen Brentano.

"Es ist richtig, dass der Begriff des Guten im weitesten Sinn ein einheitlicher ist und nicht, wie Aristoteles lehrte, bloss in analoger Weise ein solcher. Aber entsprechend den mehrfachen Arten von Betätigungen im Gebiete der dritten Klasse ist er doch wieder ein mehrfacher. Was in uns ein richtig charakterisiertes Wohlgefallen erweckt, ist nicht im selben Sinn gut, als was wir mit richtig charakterisiertem Wollen wollen. Und darauf beruht der Unterschied des Guten, wie er in der Ethik und wie er in der Ästhetik verstanden wird.

"Die Ethik gebraucht 'gut' in dem Sinne von 'sittlich gut', d.h. von dem mit richtig charakterisiertem Wollen zu wollenden. Hier bestimmt der Charakter des Willensaktes allein über Gut und Schlecht. Ja genau genommen müssten wir, um die Analogie mit dem Urteilsgebiete, das sie bei ihren Entdeckungen so trefflich geleitet hat, [zu gebrauchen], nur den Willensakt im ersten und eigentlichen Sinn für gut und schlecht erklären, das Gewollte aber gut nur in demselben übertragenen Sinn als das Anerkannte für wahr (zunächst evident wahr).

"Gegen die Erklärung, dass nur der Wille gut sei, erhebt sich ein naheliegender Einwand. Wir nennen Gemütsbewegungen jeder Art, nicht bloss Willensakte, [omit 'für'] sittlich verwerflich oder sittlich gut. Freude am Guten - Schadenfreude, niedriges Begehren etc. bieten beliebige Beispiele. Indessen löst sich dieser Einwand bei genauer Betrachtung. Nicht direkt, sondern nur mittelbar kommt diesen Akten das Prädikat 'sittlich gut' und 'sittlich schlecht' zu; nämlich insofern sie unseren Willen bestimmen. Die Ethik stellt nur Normen für unser Handeln auf. Gemütsbewegungen jeder Art können nun Motive für unseren Willen sein. Da nun ein auf Gutes im weitesten Sinne gerichtetes Wollen hierdurch selbst als richtig charakterisiert erscheint, so ist das Gute jeder Art auch als Gutes im engeren Sinne des sittlich Guten anzusehen. Aber immerhin wechselt hier die Beziehung auf den wertgebenden Akt. Und darum müsste der Unterschied hervorgehoben werden. Ebenso müssen wir das Schlechte jeder Art bekämpfen, denn es ist sittlich verwerflich, der darauf gerichtete Wille ist als unrichtig charakterisiert. (Der Charakter 'als unrichtig' muss als pos[itiver] Charakter anerkannt werden! Es sei denn, dass es einen richtig charakterisierten Widerwillen gibt.) Und es ist besonders zu bekämpfen, weil unsittliche Motive für die Zukunft gestärkt werden. Die spezifischen Unterschiede innerhalb der dritten Klasse bedingen es, dass in Rücksicht auf die Beziehung von Akten auf einander mehrere Fälle hervortreten können. Eine richtig charakterisierte Liebe irgendeiner Art ist für eine Liebe irgendeiner Art richtig charakterisierendes Motiv. Jedes Gefallen, jeder Wunsch, jede Hoffnung, jedes Begehren, jedes Wollen, das auf ein Gutes geht, ist dadurch eo ipso richtig.

"Eine richtig charakterisierte Liebe irgendeiner Art ist für einen Hass irgendeiner Art als unrichtig charakterisierendes Motiv wirksam. Das Missfallen, das Verabscheuen eines Guten ist unrichtig. Ebenso richtig charakterisierter Hass: darauf gerichtet eine Liebe unrichtig. Richtig charakterisierter Hass: darauf gerichtet ein Hass richtig.

"In der Ästhetik spielt der Begriff des Schönen eine analoge Rolle. Das Schöne ist dasjenige, dessen Vorstellung ein richtig charakterisiertes Wohlgefallen erweckt. Wiederum wäre schön eigentlich zu nennen das Gefallen, aber hier widerstrebt der Sprachgebrauch entschieden. Wir nennen schön den Gegenstand des Gefallens, den wir als Grund (Ursache) desselben auffassen. Dieser Begriff des Schönen ist Ausgangspunkt für die Ästhetik, wie der Begriff des sittlich Guten derjenige der Ethik. Ich sage bloss Ausgangspunkt, denn die Ästhetik und Ethik sind Kunstlehren. Und sie gehen nicht bloss auf die Entscheidung, darauf ob etwas schön und gut sei, sondern sie wollen auch Regeln geben für die Verwirklichung desselben. Ja noch mehr. Sie gehen auf die Verwirklichung des Besten und Schönsten. So wie die Logik in Logik der Prüfung und Logik der Entdeckung zerfällt, so würde Ähnliches für jene beiden disziplinen gelten, allerdings mit der Unterscheidung: auf dem Gebiet der dritten Klasse gibt es Wert- und Gradunterschiede, die auf dem der zweiten fehlen. Und so kommt es bei der ästhetischen Entscheidung nicht bloss darauf an, ob an ein Werk sich überhaupt ein richtig charakterisiertes Wohlgefallen knüpft, sondern ob dies in besonders hohem Masse geschieht. 'Das Beste unter dem Erzielbaren'. So findet hier ein Abwägen statt. Dafür gibt es allerdings auf dem Gebiete der Ästhetik keine bestimmte Entscheidung. Die Zahl der Mittel um einen gegebenen Zweck

In spite of Brentano's opposition against Kant, also in spite of Husserl's early tendency to share in this opposition, Husserl shows himself in the passage just cited to favor Kant over Brentano in certain important respects. One of these respects is to be found in the claim that moral goodness is most properly attributed to the will, the good will of course.[1] Another respect lies in Husserl's correlation of the beautiful with certain acts of feeling, particularly certain pleasures, rather than with desire or will.[2] We have seen that Brentano's psychology will not allow for this, for no sharp division between feelings and volitions, on his view, are to be made. If we now recall that the class of presentations for Husserl includes judgments as well as "mere" presentations, the conclusion becomes irresistible: the resulting classification of psychical acts is indeed more Kantian (thinking, feeling, and willing) than Brentanian (presentations, judgments, and phenomena of love and hate).[3] While Husserl's theory of values is therefore in large measure inspired by Brentano's, its psychological side turns out to be extremely antithetical to the teachings of his mentor.

---

zu erreichen ist nichts Dargebotenes und bei der Entscheidung zu Überblickendes. Hier hilft Ausführung und Erfahrung. Anders auf dem Gebiet des Willens. Die Überlegung erstreckt sich auf die beschränkte Zahl erreichbarer und verfügbarer Momente und darum kann man verlangen, dass nach den Umständen des Falles das Beste gewählt wird.

"Noch eins: Die Ethik geht auch, sagte ich, auf die Verwirklung des sittlich Guten. Das tut sie als sittliche Erziehungslehre. Sie lehrt die Motive kennen, welche schädlich und die welche nützlich wirken, die welche das sittlich Gute zu fördern und die es zu hemmen geeignet sind. Und auch sie ist in dieser Hinsicht auf Erfahrung angewiesen und entnimmt dieser die Momente, durch welche sittliche Ideale charakterisiert werden können."

Though the second sentence in this lengthy passage begins with "1)", this has been deleted since no other points are enumerated.

[1] Cf. Kant, *Grundlegung zur Metaphysik der Sitten*, A 1/B 1: "Nothing anywhere in the world, not even outside of it, can possibly be thought of which can be regarded as good without qualification, except only a *good* will."

[2] Kant's famous definition of "beauty" in *Kritik der Urteilskraft* is "what is cognized without a concept as an object of a necessary pleasure".

[3] This point has been made by Ulrich Melle, "Objektivierende und nicht-objektivierende Akte", in Samuel IJsseling (ed.), *Husserl-Ausgabe und Husserl-Forschung* (Dordrecht: Kluwer, 1990), pp. 35-49.

5. CONCLUDING REMARKS

In this chapter we have considered some of the ways in which Husserl's philosophical views in the *Logische Untersuchungen* depart from the doctrines which he had learned from Brentano. As far as Brentano himself was concerned, the most important departure was Husserl's espousal of a Platonistically conceived pure logic. Brentano's blindness kept him from further disappointment in his former pupil, for as we have seen, the *Logische Untersuchungen* diverge in other important ways from Brentanian doctrines. The concept of intentional reference is held to be a crucial theme for phenomenology, although it is no longer regarded as an inexistence of the object. Moreover, certain parts of consciousness, according to Husserl, are not themselves intentional in character. Besides the thesis that intentional reference is one of the distinguishing features of psychical phenomena, other doctrines which Brentano taught were to be found in the theses that psychical phenomena are inwardly perceived and that they are either presentations or founded on presentations. Both of these theses, as we have seen, also undergo considerable qualification in the *Logische Untersuchungen*.

However, as already pointed out in the introduction, such divergences from Brentano's philosophy do not entail that Husserl's views in the *Logische Untersuchungen* are no longer to be considered in the context of the school of Brentano. A good deal of this work can be considered as an alternative descriptive psychology which is best understood in relation to Brentano's descriptive psychology and to the alternative ones of other Brentanists. It is therefore no surprise that Husserl's characterization of the *Logische Untersuchungen* as a "breakthrough work" (Hua XVIII/1, 8) is not repeated by any of his fellow Brentanists.[1] It will indeed be seen that in some very important respects the descriptive psychology and the general philosophical position in that work and related ones diverge less from the doctrines of Brentano than do the positions of other Brentanists.

Even Husserl's Platonistic tendencies in the *Logische Untersuchungen* are not without parallels with the philosophical views of other Brentanists. We shall now briefly consider Husserl's relation to Bolzano, who is, after all, in large measure the one behind the Platonism in the *Logische Untersuchungen* and also an important influence on other Brentanists.

---

[1] It is however repeated by Heidegger in *Sein und Zeit* (Tübingen: Max Niemeyer, 1986).

CHAPTER TWO

HUSSERL AND BOLZANO

We now come to the discussion of the relation of Husserl to Bolzano, insofar as this relation is relevant to determining Husserl's position in the school of Brentano. The most important themes here will be the Bolzanian notion of the objects of logic and Husserl's reaction to this notion. Before I discuss these themes, however, it will be helpful to sketch the reception of Bolzano in the school of Brentano.

1. THE BRENTANIST RECEPTION OF BOLZANO

Though Bernard Bolzano (1781-1848) did not live into the second half of the nineteenth century, he had little influence prior to that time. Under the restrictions of the authorities of the Austro-Hungarian Empire he could publish only by having his manuscripts smuggled abroad.

Among the disciples who could assist him was Robert Zimmermann, who played an important role in spreading Bolzanian doctrines by writing his *Philosophische Propädeutik* which was used in gymnasia throughout the Austro-Hungarian Empire. This textbook, which went through three editions (1853, 1860, and 1867), served to initiate all of the Austrian Brentanists, including Husserl, in philosophy.[1] Moreover, as a professor of philosophy in Vienna and a colleague of Brentano, Zimmermann was in a position to promote Bolzanian doctrines at least to some extent. Here it may of course be pointed out that Zimmermann became a disciple of Herbart, who indeed had tremendous influence in Austria during the nineteenth century.[2] Though he used the

---

[1] Husserl had copies of both the second and third edition of this work. While it is reasonable to assume that he used the third as a textbook, the second bears more markings and annotations. These would have to be taken into account in a full study of Husserl and Bolzano, which is not attempted here.

[2] Fritz Mauthner testifies to this fact in Raymund Schmidt (ed.), *Philosophie der Gegenwart in Selbstdarstellungen* III (Leipzig: Felix Meiner, 1922), p. 123: "In all of Austria one appealed to Herbart when one wanted to talk scientifically about philosophical, especially about pedagogical questions [In ganz Österreich berief man sich auf Herbart, wenn man wissenschaftlich über philosophische, besonders über pädagogische Fragen reden wollte]".

terminology of Bolzano in the first edition of his *Philosophische Propädeutik*, he replaced it in the second edition with Herbartian terminology. But he points out in the preface to the second edition that "he does this, not because he has changed his *views*, for he *fortunately does not in essence have to change these*".[1] Thus, Zimmermann sees the difference between Bolzano and Herbart on logical matters as insignificant. Moreover, if we take into account Bolzano's quotations of Herbart in *Wissenschaftslehre* § 51, some of which are again repeated by Husserl in *Prolegomena* (Hua XVIII, 218 ff.), it becomes clear that there is an affinity between Bolzano and Herbart, for in the passages quoted by Bolzano and Husserl concepts are distinguished from "activities of our mind" (*Tätigkeiten unseres Geistes*).[2] According to Bolzano, this is an acknowledgment of presentations in themselves, which are regarded by him as belonging among the objects of logic

Besides Zimmermann, Brentano himself brought the work of Bolzano to the attention of his students. As already indicated, Brentano lectured on Bolzano's *Paradoxien des Unendlichen*. In a letter to Hugo Bergmann (1 June 1909) Brentano explains:

It was important not merely to stimulate the youth of Austria to study philosophy, but particularly also to inspire them. What had thus far been accomplished in the country was not very much. [...] Only Bolzano proved to be in many respects an outstanding phenomenon. In an age of extreme decay [when German idealism prevailed] he got clear about its character; he did not allow himself to be impressed by the name of Kant. He preferred Leibniz and was right in doing so. [...] If, under such circumstances, I called attention to Bolzano, this was by no means done [...] to recommend Bolzano as a teacher and leader to the young people. What they could learn from him, I would say to myself, they could better learn from me. But you understand why I found no cause to enter into a criticism of Bolzano's weaknesses. As a result, Meinong and Twardowski, as well as Husserl and Kerry -- who was in fact influenced more by me than by Zimmermann and, long after leaving Vienna, engaged in correspondence with me in the final years before his early death -- immersed themselves in the study of Bolzano. What was wrong therein they did not

---

[1] Zimmermann, *Philosophische Propädeutik* (1867), pp. vii f: "[...] so tut er das, nicht weil er seine Ansichten geändert hat, denn diese *braucht er glücklicherweise dem Wesen nach nicht zu ändern*".

[2] The passages which Bolzano cites (p. 227) are taken from the first edition (1813) of Herbart's *Lehrbuch zur Einleitung in die Philosophie*. It is interesting to note that in Husserl's copy Bolzano's *Wissenschaftslehre* Herbart's name is underlined on the relevant page and there is a downward-pointing arrow in the margin next to it. Husserl also quotes from a later edition of *Einleitung in die Philosophie*, but also from Herbart's *Psychologie als Wissenschaft*, in order to show that Herbart was an early opponent of psychologism. But he also refers to Herbart's *Lehrbuch zur Psychologie* (Hua XVIII, 220 f.) in order to show that this opposition involves a failure to appreciate the ideality of concepts. Though Husserl accordingly has reservations about Herbart in the *Logische Untersuchungen*, it is nonetheless true, as pointed out in Karl Schuhmann, "Husserls doppelter Vorstellungsbegriff", that Herbart was an important influence on his psychological views in 1893.

sufficiently recognize as such.[1]

In this connection it should be mentioned, however, that the text which inspired the Brentanists in question was primarily the *Wissenschaftslehre*, not the *Paradoxien des Unendlichen*. In this light it seems as though Brentano exaggerated his role in the spread of Bolzanian notions.

While Husserl is often given credit for being the one who discovered Bolzano, other Brentanists before him had dealt with Bolzanian themes. It is noteworthy that already in the 1880's Kerry made extensive reference to various texts of Bolzano, including the two mentioned above as well as others.[2] In the final article of the series "Über Anschauung und ihre psychische Verarbeitung" Kerry makes an attempt to assimilate the Bolzanian notion of presentations in themselves (*Vorstellungen an sich*) and points out that Bolzano was a precursor of Brentano in two important respects.[3] First of all, in the *Wissenschaftslehre* we find a clear-cut distinction between presentations and judgments.[4] In this regard Bolzano stands in sharp contrast to various nineteenth century philosophers, especially Kant, Herbart, and the disciples of either one of these. Secondly, in this work we find an acknowledgment of predicates which modify their subject.[5] We have already seen how important this notion was for

---

[1] "Briefe Franz Brentanos an Hugo Begmann", pp. 125-126: "Es galt, die Jugend Österreichs zum Studium der Philosophie nicht bloss anzuregen, sondern insbesondere auch zu ermutigen. Was bis dahin im Lande geleistet worden war, war nicht eben sehr viel. [...] Nur Bolzano zeigte sich als eine, in mancher Beziehung hervorragende Erscheinung. In einer Zeit äussersten Verfalls machte er sich deren Charakter klar; den Namen Kants liess er sich nicht imponieren. Mit richtigem Blick gab er Leibniz den Vorzug. [...] Wenn ich unter solchen Umständen auf Bolzano aufmerksam machte, so geschah dies [...] keineswegs, um den jungen Leuten Bolzano als Lehrer und Führer zu empfehlen. Was sie von ihm, das, dürfte ich mir sagen, könnten sie besser von mir lernen. Aber Sie verstehen auch, warum ich auf eine Kritik der Schwächen Bolzanos einzugehen keinen Anlass fand. Daraufhin ist nun geschehen, dass sowohl Meinong und Twardowski als Husserl und Kerry, der allerdings auch mehr von mir als von Zimmermann beeinflusst worden ist und sich, nachdem er schon lange Wien verlassen, noch in den letzten Jahren vor seinem frühen Tod in brieflichen Verkehr mit mir setzte, in das Studium von Bolzano vertieften. Das Verkehrte darin wussten sie nicht genug als solches zu erkennen".

[2] See Kerry, "Über Anschauung und ihre psychische Verarbeitung", *Vierteljahrsschrift für wissenschaftliche Philosophie* 9 (1885): 476ff., where some of Bolzano's mathematical writings are discussed.

[3] Kerry, "Über Anschauung und ihre psychische Verarbeitung", *Vierteljahrsschrift für wissenschaftliche Philosophie* 15 (1891): 135 f. n.

[4] *Wissenschaftslehre*, § 34. Cf. Hugo Bergmann, *Das philosophische Werk Bernard Bolzanos* (Halle a.S.: Max Niemeyer, 1909), pp. 42 ff.

[5] *Ibid.*, § 23 & § 29. Kerry points out ("Über Anschauung und ihre psychische Verarbeitung" (1891): 135 f.n.) that this notion is already present in the logic of Savonarola. In § 19 Bolzano cites a passage from Savonarola's work in which it is said that a dead man has the shape and likeness of a man and is

Brentano. It will be seen later on that it is crucial to Husserl's reaction to Twardowski.

While Kerry is perfectly right to point out these parallels between Bolzanian and Brentanian teachings, it is certain that more can be found. As already indicated in the above-cited letter to Bergmann, Brentano approves of Bolzano's contempt of German idealism and of his preference of Leibniz over Kant. Another parallel between Bolzano and Brentano lies in their refusal to regard linguistic structures as decisive in logical considerations. In addition to this, Bolzano's emphasis on the reference (*Beziehung*) of presentations and judgments to objects (*Gegenstände*) made his thought easily accessible to the Brentanists. In this regard, however, his allowance for objectless presentations (*gegenstandlose Vorstellungen*), as opposed to "objectual" ones (*gegenständliche Vorstellungen*),[1] stands in sharp contrast with Brentano's characterization of psychical phenomena in terms of intentional reference. According to Bolzano, objectless presentations are to be found in our grasp of terms such as "round square", "golden mountain", "nothing", and "green virtue".[2] If, however, none of the presentations in question have objects, this comes into conflict with Brentano's thesis that all psychical phenomena, including all presentations, are characterized by their reference to objects. The resulting conflict between Bolzano and Brentano is seen in Kerry's shift

---

nonetheless not a man. This point, however, had already been made in Aristotle, *Parts of Animals*, 640 b 35-36.

At the risk of digression, it may be here be suggested that the distinction between properly used terms and modified ones is in need of a supplement, namely the distinction between the *fully* modified and the *semi*-modified sense of a term. In order to make this clear let us consider the term "eye". When we speak of seeing with one's eyes, this term is obviously meant in the proper sense. If, however, we speak of the eyes of a statue, the term is used in a fully modified sense. But now let us ask whether blind people have eyes. Obviously many of them do, although the term "eye" in this context is used in neither the proper nor the fully modifified sense. In order to see that this sense is not the proper one, just consider how wrong it would be to teach a child how to use the word in question by pointing to the eyes of a blind person as exemplary. Yet, the sense in which a blind person has eyes is closer to the proper sense than is the sense in which a statue has eyes. This is not to say that, wherever a proper and fully modified sense of a given term can be identified, there must also be a semi-modified sense. One must however be careful to consider whether there is one, for sometimes the result of such considerations will be surprising. At first sight it may seem as if there were only a proper and a modified sense of "money". When we speak of German money *simpliciter*, we are using the term in the proper sense. When we speak of counterfeit money, the term is used in the fully modified sense. But when we say of a certain coin or note that it is no longer valid money, this seems to be instance of a semi-modified sense of the word in question. It would be of great interest to work out this suggestion more fully, but such a task lies beyond the scope of the present study.

[1] Objectual presentations are simply presentations which have objects. The term "objective" is avoided here, for it is used as a translation of *objektiv*. An objective presentation is simply a presentation in itself, which may be either objectless or objectual.

[2] *Wissenschaftslehre*, § 67.

from one side to the other without making this problem thematic.¹

While Kerry was the first Brentanist to attempt an explicit assimilation of Bolzanian notions, it is noteworthy that the logic textbook to take the place of Zimmermann's as a propeduetic in the gymnasia, written by Alois Höfler with Meinong as a collaborator,² contains two references to Bolzano. Höfler cites with approval Bolzano's characterization of textbooks as "books which are quite especially made for the sake of convincing".³ Höfler also cites Bolzano's rejection of the old canon of logic that the richer the content, the smaller the extension.⁴ Such a canon was allegedly exemplified by concepts such as that of a human being in relation to the concept of animal. While the former concept is richer in content than the latter (insofar as the definition of "human being" would involve mentioning more features than the definition of "animal"), the amount of individuals which fall under the concept of a human being is smaller than that of the ones falling under the concept of an animal. According to Bolzano, this rule is refuted by comparing the concept of human beings who understand all European languages and the concept of human beings who understand all *living* European languages. The latter is both richer in content and greater in extension. It is richer in content, for it contains "living" in addition to all the same elements. But Höfler leaves it up to the student to decide whether Bolzano's counter-example is acceptable.

Finally, mention should be made of Kasimir Twardowski as one of the Brentanists who helped to bring attention to Bolzano. All of the above-mentioned authors, namely Zimmermann, Brentano, Kerry, and Höfler, are cited in Twardowski's *Zur Lehre vom Inhalt und Gegenstand der Vorstellungen*. The above-mentioned problem of objectless presentations, moreover, becomes thematic there. The way in which he proposes to solve this problem was however regarded as unsatisfactory by Husserl. In the chapter on Husserl and Twardowski we shall elaborate on this topic. Twardowski is mentioned here only because he played an important role in bringing Bolzanian themes to the attention of other Brentanists, most notably Husserl.

---

[1] See Twardowski, *Zur Lehre vom Inhalt und Gegenstand der Vorstellungen*, p. 29.

[2] It should also be noted here that Höfler was the editor of the first two volumes of *Wissenschaftslehre* which were published in 1914.

[3] *Wissenschaftslehre* IV, § 393: "Bücher [...], welche für den Zweck der Überzeugung ganz vornehmlich eingerichtet sind". This phrase is quoted in a larger passage in Höfler (in collaboration with Meinong), *Logik* (Prague/Vienna: Tempsky; Leipzig: Freytag, 1890), p. vii.

[4] *Wissenschaftslehre* I, § 120, referred to in Höfler, *Logik*, p. 37.

2. BOLZANO ON THE OBJECTS OF LOGIC

In the *Wissenschaftslehre* Bolzano attempts to develop a discipline consisting of "the sum total of all those rules according to which we must proceed when dividing up the entire realm of truth into particular sciences and expositing them in special textbooks, if we want to proceed in a truly appropriate manner".[1] According to a shorter characterization of the theory of science, it is "that science which instructs us on how we are to exposit the sciences in appropriate textbooks".[2] This discipline is also called "logic" and is accordingly meant to include much of what has been traditionally presented under that name, e.g., rules of inference. However, regarding the plan in which logic is to be presented, Bolzano remarks:[3]

that a very essential difference between my plan and that of others consists first and foremost in the fact that I endeavor to speak of *presentations, sentences, and truths in themselves*, whereas in all textbooks of logic thus far (as many as I at least know) all these objects are treated only as (real or possible) appearances in the mind of a thinking entity, only as *modes of thinking*.

Here we find not only Bolzano's sharp separation of the objects of logic from psychical phenomena, but also his enumeration of the former objects as presentations in themselves, sentences in themselves, and truths in themselves. We shall now attempt to elucidate each of these notions as well as Bolzano's motivation for regarding them as the objects of logic.

In § 19 of the *Wissenschaftslehre*, a section entitled "what the author means by a sentence in itself", Bolzano contrasts both sentences in expression and sentences in thought with sentences in themselves. The term "sentence" *simpliciter* ordinarily means

---

[1] *Wissenschaftslehre*, § 2: "[...] so verstehe ich denn unter der Wissenschaftslehre den Inbegriff aller derjenigen Regeln, nach denen wir bei dem Geschäfte der Abteilung des gesammten Gebietes der Wahrheit in einzelne Wissenschaften und bei der Darstellung derselben in eigenen Lehrbüchern vorgehen müssen, wenn wir recht zweckmässig vorgehen müssen". This passage is marked in Husserl's copy. In the margin next to it is written "def" and "19", indicating tha t Bolzano here gives us a definition of "theory of science" which is referred to on page 19 of Volume I (§ 4).

[2] *Ibid.*, § 1: "[...] so könnten wir unsere Erklärung der Wissenschaftslehre kürzer auch so fassen, dass sie diejenige Wissenschaft sei, welche uns anweise, wie wir die Wissenschaften in zweckmässigen Lehrbüchern darstellen sollen". This passage is also marked in Husserl's copy of the *Wissenschaftslehre*.

[3] *Ibid.*, § 16: "Gleichwohl darf ich es nicht verhehlen, dass ein sehr wesentlicher Unterschied zwischen meinem und dem Plane Anderer zuvörderst schon darin bestehe, dass ich von *Vorstellungen, Sätzen und Wahrheiten an sich* zu sprechen unternehme, während in allen bisherigen Lehrbüchern der Logik (so viele ich wenigstens kenne) von allen diesen Gegenständen nur als von (wirklichen oder doch möglichen) Erscheinungen in dem Gemüte eines denkenden Wesens, nur als von *Denkweisen*, gehandelt wird". This passage is marked in Husserl's copy. In the right margin is written "47", referring to page 47 of volume I (§ 12) where a similar point is made.

a linguistic expression of a certain type, e.g., "a square is round". While Bolzano acknowledges this, he prefers to make his reference to these expressions clear by using special terms for them (*ausgesprochene Sätze* or *ausgedrückte Sätze*). Here we may use the English term "sentences in expression" for this purpose. Moreover, Bolzano maintains that it is quite possible to think in sentences without actually expressing them. These sentences are again indicated by a special term (*gedachte Sätze*). Here we use the English term "sentences in thought" for this purpose. Sentences in themselves, by contrast, are briefly characterized in the following way: "any assertion that something is or is not, no matter whether this assertion is true or false, put into words by someone or not, indeed even thought in the mind or not".[1] Unlike sentences in thought or expression, sentences in themselves do not have reality or existence. It is as wrong to ascribe to them an eternal existence as it is to say that they come and go together with our thoughts.

Now truth, according to Bolzano, can be ascribed either to sentences in themselves or to judgments (which are of course included among the sentences in thought).[2] Any given sentence in itself must moreover be either true or false,[3] the true ones being referred to as "truths in themselves".[4] Bolzano's defense of this notion of truth is pivotal in his rejection of the view that logic is concerned with "modes of thinking".[5] In response to those who regard the laws of logic, e.g., the law of contradiction, as laws about the conditions under which the thoughts of any rational being can be true, he

---

[1] *Ibid.*, § 19: "irgend eine Aussage, dass etwas ist oder nicht; gleichviel, ob diese Aussage wahr oder falsch ist; ob sie von irgend Jemand in Worte gefasst oder nicht gefasst, ja auch im Geiste nur gedacht oder nicht gedacht worden ist". This passage is emphatically marked in Husserl's copy of the *Wissenschaftslehre*.

[2] *Ibid.*, § 24.

[3] *Ibid.*, § 125.

[4] As far as I am aware, Bolzano does not speak of "falsehoods in themselves". But it would by no means be antithetical to his way of thinking if one were to use this term. On this point Hugo Bergmann's interpretation (op. cit., pp. 12 ff.) of Bolzano's theory of sentences in themselves is erroneous. See Edgar Morscher, *Das logische An-sich bei Bernard Bolzano* (Salzburg: Anton Pustet, 1973), p. 65.

[5] Cf. *Ibid.*, § 20: "As soon as one admits to me that it is necessary, indeed also only useful, in logic to speak of *truths in themselves*, i.e., truths regardless whether or not they are known by someone, and especially of the connection which prevails among them, one will also not deny that the concept of *sentences in themselves* [...] deserves to be adopted in logic [Sobald man mir zugibt, dass es in der Logik notwendig, ja auch nur nützlich sei, von *Wahrheiten an sich*, d.h. von Wahrheiten, abgesehen davon, ob sie von jemand erkannt oder nicht erkannt werden, und insbesondere von dem Zusammenhange, der zwischen ihnen herrscht, zu sprechen; so wird man auch nicht in Abrede stellen, dass es der Begriff von *Sätzen an sich* [...] verdiene, in die Logik aufgenommen zu werden]". Since presentations are characterized as parts of sentences in themselves (as yet to be discussed in the text), the justification of the notion of truths in themselves will also provide the justification of the notion of presentations in themselves.

raises the question how we know these conditions must obtain for any rational being. He answers:

> that we know (or believe to know) this only because we see (or in any case believe to see) that this law is a condition which holds for truths in themselves. Thus, we claim, for instance, that the *law of contradiction* is a universal law of thought and consequently belongs to the pure part of logic, only because and insofar as we presuppose that this law contains a *truth in itself* and therefore a condition with which all other truths must accord. If we know that something is a universally valid law of thought only from the fact we have known before that it is a truth and a conditional sentence for other truths, then it is obviously a shift away from the correct viewpoint if one pretends to deal with the general laws of *thought* where one is at bottom establishing the universal laws of *truth* itself.[1]

In addition, Bolzano also attacks the limitation of the laws of logic to the thoughts of human beings. This limitation is even worse than the one just dealt with, for the class of human beings is, after all, to be included in the class of rational beings. It is indeed inescapable for the logician to regard the laws of his science as *applicable* to our species. Such an application, however, in no way excludes the conception of the objects which are in no way *reducible* to our processes of thought or those of any other species.

Every sentence in itself, according to Bolzano, is made up of parts which are not themselves sentences in themselves.[2] These parts are called "presentations in themselves" or "objective presentations". As sentences in themselves sometimes have their counterparts in judgments and other thoughts, presentations in themselves likewise sometimes have their counterparts in certain psychical appearances which Bolzano calls "subjective presentations" (*subjektive Vorstellungen*). Presentations in themselves moreover sometimes have their linguistic counterparts which are to be found in the subject, the predicate, and the copula of a sentence in expression.[3] Like sentences in themselves, presentations in themselves are also denied any existence in reality. They

---

[1] *Ibid.*, § 16: "[...] dass wir dies immer nur daher wissen (oder zu wissen glauben), dass dieses Gesetz eine für alle Wahrheiten selbst stattfindende Bedingung sei. So behaupten wir z.B., dass der *Satz des Widerspruches* ein allgemeines und somit in den reinen Teil der Logik gehöriges Denkgesetz sei, bloss weil und in wiefern wir voraussetzen, dass dieser Satz eine *Wahrheit an sich*, und somit eine Bedingung, der alle andere Wahrheiten gemäss sein müssen, enthalte. Erkennen wir nun, dass etwas ein allgemeines Denkgesetz sei, nur eben daraus, weil wir zuvor erkannt haben, dass es eine Wahrheit und ein Bedingungssatz für andere Wahrheiten sei; so ist es offenbar eine Verschiebung des rechten Gesichtspunktes, wenn man dort von den allgemeinen Gesetzen des *Denkens* zu handeln vorgibt, wo man im Grunde die allgemeinen Bedingungen der *Wahrheit* selbst aufstellt". Beginning with the second sentence, this passage is marked in Husserl's copy of the *Wissenschaftslehre*.

[2] *Ibid.*, § 48.

[3] *Ibid.*, § 126.

are classified in various ways: e.g., concrete and abstract,[1] simple and complex,[2] objectual and objectless,[3] real and imaginary,[4] intuitive and conceptual.[5] By no means is it possible here to enter into these distinctions and other claims which Bolzano makes regarding the relations among presentations in themselves[6] or the relations between them and other objects.[7] Important to us here, however, are some remarks which he makes regarding the *reference* of the presentation to its object.

The claim that some presentations are objectless, as already mentioned, was confronted as a challenge to what the Brentanists learned from their mentor. According to Bolzano, such presentations are expressed in various words, e.g., "nothing", "golden mountain", "green virtue", and "round square".[8] While all of these are alleged to be cases in which there is a presentation on the one hand and no corresponding object on the other hand, one must be careful to avoid the impression that for Bolzano the object of a presentation must be something real. As it turns out, he regards the concept of an object, or *something* (or any equivalent concept), as the highest concept of all, higher than the concept of reality or being.[9] The concept of an object therefore includes in its extension objects which are not real. It is also clear *what* non-real objects are allowed for by Bolzano. They are not golden mountains and round squares, which are not objects at all, but rather presentations and sentences in themselves (including of course truths in themselves). Thus, insofar as the reference of a presentation is concerned,

---

[1] *Ibid.*, § 60.

[2] *Ibid.*, § 61.

[3] *Ibid.*, § 67.

[4] *Ibid.*, § 70.

[5] *Ibid.*, §§ 72-75.

[6] *Ibid.*, §§ 91-108.

[7] *Ibid.*, §§ 109-114.

[8] *Ibid.*, § 67. Bolzano also mentions "and" and "has" as examples of objectless presentations in ibid., § 78 (I, p. 360). Next to this passage of the *Wissenschaftslehre* Husserl writes "?!" in his copy. Bolzano's usage of these examples, it can be argued, falls prey to the same objection (discussed in Chapter Five) which Twardowski uses against the claim that the term "nothing" manifests an objectless presentation. Since this term is syncateroematic, it does not manifest any presentation at all, neither an objectual nor an objectless one. This objection applies all the more obviously to the terms "and" and "has". It is indeed surprising how a philosopher of logic as sophisticated as Bolzano could have committed such a fundamental error.

[9] *Ibid.*, § 99.

Bolzano divides them into presentations which refer to existent objects, those which refer to non-existent objects, and those which do not refer at all. This classification is of course incompatible with Brentano's early theory of presentations, insofar as we limit our consideration to subjective presentations (for objective presentations do not at all come into consideration for him). It is therefore understandable why the Brentanists, given their attempt to assimilate Bolzanian notions, were so occupied with the revision of the doctrine of intentional inexistence.

In the *Wissenschaftslehre* there is one other discussion regarding presentations in themselves which concerns us here, namely the one regarding "whether the parts of a presentation are identical with the presentations of the parts of its object".[1] Here Bolzano argues that the parts of a presentation need not be identical with the presentations of the parts of its object. This is already clear from the notion of objectless presentations. Obviously the parts of such a presentation cannot be identical with the presentations of the parts of its object, for there is no such object. If the alleged identity between parts of a presentation and presentations of the parts of its object is restricted to referring presentations, Bolzano admits that this identity can indeed obtain in some cases. But he also points out the following counter-examples: "'A country which has no mountains', 'a book which is without an etching', and the like. For via the presentations which occur in them: mountains, etching, they obviously do not refer to parts which the object subsumed under them has, but rather to ones which it lacks".[2] Other counter-examples are to be found in such cases as "the eye of man". Moreover, Bolzano adds that the presentation of a simple object can be complex. This is the case in the presentation of a spiritual entity, which, according to scholastic doctrine, is a pure form and thus not a complex of matter and form.

Before we leave this discussion of Bolzano on the objects of logic, one further issue must be raised regarding his conception of sentences in themselves. As some presentations in themselves are said to have objects, we might expect the same from sentences in themselves. If they do, then the question arises whether the objects in question are uniquely correlated with sentences in themselves or whether they may also correspond to presentations in themselves. As it turns out, Bolzano maintains that every truth in itself has an object, namely the object which corresponds to the *subject* of the

---

[1] *Ibid.*, § 63: "Ob die Teile einer Vorstellung einerlei sind mit den Vorstellungen der Teile ihres Gegenstandes".

[2] *Ibid.*, § 63: "'Ein Land, das keine Berge hat', 'Ein Buch, das ohne Kupfer ist' u. dgl. Denn diese weisen durch die in ihnen vorkommenden Vorstellungen: Berge, Kupfer, offenbar nicht auf Teile hin, welche der ihnen unterstehende Gegenstand hat, sondern vielmehr auf solche, die ihm mangeln". This passage is marked in Husserl's copy of the *Wissenschaftslehre*.

relevant sentence.[1] If, for instance, it is true that the sky is blue, then the object of this truth in itself is the sky. Thus, the object of a sentence in itself is likewise an object of a presentation in itself, not something which is uniquely correlated with a sentence in itself.

3. HUSSERL ON THE OBJECTS OF LOGIC

In the *Prolegomena zur reinen Logik* Husserl argues that, while logic in its practical application may involve psychology, it is nonetheless also dependent on a theoretical discipline called "pure logic", which is to be sharply distinguished from psychology and divided into two branches (Hua XVIII, 245 ff.). On the one hand, the fundamental concepts of pure logic are "pure or formal objective categories" (*die reinen oder formalen gegenständlichen Kategorien*), e.g., object, state of affairs, unity, plurality, and many others. The remaining branch of pure logic, on the other hand, deals with "meaning categories" (*Bedeutungskategorien*), e.g., concept, sentence, and truth. The objects which are referred to in the application of meaning categories are in short *meanings*, which are not to be confused with the psychical acts corresponding to these meanings. Meanings are ideal, whereas the acts in which meaning is given to expressions are real (Hua XIX/1, 97 ff.). The view that pure logic is concerned with ideal objects, as Husserl explicitly acknowledges, is by and large inspired by Bolzano (Hua XVIII, 227 ff.).

In Husserl's copy of the *Wissenschaftslehre* we nonetheless find annotations which indicate an exegetical problem which prompted him to work out the Bolzanian notion of the objects of logic further. A sentence in thought, as explained in § 19 of the *Wissenschaftslehre*, may be taken as the thought itself which is not put into words (and would of course be expressed as a full sentence in expression if it were put into words). "But what he usually means by this ['sentence in thought']," Husserl adds in the bottom margin, "is sentences which are *objects* of thought, as he then says further 'thoughts of it'".[2] In this case the sentence in thought would be construed as that which sometimes

---

[1] *Ibid.*, § 196. The corresponding presentation in itself is called the "substrate" (*Unterlage*).

[2] "Aber zumeist versteht er darunter Sätze, die Gegenstände von Gedanken sind, wie er dann weiter sagt 'die Gedanken an ihn'". Here reference is made by Husserl to the words "gedacht oder vorgestellt" Vol. I, p. 78, where Bolzano says: "It is certainly true that every sentence is thought or presented by God, if not by any other entity [...] [Wahr ist allerdings, dass jeder Satz, wenn sonst von keinem anderen Wesen, doch von Gott gedacht oder vorgestellt [...]]". While sentences in themselves are thus regarded here as the objects of God's thoughts or presentations, it does not follow from this that they are in every case the objects of the relevant thoughts. However, in the above-cited annotation in Husserl's copy of the *Wissenschaftslehre* reference is also made to Vol. I, p. 99 (§ 23) where Bolzano equates a sentence in thought with "the subjective presenta-

80 CHAPTER TWO

coincides with the sentence in itself (namely when thinking occurs) and sometimes does not (when thinking does not occur). Another interpretation is however suggested on the next page (p. 77) of Husserl's copy of the *Wissenschaftslehre*. Here Husserl makes the following remark in the bottom margin: "That Bolzano means the judgment *in specie* is shown by the approving quotation from Mehmel 85".[1] The reference here is to Volume I, page 85 of the *Wissenschaftslehre* where Bolzano cites the following passage from Mehmel's *Versuch einer vollständigen analytischen Denklehre als Vorphilosophie* (1803): "The judgment, considered objectively, i.e., in abstraction from the mind whose action it is, is called 'sentence'".[2] In the margin next to this quotation from Mehmel Husserl writes: "That would be the judgment *in specie*".[3] Abstraction is of course traditionally held to be the means whereby a species is accessible to cognition. By abstracting away all the individualizing properties of a judgment, the judgment *in specie* is accordingly cognized. This is not to say that we do this whenever we judge; rather, as Husserl understands the claim of Mehmel, and apparently of Bolzano too, *logicians* concern themselves with judgments *in specie*.

It thus seems to Husserl that Bolzano's conception of sentences in themselves in relation to the corresponding thoughts is equivocal. On the one hand, sentences in themselves are regarded as the *objects* of these thoughts whenever such thoughts occur. On the other hand, they are regarded as the *species* of these thoughts, more precisely of judgments. Confronted with this equivocation, Husserl naturally felt compelled to choose between one of these conceptions of sentences in themselves.[4] As is now well

---

tion of a sentence". In the margin next to this passage a question mark is written in Husserl's copy.

[1]"Dass Bolzano das Urteil in specie meint, zeigt das beifällige Zitat aus Mehmel 85." Gottlieb Ernst August Mehmel (1761-1840), professor at Erlangen, was in large measure a follower of Kant, but he was also influenced by Fichte. For further details about him, see Ludwig Noack, *Philosophie-geschichtliches Lexikon. Historisch-biographisches Handwörterbuch zur Geschichte der Philosophie* (Leipzig: Erich Koschny, 1879), p. 589; Werner Ziegenfuss and Gertrud Jung, *Philosophen-Lexikon. Handwörterbuch der Philosophie nach Personen* II (Berlin: Walter de Gruyter, 1950), p. 143; Rudolf Eisler, *Philosophen-Lexikon. Leben, Werke und Lehren der Denker* (Berlin: Ernst Siegfried Mittler und Sohn, 1912), p. 461.

[2]*Wissenschaftslehre*, § 21: "Das Urteil objektiv, das ist, mit Abstraktion von dem Geiste, dessen Handlung es ist, betrachtet, heisst ein *Satz*". Bolzano calls Mehmel's work *Analytische Denklehre*.

[3]"Das wäre das Urteil *in specie*".

[4]Cf. Dallas Willard, *Logic and the Objectivity of Knowledge: A Study in Husserl's Early Philosophy* (Athens, Ohio: Ohio University, 1984), p. 84: "For Bolzano ... the proposition primarily enters into relationship with the mind as its object, and hence through *intentionality*. For Husserl, on the other hand, the proposition ... enters into the act of thought or speech through *instantiation or exemplification*, and becomes an object, if at all, through special acts of reflection". Unfortunately, Willard here misses the ambiguity which Husserl finds in Bolzano's theory of sentences in themselves. This ambiguity is discerned

known, he chose to conceive of them as the species of judging acts. Moreover, the suggestion of Mehmel was extended to other meanings. Thus, we find Husserl referring to concepts as species of certain acts of consciousness, i.e., the meanings of names (Hua XIX/1, 223). Pure logic, insofar as it is concerned with meaning categories, therefore has the species of propositional and nominal acts as its objects. It will be seen later that Husserl's view on this matter differs sharply from Meinong's.

We have seen that Bolzano regarded sentences in themselves and presentations in themselves as non-real objects. Husserl likewise adopts this view. He equates the real with the temporal and denies that meanings have any temporal determinations at all. However, he is willing to say that they exist, insofar as certain attributes can categorically be ascribed to them. While he here speaks the language of Lotze rather than Bolzano,[1] it seems to be a mere terminological preference of Bolzano to use "existence" as a synonym of "reality". As it turns out, he is willing to say that there *are* truths in themselves in the sense that certain sentences in themselves are true.[2] Thus, it appears that Husserl's view regarding the ontological status of the objects of logic, although it is inspired by Lotzean Platonism, also has roots in Bolzano's *Wissenschaftslehre*.[3]

---

not only in the annotations in Husserl's copy of the *Wissenschaftslehre*, but also in his 1908 lectures on theory of meaning (Hua XXVI, 33, 156). Most importantly, however, it is noted in *Ideen* I (Hua III/1, 219 n.). Here Bolzano's "approving quotation from Mehmel's *Denklehre*" is again appealed to in support of the interpretation of sentences in themselves as judgments *in specie*. But in *Ideen* I they are alternatively construed as noemata rather than judgments *in specie*. Since Husserl's notion of the noema is absolutely unparalleled in the school of Brentano, this notion will not be focal in the present study, except in our consideration of Stumpf's critique of *Ideen* I.

[1] See R.D. Rollinger, *Meinong and Husserl on Abstraction and Universals*, pp. 30 f., 101 f. See also Christian Beyer, *Von Bolzano zu Husserl. Eine Untersuchung über den Ursprung der phänomenologischen Bedeutungslehre* (Dordrecht: Kluwer, 1996).

[2] *Wissenschaftslehre*, § 30.

[3] Fink (ed.), "Entwurf einer 'Vorrede' zu den *Logischen Untersuchung*", pp. 129-133. See also Husserl's criticism of Lotze (ibid., pp. 323-326) and also that of Bolzano (pp. 326-329). The gist of both criticisms is nothing like a retraction of Husserl's Platonism, for he rather accuses both of these thinkers of back-sliding into the opposing tendencies, namely psychologism and empiricism.

4. CONCLUDING REMARKS

While Bolzano had already been an important figure in the school of Brentano before Husserl assimilated some of his doctrines, this assimilation is peculiar insofar as it involves the acceptance of the view that the objects of logic are sentences in themselves and their parts. According to Bolzano, these are not to be confused with judgments or other psychical phenomena and are indeed denied "reality" altogether. Husserl fully agrees with this view, although he insists that sentences in themselves are the *species* and not the *objects* of acts of judging. He also adds that, while the objects of logic do not have the sort of being which physical and psychical objects (real being) have, they nevertheless have an ideal being. This Platonistic twist, however, must at least in part be attributed to Lotze. Besides this view on the objects of logic, another Bolzanian doctrine found its way into Husserl's thinking, namely the doctrine of objectless presentations, which will be fully discussed in the chapter on Husserl and Twardowski.

CHAPTER THREE

HUSSERL AND STUMPF

1. STUMPF AS A PUPIL OF BRENTANO

Carl Stumpf was Brentano's "oldest pupil",[1] for he began attending lectures of his mentor before any of the other Brentanists. He was already studying law in Würzburg (not because a career in this area interested him, but rather because it would allow him the leisure to occupy himself with music) when a transformation was initiated by Brentano's defense of a number of theses for the sake of habilitation in 1866. Stumpf describes the impression which Brentano then made on him as follows:

Everything folded before the great tasks of philosophical and religious rebirth. Sharp thinking was in fact not my inclination until then; on the contrary, it was rather unpleasant to me. Only Brentano's iron discipline made the need for logical clarity and consistency second nature. [...] The thesis which he defended in his habilitation, that the true philosophical method is none other than the one of natural science, was and remained for me a guiding star.[2]

In the winter semester of 1866/67 Stumpf attended Brentano's lecture on the history of philosophy. In this lecture, which began with an introduction concerning the concept and method of philosophy, Brentano presented his view that each period of the history of philosophy goes through four phases. The deep impression which Brentano made through this lecture, also of course through his habilitation defense, caused Stumpf to give up his study of jurisprudence and devote himself to philosophy and theology. Thereafter he stayed in very close contact with Brentano.

In order to pursue a career in philosophy, Stumpf needed to take a doctorate. Since

---

[1]Carl Stumpf, *Erkenntnistheorie* II (Leipzig: Johannes Ambrosius Barth, 1940), p. 428: "ältester Schüler". Here Stumpf does not mean "oldest" in the sense of being born the earliest, for in this sense Marty was the oldest disciple.

[2]*Die Philosophie der Gegenwart in Selbstdarstellungen* V, edited by Raymund Schmidt (Leipzig: Felix Meiner, 1924), p. 208: "Alles versank vor den grossen Aufgaben der philosophischen und religiösen Wiedergeburt. Scharfes Denken war eigentlich bis dahin nicht mein Fall, vielmehr mir etwas unbehaglich. Erst Brentanos eiserne Diszipline machte mir das Bedürfnis logischer Klarheit und Folgerichtigkeit zur zweiten Natur. [...] Seine Habilitionsthese, dass die wahre philosophische Methode keine andere sei als die naturwissenschaftliche, war und blieb mein Leitstern".

Brentano was only a *Privatdozent* at the time, a dissertation had to be written under someone else's supervision. He accordingly advised Stumpf to go to Göttingen where he could write it under the supervision of Lotze. This recommendation was by no means insignificant, for Stumpf says in his memoires regarding Lotze: "None of the German teachers of philosophy could be put on even just approximately the same level with him, if one considered the natural scientific method of thinking, as Brentano did, to be exemplary for the philosophical one, and close contact with the natural sciences to be the condition of successful philosophizing".[1] Stumpf stayed in Göttingen for three semesters (from the summer of 1867 to the summer of 1868). After finishing a dissertation on Plato (1868), he returned to Würzburg "in order to continue the philosophical studies with Brentano, but at the same time to begin theological ones".[2] In the following year he began attending the seminary in Würzburg, where he "diligently studied Thomas Aquinas and other scholastics".[3] At the same time he followed lectures of Brentano.

Among the lectures which Stumpf attended was the one on metaphysics (SS 1868), which was later expanded into a course which took up two semesters (WS 1868/69, SS 1869). The first part was concerned with transcendental philosophy (i.e., epistemology) and ontology. Here Brentano painstakingly argued in reply to various sceptical objections against the two types of immediate knowledge, namely inner perception and the cognition of axioms. "The necessity to assent to them", according to Stumpf's paraphrase:

is not rooted in a blind psychological compulsion, but rather in their inner, self-luminous evidence. [...] He [Brentano] concluded further that what is evident is true not only for our understanding, but for every possible understanding, for it is only the special light of the thing itself. He was therefore miles and miles away from psychologism, which wants to derive logical necessity from a psychological one.[4]

---

[1]Stumpf, "Zum Gedächtnis Lotzes", *Kantstudien* XXII (1918), p. 2: "Keiner unter den deutschen Lehrer der Philosophie konnte ihm auch nur annähernd gleichgestellt werden, wenn man wie Brentano selbst die naturwissenschaftliche Methode des Denkens als vorbildlich für die philosophische, und enge Fühlung mit den Naturwissenschaften als die Bedingung erfolgreichen Philosophierens".

[2]*Ibid.*, p. 209: "um die philosophischen Studien bei Brentano fortzusetzen, zugleich aber theologische zu beginnen".

[3]*Ibid.*, p. 210: "Daneben studierte ich fleissig Thomas von Aquino und andere Scholastiker".

[4]"Erinnerungen an Franz Brentano", pp. 100 f.: "Die Notwendigkeit, ihnen zuzustimmen, wurzelt nicht in einem psychologischen Zwang, sondern in ihrer inneren, selbstleuchtenden Evidenz. [...] Er folgerte weiter, dass das Evidente nicht nur für unseren Verstand, sondern für jeden möglichen Verstand wahr sei, weil es eben nur das eigene Licht der Sache selbst sei. Vom Psychologismus also, der die logische Notwendigkeit aus einer psychologischen herleiten will, war er himmelweit entfernt". Here Stumpf is obviously defending Brentano against Husserl. As we have already seen, Brentano was emphatically opposed to psychologism

As far as ontology is concerned, Brentano was occupied with the derivation of the Aristotelian categories and the Aristotelian distinction between matter and form. In the second part of the metaphysics lecture he defended theism and a concomitant teleological view of the cosmos from the standpoint of probability theory. According to Brentano, there is only an infinitesimal probability that the world is as it is without a deity who is at work in it.

The notion of probability again played an important role in Brentano's lecture on deductive and inductive logic,[1] which Stumpf also attended. In this lecture Brentano "distinguishes, in the case of both names and assertions, what they *express* (the psychical functions which are manifested in them) from what they *mean*".[2] While an assertion manifests an act of judging, which is reduced to affirming or rejecting a presented object (the matter of the judgment), the meaning of the assertion is the *content* of the judgment. "It can be linguistically expressed in infinitival form or in 'that' clauses. This concept (later designated by me as 'state of affairs') is for one reason, among others, important: because the whole class of indirect judgments (It is possible, necessary, probable, true, false that ...) is, according to his account at that time, tied to properties of such contents of judgments".[3] In the first chapter we have already encountered Brentano's concepts of quality and matter of judgment. These

---

insofar as this is to be construed as a sort of relevativism.

The term "psychologism", says Husserl, is used by him "without any derogatory 'coloring'" (Hua XVIII, 64). He attributes the same sort of usage to Stumpf in "Psychologie und Erkenntnistheorie", *Abhandlungen der bayrischen Akademie* (1891). While he may be right in his assessment of Stumpf's usage of this term, it is rather bizarre and altogether unconvincing for Husserl to say that he does not mean to denigrate the very viewpoint which he is attacking.

[1] As pointed out in Karl Schuhmann, "Carl Stumpf (1848-1936)", in L. Albertazzi et al. (eds.), *The School of Franz Brentano* (Dordrecht: Kluwer, 1996), p. 111, the title of the lecture under consideration is "clearly reminiscent of J.S. Mill". As regards parallels between Brentano and Mill, see Wilhelm Baumgartner, "Mills und Brentanos Methode der beschreibenden Analyse", *Brentano Studien* 2 (1989): 63-78.

[2] "Erinnerungen an Franz Brentano", pp. 106 f.: "unterscheidet sowohl bei den Namen wie bei den Aussagen das, was sie *ausdrücken* (die psychischen Funktionen, die sich in ihnen kundgeben) von dem, was die *bedeuten*".

[3] *Ibid.*, p. 107: "Er kann sprachlich in infinitivischer Form oder in Dass-Sätzen ausgedrückt werden. Dieser (von mir später als 'Sachverhalt' bezeichnete) Begriff ist u.a. darum wichtig, weil die ganze Klasse der indirekten Urteile (Es ist möglich, notwendig, wahrscheinlich, wahr, falsch, dass ...) sich nach seiner damaligen Darstellung auf Eigenschaften solcher Urteilsinhalte bezieht". This passage, written in 1919, is a repetition of what Stumpf had already said in 1907 (*Erscheinungen und psychische Funktionen*, p. 29). We have already encountered the notion of the state of affairs in Husserl's philosophy. He had a copy of the lectures in which Stumpf began to use this notion under the heading "state of affairs" (*Sachverhalt*) (see the syllabus for logic, § 4, in Appendix Three below). More will be said about this in the present chapter.

concepts, according to Stumpf, were also used in the lecture on logic. The quality of a judgment is of course to be found in whether it is affirmative or negative. Some of these considerations, as we have already seen, are repeated and transformed in Husserl's *Logische Untersuchungen*.

In the summer of 1870 Stumpf left the seminary, deciding not to become a priest. This was of course done due to doubts which Brentano raised in him about the Catholic faith and Christianity in general. He thus returned to Göttingen in order to do his habilitation under Lotze. This was finalized in October 1870. He remained there as a *Privatdozent* until he was called to become professor at Würzburg (1873). From Würzburg he went to Prague (1879), from Prague to Halle (1884), from Halle to Munich (1889), and finally from Munich to Berlin (1894). At Berlin he became the director of the Psychological Institute. As far as professorships in philosophy and psychology are concerned, the chair in Berlin was by far the most prestigious in the German Reich. Until the death of Brentano in 1917 the contacts between him and Stumpf were very good, although Stumpf preferred Brentano's earlier views over the later ones.

2. HUSSERL AS A PUPIL OF STUMPF

After Husserl had been following lectures of Brentano in Vienna for two years, a decision had to be made about where he was to do his habilitation. On 18 October 1886 Brentano accordingly wrote the following recommendation to Carl Stumpf in Halle:

> The concern of these lines is first and foremost the request of a young man who asked me to recommend him to you. Dr. Husserl, mathematician and for some years an enthusiastic student of philosophy, wants to spend this winter in Halle. He looks forward to the advancement which he hopes to gain through your lectures and your company. Perhaps Cantor too [Stumpf's colleague] will be of use to him.
>
> He is working on a treatise about the problem of continuity. Though I have seen none of it, I have noticed only that he has spent a good deal of diligence on it. With it he would like to do his habilitation in philosophy and is thinking about doing this in Halle itself. I myself believe that this would be better for him than here in Vienna [...]. I regard him as solid in character and more hard-working than [...] most of our young people.[1]

While Brentano hesitates to say anything in favor of Husserl's philosophical talents, the only difficulties Stumpf apparently saw were in the possibility of a non-

---

[1] Brentano, *Briefe an Carl Stumpf 1867-1917*, pp. 83 f. Brentano gives two reasons why Brentano should leave Vienna. First, he says that Husserl is not much of an Austrian patriot and this could make things difficult for him there. Secondly, he does not think that Husserl, who was soon to marry, could earn enough money in Vienna in order support a family.

Protestant pursuing a career in Lutheran Halle. However, Brentano assured Stumpf that Husserl was a Protestant.[1] The recommendation was then accepted and thus Husserl began attending Stumpf's lectures in psychology in the winter semester of 1886/87. Within a year after his arrival in Halle he was done with his habilitation thesis *Über den Begriff der Zahl*. Thereafter Husserl became a *Privatdozent* at Halle and thus a colleague in the same faculty with Professor Stumpf, who left, however, for Munich in the autumn of 1889.

In subsequent years the two men stayed in contact through correspondence and visits, though they took divergent paths in philosophy. While not one single letter from Stumpf to Husserl is available to us,[2] and while only one actual letter (*Briefwechsel* I, 157-164) and a few drafts of letters (*Briefwechsel* I, 169-178) from Husserl to Stumpf have survived,[3] what can be gathered from this material nevertheless indicates that the relationship between them was personally cordial and philosophically open. In the extant letter from Husserl to Stumpf (c. February 1890), for instance, there is a rather extensive description of how the work on *Philosophie der Arithmetik* is progressing. The philosophical openness between the two Brentanists is however especially shown by the draft of a letter (21 June 1899) in which Husserl felt free to criticize Stumpf's attempt to work out a theory of the calculation of probability (*Briefwechsel* I, 165-168).[4]

As we may recall from the first chapter, there was a lack of such openness in the relationship between Husserl and Brentano. Even though Husserl had already in the 1890's adopted positions which significantly diverged from those of his mentor, this divergence was not conveyed to Brentano until after the publication of the *Logische Untersuchungen*. Moreover, Husserl played down any suggestion that Brentano was guilty of psychologism, but we have also seen that there are reasons to regard him as somewhat insincere in doing so. In his relation with Stumpf, however, he felt very free to express his opposition. The reason for this openness cannot be due to a lack of respect, for the fact that the *Logische Untersuchungen* are "dedicated to Carl Stumpf in

---

[1]*Ibid.*, p. 85. Stumpf must have thought that Husserl, coming from Austria, was a Catholic. There is nothing at all to suggest that Husserl's Jewish origins were known by Stumpf at this time.

[2]Most of the letters from Stumpf were probably destroyed in the bombing of Antwerp.

[3]Stumpf's *Nachlass* was destroyed in the bombing of Berlin.

[4]The relevant literature by Stumpf and by others is indicated in the annotations to the letter in question. As we have already seen, the topic in question was crucial to Brentano's theory of induction. It was later to be treated extensively by Stumpf in *Erkenntnistheorie* II, pp. 429-534. Two other Brentanists, namely Masaryk and Meinong, were also very much concerned with the concept of probability. It is not treated in the present study because it was not central in the work of Husserl, especially not in his early work.

veneration and friendship" certainly indicates the contrary. The plain fact of the matter seems to be that Stumpf, unlike Brentano, did not demand devotion to his doctrines. In spite of the fact that Husserl had developed heretical views, Stumpf did everything he could to secure an appointment for Husserl in Göttingen. This involved going there personally and persuading faculty members that Husserl would be worthy of such an appointment.

It might also be mentioned here that Stumpf, who was in close contact with William James, was the one who introduced Husserl to the *Principles of Psychology* in 1894 (*Husserl-Chronik*, 41). This latter work must indeed be counted among one of the important influences on Husserl's philosophical development.

Though the path which Husserl took diverged more from Brentanian orthodoxy than did Stumpf's path, this was not because Stumpf was unaware of the turn taken in the *Logische Untersuchungen*. In fact he was quite well informed of the new developments soon after the publication of the work in question. This is shown by the draft of a letter to Stumpf of 11 May 1902 (*Briefwechsel* I, 169-173) in which Husserl replies to a question which Stumpf had raised about the standpoint in the *Logische Untersuchungen* regarding universals and abstraction. While Stumpf later showed some sympathy for some of Husserl's positions in that work, he was very dissatisfied with the transcendental turn taken in later years.[1]

Before we concern ourselves with Husserl's reaction to Stumpf's philosophical views, it will be helpful to say a word about the material under consideration here. As far as works published by Stumpf in the nineteenth century are concerned, there are two which are of some importance here: *Über den psychologischen Ursprung der Raumvorstellung* (1873) and *Tonpsychologie* (1883/90). Husserl's copies of these works bear some markings and annotations. The works in question, however, are unfortunately concerned with rather peripheral matters. As far as Stumpf's views on more central matters are concerned, we shall rather draw upon his lectures on psychology (1886/87) and on logic (1888). Especially the former lecture is important, for Husserl's own notes of this lecture (for the most part in Gabelsberger stenography) are quite extensive, filling up two whole notebooks.[2] By drawing on this lecture, together with the one on logic, we may rest assured that we are in touch with precisely the views of

---

[1] Thus in *Erkenntnistheorie* I (p. 194) Stumpf concedes that Husserl had contributed "something of merit" (*Verdienstliches*) in the *Logische Untersuchungen*, but this congratulatory remark is made in the context of a scathing attack against the standpoint adopted in *Ideen* I. This attack will be discussed further below.

[2] These notebooks are to be found in the Husserl Archives (Louvain) under the signature Q 11/1 and Q 11/2. The central theses which were presented in them are translated in Appendix Two of the present study. As far as the lecturs on logic of 1888 are concerned, their central theses are also to be found in the Husserl Archives (Louvain) under the signature Q 13 and translated in Appendix Two below.

Stumpf most familiar to Husserl. Two other works which Stumpf published in 1907, namely *Erscheinungen und psychische Funktionen* and *Zur Einteilung der Wissenschaften*, are also to be taken into consideration, for Husserl's markings and annotations in his copies of them clearly show that he read them quite thoroughly.

3. INTENTIONAL REFERENCE

We have seen that Brentano characterizes psychical phenomena in terms of their peculiar intentional reference. This is moreover, on his view, an intentional inexistence of the object. If I imagine, then I imagine something. Whether or not there is something which corresponds in actuality to *what* I imagine, the imagined object is nonetheless immanent in the act of imagining. This conception of intentional reference, here called "immanentism", is adopted in Stumpf's lecture on psychology.

My psychical states need not be directed at something actual. What is here called 'content' has occasionally been called 'object'. My thinking must have an object. In this case, however, the mentioned confusion [that thinking must be directed at something actual] is suggested. It does not need an additional object obtaining outside of my consciousness. Hence, some psychologists add: there must be a mental object, immanent object. In that case these expressions are certainly unobjectionable.[1]

For the most part, however, Stumpf simply speaks of the content of consciousness, not of the mental or immanent object.

3.1. The Immanence of States of Affairs and Other Objects

It should be pointed out here that "content" for Stumpf is used in a peculiar sense when he speaks of contents of judgments. As we have seen above, he had attended Brentano's lecture on logic where these are distinguished from the matter of the judgment, i.e., from the content of the underlying presentation. This same distinction is highlighted in Stumpf's 1888 lecture on logic (§ 4 in the syllabus for logic in Appendix Three), where the content of a judgment is also called "state of affairs" (*Sachverhalt*). If, for instance, one person judges that God exists and another judges that God does not exist, these two judgments, to be sure, have the same matter (God), but the states of

---

[1] Q 11 I/70: "Meine psychischen Zustände brauchen nicht auf etwas Wirkliches gerichtet sein. Was wir hier Inhalt nennen, hat man mitunter Gegenstand, Objekt genannt. Mein Denken muss ein Objekt haben. Dann liegt aber die genannte Verwechslung nahe. Es braucht nicht ein ausser meinem Bewusstsein bestehender Gegenstand bei. Deswegen fügen manche Psychologen bei: es muss ein mentaler Gegenstand, immanenter Gegenstand vorhanden sein. Dann sind diese Ausdrücke allerdings ohne Bedenken."

affairs differ in the two cases. While the state of affairs in the one case is the being of God (or that God is), the state of affairs in the other case is the non-being of God (that God is not).

Husserl accommodates this notion of a state of affairs. One of the differences between him and Stumpf, however, lies in the fact that for Husserl states of affairs are regarded as ideal objects (perceivable only by categorial intuition) and therefore as existing independently of consciousness; Stumpf, on the other hand, makes no effort at all in his early philosophy to denounce the immanence of the state of affairs, however peculiar it is regarded in comparison with the contents of presentations or feelings. Moreover, as we shall soon see, in 1907 he argues explicitly that a state of affairs is real only insofar as it is immanent in the judging act.

While Stumpf and Husserl thus disagree regarding the immanence or transcendence of states of affairs, there are two other important differences which should be mentioned here. One of these is to be found in Stumpf's claim that the notion of a state of affairs can be traced back not only to Brentano's notion of a content of judgment, but also back to Bolzano's notion of a sentence in itself.[1] We have of course seen in the last chapter that Husserl takes pains to distinguish states of affairs from sentences in themselves (propositions) by construing the former as *objects* of certain acts, e.g., judging, and the latter as *species* of these acts (species which are moreover the same as the meanings of assertions rather than those of names or syncategorematic expressions).[2] One other difference to be noted here lies in the fact that Stumpf maintains that states of affairs are uniquely correlated with judgments,[3] whereas Husserl takes the view that they can be not only named and therefore presented in nominal acts, but are also the correlates of certain non-positing acts which are no less "propositional" than judgments. There will be more about Husserl's views on these matters in the chapter on him and Meinong.

In 1907 Stumpf's immanentism remains fully intact, and with special reference to states of affairs as immanent in consciousness. While he does not at this time simply

---

[1]*Erscheinungen und psychische Funktionen*, pp. 29 f.

[2]The distinction between propositions and states of affairs was also made by the Munic phenomenologist, Adolph Reinach, who thus complains in *Sämtliche Werke* I, edited by Karl Schuhmann and Barry Smith (Munich: Philosophia, 1989), p. 526 n.: "Stumpf, Bergmann, also Bolzano - all Austrians continually confuse proposition and state of affairs". As will become apparent in Chapter Six, one of the Austrians who could be accused of such confusion is Meinong. It must however be added that, while Reinach insists on the distinction in question, he maintains, contrary to Husserl, that propositions are formed by positing acts of consciousness.

[3]Stumpf puts forward this view in opposition to Meinong in particular. See *Erscheinungen und psychische Funktionen*, p. 30 n.

use the terms "content" and "object" as synonyms, this is not to be construed as an retraction of immanentism. An object, according to him, is a "conceptual formation" (*begriffliches Gebilde*),[1] which is simply a content of a certain type, for "the formations are facts in the first place only as contents of psychical functions [i.e., of psychical acts]".[2] Other formations are states of affairs, collectives, and values.[3] All of these stand in contrast with other contents, called "appearances" (*Erscheinungen*), which are primarily the contents of sensation and secondarily the corresponding contents of imagination.[4] We have already seen that Brentano had regarded the objects of sensations as existing only intentionally and never actually. Stumpf adopts a similar view, although he warns against regarding appearances as "a complete nothing" (*ein völliges Nichts*). "Appearances only do not belong to that reality to which naive thinking at first ascribes them, namely to an actuality independent of consciousness".[5] Accordingly, Stumpf does regard immanent existence as an existence in the proper sense. As far as the existence of formations is concerned, the state of affairs is used as an example to argue as follows:

---

[1] *Zur Einteilung der Wissenschaften*, p. 6.

[2] *Erscheinungen und psychische Funktionen*, p. 32: "die Gebilde aber sind Tatsachen überhaupt nur als Inhalte von Funktionen". Underneath the word *Tatsachen* Husserl writes: "= immediate givennesses, or givennesses as such [= unmittelbare Gegebenheiten, oder Gegebenheiten überhaupt]".

[3] *Ibid.*, pp. 28 ff.

[4] *Ibid.*, p. 4.

[5] *Ibid.*, p. 10: "Die Erscheinungen gehören nur nicht *der* Wirklichkeit an, der sie das naive Denken zunächst zuschreibt, nämlich einer vom Bewusstsein unabhängigen Wirklichkeit". To this passage Husserl appends the following annotation: "We must distinguish: the naivety of perception and the naivety of reflection of the everyday person and of the philosopher prior to epistemology. In the naivety of perception the thing is there as colored etc. The thing with its colors, which are however not the appearances, is not there as something outside of consciousness. Only reflection, the naive philosopher, posits the thing outside of 'consciousness' (and not merely outside of one's own ego-body) [Wir müssen unterscheiden: die Naivität der Wahrnehmung und die Naivität der Reflexion des Alltagsmenschen und des Philosophen vor der Erkenntnistheorie. In der Naivität der Wahrnehmung steht das Ding da als gefärbt etc. Das Ding mit seinen Farben, die aber nicht die Erscheinungen sind, steht nicht als etwas ausser dem Bewusstsein da. Erst die Reflexion, der naive Philosoph, setzt das Ding ausserhalb des 'Bewusstseins' (und nicht bloss ausserhalb des eigenen Ichkörpers)]". What is under attack here, however, is not Stumpf's immanentism as such. The charge is rather that Stumpf fails to distinguish between two types of naivety. In the naivety of perception, says Husserl, there is no question of positing the thing as outside of consciousness. We must ask, however, whether he thereby means to say that the thing is posited as "inside" consciousness. Perhaps he only means that at this level there is no question of "outside" or "inside". This question arises only when we philosophize naively.

> The state of affairs cannot be immediately given alone, independently of any psychical function and thereby also be real. Only as a content of a current judgment can it be real. Otherwise any state of affairs, even the certainly false, indeed absurd one, would not only be true, but even real.

The conclusion is that states of affairs and in general all formations are real only as contents, but that *as such* they *do* indeed have reality.

In 1907 Husserl expresses great dissatisfaction with this immanentism. In response to the above-cited claim, that the formations are facts only as contents of functions, Husserl writes the following in the margin of the relevant page (32) of his copy of *Erscheinungen und psychische Funktionen*: "Here Stumpf confuses 'real' in the sense of the 'actuality' of the state of affairs, of its true subsistence, and reality in the sense of the fact of consciousness (in his earlier defined sense)."[1] By "his earlier defined sense" Husserl means Stumpf's claim: "The totality of the immediately given is real".[2] The charge against Stumpf is accordingly that the immanentist theory of formations is based on an inference from their reality in the sense of their immediate givenness to their reality in the sense of their actuality or subsistence. The result is that this actuality can be regarded only as one which is dependent on consciousness. In the *Logische Untersuchungen*, however, Husserl adopts the view that the existence of states of affairs and other ideal objects is timeless and as such cannot be dependent on time-bound acts of consciousness.

While Husserl's view concerning states of affairs is certainly incompatible with immanentism, we must however keep in mind that it is not the only alternative to immanentism. Another alternative, after all, is to be found in the thesis that these are not immanent in judgments or other psychical phenomena and still just as temporally determined as both psychical and physical phenomena. Such a view was indeed held by Marty in his work of 1908, to be discussed further below. Though I shall not at present argue in favor of this view, it can be said here that Husserl offers us very little in favor of his Platonistic conception of states of affairs. In the *Prolegomena zur reinen Logik* he argues, to be sure, that propositions must be regarded as timeless entities in order to avoid sceptical relativism. In the first chapter we have already raised doubts about this argument, since truth and falsity can apparently be ascribed first and foremost to acts of judging without succumbing to relativism. If a given judgment is now true, it does not follow, as Husserl suggests in opposition to Sigwart (and by implication in opposition to Brentano) that it was false before it or judgments of the exact same kind

---

[1] "Hier verwechselt Stumpf 'real' im Sinn der 'Wirklichkeit' des Sachverhalts, seines wahren Bestandes, und Realität im Sinn der Bewusstseinstatsache (in seinem früher definierten Sinn)".

[2] *Erscheinungen und psychische Funktionen*, p. 10: "Die Gesamtheit des unmittelbar Gegebenen ist *real*". Husserl underlines the last word of this sentence.

came into being. Where no judgment at all occurs, there is, strictly speaking, no truth or falsity, though there may well be an *actuality* which would make a judgment true or false if a judgment would come into being. Moreover, even if we accept Husserl's view that propositions are timeless, it does not follow that the same must be said about states of affairs, which are, after all, allegedly distinct from propositions. One is indeed hard pressed to find any argument at all on Husserl's part to make good the claim that states of affairs are ideal.

Now let us consider Stumpf's immanentism and Husserl's rejection of it with regard to physical objects. Stumpf has this class in mind when, after making the above-cited claim that the totality of the immediately given is real, he says: "For it is that from which we obtain the concept of the real, in order then only to transfer it to something else,"[1] namely to reality as entertained by natural science. Here, again, Husserl objects that Stumpf confuses two senses of "real". Thus, he writes: "Yet, 'real' in this sense and 'real' in the sense of a physical thing are essentially different, and the talk of transference very objectionable".[2] As Stumpf allows for an inference from the immediate givenness of formations to their subsistence, he likewise allows for an inference from the contents of sensations to external things. In either case, however, Husserl maintains that the inference is objectionable due to an equivocation of "real". Accordingly, he will not allow immanentism any opportunity to accommodate the real existence of physical things or the ideal existence of states of affairs and other formations.

3.2. Apprehension of Contents and Objects

In 1907 Husserl lectured on thing and space. In this lecture he found an occasion to refer to Stumpf with approval: "the ambiguous word 'apperception' we prefer to avoid completely; 'apprehension' suffices, as Stumpf has already advocated for a long time" (Hua XVI, 49). We have already seen that the notion of apprehension (or apperception) for Husserl goes together with the notion of sensations and other phenomenological contents of consciousness. Insofar as these contents are apprehended (or apperceived), an object is intended. The above-quoted reference to Stumpf can be traced back to the following passage from *Tonpsychologie* I:

---

[1] *Ibid.*: "Denn sie ist das, wovon wir überhaupt den Begriff des Realen gewinnen, um ihn dann erst auf anderes zu übertragen".

[2] "Und doch ist 'real' in diesem Sinn und 'real' im dinglichen Sinn wesentlich verschieden, und die Rede vom Übertragen sehr bedenklich".

Judging, as we understand it, does not always arise from deliberation and is not always fixed in language, not even in inward speech. [...] We may now deliberate whether two tones possess equal or different pitches, especially if we are asked about this, doubting and then deciding. But differences, similarities, etc. are certainly noticed, apprehended from the outset and still before the beginning of speech, albeit in a crude way, without a preceding doubt about the correctness of the apprehension or also only a "whether - or", a question arising from within or without. Doubt itself is possible only if some spontaneous apprehension was there to which it refers.

For such rudimentary or, better, elementary judging the term just used, "apprehension", appears to be linguistically more expedient (replacing, by the way, also completely the barbaric "apperception") [...].[1]

While apprehension, as Stumpf understands it, is thus an elementary judging, as when we simply notice at once that two colors, for instance, are different, it still differs from apprehension in the Husserlian sense. For Husserl does not regard apprehension as an act of any kind; it is at best, like the phenomenological contents themselves, only part of an act.

As apprehension in this sense is even more elementary than the elementary judging which Stumpf has in mind, the same can be said for sensations, according to Husserl's conception, in comparison with sensations à la Stumpf which are simply the presentations which characteristically underlie outer perceptions. Together with sensations Husserl includes certain feelings in the same class. Thus, in reply to the question whether there are non-intentional feelings Husserl answers that there most certainly are (Hua XIX/1, 406-410). Though he concedes that such feelings, e.g., the pain of being burnt, are felt in reference to something objective, "on the one hand to the ego, more precisely to the burnt member of the body, on the other hand to the burning object" (Hua XIX/1, 406), he adds that they have this reference only as color-sensations and tone-sensations do, namely by virtue of being apprehended. In this regard Husserl stands in stark contrast with Stumpf, who does his best in his 1886/87 lecture on psychology to construe the feelings in questions as intentional.

Husserl's understanding of intentional reference as something brought about by the apprehension of phenomenological contents continues to be upheld in later investigations. In *Ideen* I the moment of apprehension is called *morphé* and the

---

[1]*Tonpsychologie* I, pp. 4 f.: "Beurteilung, wie wir sie verstehen, entspringt nicht immer aus Überlegung, wird auch nicht immer in der Sprache, nicht einmal im innerlichen Sprechen, fixiert. [...] Ob zwei Töne gleiche oder verschiedene Höhe besitzen, mögen wir jetzt überlegen, zumal wenn wir danach gefragt sind, zweifelnd und uns dann entscheidend. Aber gewiss werden von Anfang an und noch vor Beginn des Sprechens Unterschiede, Ähnlichkeiten u.s.w., wenn auch gröberer Art, als solche bemerkt, aufgefasst, ohne dass ein Zweifel an der Richtigkeit der Auffassung oder auch nur 'ob - oder', eine von aussen oder innen angeregte Frage vorausging. Der Zweifel selbst ist erst möglich, wenn irgend eine spontane Auffassung da war, auf welche er sich bezieht.

Für solche rudimentäre oder besser elementare Beurteilung erscheint wohl der eben gebrauchte Ausdruck *Auffassung* sprachgemässer (ersetzt nebenbei auch vollkommen die barbarische 'Apperzeption') [...]." Husserl underlines both the terms *Auffassung* and *Apperzeption* in the last paragraph.

phenomenological contents *hylé*. With this model in mind he criticizes the conception of phenomenology which Stumpf puts forward in *Zur Einteilung der Wissenschaften*. According to this conception, phenomenology is concerned with appearances, i.e., first and foremost with the contents of sensations.[1] In a remark in *Ideen* I (Hua III/1, 199) Husserl maintains that phenomenology in this sense would be a "hyletics" (*Hyletik*), restricted to a consideration of the *hylé* without taking into account the *morphé*. The phenomenology which Husserl advocates is of course not to be restricted in this way. This comment, however, involves a misunderstanding of Stumpf's notion of appearances, for these are understood as *contents* of sensation and not as sensations themselves. Sensations, according to Stumpf, are acts (in his terms: psychical functions) which have appearances as their intentional correlates. While they accordingly *have* contents, they as such *are not* contents. If these contents are conceptualized, they are moreover made into objects. All of this is of course very alien to Husserl's way of thinking, especially in *Ideen* I, and thus it is no wonder that he misunderstands Stumpf. As it turns out, Stumpfian phenomenology is allied with various "neutral sciences", including eidology (concerned with the psychical formations),[2] the general theory of relations,[3] and metaphysics,[4] whereas the theory of psychical functions is to be treated in psychology, which is indeed not to be detached from the previously mentioned disciplines since their subject matter in each case depends on psychical functions. Whether we prefer Husserl's division of sciences as less "psychologistic" or not, and of course whether we accept Stumpf's immanentism or not, it must be said in favor of Stumpf's division of the sciences that it has the advantage of leaving no subject matter, except perhaps contradictory ones,

---

[1] *Zur Einteilung der Wissenschaften*, pp. 26-32.

[2] *Ibid.*, pp. 32-37. The term *Phänomenologie* had of course been used long before Husserl. Stumpf's usage of it should therefore not be construed as as a borrowing from Husserl. The term *Eidologie* had already been used by Herbart to designate "investigations whereby it is decided the extent to which our presentations provide us with genuine cognition [*Untersuchung, durch welche entschieden wird, in wiefern unsere Vorstellungen uns wahre Erkenntnis liefer*]", *Allgemeine Metaphysik nebst den Anfängen der philosophischen Naturlehre*, in *Sämtliche Werke in chronologischer Reihenfolge*, edited by Karl Kehrbach (Langensalza: Hermann Beyer & Söhne, 1892), p. 53. Such investigations are however identical with what would now be called "epistemology" and not to be identified with eidology in the Stumpfian sense.

[3] *Ibid.*, pp. 37-42.

[4] *Ibid.*, pp. 42-44.

"homeless".[1]

Before leaving this discussion of apprehension, it should be noted that Husserl sometimes uses the term "apprehension" (*Auffassung*) in a way which can apparently be dissociated from the otherwise correlative notion of phenomenological contents. This other usage comes into play in his formulation of the concept of *matter*, namely as that "peculiarity which determines what the act apprehends the object *as*" (Hua XIX/1, 430). In this sense it is accordingly the *object*, not the *phenomenological content*, which is apprehended. I can accordingly apprehend one and the same *object* now as the victor at the battle of Jena, now as the vanquished at the battle of Waterloo. While apprehension in this sense may come somewhat closer to the elementary judging which Stumpf refers to under the same heading, it must be kept in mind that Husserl ascribes matter to acts of all kinds and not only to judgments.

There is however one other respect in which the apprehension of objects, as understood by Husserl, may be related to a similar notion which appears in Stumpf's works of 1907. As we have already seen, Stumpf uses the term "objects" in reference to conceptual formations. These are for him either general concepts, e.g., "man", or also those contents which are *subsumed* under general concepts, e.g., individual men insofar as they are conceived as men. If we now leave aside the issue of immanentism and accordingly disregard Stumpf's usage of the term "contents" in this context, we may ask whether the subsumption under general concepts is to be equated with what Husserl has in mind when he speaks of the apprehension of an object as this or that. This very question is addressed by Husserl in the following passage where Stumpf is under attack:

> This is not completely intelligible to me. What does "being grasped under general concepts" mean? That can indeed only be an apprehension of an object as an object of a concept, thus Napoleon I as human being, as bearing the historical spirit of the times, etc., as riding, etc. It is therefore not the case that objects are first constituted and then they are conceptually apprehended, and thought of as being such and such, but rather there are objects only by means of conceptual apprehension. Let us take perceiving. As it seems, this is for Stumpf the mere picking out of "appearances" out of the chaos. Then conceptual grasping is added to this, the grasping under the general concepts.
>
> This cannot be correct. My investigations concerning the constitution of the object teach the opposite.

---

[1] The term "homeless" (*heimatlos*) is here taken from Meinong, whose work is by no means unfamiliar to Stumpf. In many places of the writings of 1907 Meinong is referred to, often with approval. See especially *Zur Einteilung der Wissenschaften*, pp. 40-42. While both Meinong and Stumpf wish to expand the subject matter of the sciences beyond the traditionally delineated range of topics, the main differences between Meinong and Stumpf are to be found in Stumpf's continued insistence on psychology as the founding science and in his rejection of contradictory objects as a legitimate concern of scientific inquiry. In the former respect Stumpf is opposed to Husserl, whereas he and Husserl stand in opposition to Meinong on the question of contradictory objects. There will of course be more on this opposition between Husserl and Meinong in the chapter which especially treats their relation to each other.

In itself it already seems obvious to say that an object is thought of under concepts, now under these, now under others, and must thus already objectively be thought of, intuited or thought of in symbolic intentions. And I must already be directed at it before I can put it under this or that general concept. Bringing under the general concept, this is subsuming under the general concept. And can we say in this sense that we always find such subsumptions, that they are indeed necessary? Hence already in the case of simple perceiving, which is indeed the perceiving of a thing. Is the concept of the thing, of the house, etc., the "general concept" given here? Therefore in the case of animals too?

Is not the first thing the indicating function which puts unity into the manifold, e.g., of the changing, now rising, now fading tones, and then intimately intertwined with this, the generalizing, comparing, synthesizing [functions], etc.

Only if the grasping of an object-consciousness or unity-consciousness (identity-consciousness) is understood as a conceptual grasping, where however there is no mention of general concepts and also not of concepts in the sense of predicates, would what Stumpf says be correct, or there would be something correct in it. The unity-consciousness, identity-consciousness, object-consciousness, this is fundamentally and essentially a new function which makes the content (that would be the 'appearance') become the consciousness of such and such an object, the appearance in the true sense. This is objectification, which is logical consciousness in the broadest sense, whereas in the narrower sense logical consciousness is grasping and predicating and judging consciousness by means of general concepts.

What is clearly missing, after all, is a systematic exposition and a step-by-step construction of the strata of cognition. And it is understandable why Stumpf says that whenever thinking is directed at the universal, at concepts or laws, the distinction between content and object vanishes.

Also concepts, when they are objects, are "unities in contrast with multiplicities" and they, too, can be grasped either in the unity-consciousness without being thought under general concepts (in the sense of subsumption and predication) or they can be grasped in this way.

As I can perceive Napolean I without classifying him or predicating of him, and as I can think of him by means of a proper concept, whereby I therefore have no general concept in the true sense, I can attend to a universal such as redness, think of it via a proper concept "redness" (which in this respect is no general concept) and again bring it under general concepts. Red is no general concept in the sense that red is with regard to the single red-objects.[1]

---

[1] K II 4/162 f.: "Vollkommen verständlich ist mir das nicht. Was heisst das 'unter allgemeinen Begriffen erfasst werden'? Das kann doch nur Auffassung eines Gegenstandes als Gegenstand eines Begriffes [sein], also Nap[oleon] des I. als Mensch, als den historischen Zeitgeist tragend etc., als reitend etc. Also nicht konstituieren sich erst Gegenstände und dann werden sie begrifflich aufgefasst, als so und so beschaffen gedacht, sondern Gegenstände sind erst durch die begriffliche Auffassung da. Nehmen wir das Wahrnehmen. Wie es scheint, ist das für Stumpf das blosse Herausheben der 'Erscheinungen' aus dem Chaos. Dazu tritt dann die begriffliche Fassung, das unter den allgemeinen Begriffen Erfassen.

"Das kann nicht richtig sein. Meine Untersuchung über die Konstitution des Gegenstandes lehren das Gegenteil. An sich ist es schon naheliegend zu sagen, ein Gegenstand wird unter Begriffen gedacht, einmal unter diesen, das andere mal unter anderen, und muss so gegenständlich schon gedacht sein, angeschaut oder in symbolischen Intentionen gedacht sein. Und ich muss schon auf ihn gerichtet sein, ehe ich ihn diesem oder jenem allgemeinen Begriff unterstellen kann. Unter den allgemeinen Begriff bringen, das ist dem allgemeinen Begriff subsumieren. Und kann man in diesem Sinn sagen, immer finden wir solche Subsumtionen, ja sie sind notwendig? Also schon beim einfachen Wahrnehmen, das doch Wahrnehmen eines Dinges ist. Ist da der Begriff des Dinges, des Hauses etc., der 'allgemeine Begriff' vorhanden? Also auch beim Tier?

"Ist nicht das erste die indizierende Funktion, die Einheit in die Mannigfaltigkeit hinsetzt, z.B. der sich ändernden, bald anschwellenden, bald nachlassenden Töne, und dann innig damit verflochten, die generalisierende, vergleichende, synthetisierende etc.?

"Nur wenn man das Fassen eines Gegenstandsbewusstseins oder Einheitsbewusstseins (Identitätsbewusstseins) als begriffliches Fassen versteht, wobei aber nicht die Rede von allgemeinen Begriffen

From this passage it is clear that the apprehension of objects, as understood by Husserl, is not to be found in Stumpf's notion of subsumption. For Husserl mainatins that either an individual or a concept can be apprehended, e.g., Napolean I as Napolean I or redness as redness, without being subsumed under a general concept, e.g., "man" or "color". Neither the subsumption under general concepts which Stumpf thematizes in 1907 nor the older notion of elementary judging can accordingly be equated with apprehension in either of the Husserlian senses.

In this context we should be reminded of Husserl's boast in *Die Krisis der europäischen Wissenschaften und die transzendentale Phänomenologie* (Hua VI, 237), already cited in the first chapter, that in the *Logische Untersuchungen* evidence had been taken into account for the first time in connection with the concept of synthesis, and more particularly on a pre-scientific level of cognition. If we follow Stumpf's view of perception to its logical conclusion, it would have to be said that we do not perceive objects. Husserl, on the other hand, allows not only for the perception of objects, but also (and especially) for the perception of things in the narrow sense, namely the sense in which tables and chairs are things and acts or contents of consciousness are not. Such perception, according to Husserl, is possible only via a synthesis whereby the thing becomes identified throughout a series of acts. I see the table from one side and then from another side. I may also touch it and make a sound by rapping on it. The thing which is seen from one side and then another, which is also rough or smooth, as the case may be, and which is one of the factors in making the sound that I hear, is apprehended as one and the same table. This apprehension is moreover not a conceptual one, as might occur when I try to classify the table in terms of the wood from which it had been made or in reference to its design. Such pre-scientific and non-

---

einträte, und nicht von Begriffen im Sinn von Prädikaten, wäre es richtig, was Stumpf sagt, oder es steckte Richtiges dahinter. Das Einheitsbewusstsein, Identitätsbewusstsein, Gegenstandsbewusstsein, das ist die grundwesentlich neue Funktion, die aus dem Inhalt (das wäre die 'Erscheinung') das macht, wodurch er das Bewusstsein von dem und dem Gegenstand ist, die Erscheinung im echten Sinn. Das ist die Objektivikation, die das logische Bewusstsein ist im allerweitesten Sinn, während im engeren Sinn logisches Bewusstsein allgemeinbegrifflich fassendes und prädizierendes und urteilendes Bewusstsein ist.

"Es fehlt doch, das ist klar, an einer systematischen Darstellung und an einem schrittweisen Aufbau der Erkenntnisschichten. Und verständlich ist es, warum Stumpf sagt, dass wenn das Denken sich auf Allgemeines, auf Begriffe oder Gesetze richtet, der Unterschied zwischen Inhalt und Gegenstand wegfällt.

"Auch Begriffe, wenn sie Gegenstände sind, sind 'Einheiten gegenüber Mannigfaltigkeiten' und auch sie können entweder im Einheitsbewusstsein erfasst werden, ohne unter allgemeinen Begriffen (im Sinn der Subsumtion und Prädikation) gedacht zu werden, oder sie können es werden.

"So wie ich Nap[oleon] I wahrnehmen kann, ohne ihn zu klassifizieren und von ihm zu prädizieren, und wie ich ihn durch einen eigenen Begriff denken kann, wobei ich also keinen allgemeinen Begriff habe im echten Sinn, so kann ich auf ein Allgemeines wie Röte achten, es durch einen eigenen Begriff 'Röte denken (der in diesem Hinsicht kein allgemeiner Begriff ist) und wieder unter allgemeine Begriffe bringen. Das Rot ist kein allgemeiner Begriff in dem Sinn wie Rot es ist hinsichtlich der einzelnen Rotobjekte."

conceptual apprehension is indeed absolutely fundamental to our cognitive activities. Husserl is to be given credit for making this the theme of painstaking psychological description far more than Stumpf and the other Brentanists, not to mention Brentano himself.

What unfortunately becomes clear in the above-quoted attack on Stumpf and must in all fairness be pointed out is that, as far as Husserl is concerned, the apprehension of contents and the apprehension of objects are regarded by him as somehow continuous, both being crucial to the constitution of the object, and not to be viewed as separate. They have nonetheless been treated separately in the foregoing because, whereas the apprehension of an object as this or that, especially in outer perception, must be acknowledged in any fully worked out theory of consciousness, the apprehension of phenomenological contents must be rejected along with the very notion of phenomenological contents. There will be more about this in the chapter on Husserl and Marty.

3.3. Indeterminacy

While the concept of apprehension, either as related to contents or to objects, accordingly drives a wedge between Husserl and Stumpf, however contrary this fact might be to what is suggested in Husserl's 1907 lecture on thing and space, it turns out that in the *Logische Untersuchungen* Husserl does show himself to be influenced to some extent by Stumpf in the consideration of the question whether there are non-intentional feelings. In the 1886/87 lecture on psychology the question comes up whether certain moods are non-intentional, "e.g., if someone is melancholic and lost in thought. He has nothing at all in his consciousness. There is only a feeling which has taken hold of him".[1] According to Stumpf, such moods "point to their being something here presented, however indeterminately: surely certain space and time presentations, which we never get rid of, or presentation like distant images, indistinct, hazy, at the same time also restlessly changing, so that one never gains fixed stock."[2] An indeterminacy is also to be found, according to Stumpf, in the case of willing, as when we say of someone that he does not know what he wants. "One walks around in the room and

---

[1] Q 11 I/75: "z.B. wenn einer melancholisch ist und [vor sich] hinbrütet. Der hat gar nichts in seinem Bewusstsein, nur ein Gefühl ist es, das ihn in Beschlag genommen hat."

[2] Q 11 I/76: "weisen darauf hin, dass irgendetwas dabei, wenn auch unbestimmt, vorgestellt wird. Sicherlich gewisse Raum- und Zeitvorstellungen, die wir nie loswerden, oder Vorstellungen wie entfernte Bilder, undeutlich, verschwommen, zugleich auch unruhig wechselnd, so dass [man] keinen festen Bestand gewinnt"

looks for something and has forgotten what one is actually looking for. The person in question nonetheless knows that he wants an external object, and that the object is in the room. A content of presentation is there".[1]

The same considerations come into play for Husserl when he allows for indeterminately directed desires and volitions (Hua XIX/1, 410), "whereby the 'indeterminacy' of the objective direction does not have the significance of a privation, but rather a descriptive character, and would indeed have to designate a presentational character. This is indeed the case with the presentation which we perform when 'something' stirs, 'it' is rustling, when 'someone' is ringing at the door, etc." Thus, it turns out that, in spite of Husserl's rejection of immanentism in the *Logische Untersuchungen*, his views on intentional reference still exhibit parallels with those of his second mentor in philosophy. It is indeed instructive to make note of this, for immanentism may seem so repellent to many of us that we forget that not every point in a theory of intentional reference turns on whether or not the object of consciousness is construed as a content. This is by no means the case, no more than it is the case that every point in such a theory turns on whether Husserl's doctrine of apprehension is accepted - a doctrine which, as will be argued below, is no less dubious than the immanentism of Stumpf. While both Stumpf and Husserl adopt theories of intentional reference which are in need of revision, the flaws in their respective theories do not prevent them from seeing certain important points regarding intentional reference. One of these points is without a doubt that a psychical phenomenon can refer to an object indeterminately. It will indeed be seen that Husserl maintains that any division of *objects* into determinate and indeterminate ones is derived from the corresponding division of *presentations*.

4. PARTS AND WHOLES

Though Husserl found no occasion in his habilitation thesis to make any special reference to Stumpf, his *Philosophie der Arithmetik* - even the part which corresponds, sometimes verbatim, to the habilitation thesis - contains various references to his second mentor in philosophy. In this work Stumpf inspires Husserl to say that relations are not created through our psychical activities (Hua XII, 42),[2] that there is no

---

[1] Q 11 I/76: "Man geht im Zimmer herum und sucht etwas und hat vergessen, was man eigentlich sucht. Der Betreffende weiss doch, dass er einen äusseren Gegenstand will, und dass der Gegenstand im Zimmer vorhanden ist. Ein Vorstellungsinhalt ist da."

[2] Husserl here refers to *Tonpsychologie* I, p. 105 and the following pages. At the top of the right margin of page 105 Husserl writes "NB" with a downward pointing arrow underneath to indicate that this entire page is to be well noted. As an example of how "the result of our judgment" is "in large measure in our power",

psychical activity which makes a plurality out of what was previously "an unanalyzed unity" (Hua XII, 63),[1] that we can notice equality between two sensory objects "in a glance, without noticing the least bit of the great diversity of simple relations which can take place between any pair of the objects" (Hua XII, 70 f.),[2] and that equality is simply "extreme similarity" (Hua XII, 207).[3] While these are statements made in passing and can hardly provide us with material for extensive discussion in the present context, the concept of fusion (*Verschmelzung*) which is used in *Philosophie der Arithmetik* and explicitly taken from Stumpf is in need of a detailed examination here, for it turns out to be of considerable importance for both phenomenological analysis and also for the general theory of parts and wholes.

The concept of fusion is used not only in *Philosophie der Arithmetik*, for it turns up again in the *Logische Untersuchungen* with an explicit reference to Stumpf's *Tonpsychologie*. Between *Philosophie der Arithmetik* and the *Logische Untersuchungen*, however, Husserl began to focus on another topic which had been of great interest to Stumpf in *Über den psychologischen Ursprung der Raumvorstellung*. This topic is treated in the work just mentioned under the headings "independent" and "partial contents", whereas Husserl treated it in his *Psychologische Studien zur elementaren Logik* under the headings "independent" and "dependent" content (Hua XXII, 94-100). Stumpf's book on the origin of space-presentation, especially § 5 thereof, "to which I [Husserl] here and elsewhere owe a great deal" (Hua XXII, 94 n), is held in high esteem for the distinction between the two types of content just mentioned. In the *Logische Untersuchungen* Husserl returns to a discussion of the same distinction, but in this work it is treated in close connection with the notion of fusion.

Let us now examine the views of both Stumpf and Husserl regarding parts and

---

Stumpf points out: "The two successive tones C and a3 we must distinguish, whether we want to or not, and must notice that they are less similar than C and D, and more similar than either one of them is to a color [Die beiden aufeinanderfolgenden Töne C und a3 müssen wir unterscheiden, mögen wir wollen oder nicht, müssen auch bemerken, dass sie einander weniger ähnlich sind als C und D, und ähnlicher als jeder von ihnen mit einer Farbe]". Next to this passage Husserl writes a question mark. Of course, the point which Stumpf is making here is rather different from the thesis that relations are not made by us. But Stumpf clearly thinks that they are not and are thus "forced on us" just as the contents of sensation are.

[1]Husserl here refers to Stumpf's definition of "analysis" as "the noticing of a multiplicity" (*das Bemerken einer Mehrheit*) in *Tonpsychologie* I, p. 96.

[2]Here Husserl refers to *Tonpsychologie* II, p. 310.

[3]Here Husserl refers to *Tonpsychologie* I, p. 111, where Stumpf emphatically says: "Equality of sensory appearances is nothing but extreme similarity [Gleichheit sinnlicher Erscheinungen ist nichts anderes als extreme Ähnlichkeit]". Next to this passage Husserl writes "NB" with a downward pointing arrow underneath.

wholes, particularly those which pertain to fusion and of course independent and dependent contents. Though the doctrine of Brentano, namely that a part can be one of four kinds (physical, metaphysical, collective, and logical) is espoused in Stumpf's lectures, Husserl (who is, as we have already seen in Chapter One, critical of the notion of logical parts) draws more from Stumpf's published work than from lectures as regards the topic of parts and wholes.

We shall begin by discussing the treatment of this topic in *Über den Ursprung der Raumvorstellung* (§ 5) and *Tonpsychologie*. Then we shall turn to Husserl's treatment of fusion in *Philosophie der Arithmetik*. Finally, we shall consider his treatment of this topic, as well as independent and dependent contents, in the *Logische Untersuchungen*.[1]

4.1. Über den Ursprung der Raumvorstellung

In the book on the origin of space-presentation the views on independent and partial contents are developed especially, as the title of the work in question indicates, in connection with Stumpf's views on the presentation of space. While some have maintained that the presentation of space is not original, i.e., that such a presentation arises from various other presentations and feelings (e.g., muscle sensations), Stumpf maintains that it is no less original than the presentation of color. This is of course to say that it cannot be accounted for by tracing it back to more primitive presentations, for the presentation of color cannot be traced back in this manner.

As a good Brentanist, Stumpf insists upon the priority of descriptive investigations over genetic ones. Thus, while one may call the concern with the origin with the presentation of space "genetic", Stumpf regards it as "above all matters desirable and necessary to remind oneself of the phenomena of ordinary consciousness, which, after all, prompt scientific inquiry in this case, as they do in every case".[2] A more succinct statement in favor of the precedence of phenomenological considerations could hardly be hoped for.

Let us now consider how Stumpf describes the phenomena under consideration, namely presentations of space, more particularly those which are visual as opposed to

---

[1]*Psychologische Studien zur elementaren Logik* will not be discussed separately, since the relevant part of it is taken up into the third "Logical Investiation".

[2]*Über den psychologischen Ursprung der Raumvorstellung*, p. 106: "vor allen Dingen wünschenswert und notwendig, sich der Phänomene des gewöhnlichen Bewusstseins zu erinnern, die ja in diesem wie in jedem Fall die wissenschaftliche Nachforschung anregen".

tactile ones. "The question which we at first put to ourselves is now not the one concerning the origin of the presentation of space, but rather the following: *how space and quality are related to each other in the presentation*".[1] This question is answered by considering various ways in which contents can be presented together, although Stumpf does not mean to give an exhaustive list of these. First of all, there are cases where two contents are incompatible, as when we present black red or wooden iron. It must indeed be admitted, says Stumpf, that such presentations occur, for they are the foundations of judgments such as "wooden iron is impossible". Secondly, one can present qualities together which belong to different senses, e.g., colors and sounds. A joint presentation of this kind already involves a closer togetherness than the one in the previous case. "But one can thirdly present qualities of the same sense together, where a positive affinity arises",[2] as in the case when several sounds are presented together in a single chord. Still a closer connectness among the contents is possible, "so that one will here want to acknowledge not so much a presenting-together of several items as a distinguishing of one single item as regards several respects".[3] This is the fourth case of presenting together. Insofar as space and color are presented together in a spatially extended and colored surface, this is an instance of the fourth way of presenting together.

According to Stumpf, the consideration of four different ways of presenting together brings to light a distinction between "two main classes: independent contents and partial contents, and [we] determine as the definition and criterion of this difference: independent contents are given wherever the elements of a presentational complex can, by their nature, also be separated; partial contents wherever this is not the case".[4] In this regard the fourth of the above-considered cases consists of the presenta-

---

[1] *Ibid.*, p. 107: "Die Frage, welche wir uns an erster Stelle vorlegen, ist nun nicht die nach dem Ursprung der Raumvorstellung, sondern folgende: *wie sich Raum und Qualität in der Vorstellung zu einander verhalten*".

[2] *Ibid.*, p. 108: "Man kann aber drittens Qualitäten desselben Sinnes zusammen vorstellen, wobei eine positive Verwandtschaft auftritt".

[3] *Ibid.*: "sodass man nicht sowohl ein Zusammenvorstellen von Mehrerem, als ein Unterscheiden eines Einzigen nach mehreren Beziehungen hier wird anerkennen wollen".

[4] *Ibid.*, p. 109: "zwei Hauptklassen: *selbstständige Inhalte* und *Teilinhalte*, und [wir] bestimmen als *Definition und Kriterium* dieses Unterschiedes: *selbstständige Inhalte sind da vorhanden, wo die Elemente eines Vorstellungskomplexes ihrer Natur nach auch getrennt werden können; Teilinhalte da, wo dies nicht der Fall ist*". While the term "partial contents" (*Teilinhalte*) may include more than metaphysical parts, it is clear that it includes at least these. Here one may think of logical parts as also belonging to the class in question, although these do not come into consideration in Stumpf's discession here. The passage just cited is partly underlined in Husserl's copy of the text under consideration. Moreover, he cites it almost verbatim (Hua XIX/1, 233), replacing the term "partial contents" with "dependent contents" (*unselbständige Inhalte*).

tion of partial contents, whereas all the others consist of the presentation of independent contents. When Stumpf regards the presentation of a colored and spatially extended surface as an instance of the fourth type, he accordingly claims that the color and extension of this presented surface are partial contents and therefore by their nature inseparable from each other.[1]

The fact that the presentation in question meets the criterion which Stumpf puts forward for partial contents might be affirmed by some, simply because their efforts to present the extension and color of the surface separately are in vain. Against concluding from our vain efforts Stumpf however warns us, not because the presentation of extension together with color could be one of a fixed association, but rather because physiological factors may determine the togetherness of the two contents in presentation.[2] Rather, it is the following consideration which Stumpf finds compelling in his decision that the extension and color of a visually presented surface are indeed partial contents:

In general it holds good that they *change independently of each other*. That is to say, the extension can change while the color remains the same, and the color can change while the extension remains the same. Nevertheless, the *quality participates in a certain way in the change of the extension*. We express this linguistically by saying: the color diminishes, becomes smaller, until it vanishes. "Increasing and diminishing" is the designation for quantitative changes.

As a matter of fact, the quality is also affected by the change of the extension, although its peculiar manner of change does not depend on it. It does not here become less green or red; it as such has no degrees, but only kinds, and cannot in itself increase and diminish, but only be altered. In spite of this, however, if we allow it to remain with regard to its peculiar manner unchanged, to remain green for instance, it is still also affected by the quantitative change. And this is certainly not just an improper expression of language or a deceptive transference, as is shown by the fact that it *diminishes to the point of vanishing*, that it eventually becomes *zero through the mere change of the quantity*.

From this it now follows that the two are by their nature inseparable, that they in some manner form a single content of which they are only partial contents. If they were merely members of a sum, then it would perhaps be thinkable that, simply speaking, if the extension is omitted, the quality too is omitted (that they do not exist independently); but it would be inconceivable that the quality gradually diminishes in such a manner and disappears through the mere diminishment and disappearance of the quantity without thereby changing in its manner as a quality. [...] In any case [...] [they] can not be independent contents, cannot by

---

[1] The influence which Stumpf had on Husserl regarding this fourth case and others like it has already been appreciated in Barry Smith, "Ontologische Aspekte der Husserlschen Phänomenologie", *Husserl Studien* 3 (1986): 115-130.

[2] *Über den psychologischen Ursprung der Raumvorstellung*, pp. 111 f. See ibid., pp. 49 f. for Stumpf's argument that the case in question cannot be one of fixed association.

their nature be separated and exist independently from each other in the presentation.[1]

While Stumpf accordingly concludes that the extension and the color of an extended colored surface are inseparable by their nature, this also helps him to decide the genetic question whether the presentation of space is original. He answers "that space is as originally and directly perceived as quality is".[2]

While we may grant that Stumpf's interesting and illuminating thought-experiment yields the desired conclusion here, one observation is in order. The extension and color of the extended colored surface, according to Stumpf, are inseparable *from each other*. While this certainly seems to be the case, it should also be pointed out that Stumpf's thought-experiment can be pursued further to show that the extension is not related to the color precisely as the color is related to the extension. It is indeed quite clear that changes in the color participate in changes in the extension, that there is, as it were, less color if there is less extension, and again more color with more extension. It must be asked, however, whether the extension likewise changes in accordance with changes in the color. If a red surface has yellow added to it and thereby becomes orange, while it remains the same in other possible respects, does its extension in any way at all change? Apparently it does not. The surface may become more and more yellow until it is finally no longer orange, or its color may change in any other direction, but this does not in the least affect the extension as changes of the extension affect the color. As the extension diminishes, the color approaches zero, whereas the extension does not

---

[1] *Ibid.*, pp. 112 f.: "Im Allgemeinen gilt, dass sie sich *unabhängig verändern*, i.e., es kann die Ausdehnung sich ändern, während die Farbe die gleiche bleibt, und kann die Farbe sich ändern, während die Ausdehnung gleich bleibt. Aber dennoch *partizipiert die Qualität in gewisser Weise an der Änderung der Ausdehnung.* Wir drücken dies sprachlich aus, indem wir sagen: die Farbe nimmt ab, wird kleiner, bis zum Verschwinden. Wachsen und Abnehmen ist die Bezeichnung für quantitative Änderungen.

In der Tat wird die Qualität durch Änderung der Ausdehnung mit affiziert, obgleich die ihr eigentümliche Änderungsweise davon unabhängig ist. Sie wird dabei nicht weniger grün oder rot; sie selbst hat nicht Grade, sondern nur Arten, kann an sich nicht wachsen und abnehmen, sondern nur wechseln. Aber trotzdem, wenn wir sie nach dieser ihr eigentümlichen Weise ganz unverändert z.B. grün bleiben lassen, wird sie doch durch die quantitative Änderung mitaffiziert. Und dass dies nicht etwa nur ein uneigentlicher Ausdruck der Sprache oder eine täuschende Übertragung ist, zeigt sich daran, dass sie bis *zum Verschwinden abnimmt,* dass sie schliesslich *durch blosse Änderung der Quantität Null wird.*

Hieraus nun folgt, dass beide ihrer Natur nach untrennbar sind, dass sie in irgend einer Weise einen einzigen Inhalt bilden, von dem sie nur Teilinhalte sind. Wären sie bloss Glieder einer Summe, so wäre es vielleicht denkbar, dass schlechthin gesprochen, wenn die Ausdehnung hinwegfällt, auch die Qualität hinwegfällt (dass sie nicht unabhängig existieren); aber dass die Qualität auf solche Art allmählig abnimmt und verschwindet durch blosses Abnehmen und Verschwinden der Quantität, ohne sich dabei als Qualität in ihrer Weise zu ändern, wäre unbegreiflich. [...] Jedenfalls [...] können [sie] nicht selbständige Inhalte sein, können ihrer Natur nach nicht getrennt und unabhängig von einander in der Vorstellung existieren." This passage is partly underlined by Husserl.

[2] *Ibid.*, p. 115.

approach anything at all while the color changes. Thus there seems to be an asymmetry between the two parts under consideration, in spite of their mutual dependence on each other.

It may be added, however, that for Stumpf's purposes in the book on the origin of the presentation of space it is most important to show that color is dependent on extension, for it is granted by all that the presentation of *color* is original and needs to be shown that the presentation of *extension* (space) is no less so. As long he can show that color is dependent on extension, as he does by illustrating that the color is by its nature affected by changes in the extension, he effectively demonstrates the originality of the presentation of space.

4.2. Tonpsychologie

Now let us turn to Stumpf's treatment of the topic of fusion in *Tonpsychologie*. In the first volume of this work this topic is touched upon only in passing. "The consonance of two tones," says Stumpf, "is based on a peculiar sensory relation of these to each other, a relation whereby they are less easily and perfectly discerned as a plurality than the dissonant tones".[1] The peculiar sensory relation in question is of course fusion, but a more thorough-going discussion of this is left for the second volume. What is however clear at once is that fusion for Stumpf takes place among sensory contents, not among acts of sensation or of any other kind, but also not among contents which are correlated with non-sensory acts.

In *Tonpsychologie* II fusion is contrasted with relations of two other kinds, namely the one which occurs between "moments" (or what had been called "partial contents" in the book on the origin of the presentation of space), e.g., the quality and intensity of a tone, and the relation whereby elements belong together in a collection ("mere sum"). If we wish to make clear what a whole is in contrast with a mere sum, the relation between moments, says Stumpf, serves us best. "A looser unity," he continues, "albeit one still quite distinct from the merely collective unity, is that of the simultaneous sensory qualities among each other. We want to call this especially 'fusion'. It is analogous to the previously mentioned one [between moments] insofar as here, too, different contents form a whole with each other; but the parts are no longer inseparable, as they were in the other case. I cannot have a sensation of intensity without quality and vice-versa, but I can indeed have a sensation of one of the simultaneous tones also

---

[1] *Tonpsychologie* I, p. 101: "Die Konsonanz zweier Töne beruht [...] auf einem eigentümlichen sinnlichen Verhalten dieser zu einander, demzufolge sie weniger leicht und vollkommen als eine Mehrheit erkannt werden als die dissonierenden". This passage is underlined by Husserl. In the margin he also marks "NB".

without the other. *If* only they are sensed at same time, it is impossible to avoid sensing them as a whole, to avoid sensing them in the relation of fusion".[1] There are, Stumpf adds, greater and lesser degrees of fusion. In cases where the sensations belong to one sense the contents are fused together to a greater degree than in cases where the sensations belong to different senses. However, even if the sensations belong to different senses, the fusion between tastes and odors is stronger than that between colors and tones. Moreover, if the sensations belong to one sense, the fusion between the contents can vary in degree. "The strongest fusion", says Stumpf, "occurs here in the case of the octaves".[2] This example, according to him, illustrates best what fusion is, just as the union of moments in a content of sensation provides the best example of a sensory whole.

4.3. *Philosophie der Arithmetik*

The question still remains how a fused whole differs from a collection. We shall return to this question after we have considered Husserl's usage of the concept of fusion in *Philosophie der Arithmetik*. In this work, published just one year later than *Tonpsychologie* II, Husserl uses the concept of fusion in connection with his theory of figural moments. These are exemplified by a row of soldiers, a pile of apples, a boulevard of trees, a swarm of birds, a gaggle of geese. The difference between these cases and ones in which we simply use the appropriate plurals, e.g., "soldiers", "apples", and so forth, is to be found in "a certain characteristic feature of the whole intuition of the collection which can be grasped in a glance and in its well determined forms makes up the most essential part of the meaning of those expressions, 'row', 'pile', 'boulevard', 'covey', 'flock', 'gaggle', etc., which introduce the plural" (Hua XII, 204). Such features differ, according to Husserl, depending not only on inner features of the "sub-intuitions" (*Teilanschauungen*), but also depending on "certain relations and complexes of relations which link the sub-intuitions with each other" (Hua XII, 204).

---

[1]*Tonpsychologie* II, p. 65: "Eine losere, gleichwohl aber von der bloss kollektiven noch wohl zu unterscheidende Einheit ist die der gleichzeitigen Empfindungsqualitäten unter einander. Diese speziell wollen wir *Verschmelzung* nennen. Sie ist der vorhin genannten insofern analog, als auch hier verschiedene Inhalte ein Ganzes miteinander bilden; aber die Teile sind nicht mehr wie dort untrennbar. Ich kann eine Intensität nicht ohne Qualität und umgekehrt empfinden, wohl aber einen der gleichzeitigen Töne auch ohne den andern. Nur *wenn* sie zugleich empfunden werden, dann ist es unmöglich, sie nicht als Ganzes, nicht im Verschmelzungsverhältnis". Husserl partly underlines this passage and writes "NB" alongside the last sentence.

[2]*Ibid.*, p. 66: "Die stäkste Verschmelzung findet sich hier bei den Oktaven".

The inner features or relations in question are moreover said to be fused.[1]

While Husserl is content here to apply what he regards as the Stumpfian concept of fusion, we may have doubts whether this is in fact the concept he applies. It has already been pointed out that, while the equality or similarity of the members belonging to a collection in which fusion occurs is regarded by Husserl as essential (Hua XII, 124), this is by no means the case regarding the Stumpfian concept of fusion.[2] As far as Stumpf is concerned, fusion occurs wherever contents are sensed at the same time. In this regard Stumpf would have to say that all that one is at any given moment hearing, seeing, tasting, smelling, and feeling (by touch) belongs to one single fused whole. This being sensed at the same time may of course guarantee only the minimum degree of fusion, but this minimum is already sufficient to bring to light another divergence in the Husserlian and Stumpfian concepts of fusion, a divergence even greater than the one just mentioned.

In order to see this second divergence one must consider how Husserl regards collective combination already in his habilitation thesis and again in *Philosophie der Arithmetik*. According to Husserl, we cannot draw the concept of a collection only from the presentations of the collective members; rather, we must take into account the peculiar relation which occurs between these members, the relation of collective combination (*kollektive Verbindung*). Unlike certain other relations, such as the relation of similarity, collective combination is a psychical rather than a primary relation. A psychical relation, in contrast with a primary relation, cannot be conceived without reflecting on an act in which both of the members (or "foundations") of the relation are presented. While a similarity obtains merely due to intrinsic features which the similar contents have (e.g., they are both red), two or more contents belong together in a collection merely because they are collected. Thus, objects of all kinds - physical, psychical, and any others which one may care to admit - can belong together in the

---

[1] What Husserl calls "figural moments" in *Philosophie der Arithmetik*, as he says in a footnote (Hua XII, 210 f.) can be compared with Gestalt qualities as investigated in Christian von Ehrenfels, "Über 'Gestaltqualitäten'", *Vierteljahrsschrift für wissenschaftliche Philosophie* 14 (1890): 249-292. This article, Husserl explains in the footnote just mentioned, was not available to him while writing *Philosophie der Arithmetik*. His own copy of it bears no markings or annotations. While he apparently did not draw anything from von Ehrenfels' article, he explains that the two of them hit upon the same notion due to the influence of Ernst Mach's *Beiträge zur Analyse der Empfindungen* (Jena, 1886). In the *Logische Untersuchungen* he again uses this notion (Hua XIX/1, 287 f.), this time under the heading "unity moments" (*Einheitsmomente*), but there is no attempt to examine the nature of such moments further. For an extensive discussion of the Ehrenfelsian notion of Gestalt qualities and the closely related notions which occur in the work of Husserl, Meinong, Stumpf, and the Berlin School, see Barry Smith, *Austrian Philosophy*, pp. 243-280.

[2] Elmar Holenstein, *Phänomenologie der Assoziation*, p. 124.

same collection.

In his attempt to stress the *sui generis* character of collective combination, Husserl discusses various alternative ways of conceiving of collective combination. One of these ways involves regarding all contents which are given together in the same consciousness as collectively combined. Against this view Husserl's main argument runs as follows (Hua XII, 23):

Various phenomena make up the stock of our total consciousness at any moment; but special interests are involved in picking out and collectively unifying certain presentations from this fullness. And this is done without all remaining presentations vanishing from consciousness. If that view were correct, then there would be at any moment only one single collection, consisting in the totality of the given sub-contents of our consciousness; while we can however form various collections at any time and arbitrarily, expand an already formed one by adding new contents and contract it by omitting others without the excluded ones having to go out of consciousness; in short, we are conscious of a spontaneity which would otherwise be inconceivable.

This argument is indeed a very strong one, for it makes clear that certain collections can be marked off from a larger fullness of presented objects. In this way we are indeed able to add and subtract. We are also able to think of distinct collections at the same time, e.g., the pile of apples next to the pile of pears. If the view of collective combination which Husserl argues against here is further developed and one stresses that the contents in question must be *simultaneously* given in the same consciousness, the same argument which has just been quoted still holds good (Hua XII, 24). For it is obvious that we can think of distinct collections at the same time.

Another way in which collective combination might be regarded is in terms of *successive* contents of consciousness. While Husserl puts forward several arguments against this view, he most effectively deals with it by asking one simple question: "What would otherwise be the sense of speaking of a plurality [or a collection] of *simultaneous* contents? The origin of the concept of temporal co-existence would be an incomprehensible enigma from this standpoint" (Hua XII, 29).

What we must now note is that both Stumpf and Husserl contrast the case of a fused whole with a "mere sum". This is already stated clearly by Stumpf in the first characterization of fusion quoted above. Husserl, too, says "that the unitary [i.e., figurative] moments are simply different from mere sums" (Hua XII, 204). If we understand a mere sum as a collection (and there is apparently no other way to understand this term), then we might ask what the difference is between a collection and a fused whole. The term "mere" is well chosen because, in order for contents to be fused, they must be presented together in a collection. What, then, must in addition occur so that the collected contents are fused? Of course, Husserl speaks of similarity or equality. But he also admits that this is not enough, that there is some "characteristic feature of the whole intuition" which makes the pile of apples a *pile* and not just apples, let alone a row, a flock, etc.

If we now consider Stumpf's view on this matter, things are quite different. There is no talk of such a characteristic feature. All that is needed for fusion is the simultaneity of the contents in a single consciousness. If we ask what distinguishes a fused whole from a mere sum, we get the following answer: "Successive sensations form as sensations a mere sum, simultaneous ones already as sensations a whole".[1] Hence, a fused whole is not something which results from adding something to a collection. The fused whole and the collection are indeed mutually exclusive. This not only makes it hard to understand why Stumpf speaks of a "mere" sum, but his characterization of a sum in terms of succession opens him up to the above-quoted objection which Husserl raises against this characterization. Since his notion of fusion is formulated in contrast with this dubious notion of a mere sum, his notion of fusion turns out to be equally dubious.

4.4. Logische Untersuchungen

Let us now consider Husserl's application of the notion of fusion in the *Logische Untersuchungen*. This notion, first of all, comes into play in the first "Logical Investigation". It is used here in order to illuminate the relation between the perception of an expression, whether it be spoken or written, and the act of consciousness which gives this expression meaning. These acts, says Husserl (Hua XIX/1, 45):

form in consciousness no mere 'together', as if they were merely simultaneously given. They rather form an intimately fused unity with a peculiar character. Familiar to everyone from his inner experience is the unequivalence of the two constituent pieces, in which the unequilateralness of the relation between the expression and the object, expressed (named) by means of the meaning, is mirrored. Both of them, word-presentation and sense-giving act, are lived through; but while we live *through* the word-presentation, we still by no means live *in* the presenting of the word, but exclusively in the execution of its sense, its meaning.

While Husserl's discussion of this matter continues in a way which does not shed special light on the concept of fusion, the passage just quoted confirms once again what had already been seen, namely that Husserl's concept of fusion differs from Stumpf's. This is made clear by the contrast between fusion and being "merely simultaneously given", for the latter is simply synonymous with "fusion" as understood by Stumpf.

---

[1] *Tonpsychologie* II, p. 64: "Aufeinanderfolgende Empfindungen bilden als Empfindungen eine blosse Summe, gleichzeitige schon als Empfindungen ein Ganzes".

The fusion between the perception of an expression and the meaning-giving act is moreover worth mentioning, for it relevant to a recent controversy. The charge has been raised that Husserl's view is "a Humpty-Dumpty view of this matter: the view, namely, that an utterance assumes the meaning that it bears by an interior act of investing it with that meaning".[1] Another commentator has defended Husserl, saying that his view "is safe against such criticisms, however, for the expression and the sense which animates it are not conceived by Husserl as separate and distinct, but as one 'concrete phenomenon' within which different sides (dependent parts or moments) can be distinguished at best only abstractly (like North and South poles of a magnet)".[2] Yet, Husserl's view is not to be defended in this way, for as we shall see, he maintains that there is a difference between parts which are *fused together* and those which are *dependent on each other*. A discussion of this point will take us into considerations of the third "Logical Investigation", where the concept of fusion again comes into play, and of the Stumpfian background of this text.

Here Husserl fully endorses Stumpf's classification of objects into independent and partial contents, though he prefers to speak of dependent contents (*unselbständige Inhalte*) instead of partial ones (Hua XIX/1, 232). Moreover, Husserl also speaks in favor of Stumpf's manner of demonstrating the dependence of the color of the colored extended surface on extension and the extension thereof on the color (Hua XIX/1, 235 f.). This is of course not to say that, whenever one content depends on another, the latter also depends on the former, for Husserl also allows for cases of one-sided dependence. Such cases had of course already been admitted in Brentano's psychology, for acts of judging and acts of feeling and willing were regarded as dependent on presentations, whereas it was also held that presentations could exist independently. In the third "Logical Investigations" Husserl enters into various refinements in the theory of parts and wholes which, though well worth detailed considerations,[3] would take us too far afield in the present context.

It should be pointed out however that this theory, as useful as it is in phenomenological investigations, is by no means limited to the sphere of psychical phenomena; rather, the distinction between dependent and independent objects, says Husserl, "extends in this case beyond the sphere of contents of consciousness and

---

[1] Michael Dummett, *Ursprünge der analytischen Philosophie* (Frankfurt: Suhrkamp, 1988), pp. 45 f.

[2] Barry Smith, "Husserl's Theory of Meaning and Reference", in L. Haaparanta (ed.), *Mind, Meaning and Mathematics*, 173 f.

[3] See Barry Smith (ed.), *Parts and Moments: Studies in Logic and Formal Ontology* (Munich: Philosophia, 1981).

becomes a theoretically most significant distinction in the realm of *objects as such*" (Hua XIX/1, 227). After examining this distinction with explicit references to Stumpf Husserl tells us (Hua XIX/1, 247):

> that cutting across the distinction considered thus far between independent and dependent contents there is in the phenomenological sphere, but also only in the phenomenological sphere, a second distinction which is confused with the former: namely the distinction between the *intuitively "separate"* contents, which are *"marked off"* or "kept apart" from connected contents, and those which are *fused* with the connected ones, running into them without delineation. The expressions are, to be sure, ambiguous, but already their juxtaposition will make clear that there is indeed an essentially new distinction under consideration.

The extension and the color of the extended colored surface, though inseparable from each other, are nonetheless marked off from each other in the sense under consideration, whereas this surface consists of parts which are "independent, but not separate". The surface can be sliced in half, for instance, making the two halves separate; otherwise, the two halves, as independent as they may be, are fused into one whole, the colored extended surface. The color may gradually change from one side of the surface to the other, or it may remain the same color all over the surface; in either case there is a continuity which obtains here in spite of the separability of the parts. This continuity is to be found in all instances of fusion according to Husserl's conception.

If for the moment we keep this conception in mind, not worrying about how it compares with Stumpf's or indeed with Husserl's earlier conception, we may consider the case of fusion between the presentation of an expression and the act which gives the expression meaning. The assertion of this fusion is not to be regarded as "Humpty-Dumpty theory", if what is meant by this is a theory which asserts that we can *arbitrarily* give this or that meaning to this or that expression.[1] Just as the colored surface is given as one fused whole in our experience, whether we like it or not, the same can be said of the presentation of the expression and the meaning-giving act. There is indeed one concrete phenomenon within which different sides can be distinguished, but these sides are not to be distinguished "abstractly", i.e., as dependent parts, since they can obviously exist separately from each other. Obviously the presen-

---

[1] Much of the later Wittgenstein's work may be regarded as a critique of the Humpty-Dumpty theory of meaning. While he often seems to draw the conclusion that there is no act of meaning which goes together with the usage of words, he at best demonstrates that words cannot be given meaning by sheer fiat. In *Zettel* (§ 5), for instance, he asks, "Can I mean with words whatever I will?", and answers, "Look at the door of your room while saying a series of random sounds, and mean by them a description of the door!" The result of this experiment may well be that there is no *voluntary* act which gives words meaning, but it does not follow from this, as Wittgenstein sometimes suggests, that there is no act of meaning at all. An act, after all, is only a psychical phenomenon, which is distinguishable by its intentional reference and perhaps other characteristics, but not by its being a volition.

tation of the expression, i.e., of the written or spoken sign, can exist without being given meaning. Moreover, while we may have misgivings about there being meaning-giving acts without there being written or spoken signs, it is nonetheless clear that the particular signs to which a meaning is given can vary indefinitely, as is made evident by the existence of many different languages and by synonyms in one and the same language.

It had of course been stressed by Stumpf in *Tonpsychologie*, as we have already seen, that the fused whole is "looser" than a whole consisting of moments. Moreover, as Husserl referred in *Philosophie der Arithmetik* to the Stumpfian concept of fusion (in spite of divergences between this concept and his own), in the *Logische Untersuchungen* he again makes reference to Stumpf, now saying (Hua XIX/1, 249 n): "Stumpf, as is well known, defines fusion at first in a narrower sense, as a relation of simultaneous *sensory qualities* by virtue of which they appear as parts of a sensory whole. He forgoes, however, drawing attention to the broader concept which is relevant to us here." Fusion in this broader sense may take place between acts as well as sensory qualities and moreover between acts *of all kinds*. Thus it could be said in the first "Logical Investigation" that fusion occurs in the case of the presentation of an expression and the meaning-giving act.

While Husserl thus expands the concept of fusion beyond the sensory realm in the *Logische Untersuchungen*, the fact still remains that it, just like the concept of fusion in *Philosophie der Arithmetik*, is different from the Stumpfian notion in another important way, namely that the mere co-incidence of contents or even acts within a single consciousness is not a sufficient condition for fusion. If this were indeed the case, then it would be of little significance to say that the presentation of a word and the meaning-giving act are fused. This would only mean that the two occur simultaneously in the same consciousness. Husserl clearly means that the acts are more intimately connected than this. We may also note that the concept of fusion in the *Logische Untersuchungen* is again different from the one that had been used in *Philosophie der Arithmetik*, for the latter concept strictly applied to *collections*, whereas the fused wholes which are used for illustration in the *Logische Untersuchungen* are not mere collections. The adjacent parts of a colored surface are referred to in this regard. These are however more intimately connected than the apples which make up a pile of apples.

One of the questions which remains regarding fused parts concerns whether they are the same as *physical* parts. Husserl answers this question as follows (Hua XIX/1, 273): "If an *abstractum* [dependent content] allows for such a disintegration that the pieces [independent contents] are of the same lowest species as the one determined by the undivided whole, we call it a *physical whole*, its pieces *physical parts*". If we apply this criterion to the case of a red-moment being divided in two, then it is obvious that the resulting pieces should be called "physical parts". For both parts belong to the same lowest species as the whole red-moment. If, however, the color gradually becomes darker from one side to the other of the fused whole, the division between the darker and the lighter sides does not leave us with physical parts. The word-presentation and the meaning-giving act are for the same reason not physical parts of the concrete act of expression. It may be added here that this act is not an *abstractum* and for this reason, too, its pieces cannot be physical parts. Thus, it seems that Husserl may regard all physical parts as fused, but not all fused parts as physical.

Among the conclusions reached in the *Logische Untersuchungen*, and moreover a conclusion which diverges considerably from the doctrines of Brentano, is the application of the theory of parts and wholes to the distinction between synthetic and analytic laws. Wherever there is dependence, as there is of color in relation to extension and vice-versa, there is a obviously a necessity and a universality. It is, after all, the case that *any* color, whether it be red, blue, yellow, or some other, *cannot* be given unless it is extended. Such necessity and universality, according to Kant, are of course the distinguishing features of *a priori* judgments. As we have seen, Brentano was willing to concede that such judgments are possible, but he also maintained that they were all analytic. Husserl by contrast maintains that the cases of dependence of the kind under consideration, e.g., regarding color and extension, are precisely instances where a proposition can be stated (and thus a judgment can be made) which is *a priori* and synthetic. Only purely formal laws, according to Husserl, are to be characterized as analytic.

5. STUMPF'S CRITIQUE OF *IDEEN* I

Just as the personal relation between Stumpf and Husserl did not cease with the latter's transcendental turn, which indeed amounts to a radical departure from the school of Brentano (far more so than does the Platonism of the *Logische Untersuchungen*), the later developments in Husserl's philosophical work were not unfamiliar to Stumpf. In his posthumously published *Erkenntnislehre* he criticizes Husserl's literary product of 1913, the celebrated *Ideen zu einer reinen Phänomenologie und phänomenologischen Phänomenologie* I. The standpoint of Stumpf's critique is moreover still closely affiliated with the doctrines which he had learned from his mentor.

The main features of the program which Husserl advocates in *Ideen* I are of course well known. Phenomenology is characterized as an eidetic science, i.e., one which aims at cognition *a priori* rather than factual knowledge. Such sciences are divided up into the purely formal ones and the material ones. Here we must keep in mind that Husserl at this stage in his development makes a sharp distinction between two different types of concepts or, in his more ontologically ambitious terminology, essences, namely the formal and the material. While the concept "something" is a purely formal one, the concepts "man", "animal", and "living entity" are material ones. All the sciences which strictly deal in formal concepts belong together in a formal ontology, whereas all the other disciplines are founded on or are themselves material or "regional" ontologies.

Though this division leaves us no choice but to regard phenomenology as one of these regional ontologies, it is not merely one of them alongside the others, but is rather given a special status under the headings "pure" and "transcendental" phenomenology. This is because it is concerned with pure consciousness, which is characterized by the fact that it is given absolutely and not merely in perspectives, as of course physical things are given. In our normal dealings, however, we are immersed in the natural attitude which is characterized by a naive and unquestioned acceptance of the perspectively given things. Pure consciousness can become a scientific subject-matter only if we suspend the natural attitude and adopt the phenomenological attitude. In this attitude we do not by any means doubt the existence of the things accepted in the natural attitude, but we simply make no use of our belief in their existence.

In Husserl's attempt to state the project of pure phenomenology as a science which requires the suspension of the natural attitude, he thematizes the concepts of noesis and noema. While the former is the transcendental counterpart of the psychological concept of an act, the latter is something new. The noema is not to be identified with the object of consciousness *simpliciter*, but rather with the object as perceived, as imagined, etc. While this concept cannot here receive the attention which it has attracted in recent years in much of the literature on Husserl,[1] it is mentioned only because it comes into play in Stumpf's criticisms of *Ideen* I.

While the talk of essences harkens back to the Platonism which had decisively made its appearance in the *Logische Untersuchungen*, and while the talk of an "intuition of essences" (*Wesensschau*) is accordingly alien to a Brentanist as orthodox as Stumpf, a good deal of the cognition Husserl accounts for under this mystical-sounding heading is by no means dismissed by Brentano, Stumpf, or other members of the school. It is indeed Brentanian orthodoxy, and indeed a view which had already been espoused by empiricists such as Locke and Hume (unlike John Stuart Mill), that axioms of logic and mathematics are immediately cognized and by no means inductively inferred. As we may also recall, Stumpf insisted on a distinction between partial contents, e.g., the color and the extension of a colored extended surface, and independent contents. Such a distinction can be known in an immediate grasp which is

---

[1] See especially Rudolf Bernet, "Husserls Begriff des Noema", in IJsseling (ed.), *Husserl-Ausgabe und Husserl-Forschung*, pp. 61-80.

just as *a priori* as any mathematical or logical knowledge, but by no means identified with the cognition which takes place in these disciplines. It is therefore no surprise that in Stumpf's *Erkenntnislehre* I he makes room for axioms which he alternatively calls "objective", "regional", and "material" and are characterized as no less *a priori* than the formal axioms. In his discussion of these material axioms Stumpf comes face to face with Husserl.

The possibility of *a priori* cognition which is not purely formal, says Stumpf, can be found in various examples. There are many such instances of cognition which we can have about sensory contents. We can know, for instance, that the degree of fusion between certain contents is greater than in others, the highest in the case of octaves, but we can also know that something colored must also be extended, that perceived space is three-dimensional, that all sensory contents are temporal. The discipline in which these instances of cognition belong is phenomenology, whereas other instances of cognition of the same kind belong to psychology and eidology, i.e., insofar as they concern psychical functions (acts) and psychical formations (concepts, states of affairs, collections, etc.) respectively.

Now the "most general tendency" of *Ideen* I, according to Stumpf, is "the search for objective axioms and especially those which are fundamental to philosophy".[1] Pure phenomenology is to be the science to which these axioms belong. Whether or not phenomenology is also to derive theorems, as it were, from the axioms, Stumpf's interpretation of Husserl's project in *Ideen* I, as regards both the axiomatic status of the cognition belonging to pure phenomenology and its alleged significance, is correct. While Stumpf attributes this significance to the disciplines already mentioned, namely phenomenology (concerned with sensory contents), psychology (concerned with psychical functions), and eidology (concerned with psychical formations), the Husserlian project of a pure or transcendental phenomenology is rejected by him.

It is difficult to evaluate this project, says Stumpf, because "illuminating adequate examples for the type of cognition which he [Husserl] has in mind are all but completely missing".[2] To be sure, Husserl is perfectly right to say that we can have an *a priori* cognition of the difference between color and sound. But this cognition does not belong in the framework of pure phenomenology. Another instance of *a priori* cognition which Stumpf finds in *Ideen* I is the knowledge that everything material is extended. This knowledge, however, is characterized by him as "no substantive

---

[1]*Erkenntnislehre* I, p. 186: "die Aufsuchung gegenständlicher Axiome [...] und insbesondere, die der Philosophie zugrunde liegen".

[2]*Ibid.*, p. 188: "[weil] erläuternde adäquate Beispiele für die Art von Erkenntnissen, die er im Auge hat, so gut wie gänzlich fehlen".

judgment, but rather a mere explanation of a name".[1] Besides the conspicuous lack of examples of phenomenological cognition, other shortcomings in *Ideen* I are pointed out by Stumpf.

While Stumpf naturally allows for regional ontologies, as indeed he himself recommends at least three of them (phenomenology, psychology, and eidology), he nonetheless warns that the cognition of the material *a priori* is limited:

to elementary intuitions, never to the essence of *things* in whose presentation there is joined together a multiplicity of properties and manners of conduct, about whose belonging-together an *a priori* inspection cannot inform us. We can, to be sure, talk of a *Wesenschau* of tones, of colors, of the course of time, but not of a *Wesensschau* of liverworts or eye diseases. Nor does Husserl do so, but we miss the sharp drawing of boundaries in this regard.[2]

In connection with the restriction which Stumpf puts on the material ontologies, it is no surprise that the ontology of nature, which Husserl endorses as a legitimate concern, is regarded by Stumpf as "not an *a priori* science of the *things* of nature or also only the *occurrences* of nature, but rather a summary of the cognition regarding *sensory phenomena as such*."[3] Thus, everything which had fallen under the heading "phenomenology", as this term had been used in 1907 by Stumpf, is to be identified as the regional ontology of nature.

Although Stumpf is in large measure sympathetic with the epistemological and methodological tendencies which are exhibited in the first main section of *Ideen* I ("Wesen und Wesenserkenntnis"), he finds the thrust of the rest of this work to be fundamentally flawed. The very nature of a pure phenomenology is called into question. Insofar as "pure" is contrasted with "regional", the only discipline which is to be regarded as pure is formal logic which is of course by no means concerned with phenomena as such, e.g., with sensory contents or psychical functions. "There is therefore simply no room", says Stumpf, "for [pure] phenomenology. It is indeed a contradiction in itself, a phenomenology without phenomena. And now it is of course also

---

[1] *Ibid.*, p. 189.

[2] *Ibid.*, p. 190: "auf elementare Anschauungen, niemals auf das Wesen von *Dingen*, in deren Vorstellung immer eine Mehrzahl von Eigenschaften und Verhaltungsweisen verknüpft ist, über deren Zusammengehörigkeit uns niemals eine apriorische Schau belehren kann. Wir können wohl von einer Wesensschau der Töne, der Farben, des Zeitverlaufes reden, aber nicht von einer Wesensschau der Lebermoose oder Augenkrankheiten. Das tut Husserl nicht, aber wir vermissen die scharfe Grenzziehung nach dieser Richtung hin".

[3] *Ibid.*, p. 191: "nicht eine apriorische Wissenschaft von den Natur*dingen* oder auch nur den Natur*vorgängen*, sondern nur die Zusammenfassung der auf *sinnliche Phänomene als solche* bezüglichen apriorischen Erkenntnisse".

understandable why there must be a lack of adequate examples for the principles of this science".[1] If one turns to § 60 of *Ideen* I for help, where Husserl speaks of the "suspension of material-eidetic disciplines" as necessary for pure phenomenology, the result is especially disappointing. For, as Stumpf points out, we only get a notion of what pure phenomenology is *not*, without the slightest positive clarification of the notion of a "transcendentally purified consciousness" which concerns it. "The pure ego which is to be viewed by the 'pure ego-gaze'", Stumpf says sarcastically, "is indeed all too strongly reminiscent of the Nirvana of the Indian penitents who relentlessly look at their navel".[2] Until we are actually given examples of this pure phenomenology, Husserl's programmatic statements in favor of it remain empty and vain.

Stumpf also takes issue with Husserl's characterization of *psychology* as a science of matters of facts, for he insists that since Aristotle its aim has been the establishment of laws, not only those which are arrived at by induction but "also laws of essence or structure which are discerned by observation and analysis of psychical functions".[3] A psychology which allows for laws of both kinds is of course the descriptive psychology of Brentano, but also that of Lotze and indeed of Husserl in the *Logische Untersuchungen*. While Stumpf accordingly pays Husserl a high compliment for making a significant contribution to descriptive psychology, he also maintains that a search in *Ideen* I for additional contributions to this discipline is disappointing. In this regard he cites Husserl's description of *attention* as a ray from the ego (Hua III/1, 211 ff.). Though Stumpf sees attention as an important topic for descriptive psychology, still very much in need of further treatment, he doubts:

that the ray theory guarantees a deeper insight into the essence of attention. It seems, on the contrary, to come down to nothing else but the oldest and most popular standpoint which (according to Lotze's sneering remark) represents attention as a light with which the soul wanders around in its dark attic and shines now on this, now on that old household item. These however are only metaphors, stones instead of the bread of actually clarifying cognition.[4]

---

[1] *Ibid.*, p. 192: "Es ist also für die 'reine Phänomenologie' schlechterdings kein Platz. Ja sie ist ein Widerspruch in sich selbst, eine Phänomenologie ohne Phänomene. Und nun begreift sich freilich auch, warum es an adäquaten Beispielen für die Grundsätze dieser Wissenschaft fehlen muss".

[2] *Ibid.*: "Das durch den 'reinen Ichblick' zu erschauende reine Ich gemahnt doch allzu stark an das Nirwana der indischen Büsser, die unverwandt auf ihren Nabel schauen".

[3] *Ibid.*, p. 194: "auch Wesens- oder Strukturgesetze, die direkt durch Beobachtung und Analyse der psychischen Funftionen ermittelt werden".

[4] *Ibid.*, p. 195: "dass die Strahlentheorie eine tiefere Einsicht in das Wesen der Aufmerksamkeit gewährt. Sie scheint im Gegenteil auf nichts anderes als auf den ältesten und populärsten Standpunkt hinauszulaufen, welcher (nach Lotzes spottender Bemerkung) die Aufmerksamkeit wie ein Licht hinstellt, mit dem die Seele

Here Stumpf not only has his finger on a grave shortcoming of utterances which Husserl makes under the heading "pure phenomenology", but his criticism is very relevant to much of what has issued from the phenomenological movement in its development beyond the school of Brentano. Too often phenomenology is nothing more than a free play of metaphorical speech, often indistinguishable from poetry. While metaphors may have their place in description, they must surely be used with more caution than they are in the ray theory of attention.

The only way possible to attach any meaning at all to "pure phenomenology", according to Stumpf, is to regard it as equivalent to descriptive psychology, for attention, perception, judgment, and all the familiar themes of descriptive psychology are dealt with in pure phenomenology. As we have seen, the concern with the essence of these phenomena does not distinguish pure phenomenology from psychology. We have also noted in the introduction that shortly after the publication of the *Logische Untersuchungen* Husserl held that the two disciplines in question are separated only by a "slight nuance". The problem of separating them was indeed one that stayed with Husserl for the rest of his philosophical career. Whether this was ever done in any legitimate way ultimately turns on whether the phenomenological reduction could ever prove itself as a viable methodological procedure.

We have already gotten a glimpse into Stumpf's misgivings about this methodological procedure. The "suspensions" (*Ausschaltungen*) which are recommended by Husserl would set pure phenomenology apart from other disciplines by making it totally empty. Another way of separating it from descriptive psychology which Stumpf considers is to be found in the notion of the noema. Perhaps pure phenomenology is distinguishable from descriptive psychology insofar as the noema is exclusively the subject-matter of pure phenomenology. In this regard Stumpf reminds us that for Husserl the noema is always exactly parallel with the noesis. "Perception, for instance, has its noema, at bottom its perceptual sense, i.e., that which is *perceived as such*. Likewise *memory* has its *remembered as such* [...]; again judging the *judged as such*, enjoyment the enjoyed as such, etc." (Hua III/1, 203). Given this exact parallelism, Stumpf replies, "In this case there can no more be a phenomenology of acts [noeses] and one of contents [noemata] than there can be an arithmetic of pears and an arithmetic of nuts".[1] In light of Husserl's further confirmation of this parallelism by

---

in ihren dunklen Bodenkammern herumwandert und bald dieses, bald jenes alte Stück beleuchtet. Das sind doch nur Bilder, Steine an Stelle des Brotes wirklich aufklärender Erkenntnis".

[1] *Ibid.*, p. 196: "Es kann dann ebensowenig eine Phänomenologie der Akte und eine der Inhalte geben, wie es eine Arithmetik der Birnen und eine Arithmetik der Nüsse geben kann".

asserting that matter and quality can be understood "noematically" (Hua III/1, 298), Stumpf's reply is here all the more justified. Accordingly the concept of the noema will not help Husserl in separating pure phenomenology from psychology.

Finally, Stumpf has misgivings about Husserl's methodological strictures against experiment and indeed against any reliance on actual perceptions of individual phenomena. According to Husserl, we can just as well *imagine* the examples we need for *Wesensschau*. While Stumpf agrees that imagination can be of great service in this regard, as we have indeed seen in his attempt to argue for the inseparability of color and extension, he nonetheless cautiously notes "that mere presentations [i.e., phantasy presentations] are generally far inferior to sensory perceptions in forcefulness, distinctness, and clarity".[1] Wherever actual perceptions are readily available to us they are accordingly to be preferred over corresponding presentations. In this regard he points out that some of Husserl's pupils have let their imaginations run wild, resulting in very dubious claims:

e.g., that we *see* the hardness and heaviness of an iron rod, or that in hearing a melody the forces and tensions existing between the notes are directly perceived, forming even the basis for whole aesthetics of music and totally in contradiction with the demonstration, which has unquestionably been provided by Hume, that sensory perception can show us nothing at all of forces and causal connection.[2]

We have of course already mentioned how much of what has been done in the name of phenomenology is far too metaphorical to be regarded as work of genuine scientific interest. Perhaps this is again due to the reliance on imagination. In any case Stumpf's warning should be taken to heart, not only because the imagination might be too active or in any case wrongly applied (speaking of course from a scientific standpoint), but also because our perceptions often bring to us fresh phenomena which we would have never been constructed through imagination.

There is however much which gives way to doubt in Stumpf's own approach to the material ontologies. While his notion of a phenomenology in the sense of an ontology of the sensory realm is certainly a fruitful one, which can moreover be cashed in with

---

[1] *Ibid.*, p. 197: "dass blosse Vorstellungen im allgemeinen an Stärke, Deutlichkeit und Klarheit weit hinter den Sinneswahrnehmungen zurückstehen".

[2] *Ibid.*, p. 199: "z.B. dass wir Härte und Schwere eines Eisenstabes *sehen* oder dass man beim Hören einer Melodie die zwischen den Tönen obwaltenden Kräfte und Spannungen direkt wahrnimmt, worauf sogar ganze Ästhetiken der Musik gegründet worden sind, im vollen Widerspruch mit dem von Hume zweifellos erbrachten Nachweis, dass die sinnliche Wahrnehmung uns nirgends etwas von Kräften und Kausalzusammenhängen zeigen kann". Here Stumpf refers to a later part of his work (ibid., p. 319), where such products of a wild imagination are located in the dissertation which Wilhelm Schapp had written under Husserl: *Beiträge zur Phänomenologie der Wahrnehmung* (Göttingen, 1910), pp. 49 f., 119. A second edition of this work by Schapp also appeared (Erfurt, 1925) (see pp. 46 ff., 116 of this edition).

actual examples of what can be said in such a discipline, and while his notion of a descriptive psychology which contains a certain amount of *a priori* theses is by no means to be dismissed, we may of course raise the question whether a sharp division between the material ontologies is advisable. This is not to say that the distinction between their subject-matters should be forgone, for the intentional reference which is to be found in psychical phenomena can never be found in physical ones. It would simply be absurd to say that a color, for instance, refers to an object as does a perception or an act of imagining. This would indeed be no less absurd than it would be to say that a color without an extension could be seen. However, when we wish to describe acts of perception, it is difficult to see how this can be done without describing their objects as they appear in perception, as they are "given". The same can be said about the description of those acts which have psychical formations, if one may so speak, as their objects. Such a description cannot be accomplished in isolation from any consideration of the relevant objects. Perhaps it is therefore advisable to bring all of the material ontologies together into one single discipline, and perhaps it is *this* discipline which is best called "phenomenology".

In any case this discipline or group of disciplines is not to be supplemented or overshadowed by a pure phenomenology which cannot even be illustrated by examples. Not only does Stumpf see clearly that a pure phenomenology is simply a vacuous notion, but also an open invitation to free-wheeling flights of fancy which are inherently antithetical to the ideal of philosophy as rigorous science . In this regard it is indeed sad that so many of Husserl's admirers and critics nowadays regard an evaluation of his pure phenomenology, and its concomitant notions of a phenomenological reduction and the noema, as the definitive task in deciding the fruits of his philosophical labors.[1] As Stumpf was well aware, his pupil had made his most important philosophical contributions long before there was any talk at all of a pure phenomenology.

One final criticism which Stumpf puts forward concerns Husserl characterization of the material ontologies as involving synthetic *a priori* cognition in contrast with formal ontology which is said to be analytic in character (Hua III/1, 27). Here Husserl

---

[1]In his introduction to *Husserl, Intentionality and Cognitive Science* (Cambridge, Massachussetts: MIT, 1982) Hubert Dreyfus says that "Husserl was, regrettably, right" in his belief "that none of his students [...] had understood the nature and significance of what he considered his most important discovery: the special realm of entities revealed by the transcental phenomenological reduction" (p. 1). Here we may indeed question just how regrettable this failure in understanding is, for if the whole project of pure phenomenology is as vacuous as Stumpf says it is there is no understanding possible here. As far as the "entities" which are allegedly discovered in the phenomenological reduction are concerned, no one has yet shown that these, including the pure ego and the noema, are anything but ontological monstrosities, to be included among the many others, such as the Absolute, which philosophers time and again dream up in their efforts to be profound. Such monstrosities are at best museum pieces for historical exhibits.

refers back to his discussion of parts and wholes in the *Logische Untersuchungen*, where it is maintained that the dependence of color on extension is precisely an example of a matter that can be cognized both *a priori* and synthetically in contrast with the purely formal laws of logic. It is indeed ironic that the very example of a synthetic *a priori* cognition here is taken from Stumpf, who so emphatically denounces the possibility of such cognition altogether. Stumpf's criticism of this point however fails to enter into Husserl's own efforts to defend this possibility in the *Logische Untersuchungen* and to this extent exhibits a certain weakness.

6. CONCLUDING REMARKS

t is very clear from the discussion in this chapter that Stumpf was an important influence on Husserl in various respects. While he had felt restricted by Brentano to walk the straight and narrow path of rigid orthodoxy, his tutelage under Stumpf was a liberating experience. Not only could he develop views which were fundamentally opposed to Brentano's, but Stumpf also introduced him to James' *Principles of Psychology*, a work which was by no means written from a Brentanian standpoint.

Moreover, Stumpf also had an influence on some of Husserl's own doctrines. To be sure, Husserl gave up the old immanentism to which Stumpf held on until the very end of his life. But we have seen that not all aspects of a theory of intentional reference turn on the acceptance or rejection of immanentism. One of the issues to be addressed in such a theory concerns the indeterminacy of feelings, and indeed of acts of any kind. As we have seen, by maintaining that certain feelings could be indeterminate in their reference, Stumpf attempted to avoid conceiving of them as being non-intentional in character. Although Husserl was prepared to regard certain experiences, including certain "feelings", as non-intentional, he nonetheless accepted Stumpf's view that some of the feelings which might be construed as non-intentional are in fact indeterminate in their reference and not simply devoid of reference.

We have also seen that Husserl took the term "state of affairs" from Stumpf. While Brentano had spoken of contents of judgment in this connection, the term which Stumpf introduced, in spite of his own immanentism, could easily be used in an anti-immanentist theory of intentional reference without any suggestion of a contradiction.

Another way in which Stumpf influenced Husserl is to be found in the theory of parts and wholes, most notably in the conception of some parts as independent and others as dependent. The concept of fusion is also one that Husserl takes from Stumpf, but we must of course be careful to note that Husserl refashions this concept in important ways too. In *Philosophie der Arithmetik* he applies it only to collections which are moreover construed as irreducible to the mere simultaneous or successive presence of contents in the same consciousness, whereas Stumpf regards contents as fused together simply by virtue of being present in the same consciousness. In the *Logische Untersuchungen* Husserl moreover applies the concept of fusion beyond the purely sensory sphere, contrary to Stumpf's original suggestion.

We have finally discussed Stumpf's critique of *Ideen* I. The outstanding feature of this critique is Stumpf's rejection of the notion of a pure phenomenology. Husserl's failure to give examples of purely phenomenological cognition and also his tendency to say only what this discipline is *not*, not to mention his undisciplined usage of metaphors (e.g., in the theory of attention), all give credence to the conviction that he had made little progress since the *Logische Untersuchungen*, that the work of 1913 in many respects even represents a degenerate phase in Husserl's philosophical development.

CHAPTER FOUR

HUSSERL AND KERRY

Very little is known about Benno Kerry (born as Benno Kohn).[1] On 20 May 1889 he died of an ear infection at the young age of 30. Before this early death, however, he managed to launch the publication of a series of eight articles, "Über Anschauung und ihre psychische Verarbeitung".[2] Though he finished his studies in Strassbourg in 1885, with a habilitation thesis entitled *Grundzüge einer Theorie der mathematischen und nicht-mathematischen Grenzbegriffe*, he often visited relatives in Vienna, where he also attended lectures, including at least one by Brentano (Philosophy of Aristotle, WS 1877/78), with whom he also corresponded on a regular basis. In 1888 he decided to publish a book which was to encompass both the results of his habilitation thesis and further developments in his investigations. Most of the resulting work was published posthumously as the first volume of *System einer Theorie der Grenzbegriffe. Ein Beitrag zur Erkenntnistheorie* (1890), though material for a second volume was left unpublished.

There is no indication that Husserl's sojourns in Vienna (1881-1883, 1884-1886) included any personal encounter with Kerry. Nor did the two apparently correspond with each other. Nonetheless, Husserl had offprints of the first five articles from the series "Über Anschauung und ihre psychische Verarbeitung". He also had an offprint of Kerry's review of Georg Cantor's *Grundlagen einer allgemeinen Mannigfaltigkeitslehre*.[3] This offprint bears a dedication from Kerry to Brentano, whereas the offprints of the five articles from "Über Anschauung und ihre psychische Verarbeitung" were dedicated to Stumpf. Apparently Brentano and Stumpf, who were naturally well aware of Husserl's background in mathematics and his projected work in the philosophy of mathematics, passed on these offprints to Husserl, to whom they could be of some use. Moreover, a copy of the posthumously published volume of

---

[1] See Volker Peckhaus, "Benno Kerry: Beiträge zu seiner Biographie", *History and Philosophy of Logic* 15 (1994): 1-8.

[2] These were published in the following volumes of *Vierteljahrsschrift für wissenschaftliche Philosophie*: 9 (1885): 433-493; 10 (1886): 419-467; 11 (1887): 53-116, 249-307; 13 (1889): 71-124, 392-419: 14 (1890): 317-353; 15 (1891): 127-167. Each article will henceforth be cited by year and relevant page number.

[3] Kerry's review, "Über G. Cantor's Mannigfaltigkeitsuntersuchungen", *Vierteljahrsschrift für wissenschaftliche Philosophie* 9 (1885): 191-232, was published two years after Cantor's controversial work (Leipzig: B.G. Teubner, 1883). While Kerry tried to derive infinitesimals from Cantor's transfinite numbers, this attempt was not regarded by Cantor as a successful one. See Joseph Warren Dauben, *Georg Cantor* (Princeton, New Jersey: Princeton University, 1979), pp. 129 f.

System einer Theorie der Grenzbegriffe was also in Husserl's possession, though there is no indication of how he acquired it. All of this material bears markings and annotations.

Though Kerry is not mentioned in Husserl's habilitation thesis of 1887, he is mentioned in *Philosophie der Arithmetik* I of 1891 (Hua XII, 123-124, 165). He is also mentioned in some of Husserl's 1893 texts (Hua XXI, 286, 403-404) in preparation for a book on space which was never completed. In this chapter I shall not draw upon writings of Husserl later than the ones just mentioned. There is good reason for this restriction. Not only do these early texts share Kerry's concern with the philosophy of mathematics, but they are moreover closely related to Kerry's writings insofar as their standpoint is an explicitly psychological and empirical one.

The issues under consideration in the Husserl-Kerry relation are, to be sure, rather peripheral as compared with the ones discussed regarding Husserl's relations with other Brentanists, making the present chapter somewhat of an excursus. It will however prove worthwhile to take the Husserl-Kerry relation into account here, for in Husserl's early work, devoted to the development of a Brentanian philosophy of mathematics, Kerry is the only other Brentanist whose alternative views on the same subject receives attention.[1]

1. REMARKS ON KERRY AND THE PSYCHOLOGICAL METHOD

In Vienna Kerry conversed on a regular basis with Alois Höfler, who was a pupil of both Brentano and Meinong. While Kerry began in philosophy with an interest in Schelling and also exhibited neo-Kantian influences, Höfler significantly tells us further:

---

[1]Another Brentanist who also developed views on the same matters is Christian von Ehrenfels, who wrote "Zur Philosophie der Arithmetik", *Philosophie für wissenschaftliche Philosophie* 15 (1891): 285-347. Husserl received a copy of this article from the author in 20 August 1891, a few months after the publication of *Philosophie der Arithmetik*. Though his copy bears some markings and annotations, these do not provide enough material for a discussion of his relation to von Ehrenfels regarding philosophy of mathematics or of arithmetic in particular. In Husserl's continued attempts to work out a philosophy of mathematics there is moreover no consideration of von Ehrenfels' views on these matters. It is however worth mentioning that von Ehrenfels regards the extent to which mathematics involves inauthentic presentations as one of the crucial questions for the philosopher. While his views on the more objective side of mathematics has received some attention in Peter Simons, "Mathematik als Wissenschaft der Gestalten", in Reinhard Fabian, *Christian von Ehrenfels. Leben und Werk*, pp. 136-149, there is no consideration here of psychological matters, which are regarded as being of only historical interest (*ibid.*, p. 136). In this chapter I try to argue, at the risk of looking outdated, in favor of a psychological orientation in the philosophy of mathematics.

I could cite no moment of greater importance from Kerry's educational development than the fact that he began to become increasingly convinced and convincing in his application of that psychological method which had become a scientific habit for me, too, in accordance with the example of Brentano and Meinong.[1]

While Kerry's work thus bears this psychological mark of the school of Brentano, it should also be noted that he was aware of anti-psychologistic alternatives. As already noted, he was quite familiar with the work of Bolzano. He also knew the work of Gottlob Frege, in which the anti-psychologistic tendency is clearly pronounced. Neither Bolzano nor Frege, however, dissuaded Kerry from utilizing the psychological method.

Far from being influenced by Frege in this regard, Kerry was rather one of the early critics of the Fregean attempt to "logicize" arithmetic.[2] One of Kerry's main criticisms is that Frege never clarifies what it means to characterize both statements and concepts as "logical". To be sure, Frege offers a definition of "analytic statements".[3] However, Kerry is not only dissatisfied with this definition in application to statements, but he also points out that it leaves unclear in what sense *concepts* are said to be "logical".[4] Though Frege wrote an article in reply to some of Kerry's criticisms,[5] other criticisms,

---

[1] Höfler, Review of *System einer Theorie der Grenzbegriffe*, p. 231: "Ich wüsste kein wichtigeres Moment aus dem Bildungsgange Kerrys anzuführen, als dass er immer überzeugter und überzeugender jene psychologische Methode in seinen Arbeiten zu betätigen anfing, welche auch mir insbesondere nach dem Beispiele Brentanos und Meinongs zu wissenschaftlicher Gewohnheit geworden war."

This interesting remark raises the question whether Meinong had any influence on Kerry. The many references to Meinong in Kerry's writings clearly indicate that this is indeed the case, although some of these are polemical. See "Über Anschauung und ihre psychische Verarbeitung" (1885): 439n, 441n, 461n, 472n; (1886): 443-444n; (1887): 90n, p. 254n; (1889):116n; (1891): 140n. Since it is known that Kerry attended Brentano's lecture on the philosophy of Aristotle in the winter semester of 1877/78, he could have quite easily have come into contact with Meinong who also was attending one of Brentano's lectures in the same semester, though not the lecture on Aristotle's philosophy. See the list of lectures attended by Meinong at the beginning of Chapter Six. Finally, it should be mentioned that Meinong and Kerry did write to each other, as is indicated in Reinhard Fabian and Rudolf Haller (eds.), *Alexius Meinong. Ergänzungsband der Gesamtausgabe* (Graz: Akademische Druck- und Verlagsanstalt, 1978), pp. 440 & 452.

Höfler's description of his meetings with Kerry is moreover confirmed in the first article "Über Anschauung und ihre psychische Verarbeitung" (1885): 437, where it is acknowledged that the very concept of psychical labor was taken from Höfler. The habilitation thesis of Höfler is moreover entitled "Psychische Arbeit", *Zeitschrift für Psychologie* 8 (1894). Though Husserl had a copy of this article, his copy bears no markings or annotations.

[2] This critique is to be found in "Über Anschauung und ihre psychische Verarbeitung" (1887): 249-307. The Frege-Kerry relation certainly deserves a fuller discussion than the few remarks which I make here. See Eva Picardi, "Kerry und Frege über Begriff und Gegenstand", *History and Philosophy of Logic* 15 (1994): 9-32, where the focus is however on those criticisms from Kerry to which Frege responded.

[3] *Die Grundlagen der Arithmetik. Eine logisch mathematische Untersuchung über den Begriff der Zahl* (Breslau: Wilhelm Koebner, 1884), §3.

[4] "Über Anschauung und ihre psychische Verarbeitung" (1887): 251n ff. Doubts about Frege's concept of analyticity have recently been expressed in Michael Dummett, *Frege: Philosophy of Mathematics* (London: Duckworth, 1991), pp. 23 ff.

[5] "Über Begriff und Gegenstand", *Vierteljahrsschrift für wissenschaftliche Philosophie* 16 (1892): 192-205.

including the one just touched upon, are left unanswered.

It is advisable here to say a word about Frege's critique of the psychological method, for it is often thought that this was definitive. His statement that psychology cannot contribute anything to the foundation of arithmetic has in fact been recently declared as an "incontestable truth".[1] The sense in which "foundation" is spoken of here is of course the sense in which definitions and axioms make up the foundation of the relevant discipline. In this sense the foundation is to consist of formulae from which theorems can be derived. It may be granted without hesitation that psychology cannot add one single formula to such a foundation. Only mathematics itself can make a contribution here. Philosophy of mathematics, by contrast, may be construed as a whole different enterprise, either not concerned with foundations at all or concerned with them in a different sense.[2] If we choose to say that it is concerned with them in a different sense, then it is plausible to maintain that it is occupied with questions about if and how mathematical cognition takes place.

Mathematical cognition is indeed a source of puzzlement. Even if we leave aside the properly epistemological difficulties here, it is by no means easy to state how cardinal numbers - not to mention negative, imaginary, and transfinite numbers - may be objects of thought. One can of course ignore such difficulties as of no interest to mathematics, just as one can ignore a thousand other philosophical difficulties as irrelevant to this or that endeavor. The motive for solving philosophical problems, after all, is often (if not always) to be found only in the perplexity which they produce in us. If solutions are obtained, it is therefore hardly to be expected that any change should occur besides the disappearance of perplexity. Since there is no apparent reason to expect something more from philosophy of mathematics, the inability of psychological theories to add to the stock of mathematical axioms and definitions must not constitute a motive for excluding such theories from the area in question.

In light of these remarks I suggest that the psychologistic tendency of Kerry's work in the philosophy of mathematics, as well as Husserl's early work in this area, must not be dismissed out of hand.

---

[1] *Die Grundlagen der Arithemtik*, p. vi. See Michael Dummett, *Frege: Philosophy of Mathematics*, pp. 18-19.

[2] As Wittgenstein says of philosophy in relation to mathematics, it "leaves mathematics, too, as it is, and it can promote no mathematical discovery" (*Philosophische Untersuchung*, § 124).

2. RELEVANT DOCTRINES IN KERRY'S WORK

Central in Kerry's work is a distinction between two types of modes in which the human mind manifests itself (*Äusserungsweisen des menschlichen Geistes*). "One of them consists in either the mere continuation of a psychical state or its change into another without our doing anything, the other in 'our' active intervention in some way into that psychical occurrence, insofar as we try to stay aloft in its flow or to guide it according to our ends".[1] The former mode of manifestation is called "intuition" (*Anschauung*),[2] while the latter is called "psychical labor" (*psychische Arbeit*) or "psychical processing" (*psychische Verarbeitung*).

Examples of intuition are found not only in sensation, but also in imagination. If, for instance, we hear a clock strike, we may continue to have an auditory impression of the same sort even after the clock has ceased to strike.[3] In this regard Kerry cites Hume's comparison between imagining and "a galley put in motion by the oars".[4] "From considering all these cases", Kerry adds:

one may already be sufficiently prepared for the quite general case, especially decisive also for our ensuing investigations, namely the case where, if something presented can at all be arranged in steps, ordered, and put into a series, we do not rest with a few members of the series; rather, we are inclined to continue the established series in one of its possible directions, according to the previously accepted laws of series, towards something presented of the same genus.[5]

---

[1]*System einer Theorie der Grenzbegriffe*, p. 1: "Die eine besteht darin, dass irgend ein psychischer Zustand entweder schlankweg sich fortsetzt oder doch ohne unser Zutun in einen anderen übergeht; die andere darin, dass 'wir' irgendwie tätig eingreifen in jenes Geschehen, indem wir in dem Strome desselben obenauf zu bleiben oder ihn gar unseren Zwecken entsprechend zu leiten trachten." Various words from this passage are underlined in Husserl's copy of the work in question.

[2]In "Über Anschauung und ihre psychische Verarbeitung" (1885): 433-435 Kerry opposes his characterization of intuition to the ones defended by Kant and Bolzano. There is no explicit discussion of the concept of intuition in the work of Brentano or the Brentanists. Though Husserl has nothing to say about Kerry's distinction between intuition and psychical labor, it is so central in Kerry's work that they could not be left undiscussed here.

[3]*Ibid.*, p. 436.

[4]*System einer Theorie der Grenzbegriffe*, p. 3. Cf. *ibid.*, pp. 18-21, where Hume is regarded favorably, though not uncritically, in comparison with Descartes, Locke, Leibniz, Kant, Hegel, Fichte, Herbart, Beneke, and Sigwart. The passage from Hume's *Treatise of Human Nature* to which Kerry refers can be found in the Selby-Bigge edition (Oxford: Clarendon, 1888), p. 198.

[5]*Ibid.*, p. 4: "Und durch die Erwägung aller dieser Fälle dürfte man bereits vorbereitet genug sein auf den ganz allgemeinen und insbesonders auch für unsere nachfolgende Untersuchung massgebenden Fall, wonach, wenn überhaupt ein Vorgestelltes irgend einer Gattung nach gewissen Hinsichten abgestuft, angeordnet und in eine Reihe gebracht werden kann, wir nicht bei einigen wenigen Reihengliedern beruhigt stehen bleiben, sondern die gestiftete Reihe nach der einen oder anderen der in ihr möglichen Richtungen um ein Vorgestelltes derselben Gattung und nach den einmal angenommenen Reihengesetzen weiterzuführen geneigt sind." Beginning with the words "wenn überhaupt", this passage is underlined in Husserl's copy of the work cited. "NB" (for *nota bene*) is moreover written in the margin next to this

This expansion of series, which is classified among intuitions and not among instances of psychical labor, is called "idealizing".[1] In this regard it is to be observed that Kerry speaks of intuition in a sense somewhat broader than usual.

Two of the examples of psychical labor which Kerry gives are important here. One of them is attention, also called "abstraction", which is crucial for the formation of certain concepts. The other is the activity of relating one content to another, whether the relation in question is similarity, incompatibility, or some other one. The view that attention allows us to have certain concepts was defended by Stumpf and Meinong. Kerry's suggestion that certain other concepts are obtained via relations was taken from Meinong.[2] In this case, he maintains, one of the foundations of a relation is presented intuitively and is moreover related, either as similar, as different, as incompatible, etc., to something which lies beyond our intuitive grasp.[3] Concepts which are obtained via relations are called "synthetic",[4] while those which we have thanks to the focus of attention on certain features and the disregard of certain others are called "abstractive".

As far as our concepts of numbers are concerned, Kerry acknowledges certain judgments in which these concepts are applied with little psychical labor. We may, for instance, simply apprehend the difference in amount between a group of four objects of a certain kind and another group of five objects of the same kind. In such cases we rely on naive counting. Such counting is no doubt of fundamental importance, but the *technique* of counting objects (*Zähltechnik*), which goes beyond naive counting, already involves considerably more psychical labor. The following passage is a description of the counting technique; it is quoted at length because it elicits from Husserl a comment which we shall later on consider in detail.

One only needs to consider the basics of our counting technique: [1] the methodical subsuming of every object to be counted under the concept which is given by the task of counting and then directs the counting (unity-positing); [2] the abstracting from all those properties of the present objects which are unessential to the unity-positings which are to be performed, whereby a lot of minor details, adhering now to this unity-positing, now to that one, are cast off like ballast; [3] the attachment of every performed unity-positing to a special sign which is familiar to us, an artifice whereby something large, which could otherwise be

---

passage. What Kerry describes here is the "continuation drive" (*Fortsetzungstrieb*) which Husserl mentions in passing in Hua XII, 271. In *System einer Theorie der Grenzbegriffe* (p. 16) Kerry explicitly contrasts this drive (*Forsetzens- oder Progressivtrieb*) with drives which involve psychical labor, so-called "thetic" and "synthetic" drives.

[1] This word (*Idealisieren*) is underlined in Husserl's copy of the work cited (*ibid.*).

[2] See "Über Anschauung und ihre psychische Verarbeitung" (1885): 461n.

[3] "Über Anschauung und ihre psychische Verarbeitung" (1885): 445 ff.

[4] See *System einer Theorie der Grenzbegriffe*, p. 14: "... in contrast to ... abstractive concepts, they might be called synthetic ones [... man könnte dieselben im Gegensatze zu den ... abstraktiven Begriffen: synthetische Begriffe nennen]". In Husserl's copy of this work the word "synthetische" is underlined.

removed only with difficulty or not at all, is broken down into parts which are mastered with great confidence [...].[1]

Kerry adds "that by means of this [counting technique] we can, first of all, solve innumerably more number problems than naive counting can, however much this is exercised, and secondly, that we more reliably and more precisely solve problems which are still solvable for naive counting".[2] The distinction between naive counting and the counting technique is accordingly a very important one for Kerry.

If it is granted that both the counting technique and naive counting involve psychical labor, the question arises as to what kind of psychical labor this is. As we have already seen, Kerry distinguishes between two kinds in connection with the formation of concepts. To be sure, he regards abstracting as one type of psychical labor which occurs in the process of counting. The fact that he does this, however, does not mean that the concepts of cardinal numbers are abstractive. Even synthetic concepts, on his view, require abstraction;[3] abstractive concepts are simply those which require no other kind of psychical labor besides this. As the above passage indicates, counting also requires at least two other processes, namely unity-positing and the application of signs. However, given Kerry's characterization of synthetic concepts in terms of relations, we should expect an analysis of the concept of a cardinal number, either in general or of a particular cardinal number, as something which is presented by means

---

[1]*Ibid.*, p. 15: "Man braucht nur die Grundzüge unserer Zähltechnik zu bedenken - : [1] das planmässige Subsummieren jedes zu zählenden Gegenstandes unter den durch die Zählaufgabe gegebenen und dann das Zählen lenkenden Begriff (Einheitsetzungen); [2] das Abstrahieren von allen denjenigen Eigenschaften der vorgelegten Gegenstände, wleche für die zu vollziehenden Einheitsetzungen unwesentlich sind, wodurch eine Menge Nebenumstände, die bald dieser, bald jener anhaften, wie Ballast abgeworfen werden; [3] die Zuordnung jeder vollzogenen Einheitsetzung an ein besonderes und uns vertrautes Zahlzeichen, ein Kunstgriff, vermöge dessen ein Grosses, das sonst nur schwer oder gar nicht fortzubringen wäre, in kleine Teile zerlegt wird, die man mit grosser Sicherheit bewältigt ..." In Husserl's copy of the work in question various words in this passage are underlined. The comment which he makes in the margin next to this passage will be cited and discussed below.

[2]*Ibid.*, pp. 15 f.: "[...] dass wir vermöge derselben *erstens* unabsehbar mehr Zählaufgaben lösen können, als das naive Zählen, so geübt dieses auch sei, und dass wir *zweitens* die dem naiven Zählen immerhin noch lösbaren Aufgaben zuverlässiger und präziser lösen". This passage is partly marked in the margin and underlined by Husserl. The comment which he makes in the margin next to it will be quoted and discussed below.

[3]"Über Anschauung und ihre psychische Verarbeitung" (1885): 460 n. In this regard Kerry's theory of concepts is comparable to the one which Meinong developed in the late nineteenth century. See R.D. Rollinger, *Meinong and Husserl on Abstraction and Universals*, pp. 59 & 83.

of relating it to something intuited.[1] Unfortunately, it is difficult to find any such clear-cut analysis in Kerry's writings.

In *Philosophie der Arithmetik* Husserl attacks Kerry's attempt to formulate the cardinality (*das Anzahlenmässige*) which two sets may have in common. According to Kerry, this is to be found in a one-to-one correspondence between the objects of one set and those of the other, in spite of any other changes (in size, shape, etc.) which these objects may undergo.[2] As it turns out, however, he does not wish simply to equate cardinality in this sense with cardinal number (*Anzahl*). The latter he identifies with the cardinality of a special set, namely of the unity-positings which belong to the psychical labor of counting. If, for instance, I count 4 nuts, the cardinal number 4 is not to be identified with the cardinality of this set of nuts, but rather with the cardinality of the unity-positings which take place in counting the four nuts. Thus, even though Kerry does not simply identify cardinal number as such and cardinality as such with each other, he nonetheless defines the former as a special case of the latter.

If we look at Kerry's own criterion for a definition, there is one requirement which the above-stated definition must meet. This becomes clear in his criticism of Cantor's definition of cardinal number:

From a logical standpoint a definition, like the one that Cantor gives of cardinal number, could also be called *unsatisfactory* if it were not *incorrect*. For it is the delimitation of the extension of the concept, whereas a definition should be, at least immediately, only an analysis of the content of the concept. What is meant by 'cardinal number', e.g. four, on Cantor's view is 'the' general concept under which all sets of four elements, and only these, fall. This tells me *at best* what sorts of objects of the concept fall under the concept to be defined and what sorts do not.[3]

It is easy to understand this charge by means of another example. Suppose that someone defined "equilateral triangle" as any triangle which has three equal *angles*. In this case one would precisely delineate the extension of the concept under

---

[1] See Kerry's claim, in "Über Anschauung und ihre psychische Verarbeitung" (1885): 448, "that we are constantly compelled to think of numbers as results of certain operations (unity-positings and relation-positings) which we can perform within narrow limits and, because of their homogeneity, accept as performable within broader limits [dass wir Zahlen *stets* nur zu denken haben als die Resultate gewisser Operationen (Einheits-und Relationssetzungen), die wir innerhalb enger Grenzen vollziehen können, und vermöge ihrer Gleichartigkeit als innerhalb weiterer Grenzen vollziehbar annehmen]".

[2] *Ibid.* (1887): 79 n.

[3] *Ibid.* (1889): 343 f.: "Vom logischen Standpunkte aus wäre eine Definition, wie sie C[antor] von der Anzahl gegeben hat, auch dann *unbefriedigend* zu nennen, wenn sie nicht *unrichtig* wäre: denn sie ist die Abgrenzung eines Begriffsumfangs, während doch eine Definition, wengistens unmittelbar, nur Zergliederung eines Begriffsinhalts sein soll. Unter der Anzahl, z.B. vier, wäre nach C[antor] 'der' allgemeine Begriff zu verstehen, worunter alle Mengen von vier Elementen, und nur diese, fallen. Hiermit erfahre ich *bestenfalls*, was für Begriffsgegenstände unter den zu definierenden Begriff fallen und was für welche nicht, es wird mir also der Umfang dieses Begriffes 'definiert'".

consideration, but this definition, which says nothing about lines, would fail to analyze the content of the concept.

The question arises whether Kerry's definition of "cardinal number" falls prey to the same criticism which he makes of Cantor's definition. What Cantor has in fact defined, says Kerry, is "cardinality", but Kerry adds that his own definition of cardinality is preferable.[1]

> For it actually aims at the content and not at the extension of what is meant by "cardinality of a plurality". If one had to explain what red is to someone, the best thing to do is not to say to him, "red is a general concept under which all objects fall whose surface reflects light of such and such a wave length", but rather to show him some red object and hereby to say, "what you see here is red". My manner of definition is analogous to this procedure, which is the only effective one [...].

Here one may of course object that such a definition, though preferable to stating the wave-length in question, is by no means a case of "analysis of the content", as Kerry had characterized a definition in the proper sense. If, however, this objection is left aside, the question still remains whether Kerry adequately defines cardinal number in terms of the cardinality of unity-positings, and thus ultimately in terms of a special case of one-to-one correspondence. We shall see that Husserl claims that this definition is inadequate.

3. HUSSERL'S REACTION TO KERRY

Let us begin with Husserl's attack on Kerry's notion of cardinality. While he realizes that cardinality merely as such is not equated by Kerry with cardinal number as such, he nonetheless maintains that the former notion is "worthless" (Hua XII, 125). According to Husserl, such attempts to illuminate the concept of number tell us only what the *extension* of this concept is (Hua XII, 124). "We wish to find out something about the content of the concept of cardinal number, and we are given only the name of the extension. Kerry's definition is nothing but the paraphrase of the sentence 'Cardinal number of the set P is that which it has in common with all other sets of the same amount'". As Husserl notes in his own copy of *Philosophie der Arithmetik*, he uses Kerry's own criterion for definition (as applied in the criticism of Cantor's definition

---

[1] *Ibid.* (1890): 351: "Sie zielt nämlich wirklich auf den Inhalt und nicht auf den Umfang dessen, was man unter dem Anzahlenmässigen einer Vielheit versteht. Wenn man jemandem zu erklären hätte, was rot sei, so wird man am besten tun, ihm nicht etwa zu sagen: rot sei der Allgemeinbegriff, unter welchen alle Gegenstände fallen, deren Oberfläche Licht von der und der Wellenlänge zurückwirft, sondern ihm irgend einen roten Gegenstand zu zeigen und hiebei zu sagen: das, was du da siehst, ist rot. Diesem einzig wirksamen Vorgehen ist meine Definitionsweise analog [...]."

of cardinal number) against Kerry himself (Hua XII, 514). "Kerry, as if he had a premonition of my objection", Husserl notes on the same page, "defends himself by saying that his way of defining cardinal number is a definition via the extension. He conceives it as similar to pointing to the content, as we define the concept red". As we have seen, however, Kerry makes this analogy in connection with his definition of "cardinality", not his definition of "cardinal number".

Husserl maintains, moreover, that his formulation of Kerry's definition of cardinal number ("cardinal number of the set P is that which it has in common with all other sets of the same amount") is even preferable to the one which Kerry gives, "since Kerry's has the strong suggestion of the erroneous notion that the cardinal number is a partial content, an intrinsic feature" (Hua XII, 124). Here Husserl has in mind his own characterization of amounts in terms of collective combination (*kollektive Verbindung*) (Hua XII, 64 ff.). In this case it is not at all an intrinsic feature of these objects which makes them belong to one and the same collection. It is rather an act of collecting which is responsible for them belonging together in one and the same collection. The further determination of collections by discerning the amount of their members is accordingly nothing that can be derived from these members as such, no more than the collective combination is something that obtains independently of the collecting activity. This view is certainly to be preferred over the conception of a cardinal number as an intrinsic feature. Otherwise we would indeed expect that counting could be performed by examining some pregiven object, whether this be the collection itself or its elements. The very phenomenon of counting, however, clearly involves a preliminary determination of what is to be counted, whereby the elements are indeed collected together. Both the ontological economy and the phenomenological simplicity of this view speak in its favor.

The main objection which Husserl raises against Kerry's characterization of cardinality is more or less the same as an objection which he raises against Frege who also characterizes amounts in terms of one-to-one correspondence (Hua XII, 111 ff.).[1] Such a characterization, according to Husserl, only states the extension of the concept of an amount, whereas he wishes to discern the content of this concept. It is interesting to note here that in the *Logische Untersuchungen* Husserl retracts this objection against Frege (Hua XII, 172n). While no mention is made here of Kerry, the implication is of course that the above-stated objection against his concept of cardinality should likewise be retracted. But Kerry had already been dead for over a decade. Since his work drew little attention from anyone else, it was not necessary for Husserl to bother himself with it.

---

[1] The criticisms of the views of Frege and Kerry belong to the same chapter, entitled "The Definition of Number via Equivalence".

Now we turn to some other remarks which Husserl makes about Kerry's work. These are to be found in annotations which were written in Husserl's copy of *System einer Theorie der Grenzbegriffe*. As we may recall, Kerry identified three types of psychical labor in the counting technique: 1) the subsumption of objects under some concept, 2) abstracting, and 3) the application of signs. In the margin next to the passage in which this technique is described by Husserl says the following regarding the first type of psychical labor: "As a rule, the totality of equal objects is already prominent before we count: e.g. seven balls, etc. Thus, there is no need for the subsumption, but only the unity-positing in the broader sense of the word".[1] As regards the second type of psychical labor, Husserl says: "Abstracting is not a new psychical activity".[2] That is to say, wherever the objects to be counted are prominent, as much abstraction is already present as is needed for counting. It thus turns out that counting, on Husserl's view, is a much simpler process than the one described by Kerry.

Husserl continues to remark in the same context: "Kerry also does not distinguish symbolic and authentic counting".[3] This is indeed an important distinction which was already acknowledged in Husserl's habilitation thesis and treated more thoroughly in *Philosophie der Arithmetik*. Authentic counting occurs whenever the amount is very small. I look at three nuts and know at once that the amount in question is three. If the amount is very large, however, I must of course use signs, as I do when I say out loud "one, two, three, four ....". It is of course obvious, as far as Husserl is concerned, that we need arithmetic precisely because authentic counting is so limited. However, it is also his view that we could not engage in inauthentic counting and the operations which are performed on symbolically presented amounts unless there were an intuitive basis. Kerry's failure to make the distinction between authentic and inauthentic counting is therefore a grave one from Husserl's point of view.

Finally, we should consider how appropriate Kerry's contrast between intuition and psychical labor is from Husserl's standpoint. During the time when Husserl took an interest in Kerry's work he raised no objection against this contrast. This is no surprise, since it fits in well with Husserl's descriptive psychology, according to which the materials given in intuition can be abstracted from in order to form general concepts, collected in order to form the concept of numbers (thereby making inauthentic counting possible), and compared in order to discern relations such as similiarity and difference. We have however already seen in the first chapter that in the *Logische Untersuchung-*

---

[1] "Der Inbegriff gleicher Objekte ist in der Regel schon herausgehoben, bevor wir zählen: z.B. Siebenzahl Kugeln etc. Es bedarf also der Subsumtion unter keinen Gattungsbegriff, sondern nur der Einheitssetzung im weiteren Sinne des Wortes".

[2] "Das Abstrahieren ist keine neue Geistestätigkeit".

[3] "Kerry unterscheidet auch nicht symbolisches und eigentliches Zählen".

enen the notion of categorial intuition is formulated for the first time. At this stage Husserl was willing to say that the objects of intuition include not only colors, sounds, psychical phenomena, and other primitive objects, but also objects of higher order such as states of affairs and concepts. The intuition of the latter objects is moreover regarded as an activity which is built upon lower-order acts of intuition. The result of these considerations is that it is no longer possible to characterize intuition by contrasting it with psychical labor. There was however no longer any necessity to engage in polemics against Kerry.

4. CONCLUDING REMARKS

We have here examined two attempts to solve some of the problems of the philosophy of arithmetic from the Brentanian point of view. Some remarks were made in defense of not only this standpoint, but also generally of a psychological standpoint (understood in a broad sense). These remarks as such were certainly not meant to endorse the particular views of either Kerry or Husserl on the issues under consideration, although there is indeed much to be said in favor of Husserl's early theory of collections as entirely dependent on the collective activity. Husserl's critique of Kerry's attempt to define "cardinal number" in terms of a one-to-one correspondence, however, has to some extent been found wanting. As regards the other issue under consideration in Husserl's criticisms of Kerry's approach to philosophy of arithmetic, namely the analysis of counting, we have seen that Husserl insists on a distinction between authentic and inauthentic counting.

It is this latter disagreement which is most relevant to the present study. The distinction between authentic and inauthentic presentations is, after all, one of the most important ones in the school of Brentano. We shall see that it is also encountered in the work of Meinong and Marty. In the present chapter we have seen that one of the tasks for a Brentanian philosophy of mathematics is to decide whether we can have authentic presentations at all in our mathematical cognition. There is certainly room for disagreement here. Kerry's insistence that mathematics is from the outset a matter of psychical labor, and indeed a type of labor which involves more than just abstracting and collecting, is *prima facie* neither more nor less an orthodox Brentanian position than Husserl's allowance for a few cases of so-called authentic counting. Perhaps this matter could be decided by further clarifying the distinction between the two types of presentation in question. Nevertheless, the agreement that there is such a distinction to be made and that it is moreover crucial to understanding mathematical cognition brings Husserl and Kerry very close together as fellow Brentanists, as opposed to the total exclusion of psychological considerations from the philosophy of mathematics espoused by Frege and his followers. It has hopefully been seen that the approach of Husserl and Kerry in this area, as much as they differ in details, is not to be regarded as philosophically insignificant.

CHAPTER FIVE

HUSSERL AND TWARDOWSKI

Kasimir Twardowski studied philosophy under Brentano and Zimmermann in Vienna from 1885 to 1889. In 1892 his dissertation on Descartes, *Idee und Perzeption*, appeared and was followed in 1894 by his habilitation thesis, *Zur Lehre vom Inhalt und Gegenstand der Vorstellungen*. He stayed in Vienna as a *Privatdozent* until 1895, when he was called to Lvov, where he was to exercise considerable influence in Polish philosophy. His influence in Poland was primarily due to his teaching activity, not to the few publications which he produced during the years in Lvov.[1] As a teacher he regarded his task as the advancement and application of the rigorous method which he had learned from Brentano, though he did not insist on promoting this or that particular doctrine. The result was in large measure the rise of the Polish school of logic, not to mention the impact which Twardowski had on phenomenologists such as Roman Ingarden and Leopold Blaustein. Here we are however concerned with the ideas which he had presented in his habilitation thesis, for Husserl's critical confrontation with these ideas was a crucial turning point in his philosophical development.

During the year 1885, when Husserl and Twardowski were both studying under Brentano, they must have had some contact with each other. But the complete lack of information about any such contact suggests that the relation need not have been a close one. Moreover, Husserl, for obvious reasons, showed little interest in Twardowski's dissertation, for his copy of it bears no markings or annotations.

While it is uncertain how Husserl obtained a copy of Twardowski's habilitation thesis, he had one already in 1894. For this is the year in which he wrote the text "Intentionale Gegenstände", both his reply to *Zur Inhalt und Gegenstand der Vorstellungen* and his own attempt to come to terms with the Bolzanian notion of objectless presentations. Two years later Husserl wrote a review of Twardowski's habilitation thesis (Hua XXII, 349-356), but this review was never published during Husserl's lifetime.[2] This review and "Intentionale Gegenstände", together with a few remarks in the *Logische Untersuchungen*, will be the main sources here for discerning the relation between Husserl and Twardowski.

---

[1]For a fuller discussion of Twardowski's influence in Poland, see Barry Smith, *Austrian Philosophy*, pp. 155-160; see also Jan Wolenski, *Logic and Philosophy in the Lvov-Warsaw School* (Dordrecht: Reidel, 1989).

[2]For the reason why this review was not published and for a few other biographical details left unmentioned here, see Schuhmann, "Husserl and Twardowski", pp. 41 ff.

Husserl's reading of Twardowski's habilitation thesis is indeed of considerable importance in his philosophical development, not because he was thereby prompted to adopt positions which Twardowski advocated, but rather because his critical reaction to Twardowski culminated in the Husserlian theory of intentionality which endured into the *Logische Untersuchungen* and was opposed to Brentano's conception of intentional reference as the inexistence of the object.

1. TWARDOWSKI ON CONTENT AND OBJECT

As the title of *Zur Lehre vom Inhalt und Gegenstand der Vorstellungen* indicates, the central theme of this work is the difference between the content and the object of presentations. By no means does Twardowski claim originality for discerning this difference. At the outset he cites Höfler's logic, where the following distinction is made:

> 1. What we above called "content of the presentation or of the judgment" is entirely within the subject, just like the act of presentation and judgment itself. 2. The word "object" is used in two senses: on the one hand, for that which obtains in itself, "thing in itself", the actual, the real [...], towards which our presenting and judging is, as it were, directed; on the other hand, for the psychical, more or less matching "image", existing "in" us, of that real object, this quasi-image (more correctly: sign) being identical with what was called "content" under 1. For the sake of distinguishing it from the object which is accepted as independent of thinking one calls the content of a presenting and judging (likewise: of feeling and willing) also the "immanent or intentional object" of these psychical phenomena [...].[1]

With some hesitation the content is referred to as an image by Höfler, though he says that it is better to call it a "sign". Such characterizations of the content of an act, especially of a presentation, are never explicitly challenged by Twardowski. Nonetheless, he says a good deal of other things which are not taken from Höfler.

Insofar as presentations have contents which are distinguishable from their object, says Twardowski, they are analogous to judgments, for in acts of the latter kind the distinction between content and object also comes into play.[2] Twardowski accepts

---

[1] *Logik*, p. 7: "Was wir oben 'Inhalt der Vorstellung und des Urteils' nannten, liegt ebenso ganz innerhalb des Subjektes, wie der Vorstellungs-und Urteils-Akt selbst. 2. Die Wörter 'Gegenstand' und 'Objekt' werden in zweierlei Sinn gebraucht: einerseits für dasjenige an sich Bestehende, 'Ding an sich', Wirkliche, Reale ..., worauf sich unser Vorstellen und Urteilen gleichsam richtet, anderseits für das 'in' uns bestehende psychische, mehr oder minder annähernde 'Bild' von jenem Realen, welches quasi-Bild (richtiger: Zeichen) identisch ist mit dem unter 1. genannten 'Inhalt'. Zum Unterschiede von dem als unabhängig vom Denken angenommenen Gegenstand oder Objekt nennt man den Inhalt eines Vorstellens und Urteilens (desgleichen: Fühlens und Wollens) auch das 'immanente oder intentionale Objekt' dieser psychischen Erscheinungen [...]." This passage is cited in *Zur Lehre vom Inhalt und Gegenstand der Vorstellungen*, p. 4.

[2] *Ibid.*, pp. 8 f.

Brentano's theory of judgment and accordingly maintains that all judgments are existential. If I judge that the sun, for instance, exists, the object of my judgment is the sun, whereas the content is the *existence* of the sun. Someone else may judge that the sun does not exist. In this case the judgment has the same object as mine, namely the sun, but the content is now the non-existence of the sun. The content of a judgment is thus always existence or non-existence. However much we find plausible in other aspects of Twardowski's views on content and object, it is of course difficult to accept that existence or non-existence is something which is in the subject just as much as the act of judging is, or that existence or non-existence is analogous to images or signs.

As we may recall, Stumpf had made a distinction between the matter and the content of a judgment and characterized the latter as a state of affairs, e.g. the existence or nonexistence of God. This distinction is moreover one that Stumpf attributes to Brentano. Thus, when Twardowski speaks of the content of a judgment as existence or nonexistence, it is the contrast between content and *matter* which he has in mind. The analogy which he makes between this content and that of a presentation, understood as an image or a sign, exhibits a confusion on his part. For the matter of a judgment is not to be held as any less immanent than the content, whereas - in speaking of the content of a presentation - it is the actual object which is contrasted with the immanent object of the presentation. Wherever this contrast comes into play the content of the presentation is indeed more immanent than the actual object, which is, after all, not immanent at all.

Another connection in which the content-object distinction comes into consideration for Twardowski is in the three functions of a name, which he enumerates as follows: "First, the manifestation of an act of presentation which takes place in the person talking. Secondly the summoning of a psychical content, the meaning of the name, in the person spoken to. Thirdly, the naming of an object, which is presented by the presentation meant by the name".[1] It is to be noted here that the meaning of a name is identified by Twardowski with the content of a presentation, and that this content is moreover called "psychical" (for it is, after all, something which exists in the subject just as much as the act itself does). The resulting view that meanings are psychical entities is of course totally unacceptable to Husserl, as we shall soon see.

When we speak of the presented object, says Twardowski, we may mean either the content or the object in the proper sense. The case is analogous to our reference to a painted landscape. Here we may mean either the painted picture of the landscape or this or that landscape, located in this or that country, etc. The content is analogous to the picture, whereas the object is analogous to the landscape. This analogy is chosen by Twardowski not only because our habit of "designating presenting as a sort of mental

---

[1] *Ibid.*, p. 12. These distinctions are taken from Marty, "Über subjectlose Sätze" (1884).

copying"[1] makes it convenient, but also because it makes clear that "presented" is used in a modifying sense in reference to the content and in a determining sense in reference to the object. As the painted landscape, insofar as this is the *picture* of a landscape, is not a landscape at all, it is not the object of the presentation in the proper sense which we mean when we call the content "presented object". The term "presented" here modifies the meaning of the term "object", just as "painted" modifies the meaning of "landscape". Otherwise these terms are determining. When we point to a landscape and say that this is a painted landscape, we mean that it has stood in a certain relation to a painter and to the resulting painting. Likewise, when an object is presented, there obtains a certain relation between the presenter and the object, indicated by saying "presented object".

One of the crucial questions for Twardowski is whether the content-object distinction applies to all presentations. As we have seen, from the standpoint of Bolzano there are both objectual and objectless presentations. Twardowski is well aware of this standpoint, but he argues against it. Taking into account some of Bolzano's examples of objectless presentations, namely "nothing", "round square", "green virtue", and "golden mountain", he classifies them in three ways: 1) "nothing" in a class of its own, 2) contradictory presentations, and 3) non-contradictory fictions.[2]

Against the claim that "nothing" is an objectless presentation Twardowski argues that the term "nothing" is syncategorematic, comparable to words such as "and" and "or", and as such does not manifest a presentation when it used.[3] First, he equates "nothing" with "not something". Then he compares this case with others which occur when "not" or "non" is put in front of names. We may, for instance, speak of non-Greeks or non-smokers. In such cases it is indeed perfectly plausible to say that the resulting terms manifest presentations of the speaker and also cause them in the listener. While Twardowski accordingly concedes that they are categorematic, he points out that they exhibit a common feature which is not found in the case of "not something". When we distinguish non-Greeks from Greeks, we tacitly assume that this is a division between two classes of human beings. Likewise, smokers and non-smokers make up two different classes of passengers. Whenever "non" is joined to a name to make a new name, there is always a higher genus, e.g. "human being" or "passenger", which is taken for granted. But this is not the case if we join "non" to "something", for there can be no higher genus than "something". Thus, given the equivalence between "nothing" and "not something", the former is no more a name than the latter. Moreover, since the acts which are correlated with names are presentations, it follows that there is no presentation corresponding to the term "nothing".

---

[1] *Ibid.*, p. 14.

[2] *Ibid.*, 21.

[3] *Ibid.*, pp. 22 ff.

As far as the other two classes are concerned, Twardowski is prepared to say that the objects of the presentations in question do not *exist* and are nonetheless *objects*.[1] If, for instance, I speak of a round square, I am presenting an object, albeit a non-existent, even impossible one. If I hear the name "golden mountain", then I start presenting a golden mountain, which is accordingly an object, albeit a non-existent (but possible) one.

There are two arguments which Twardowski uses in order to support the assertion that presentations can have objects which do not exist.[2] One of the arguments is made from the fact that some judgments are denials that certain objects exist. If one asks what object we thereby present and reject, the answer is that the object is the one whose existence we deny. If, for instance, I deny that a golden mountain exists, I must present a golden mountain and reject it. What I reject cannot be the content of my presentation, for this is obviously something which exists. The second argument which Twardowski uses in order to support his claim (that certain presentations refer to nonexistent objects) is specifically concerned with contradictory objects, such as round squares. In such cases incompatible properties are ascribed to something. What this something is cannot be the content of the presentation, for this, once again, exists and cannot as such have incompatible properties. It is therefore the object, not the content, which has the properties in question.

Someone might raise the objection here that the object of a presentation nonetheless always exists, but only *as a presented object*. In reply to this objection Twardowski says that it involves the oversight "that, if something 'exists' as something presented in the sense of the object of presentation, this existence is not existence in the proper sense".[3] Here he makes use of Brentano's distinction between actual and intentional existence, emphasizing that "intentional" in this case is a *modifying* term. Intentional existence is accordingly not existence, just as counterfeit money is not money and just as a dead person is not a person.

Twardowski's rejection of the Bolzanian doctrine of objectless presentations obviously involves extensive usage of the content-object distinction. In reply to any attempt to regard the content-object distinction as a merely logical rather than a real one, Twardowski insists not only 1) that this distinction is required for cases where the object does not exist, but also 2) that there are cases where the object has properties which the content could not have. Whenever a physical object, for instance, is the object of a presentation, this object must have the property of extension, which could never belong to the content or to any anything else psychical. 3) Moreover, he argues for the content-object distinction from cases where two presentations differ in content

---

[1] *Ibid.*, pp. 23-29.

[2] *Ibid.*, pp. 24 f.

[3] *Ibid.*, p. 24.

and yet refer to one and the same object, such as "the city which has the same location as the Roman Juvavum" and "the birth place of Mozart". While both of these have Salzburg as their object, the two are clearly different in content (meaning), again indicating a real distinction between object and content.

A fourth argument which Twardowski finds in Kerry proceeds from the consideration of general presentations.[1] While each of these has only one content, there is in each case many objects. However, Twardowski rejects this argument, since he maintains that a general presentation has only one object, a general object.[2] The presentation which we have when we use the general name "triangle", for instance, refers to the triangle in general, which is not scalene, not isosceles, not equilateral. It is nonetheless a *part* of any given individual triangle.

While Twardowski tends to regard the contents of presentations as images or signs, the question remains whether these contents fully correspond with the objects of the relevant presentations. He emphatically rejects any attempt to settle this matter by construing the content as "a psychical copy of the object" and thereby regarding the correspondence between content and object as "a kind of photographic similarity".[3] In this regard Twardowski, like Höfler, seems to prefer to view contents as signs rather than images. The question nonetheless still remains whether the *parts* of a content somehow correspond with the *parts* of the object. Here we are reminded of Bolzano's view that such presentations as "spiritual being" and "country without mountains" have parts which are not in any way reflected in the object. In the first of these cases the object is simple. In the second case there is nothing in the object which corresponds to that part of the presentation associated with the word "mountains". Let us now consider what Twardowski says about these counter-examples.

Regarding the first one he says "that there are no simple objects in the sense in which no relations to other objects could be distinguished in them".[4] Of course, one may object to this statement by saying that it should not matter whether there *are actually* such objects. As long as we present them, i.e., as long as they exist *intentionally*, they are cases where the contents of the presentations have parts which do not correspond to parts of the objects. However, Twardowski also says that we present God

---

[1] "Über Anschauung und ihre psychische Verarbeitung" (1886): 432.

[2] *Zur Lehre vom Inhalt und Gegenstand der Vorstellungen*, p. 101-111. Husserl's rejection of this theory of general presentations has already been treated in R.D. Rollinger, *Meinong and Husserl on Abstraction and Universals*, pp. 119-122. It is correctly pointed out by Marco Santambrogio, "Meinongian Theories of Generality", *Nous* 24 (1990): 550-567, that this theory is an early version of a theory which Meinong later came to hold. By rejecting this theory Husserl by implication rejects Meinong's later theory of general presentations.

[3] *Ibid.*, p. 67.

[4] *Ibid.*, p. 94.

or any other allegedly simple object "by presenting single relations of this object to other objects".[1] Such objects therefore have at least relational ("formal") parts.

Twardowski's discussion of examples such as "country without mountains" relies heavily on his claim that the content of a presentation is the *meaning* of the relevant name.[2] Moreover, he distinguishes between the meaning and the *etymon* of a name. The latter, also called "inner linguistic form" (*innere Sprachform*), provides us with an auxiliary presentation. One may here think of metaphors which give us images, but these images are not to be confused with the meaning. When we present a country without mountains, this presentation may indeed by accompanied by the image of mountains, but this image is not to be confused with the meaning of the name and therefore not to be confused with the content of the presentation. Thus, Twardowski concludes, the Bolzanian claim that "country without mountains" has parts which do not correspond to the object is to be rejected.

2. HUSSERL ON TWARDOWSKI'S THEORY OF MEANING

Though Husserl was very impressed with Twardowski's habilitation thesis (Hua XXII, 356; Hua XIX/1, 206) and continued to hold it in high regard in *Ideen* I (Hua III/1, 298), he nonetheless found difficulties with Twardowski's view on meaning, but also with Twardowski's attempt to argue against the Bolzanian thesis that there are objectless presentations. Let us first consider Husserl's objections against Twardowski's theory of meaning.

We have seen that Twardowski identifies the meaning of a name with the content of the presentation which is manifested in the utterance of the name. The meaning is accordingly something psychical and individual, just as the presentation itself is. Against this view Husserl argues (Hua XXII, 349 f.): 1) The meaning of a name can remain the same while the content, the so-called "representation" in Husserl's terminology, varies from one person to the other. If, for instance, a tree is spoken of, the content may be the image of an evergreen for one person, a linden for someone else, the written sign "tree" for a third person, whereas the meaning remains the same. 2) The contents of individually distinct presentations can at best be only more or less similar to each other, whereas the meaning of a name is in one case identical and not merely similar with that in another. 3) In whatever relation the content stands to the object - e.g. as something alien to the object, as part or aspect of the object, as similar to a part or aspect of the object - it is in all cases something *noticeable*, i.e., perceivable in the strict and narrow sense. "The meaning, however, is never something noticeable.

---

[1] *Ibid.*
[2] *Ibid.*, pp. 97 ff.

The content as such is an individual, psychical datum, something existing here and now. The meaning, however, is nothing individual, nothing real, never at all a psychical datum. For it is identically the same 'in' an unlimited manifold of individually and really separated acts" (Hua XXII, 350). While the content is really in the act, the meaning is only functionally so.

In the *Logische Untersuchungen* Husserl accuses Twardowski of "overlooking the ideal concept of meaning" (Hua XIX/1, 528). We have already encountered this concept above in Husserl's approval of the Bolzanian notion of propositions in themselves. These ideal and universal entities are simply meanings of assertions (*Aussagen*), but in the *Logische Untersuchungen* Husserl also insists that *all* meanings, including the meanings of common and proper names, are ideal and universal (Hua XIX/1, 102-112). Husserl's view in 1896, however, is ontologically less clear-cut, for the talk of a *functional* inherence of meanings in consciousness may give the impression that they are still in some manner conceived as dependent on consciousness. His emphasis on the *hic et nunc* character of the content, on the other hand, suggests by contrast the timelessness of meanings. It is in any case clear that he views meanings as having a radically different relation to acts of consciousness from the one which obtains between these acts and their contents. In this regard he finds Twardowski's identification of the content of a presentation with the meaning of the corresponding name totally unacceptable.

The meaning of a name, Husserl moreover maintains in opposition to Twardowski, can have parts which do not correspond to parts of the objects. In this regard Husserl adheres in principle to Bolzano's examples.

Instead of harkening back to antiquated metaphysical theories by appealing to examples such as "spiritual being", however, Husserl asks us to consider "simple object". "It makes no difference at all," he adds, "whether there is such an object or not" (Hua XIX/1, 304). It is of course easy to see why this makes no difference. If there is no simple object and the presentation is accordingly objectless, then it is of course impossible for the parts of the meaning to correspond with parts of the object. Twardowski's strategy for dealing with the Bolzanian notion of objectless presentations will moreover do him no good here, for "simple object" is clearly a name and not merely a syncategorematic term. Concerning the distinction between intentional and actual existence, we shall see below how Husserl dismisses this.

"Bolzano's excellent example 'country without mountains'", Husserl further claims, "has, to be sure, been disputed by Twardowski; but this is explained by the fact that he regards the direct-intuitive presentation of the meant object as the meaning, while the fundamental and only logically relevant concept of meaning escapes him. He therefore chances upon conceiving constituent parts of the meaning ('without mountains') as 'auxiliary presentations after the manner of etyma'" (Hua XIX, 305). That is to say, once the meaning is completely dissociated from the accompanying image, there is no longer any need to appeal to the notion of etyma in the example under consideration.

3. HUSSERL ON INTENTIONAL OBJECTS

Now we turn to a consideration of Husserl's critique of Twardowski's view that even a presentation which has no object in actuality corresponding to itself nonetheless has an object, namely an object which exists intentionally. Here we are also concerned with Husserl's alternative view. The text which concerns us in this connection is the one entitled "Intentionale Gegenstände" which was written in 1894, but left unpublished until 1979 (in Hua XXII, 303-348).[1] Before entering into a discussion of how Husserl argues in this text, a few words about the text itself are in order.

In the summer of 1894 Husserl wrote a lengthy essay (at least 75 pages in Ms.), entitled "Vorstellung und Gegenstand". This essay, unlike so many of Husserl's manuscripts which are accessible only to those who can read his Gabelsberger stenography, was moreover written out in longhand and was thus intended for publication. The first part of the essay (Ms. pages 1-34) is no longer extant. As the beginning of the second part indicates, in the first one Husserl had shown to his satisfaction "that a meaning-content belongs to every presentation".[2] The notion of meaning-contents is still used in the second part under the heading "objective presentation", though it is left unclear how objective presentations are to be construed ontologically. The second part, entitled "Intentionale Gegenstände", in turn consists of two parts. The first of these (Ms. pages 35-67) concerned with whether every presentation has a corresponding object. The second (Ms. pages 68-75) is a discussion of the relation between the meaning-content and the object of presentations. This discussion was in large measure taken up in the fourth "Logical Investigation" and has to this extent already been considered in the foregoing section of this chapter. Though Husserl apparently threw away the first part of "Vorstellung und Gegenstand", he clearly regarded the second part important enough to offer it to Meinong in 1902 and to Daubert in 1904. Moreover, as late as 1906 he mentions the possibility of publishing the text, though not in its existing form, but rather in connection with a critical confrontation with Meinong "in the form of several articles" (Hua XXIV, 447). Hence, Husserl's early theory of intentional reference, from 1894 to the early years of the twentieth century, must be interpreted with this text as well as the *Logische Untersuchungen* in mind.

---

[1]As already indicated in the introduction, an improved edition of this text has since appeared. Whenever I refer to "Intentionale Gegenstände", page references are made to this later edition. In the translation of this text in Appendix One the pages of the edition in question are indicated in brackets.

[2]"Intentionale Gegenstände", p. 142.

While it is primarily Twardowski's views which are criticized in "Intentionale Gegenstände", Husserl begins by attacking a popular solution to the problem posed by Brentano's thesis that intentional reference is a feature of all presentations and Bolzano's thesis that some presentations are objectless. According to this solution, the problem is to be dealt with by construing presentations as directed first and foremost at images. Every presentation thus has an object insofar as it has an image which of course exists in consciousness, although there need not be an object outside of consciousness, corresponding to the image. Though this is not Twardowski's solution to the problem under consideration, we must keep in mind that there is indeed a tendency on Twardowski's part to construe presenting as a kind of picturing. To this extent Husserl's criticisms of the image theory of consciousness is relevant here.

The claim that we present objects via images, according to Husserl, is at first plausible as long as we do not look beyond certain very simple cases. There should, for instance, be no problem in thinking of a tree via an image. It may here be pointed out that one of the reasons why Bolzano allows for objectless presentations lies in the fact that there cannot be objects which correspond to absurd concepts, such as "round square". If, however, one resorts to images in such cases, it becomes apparent how little good this will do. As it is impossible to draw a round square on paper or on a blackboard, it is likewise impossible to produce a mental image of one. However, even if one adheres to other cases of presentation where there is no absurdity, e.g., in the presentation of art, science, and the like, one does not find the "veritable whirlwinds of phantasms" which would be the appropriate images here.[1] Moreover, Husserl argues that the presence of images in consciousness would be of no use to solving the problem under consideration, for it fails to take into consideration identity, as in the case of presenting a centaur and also denying that the centaur exists.[2] The centaur which is presented and the one whose existence is denied are, after all, the same centaur. If, however, it is the image which makes up the object of the presentation, this should not be identified with the object whose existence is denied. Finally, it is pointed out by Husserl that, wherever an image is used in a presentation, it is never the object which is, properly speaking, presented.[3] Just as a picture is never to be identified with the pictured object (if indeed there is one), the mental image is likewise not to be identified with the object which is presented *by means of* the image.

While these considerations on Husserl's part are quite sound, one must however be careful to take them as effective against Twardowski's rejection of the Bolzanian thesis that there are objectless presentations. Yet, after rejecting the image theory as a solution to this problem, Husserl's attack is directed against the notion of an immanent

---

[1] *Ibid.*, p. 143.

[2] *Ibid.*, p. 144.

[3] *Ibid.*, pp. 144 f.

object, a notion which he clearly tries to pin on Twardowski. We must however be careful not to misinterpret Twardowski's position, for we have seen that he maintains that the object which does not exist is not to be identified with the content, not with that which is, prop erly speaking, immanent in consciousness. The content exists in the strict and proper sense, whereas the intentional existence of the object in the cases of the kind under consideration exists in a modified sense; that is to say, it does not exist at all.

In this regard I would insist that Husserl does not get to the heart of Twardowski's position when he suggests that it succumbs to a "false duplication which also became fatal to the picture theory".[1] This criticism would indeed be telling against a strong immanentism, such as the one we have seen in Stumpf, but Twardowski easily accommodates identities such as that between the centaur which is presented and the one which does not exist. In this case the object presented exists intentionally, but this means only that the centaur is presented. The talk of intentional existence for Twardowski is indeed little more than an after-thought, which could be removed without altering his essential point. It is, as it were, a Brentanian halo which surrounds a standpoint which actually has a greater affinity with the one later adopted by Meinong. In light of these remarks we must ask whether Husserl offers criticisms which actually get to the heart of this standpoint.

There are indeed such criticisms in "Intentionale Gegenstände", namely in connection with Husserl's penetrating considerations of improprieties of speech. As it turns out, Husserl comes to the conclusion that the claim that every presentation has an object involves precisely such an impropriety. But before he reaches this point he considers various improprieties which are, according to him, analogous to the division between "true" and "intentional" objects. These are to be found in the division between determinate and indeterminate objects, between possible and impossible objects, and finally between existent and non-existent objects. In all of these cases, Husserl insists, it is not properly a division between objects which is at stake. We may of course say "a lion" and thus allow for an indeterminacy which does not obtain when we speak of this or that lion. Nonetheless, this indeterminacy is not properly to be ascribed to lions of any kind. There are not two classes of lions, indeterminate and determinate ones, as there might be African and Asiatic ones. The same point can be vividly made regarding the other two divisions, namely between possible and impossible objects and between existent and non-existent objects. In all of these cases there are indeed genuine divisions under consideration, but these divisions pertain to our presentations and not to the objects. Thus, when we speak of *a* lion, this case differs, due to a feature of our presentation, from the ones where we speak of this or that lion.

---

[1] *Ibid.*, p. 146.

What is especially important here is the division between existent and non-existent objects, for this is precisely the one at stake in Twardowski's dismissal of the Bolzanian thesis of objectless presentations. In the cases where a genuine presentation is under consideration (unlike the case of "nothing") and there is no *existent* object which corresponds to the presentation, Twardowski tells us, we need not fear in our adherence to the Brentanian thesis of intentional reference, for these are simply cases where the object of the presentation is a *non-existent* one. Husserl in effect objects to this position: there is no genuine division between existent and non-existent objects, no more than there is a division between determinate and indeterminate objects or between possible and impossible objects; the division in question can only be construed as one which, properly speaking, pertains to the presentations, and this division is precisely the one between objectual and objectless presentations. When we speak of a non-existent object, this is only an improper way of saying that a certain presentation is objectless.

While this criticism is indeed a very plausible one, there is still one matter which is to be cleared up in understanding Husserl's reaction for Twardowski. For he does not simply embrace the Bolzanian thesis of objectless presentations and leave it at that. Rather, he also says that the Brentanian thesis of intentional reference, namely that *all* presentations refer to objects, is true in an improper sense. Part of his response to Twardowski consists of an explanation of this impropriety. His explanation is moreover closely connected with a consideration of many of the judgments we make *as if* they were true, although we would say that these judgments are false if we were forced to speak properly. Most of us would, for instance, have no trouble in saying that Zeus is the highest Olympian god. If a pupil in elementary school is taking a true-false test on Greek mythology and is confronted with this statement, he is surely expected to mark it as "true". Yet, we are not ancient Greeks. None of us believe that there is a Zeus or that there are other gods, such as Apollo and Hera, who are inferior to Zeus or related to him in any other way. What goes on in these cases, says Husserl, explains the sense in which it is true to say that all presentations refer to objects.

When we say that Zeus is the highest Olympian god we are speaking "under hypothesis" or "under assumption". The assumption in this case and in other similar ones is often left unstated, often for reasons of "thought-economy" (as Husserl says in a Machian spirit).[1] If we add "according to Greek mythology", when we say that Zeus is the highest Olympian god we thereby make the assumption explicit. But we often do not need to do this and therefore speak as if there really were different worlds - the world of myth, the world of poetry, the world of geometry. It is often simply too time-consuming to spell out all of the assumptions which would be demanded by proper

---

[1] *Ibid.*, p. 165.

speech. By doing so, we would be side-tracked from other tasks which are of vital interest to us at the moment.[1] As certain judgments which are properly false are said to be true, we may likewise say that all presentations refer to objects. Our presentation of Zeus, for instance, refers to an object in the same sense that the judgment that Zeus is the highest Olympian god is true. That is to say, if the presentation were a foundation for a true judgment, the presentation would refer to an object. Moreover, since we so often make judgments about Zeus under assumption, this makes it all the more convenient for us to say that the presentation refers to an object. Strictly and properly speaking, however, the presentation is objectless.

There is certainly much to be said in favor of Husserl's standpoint in "Intentionale Gegenstände". Here three points can be made in favor of this standpoint.

Firstly, his opposition to the image theory and any other theory which duplicates the object of presentation, including the strong immanentism that at least some Brentanists accepted, is both empirically sound and also suits our ordinary ways of making identity statements (e.g., the centaur which I present = the centaur which does not exist). In this regard it can even be said that Husserl's standpoint in "Intentionale Gegenstände" is preferable to the theory of intentionality which was later put forward in *Ideen* I, where a noema is interposed between act and object, resulting in a duplication and thereby reminding us of the old immanentism which he tried to pin on Twardowski.[2]

Secondly, his position is a very appealing alternative to what is nowadays called "Meinongianism", which is so strongly prefigured in Twardowski's habilitation thesis. The division between existent and non-existent lions is indeed as far-fetched and even absurd as the division between determinate and indeterminate lions or that between possible and impossible lions. Just as a lion is in each and every case determinate and possible, we may not speak of lions which do not exist or, if we do so, we must make it clear that these are not lions (just as Mickey Mouse is not a mouse). If the division between existent and non-existent lions is unacceptable as a genuine division, this is apparently because this division does not properly apply to objects at all. By accepting the Bolzanian notion of objectless presentations and working out the notion of judging under assumption, Husserl takes us in a more intuitively compelling direction than the proto-Meinongianism which Twardowski offers.

We have already quoted a passage in which he puts the world of geometry on a par with the worlds of myth and poetry. There are also references to mathematics in general as being subject to the same sort of impropriety of speech as in these other

---

[1] *Ibid.*, p. 159.
[2] Karl Schuhmann, "Intentionalität und intentionaler Gegenstand beim frühen Husserl", pp. 73 f. Husserl himself, after all, says in the *Ideen* I (Hua III/1, 207) that the "scholastic distinction" between the immanent and the actual object is a first attempt to grasp the distinction between the presented object *simpliciter* and the object as presented (the noema).

cases, strongly suggesting that our presentations of mathematical objects are no less objectless. We have of course already become familiar with Husserl the Platonist, but in 1894 he had at least suggested a way to escape Platonism. All of our talk about mathematical objects, even logical objects, might turn out to be improper. However, we are also faced with the fact that mathematics, unlike myth and poetry, is a discipline, one might even say a "science", which sets definite limits to our assumptions. Due to a failure to consider this point, and indeed to attempt to spell out the assumptions which are involved in mathematical thinking, Husserl's standpoint in "Intentionale Gegenstände" remains underdeveloped. As far as a suggested opposition to Platonism is concerned, the continued developments in his philosophy obviously did not go in the direction of such an opposition. Whoever wishes to pursue this direction will have to think through these matters himself.

In spite of all the advantages of Husserl's views in "Intentionale Gegenstände", it is questionable whether they allow him to accommodate the claim that all presentations have an object. For even if we accept his strategy for dealing with cases where the presentation has an object only in the improper sense, it must be stressed that this strategy does not apply to quite a few other cases, namely where there is plainly a judgment and this judgment is false. While it is only under assumption that we regard Zeus as the chief Olympian god, there were of course ancient Greeks who actually believed that Zeus existed and was more powerful than the other Olympian gods. It is certainly not merely an impropriety of speech to say that their belief had no object. As long as it granted that the belief had no object in the proper sense, there is apparently no reason for also saying that this belief has an object in the improper sense. In this case one would best say that the belief in question had no object and leave it at that. The same goes for all the false believes which people hold nowadays. Husserl's attempt to preserve the thesis of intentional reference in the case of apparently objectless presentations will not suffice in such cases.

4. CONCLUDING REMARKS

In our examination of the relation between Husserl and Twardowski we have seen a crucial aspect of Husserl's position in the school of Brentano. While Husserl's rejection of the conception of the meaning as a content is of course important in assessing this position, the importance of the theory of intentionality which is put forward in "Intentionale Gegenstände" is far greater. In the conflict between him and Twardowski on intentional reference, we see two paths which can be taken if strong immanentism is rejected. One of these paths is Meinongianis m (or weak immanentism) and the other is Husserl's Bolzano-inspired alternative. In the following chapter we shall see that this conflict continues in the relation between Husserl and Meinong, though this is not the only disagreement which arose between them.

CHAPTER SIX

HUSSERL AND MEINONG

Alexius Meinong began studying German philology and history at the University of Vienna in 1870.[1] In 1874 (the year in which Brentano began as a professor in Vienna) Meinong completed a dissertation on Arnold von Brescia and did his minor examination in philosophy with Brentano. In Brentano Meinong found someone from whom he could immensely benefit in the study of philosophy. Shortly after their encounter Meinong independently decided to pursue philosophy as a career.

An impression of what Meinong had learned in Vienna from 1875 to 1878 can be gathered from the following list of lectures by Brentano which he followed at that time:[2]

SS 1875:
Old and new logic

WS 1875/76:
Selected philosophical questions
Practical philosophy

SS 1876:
Sophisms and their application to the realm of politics
The philosophy of Aristotle

WS 1876/77:
Philosophy of the history of philosophy
Psychology

---

[1]Most of the biographical information which is used here concerning Meinong comes from his *Selbstdarstellung*, in Raymund Schmidt (ed.), *Die deutsche Philosophie der Gegenwart in Selbstdarstellung* I (Leipzig: Felix, Meiner, 1921), pp. 91-148. It will be indicated wherever other biographical sources are used.

[2]See Reinhard Fabian and Rudolf Haller (eds.), *Alexius Meinong. Ergänzungsband zur Gesamtausgabe* (Graz: Akademische Druck- und Verlagsanstalt, 1978), p. 109, where Meinong's notes from the lectures in question are listed.

SS 1877:
Logic
Questions from psychology

WS 1877/78:
Metaphysics

SS 1878:
The philosophy of Aristotle

During this time Meinong was not as close to Brentano as other eminent pupils had been. Since Brentano was a professor, he could direct dissertations and play a role in accepting habilitation theses. He asked Meinong to write a habilitation thesis on Hume, which resulted in Meinong's first major publication *Hume Studies* I.

Meinong continued to lecture in Vienna as a *Privatdozent* until 1882, upon the publication of *Hume-Studien* II, when he was called to Graz where he became a professor. In Vienna some of Brentano's pupils, particularly Alois Höfler and Christian von Ehrenfels who both later came to Graz, attended Meinong's lectures and were influenced by him at least as much as they were by Brentano. In Graz he continued to exert an influence independently of Brentano. In 1886 Meinong published "Zur erkenntnistheoretischen Würdigung des Gedächtnisses" in which he attempted to characterize the evidence of memory as immediate evidence for surmise (*unmittelbare Vermutungsevidenz*) in contrast with both mediate evidence, as obtained through inference, and evidence for certainty, as obtained in inner perception and the grasp of certain *a priori* truths.[1] This view of memory was totally unacceptable to Brentano, who was to attack it as "absurd", without mentioning Meinong by name, and further to express his regret "that lectures of mine from the time when I still took degrees of

---

[1] In a letter to Meinong (26 February 1886), already mentioned in the introduction to this study, von Ehrenfels says that he managed to convince Husserl "that he [Husserl] has not yet thought the matter [regarding the evidence of memories] through" (Quoted in Reinhard Fabian, "Leben und Wirken von Christian von Ehrenfels", p. 17). In his 1906/07 lectures on the introduction to logic and epistemology, however, Husserl says, "Although we well know, for instance, that *memory* can deceive and that it often enough does so, we trust in memory all the same. And with reason. An assertion in which I give expression to an event that I recall is, after all, not unjustified. And it is obviously justified immediately in memory, but not justified as a certainty. What it asserts is not given to me in the immediate evidence of the 'it is thus' as truth; the past episode is, to be sure, gone ... But the conviction that it has been has its reasonable 'weight', precisely 'reasons', and more particularly immediately evident ones" (Hua XXIV, 12 f.). This is clearly the view which Meinong had put forward in 1886 regarding the matter that Husserl, the beginner, had left undecided at the time. No reference is however made to Meinong in the text just quoted.

conviction for intensities of judgment seem to have been the cause of such errors".[1] As Husserl indicated in his explanation of why he and Brentano corresponded so little, Brentano was not pleased when his pupils adopted views which diverged radically from his own. Meinong was simply too independent to adhere so strictly to orthodoxy as was demanded, though he was often vexed by Brentano's attempts, such as the one exhibited in the passage just quoted, to construe Meinongian theories as mere consequences of recanted doctrines which had been learned from Brentano earlier.[2]

A few years later a decisive break occurred between Brentano and Meinong, when Höfler told Meinong that the *Logik* of 1890 (just written by Höfler himself with the assistance of Meinong) met with disapproval from the more orthodox Brentanist, Anton Marty, in a report to the Austrian ministry of education. This gave Meinong the impression "that Brentano and his loyal students had been conspiring against him, even in his own case for promotion".[3] Due to the sparse references to Meinong in Husserl's *Philosophie der Arithmetik*, Husserl, too, was suspected as part of this anti-Meinong conspiracy. Moreover, as Meinong developed his theory of objects, which allowed for objects to proliferate far beyond the realm of the real, his philosophy was regarded by Brentano on an equal footing with Husserl's.

In spite of the resulting antipathy between Brentano and Meinong, the latter wrote the following conciliatory passage at the very end of his life:

Subsequently I have often experienced how students who have just become independent try too anxiously to protect their independence against their teacher in particular, although this independence was the very thing towards which he was tirelessly working. Towards a dominant personality of someone like Brentano such anxieties may have been provoked with particular ease and suited for initiating misunderstandings

---

[1] *Vom Ursprung sittlicher Erkenntnis*, p. 84. Sigwart, whom is also under attack here, appropriately says of Brentano in a letter to Meinong (10 March 1890): "his arrogance boarders on megalomania [seine Anmassung grenzt an Grössenwahn]" (*Philosophenbriefe aus der wissenschaftlichen Korrespondenz Alexius Meinongs*, p. 87).

[2] Thus Meinong insists in his preface to *Über Annahmen* (Leipzig: Johan Ambrosius Barth, 1902) "that I have not learned *everything* from Brentano, but also something from myself or, properly speaking, from the facts in the course of scientific activity through sincere effort [dass ich nicht *Alles* von Brentano, sondern im Verlaufe meines wissenschaftliches Tuns durch redliches Bemühen auch Einiges von mir selbst oder eigentlich von den Tatsachen gelernt habe]". Only original editions of Meinong's writings will be referred to here. Wherever they have been reprinted in *Alexius Meinong. Gesamtausgabe*, edited by Rudolf Haller et al. (Graz: Akademische Druck- und Verlagsanstalt, 1968-78), the original German text will not be given in the footnotes. Since the first edition of *Über Annahmen* (1902) only partly appears in Volume IV of the collected works, quotations from it will be translated in the text and presented in the original German in the footnotes.

[3] David F. Lindenfeld, *The Transformation of Positivism: Alexius Meinong and European Thought, 1880-1920* (Berkeley/Los Angeles/London: University of California, 1980), p. 66.

whose consequences have accompanied me deep into my later activities. But that which life could no longer settle is settled by death, and as a safely kept possession there stands before the eye of my memory, as once before, the luminous figure of my honored teacher in spiritual beauty, made golden by the sunshine of his and my youth.[1]

When Husserl began attending Brentano's lectures in Vienna in 1884, Meinong had already been a professor in Graz for two years. Though it is unlikely that they ever met each other face to face, they began exchanging letters as early as 1891. Throughout the 1890's each sent his publications to the other and responded for the most part with enthusiasm regarding them.

After *Philosophie der Arithmetik* was published, Husserl sent a copy to Meinong. In a letter to Husserl (19 June 1891) Meinong notes that his work is all but disregarded in this book, which contains only one reference to Meinong, namely the distinction between direct and indirect presentations in *Hume-Studien* II. The relevant passage from *Hume-Studien* II (pp. 86-88) is merely cited in a footnote in *Philosophie der Arithmetik*, along with the suggestion that the distinction in question was derived from Brentano's distinction between authentic and inauthentic presentations. This suggestion particularly infuriated Meinong, as indicated in a draft of a letter which is much more indignant than the one actually sent to Husserl (19 June 1891),[2] for he took this as an indication of Husserl's complicity in the above-mentioned conspiracy to suppress Meinong's influence. Of course, since Husserl had dedicated *Philosophie der Arithmetik* to Brentano and at this time took criticisms from his mentor very seriously, Meinong's fear was not groundless. Nevertheless, he and Husserl continued to correspond for about a decade longer in a rather harmonious (though not particularly warm) way, though none of their publications during this period contain extensive consideration of the other's views. More about their relationship below, especially in the consideration of Husserl's reaction to *Über Annahmen*.

---

[1] Meinong, *Selbstdarstellung*, p. 94. For considerations of Meinong's relation to Brentano and also to Twardowski, see Dale Jacquette, "The Origins of Gegenstandstheorie: Immanent and Transcendent Objects in Brentano, Twardowski, and Meinong", *Brentano Studien* 3 (1990/91): 177-202. See also Dale Jacquette, "Alexius Meinong (1853-1920)", in Liliana Albertazzi et al. (eds.), *The School of Franz Brentano*, pp. 131-159. In the *Nachwort* to the *Ideen* I Husserl says that Meinong "remains tied to fundamental Brentanian views" (Hua V, 159) without specifying what views he has in mind.

[2] This letter has been published in *Briefwechsel* I, 129 f., whereas the more heated draft can be found only in *Philosophenbriefe*, pp. 94-96.

1. *HUME-STUDIEN* (1877/82)

In Husserl's library the earliest publication by Meinong to be found is *Hume-Studien* I (1877). His copy is an offprint bound together with *Hume-Studien* II (1882) in a single volume. While it is uncertain when Husserl received or purchased either of these writings, the second of these is referred to in his habilitation thesis (Hua XII, 328) of 1887 and in the *Philosophie der Arithmetik* (Hua XII, 193). On 14 February 1894 Husserl writes to Meinong: "I was just lingering in your spheres of thought (the *Hume-Studien* lie open before me) when the postman brought me your new article [*Beiträge zur Theorie der psychischen Analyse*] which aroused my most lively interest as I most hurriedly leafed through it" (*Briefwechsel* I, 133). Hence, even after the publication of *Philosophie der Arithmetik* Husserl was still reading at least one of the *Hume-Studien* or perhaps both of them.

In *Hume-Studien* I Meinong is concerned with a critique of Hume's theory of general ideas. This theory is characterized as nominalistic in the strict sense, i.e., in the sense that general names are assigned the function of making ideas general. Meinong rejects this theory in favor of an attention theory, which had been suggested by Berkeley and elaborated on by Mill and Stumpf. It is now well known that Husserl, too, accepted this theory in *Philosophie der Arithmetik* and came to reject it in the course of the 1890's, but especially in the *Logische Untersuchungen*.[1] Though the annotations in his copy of *Hume Studien* I add little to this already documented disagreement between the two Brentanists, the annotations in his copy of the more voluminous and philosophical more substantial *Hume Studien* II tell us about other matters on which the two did not see eye to eye.[2] These are the topics of indirect presentations, the origin of the concept of causation, and identity.

---

[1] Rollinger, *Meinong and Husserl on Abstraction and Universals*, pp. 184-132.

[2] Meinong's pupil, Konrad Zindler (later to become professor of mathematics at Innsbruck), adopted the views which were developed in *Hume-Studien* II and applied them to the philosophy of mathematics in *Beiträge zur Theorie der mathematischen Erkenntnis* (Vienna: Kaiserliche Akademie der Wissenschaften, 1889), a work which Meinong later significantly referred to as "the only monograph concerning *a priori* cognition that permits a look into the most immediate needs from which the conception of the theory of objects arose" ("Selbstdarstellung", p. 142). Though Husserl's copy of this work bears markings and annotations, it does not receive any attention in his writings. Unfortunately, the annotations are not extensive enough to warrent a discussion here on the relation between Husserl and Zindler.

1.1. Indirect Presentations

In *Hume Studien* II Meinong is primarily occupied with the theory of relations. In *Philosophie der Arithmetik* Husserl, too, shows some concern with this topic by distinguishing between primary and psychical relations (Hua XII, 68 ff.), and again between simple and complex relations (Hua XII, 70 f.). Though he makes no explicit reference to Meinong in this context, his proposal "that by 'foundation of relation' (in agreement with the currently generally customary linguistic usage) each of the related contents be meant" (Hua XII, 67) is apparently an implicit reference to Meinong, who maintains that one may speak of a *fundamentum relationis* only in reference to "the compared contents of presentation themselves".[1] Given Husserl's familiarity with this text while writing *Philosophie der Arithmetik*, it is understandable that Meinong remarks in a letter (19 June 1891) that Husserl "seems to have been cautious to betray none of this familiarity to the reader" (*Briefwechsel* I, 129). The question however arises whether this familiarity involves an actual influence. If we consider what Meinong says about the role of relations in indirect presentations and Husserl's comment about this, we find a disagreement rather than an influence, at least as far as this matter is concerned.

In a footnote of *Philosophie der Arithmetik* (Hua XII, 193 n) Husserl shows particular interest in this notion as this is put forward in Meinong's *Hume-Studien* II.[2] If we turn to the pages 86-88 of *Hume-Studien* II, to which Husserl refers in the footnote just mentioned, we find in his copy markings and annotations. Here Meinong considers the case where a human being is described by saying "he is as tall as I am, has chestnut brown hair, and so forth".[3] Whoever does not know the person being described, he says, "is able to constitute to some extent from the only foundation given to him and from the relation the other foundation".[4]

The notion of indirect presentation for Meinong is obviously linked to relations,

---

[1] *Hume-Studien* II, pp. 44 f. In Husserl's copy the last three words in the phrase "die verglichenen Vorstellungsinhalte selbst" are underlined.

[2] The claim which Husserl makes in this footnote, however, namely that the same distinction had always been made in Brentano's lectures, was rejected by Meinong in the letter to Husserl of 19 June 1891 (*Briefwechsel* I, 129 f.). In this letter Meinong claims not to have been aware of any such distinction from Brentano's lectures. We have already seen in Chapter One that in 1883, one year *after* Meinong left Vienna, Brentano's lecture on psychology (Q 9) contains no mention of a division between authentic and inauthentic presentations.

[3] *Hume-Studien* II, p. 86.

[4] *Ibid.*, p. 87.

e.g., similarity, and also to relative determinations, as when we say that one thing is similar to another.[1] The ability to function in the service of indirect presentations is indeed, on his view, the one thing which relative determinations have in common.[2] Next to the passage where he makes this claim Husserl writes: "Not mere relative data, also absolute features, if they serve as determinations, are relative".[3] This claim is strikingly close to the following remark from the posthumously published text, *Zur Logik der Zeichen (Semiotik)* (1890):[4] "[...] that also the absolute features, if considered precisely, represent relative determinations" (Hua XII, 342). Let us now consider what Husserl has in mind here.

The remark just quoted is made in the context of a division of signs into external and conceptual ones. An external sign is a sign in the narrower sense, as a name functions as a sign for a certain person, whereas a conceptual sign is a feature.[5] Even the features which are not relative in the ordinary sense ("intrinsic"), Husserl explains, are nonetheless relative as determinations of the thing in question. Red, for instance, is a feature of the red *thing*, and in this sense it is a relative determination. If, however, we speak of relative determinations in this sense, it must still be asked whether this has any bearing at all on Meinong's discussion of indirect presentations. Here we should note that Meinong says of relative determinations "that their function primarily consists in more or less precisely determining a previously unknown attribute".[6] The relation

---

[1] The notion of a relative determination in this sense is not to be confused with the one which will later be discussed in the chapter on Husserl and Marty.

[2] *Hume-Studien* II, p. 87.

[3] "Nicht blosse relative Daten, auch absolute Merkmale, wenn sie als Bestimmungen dienen, sind relativ".

[4] In the footnote in *Philosophie der Arithmetik* Husserl says: "More detailed investigations concerning symbolic presentations and the methods of cognitions based on these I plan to communicate in an appendix to the second volume of this work" (Hua XII, 193). Though the second volume never appeared, the 1890 text discussed here was apparently meant as the appendix to this volume.

[5] While it is puzzling to speak of a feature in English as a sign, the German word *Merkmal* is not so puzzling in this context. But it is easy to see in what sense a feature can be a sign, e.g., the redness of someone's face can be a sign of embarrassment. A sign in this sense, however, is a mark (*Anzeige*) as conceived in the *Logische Untersuchungen*, namely as indicating the existence of something else (Hua XIX/1, 31 f.). A name, on the other hand, is certainly not a sign of the named object if by "sign" we mean a mark. "Zeus" is a name, but it certainly does not indicate the existence of anything. In 1890 text Husserl had not yet come to distinguish between signs in two senses, namely between marks and expressions. Once this distinction is made, it is clear that the term "sign" is simply equivocal, and thus it is highly misleading to speak of external and conceptual signs as if two species of one genus were under consideration here.

[6] *Hume-Studien* II, p. 87.

which allows for this function is accordingly one which obtains *between attributes* or, as one could just well say, features, whereas *all* features are relative only in the sense that every feature is at least related to the *thing* which has the feature. Husserl's implicit criticism of Meinong on this point is accordingly not appropriate. Moreover, it is not entirely clear how the theory of indirect presentations is advanced by the above-cited remarks, for the only thing which could apparently be indirectly presented by means of the absolute data would be a substratum in the most metaphysically dubious sense. However, though this might suggest that it would be better to adhere to relations as the proper vehicles of indirect presentations, it will be seen in the following chapter that difficulties in this manner of regarding them do not escape Husserl's notice in his confrontation with Marty.

1.2. Causation

Meinong's views on causation in *Hume-Studien* II are also criticized by Husserl. Though Meinong feels no need to argue that causal relations cannot be outwardly perceived, he finds it necessary to criticize the view stated by Schopenhauer: "Motivation is causality seen from within".[1] As he understands this view, it is the act of willing (not outwardly perceivable behavior) which can be inwardly perceived as the effect of a motive. Against this claim Meinong argues:

The presentation which arises on one occasion as motive, can obtain on another occasion without being followed by an act of will; it is only a motive under the presupposition of a determinate psychical, perhaps even physical disposition. But inner perception yields no awareness of this disposition.[2]

A disposition, after all, is not something which can be perceived at all. And it must be part of the cause, because the presentation in question could occur without being followed by willing. I may present an ice-cream cone on one occasion and immediately thereafter want one. On another occasion there is not the slightest occurrence of willing followed by presenting an ice-cream cone. The only difference between these two cases, says Meinong, is to be found in a disposition which is in principle imperceivable.

In reply to this argument Husserl says the following: "But the motivating presenta-

---

[1] *Über die vierfache Wurzel des Satzes vom zureichenden Grunde*, Chapter VII. § 43. This statement is cited in *Hume-Studien* II, p. 119.

[2] *Ibid.*, p. 122.

tion and the presentation which is equal in content, excluding the motivating aspect, are still not the same. The character of motivatedness is still present, as the motivation is on the side of willing. And for this reason the argument comes to nothing".[1] Thus Husserl insists that when a presentation motivates it has a motivating character which can be inwardly perceived, just as the ensuing act of willing has the character of being motivated which can be inwardly perceived.

Meinong also thinks that what he says about the relation of the motivating presentation to the motivated act of willing is applicable to other cases where one might wish to insist on the inner perceivability of causation. Such a case is the one which obtains when a conclusion is inferred from premises. Causation is not perceived here, for one can judge in accordance with the premises without drawing the conclusion. Husserl writes in the margin:

To this one might however object: Only popularly and also logically speaking are premises and conclusion in both cases the same ones. In truth they obtain, whenever the evident conclusion is drawn, another character, and indeed psychologically. The concluding judgment which is endowed with this character is the effect of the premises viewed with the character of grounding.[2]

Husserl's reply here is, again, when the conclusion is drawn from the premises the judgments involved have a different character from the one which they otherwise have.

It is interesting to note here that both of the cases under consideration here regarding causation, namely the case of motivation and that of inference, are appealed to by Brentano in *Vom Ursprung sittlicher Erkenntnis* (p. 51) in order to prove that causation is inwardly perceivable. While *Hume-Studien* II was written earlier than the work just mentioned, it is unlikely that Meinong had not heard the arguments in question from Brentano's lectures. In this case he would be attacking his mentor without mentioning him. Nevertheless, he certainly attacks a position which Brentano later defends and which Husserl, too, defends. The point is particularly important here, for Brentano defends this position in a larger context, namely in his espousal of old-fashioned Lockean empiricism, according to which all concepts are derived from inner or outer perception. Husserl, too, embraced this empiricism in his earlier work, until he

---

[1] "Aber die motivierende Vorstellung und die inhaltlich bis auf das Motivierende gleiche Vorstellung sind doch nicht dasselbe. Der Charakter des Motivierens ist eben noch da, wie auf seite des Willens die Motiviertheit. Und darum bewirkt das Argument nichts."

[2] "Darauf könnte man aber einwenden: Nur populär und auch logisch geredet sind Prämisse und Conclusio in beiden Fällen dieselben. In Wahrheit erhalten sie, wenn der einsichtige Schluss gezogen wird, einen anderen Charakter, und zwar psychologisch. Das mit diesem Charakter begabte Schlussurteil ist Wirkung der mit dem Charakter der Begründung angeschauten Prämissen".

arrived at the notion of categorial perception. In his period of orthodox Brentanism, however, he correctly identified Meinong as a heretic who raised doubts about the inward perceivability of causation. It may moreover be doubted whether Husserl effectively dealt with this particular item of heresy. His claims about motivatedness and the peculiar character which the premises have when the conclusion is drawn are, after all, reminiscent of attempts to defend the *outward* perceivability of causation by saying that forces and tensions are actually seen.

1.3. Identity

In Meinong's early work on relations we find an attempt to come to terms with the notion of identity. Many of the assertions about identity, according to Meinong, can be construed as follows: "Identity is said of something insofar as it stands in relation at the same time to different things".[1] In this sense "one says of two houses that they have the same owner, of two rings that they belong to the same chain, of two properties that they are qualities of the same thing [...]".[2] Even if we accept this analysis in some cases, problems still remain.

One of the problems concerns how it is possible for two presentations to have the same object. Here we must keep in mind that under the presupposition of immanentism, which Meinong accepts at this stage, presentations and other acts of consciousness refer to contents. Under this presupposition it is easy to see how it becomes problematic for us to say that two different presentations have one and the same object, for what each presentation primarily refers to is its very own content, which could never be identical with the content of another presentation. If we now keep in mind that equality is not identity, as we may indeed say that the red-moment one thing is *equal to* and by no means *identical with* the red-moment of another, it is understandable why Meinong says "that two different presentations must, strictly speaking, also have two

---

[1] *Hume-Studien* II, p. 138. This sentence is underlined by Husserl. Next to it he writes: "X is red. The same X is round [X ist rot. Dasselbe X ist rund]". This is of course meant as an example of what Meinong means here.

It must be stressed here that by "identity" for Meinong is not synonymous with "quality". While two red-moments, for instance, may be equal, their equality does not make them identical. When he speaks of "agreement" (*Übereinstimmung*) in a later text (*Über die Erfahrungsgrundlagen unseres Wissens*, p. 21), this term is used to mean the same as "equality" and therefore not to be confused with "identity", though such a confusion occurs in Jaakko Hintikka, "Meinong in a Long Perspective", *Grazer Philosophische Studien* 50 (1995): 29-46.

[2] *Ibid.*

different contents which can be fully equal, but never one content, therefore also not identical".[1] While this remark is perhaps consoling, Meinong's explanation of it creates further difficulties: "If one therefore says that two people present the same thing, or also that a person presents the same thing at different times, this can mean only the presenting of contents which can be adequate only to one thing, regardless as to whether it exists or not".[2] By introducing the object here as something in addition to the contents of the presentation, Meinong apparently reduces the equality of the contents to the identity of the relevant object and thereby stumbles into an anti-immanentist position. While the desirability of such a position has already been endorsed in the previous chapter, we find Meinong also hinting at non-existent objects here, though not as outspokenly or consciously as he was to allow for them in later writings or even as Twardowski was to do so in 1894. In this regard we may understand Husserl's puzzlement when he writes alongside the passage just cited: "What does 'adequate' mean?" The term "adequate" is, to be sure, used by Husserl and many others, but Meinong gives it a new twist by saying that the content can be adequate to a non-existent object. We have of course seen that in 1894 Husserl rightly called into question the division of objects into existent and non-existent. If we may not speak of non-existent objects, then it is certainly impermissible to speak of a relation of adequacy between them and the contents of our presentations.

Here we may note that, if identity is construed as a standing in relation of two things (or properties) to one and the same thing *at the same time*, an account must still be given regarding identity across time. Plants and animals, for instance, are known to grow and develop. Thus, individual one undergoes considerable change through time and still remains the same. Regarding the identity which obtains in cases such as these Meinong says:

> that, in order to trace back two temporally separate appearances to the same thing, hardly more seems required than the presupposition that certain attributes or constituent parts - if possible, essential ones - have remained constant whereas the changes, or at least most of them, represent a never disrupted series - and if possible, with members continuously passing over into each other.[3]

In the margin alongside this passage Husserl writes: "Individually identical? But is an

---

[1] *Ibid.*, p. 139. The words "fully equal" (*völlig gleich*) are underlined by Husserl.

[2] *Ibid.* This passage is marked in the margin by Husserl.

[3] *Ibid.*, p. 141.

abstract moment the same now and an hour ago? one might ask".[1] First it is asked here whether it is the constancy of "attributes or constituent parts" to which Meinong refers is an identity of individuals. Apparently it is, for it would otherwise be inappropriate to speak of constancy here. The attributes under consideration would accordingly be abstract moments, which are indeed individuals, albeit ones which cannot exist separately from other individuals. Here we may again think of the red-moment and the extension of a red patch. Identity across time, as Meinong conceives of it, would therefore have to involve an identity of certain moments across time. The question which Husserl raises is whether we may speak of such an identity. Here is, for instance, a patch of red to which a certain red-moment belongs. Can this red-moment be identical with one which existed an hour ago? Or would it be better to say that at each instant of time there is a new red-moment? Certainly how we understand identity across time in general will turn on our answer to this question, though Meinong does not even raise it here and Husserl, though he raises it, does not give us an answer. We shall soon see, however, that closely related matters come back to haunt both Meinong and Husserl in their attempts to work out a theory of time-consciousness.

2. *ZUR PSYCHOLOGIE DER KOMPLEXIONEN UND RELATIONEN* (1891)

This short article is Meinong's first reaction to Christian von Ehrenfels' "Über Gestaltqualitäten".[2] A copy of it was sent to Husserl along with the letter of 19 June 1891, already referred to above, where Meinong says that it implies some disagreement with views expounded in *Philosophie der Arithmetik* (*Briefwechsel* I, 129). Most of the markings in Husserl's copy indicate only points of interest, while most of his annotations do not convey much about Husserl's opinion about the article in question. One annotation, however, is worth noting here, for it indicates one of the points of disagreement which, to Husserl mind, Meinong meant in the above-mentioned letter.

In the margin alongside the following passage Husserl writes "against *Philosophie der Arithmetik*".

If I compare A with B, this brings about a complex psychical reality whereby the presentation of A and that of B are in a determinate relation to each other and to the whole complexion, a relation whose peculiar

---

[1] "Individuell identisch? Aber ist ein abstraktes Moment jetzt und vor einer Stude dasselbe? so könnte man frage."

[2] Both the article by von Ehrenfels and the one by Meinong are referred in Husserl's "Psychologische Studien zur elementaren Logik" (1894) (Hua XII, 95 n.).

nature is revealed through psychological observation. But in addition the comparison still usually leads to something which can be called the result of the comparison: A proves to be equal or more or less similar to B, and these expressions designate contents of presentation which essentially belong so little to the forum of inner perception, so little, say, to reflection regarding the act of comparison, that they much rather apparently rank together with A and B on the same level.[1]

Though Meinong himself does not refer to Husserl in this passage, Husserl nonetheless feels that he is under attack here. Where in the *Philosophie der Arithmetik* does Husserl say that the presentation of a relation belongs to the forum of inner perception or reflection?

Husserl claims that the concept of a plurality involves the reflection on "the *combination* of the single elements to the whole. And here," he adds, "it is as it is in the case of many other classes of relations" (Hua XII, 18). The other relations which Husserl explicitly mentions here are those which obtain between "points of a line, moments of a temporal duration, the shades of a continuous series of colors, of the tone qualities of a 'tone-movement'", but also those which obtain between "metaphysical" or "psychological" parts, such as the extension and the color of a visually presented whole (Hua XII, 19). "We can on the whole quite generally say", he however concludes: "Wherever we meet with a special class of wholes, the concept of them can have arisen only by reflection on the well characterized manner of combination which is the same for every whole of this class" (Hua XII, 20). This claim would therefore apply to the wholes which result from acts of comparison. But we must carefully note that, whatever misgivings we may have about this claim, it is made concerning only the *concept*, i.e., the general presentation, of a whole. Husserl fails to point this out in his defence.

3. *BEITRÄGE ZUR THEORIE DER PSYCHISCHEN ANALYSE* (1894)

Since the main problems which concern Meinong in *Beiträge zur Theorie der psychischen Analyse*, primarily the problem concerning whether the analysis of a whole into its parts brings about a new content, do not particularly concern us, it would take us too far afield to enter into a general exposition of the text under consideration. Nonetheless, Husserl does raise questions and make comments in his annotations concerning certain points.

---

[1] "Gegen Ph. d. Ar." *Zur Psychologie der Komplexionen und Relationen*, p. 257. This pasage is partly underlined by Husserl. Moreover, alongisde the last sentence he writes "NB".

3.1. Analysis, Founded Contents, and Relations

Besides the obvious alternatives, namely 1) that the parts of an analyzed whole already belonged to this whole prior to analysis, or 2) that through analysis a new content replaces a simple whole, Meinong also considers another, namely 3) that the whole consists of *different* parts from the ones which result from analysis.[1] From this third standpoint there occurs a transition whereby each of the parts (x, y, z) are, as it were, replaced by others (a, b, c). One of the difficulties with this third alternative, according to Meinong, is that there would have to be a continuum in the transition from x to a, from y to b, and from z to c. "The question thus arises," says Meinong, "how it happens that this motion each time leads just to a, or to b or c and never beyond them; for the fact that a, b, and c themselves would already be at the natural end of the relevant continuum could nonetheless be taken into account as a very special exception".[2] Meinong must refute this alternative in his attempt to support the thesis that the parts which come into view through analysis had already been present in the whole.

Next to the passage just cited Husserl raises the apparently rhetorical question: "Does this difficulty not arise also regarding the intensity of presenting? And cannot this be subject to analogous doubts?"[3] This question can be understood in reference to Meinong's claim that his preference for the first alternative is meant only in application to *qualities* and not to *intensity*.[4] He agrees with Stumpf that the intensity of the parts of the content increase in intensity through analysis.[5] Husserl, however, maintains that this increase also occurs within a continuum which reaches a certain limit. Yet, if

---

[1] Theses alternatives are listed as 1, 3, and 2 respectively in *Beiträge zur Theorie der psychischen Analyse*, p. 10.

[2] *Ibid.*, p. 12.

[3] "Ergibt sich diese Schwierigkeit nicht auch in betreff der Intensität des Vorstellens? Und lassen sich auf diese nicht überhaupt analoge Bedenken gründen?"

[4] *Beiträge zur Theorie der psychischen Analyse*, pp. 8 f. To be precise, Meinong speaks here of the intensity of *contents*, whereas Husserl speaks of the intensity of *presenting*. Though Husserl's manner of speaking clearly makes us think of the intensity of the *act* of presentating, he perhaps shows himself here to embrace the
view of Brentano and Stumpf, who both held that, in spite of the distinction between intensity of act and that of content in the case of judgments and in the case of phenomena of love and hate, there is no such distinction to be made between the intensity of the act of presenting and that of the content of presenting. In 1883/84, however, Meinong took the heterodox Herbartian view that there is such a distinction.

[5] *Tonpsychologie* I, pp. 373 ff.; II, pp. 290 ff.

Meinong finds it difficult to see how a, b, and c could be limits in quality, there is no reason why the same difficulty could not be posed regarding the alleged increase in intensity. A related difficulty is pointed out by Husserl again where Meinong concludes "that there is never analyzed from a presentation a quality which was not contained in it".[1] Husserl underlines "a quality" (*eine Qualität*) and writes in the margin: "There was however no mention of this".[2] That is to say, Meinong criticizes the competing alternatives, at first using only letters (a, b, c) and suddenly restricts his conclusion to qualities. The exclusion of intensity therefore appears to be *ad hoc*.

The claim that analysis changes the content is not one which Meinong attacks as a mere theoretical possibility, but rather one that had actually been made in two articles by Hans Cornelius,[3] who also makes another claim which Meinong attacks: namely, that a founded content is "obviously nothing but the totality of the relations of the content-parts".[4] While Meinong is willing to admit that founded contents are presented, he insists that it is far-fetched to say "that when presenting a figure, for instance, the distances between all local determinations which make up the figure are in fact presented. [...] But relations which are not presented cannot be identical with the founded content which is presented".[5] Alongside this passage Husserl indicates a comparison between it and certain passages from his *Philosophie der Arithmetik*.[6] In one of these passages he says: "Under favorable and frequently realized circumstances we can grasp in a single glance an equality between more than two sensory objects without having noticed anything in the least of the great manifold of simple connections (Hua XII, 70 f.). In the other one he says: "The claim that the presentation of the figure would consist in the presentation of the *sum* of those relations would entail, after all, the generally quite unfulfillable requirement that we would hold in an actual collective presentation all the single point-objects in their mutual relations" (Hua XII, 205). While Husserl accordingly seems to have adopted a position in *Philosophie der Arithmetik* similar to Meinong's, he writes: "I say only 'not noticed singly' and do not

---

[1] *Beiträge zur Theorie der psychischen Analyse*, p. 13.

[2] "Davon war doch keine Rede".

[3] "Über Verschmelzung und Analyse. Eine psychologische Analyse", *Vierteljahrsschrift für wissenschaftliche Philosophie* 16 (1892): 404-446; 17 (1893): 30-75.

[4] *Ibid.* (1893): 65.

[5] *Beiträge zur Theorie der psychischen Analyse*, p. 16.

[6] The pages referred to here are pp. 75 f., 229 f. of the original edition.

say that the founded content is identical with their sum".[1] The upshot of this is that, while Husserl agrees with Meinong that the founded content is not identical with the sum of relations, he nonetheless will not go so far as to say that these relations are not presented; he more cautiously says that these relations are not noticed singly.

Let us consider another comparison which Husserl makes between one of Meinong's claims and one of those made in *Philosophie der Arithmetik*. This is the claim that the founded content is "the relation of all constituent parts which enter into the complexion".[2] A melody, for instance, is thus conceived, not as a sum of relations between the notes, but rather one single relation which obtains among all the notes. Next to this passage Husserl indicates that several passages in *Philosophie der Arithmetik* should be examined, "where I seem to adopt the same standpoint as Cornelius".[3] Since these passages encompass the others already cited and do not suggest that Husserl wishes to regard the founded content as the sum of relations, he seems to adopt a standpoint like Cornelius' only in the sense that, unlike Meinong, he does not claim that all of these relations are not presented.

Given Meinong's characterization of founded contents as relations, he realizes that he must expand the extension of the concept of relation and thereby accept the consequence "that much of what is accordingly to be designated as relation might present an aspect other than the one which has thus far customarily been attached to this word".[4] The timbre of a sound, for instance, is regarded as a founded content and accordingly as a relation.[5] Next to the passage just cited Husserl remarks: "In this case Meinong is not so far from Mill's concept of relation and from the standpoint which I advocate in *Philosophie der Arithmetik*".[6] What Husserl means by "Mill's concept of relation" is cited in *Philosophie der Arithmetik* (Hua XII, 66). Objects are related, says

---

[1] "Ich sage nur: nicht für sich bemerkt und sage nicht, dass der fundierte Inhalt mit ihrer Summe identisch ist".

[2] *Beiträge zur Theorie der psychischen Analyse*, p. 18.

[3] "[...] wo ich denselben Standpunkt wie Cornelius einzunehmen scheine". The pages referred to here are pp. 229-233, 70-71, 75 of the original edition.

[4] *Beiträge zur Theorie der psychischen Analyse*, pp. 21 f.

[5] *Ibid.*, pp. 20 f.

[6] "Dann ist aber Meinong vom Millschen Relationbegriff nicht weit und von dem Standpunkt, den ich [in] in der *Philosophie der Arithmetik* vertrete".

Mill, "in virtue of any complex state of consciousness into which they both enter".[1] While Husserl suggests that this definition be somewhat revised (Hua XII, 67), the comment just quoted concerning Meinong's concept of relation seems to suggest that Meinong expands the concept just as he does, namely on the basis of Mill's definition. It is however clear that Meinong's expansion of the concept in question is based on the conception of founded contents as relations.[2] Hence, Husserl misreads Meinong on this point.

While founded contents are conceived as relations, Meinong maintains that the members of the relation must not always be separated: "[...] in the case of the figure or melody, moreover in the case of timbre, the separation of the founding materials into distinct parts is [...] so little required that it can be downright detrimental to the founding. But wherever one is to compare, to count, to ground that separation is already indispensable for the founding".[3] Husserl marks this passage with "NB" and raises the following question concerning the notion of founding which is suggested here: "Does this not bring to mind that in the two cases the situation is different: in the one case a founded content, in the other case a psychical act?"[4] Thus, where the parts are not to be separated, what is founded is the whole content, e.g., the figure or the melody, on its parts; in the case where one is engaged in counting, comparing, or grounding, it is a psychical act which is founded on those acts in which the objects to be counted, compared, or grounded are presented. We shall see below that Husserl also has difficulties with Meinong's conception of founding as presented in *Über Gegenstände höherer Ordnung*.

---

[1] James Mill, *Analysis of the Phemomena of the Human Mind*, ed. with additional notes by John Stuart Mill, II (London, 1879), p. 10 n. Though this passage is quoted in English in *Philosophie der Arithmetik*, a German translation of it was quoted in *Über den Begriff der Zahl* (Hua XII, 328 f.). The translation was moreover taken from *Hume-Studien* II, p. 40. The translated quotation which is found there is partly underlined in Husserl's copy of the work; it is also marked "NB" in the margin.

[2] As it turns out, in *Hume-Studien* II (pp. 40 f.) Meinong says "that the mere obtaining together of presentational objects [...] in consciousness does not yet make a relation [except the relation of obtaining together itself, it is added in a footnote]; everyone will be able to recall cases where he has seen two objects next to each other for some time or has thought of them at the same time, without being struck, say, by a certain similarity or a contrast between them which he subsequently notices. But it is correct to say that such an obtaining together is an indispensable requirement of every relation between presentational objects". This passage is partly underlined by Husserl.

[3] *Beiträge zur Theorie der psychischen Analyse*, pp. 42 f.

[4] "Macht das nicht aufmerksam darauf, dass beiderseits die Sachlage anders ist: einerseits ein fundierter Inhalt, andererseits ein psychischer Akt?"

3.2. The Temporal Principle of Extension

The final section of *Beiträge zur Theorie der Analyse* (1894) is an appendix which concerns "the temporal principle of extension and successive analysis", where Meinong defends the thesis that, given certain qualifications which will henceforth be stated, only temporally extended wholes are presentable.[1] While Husserl does not attack this thesis as such, he expresses misgivings concerning some of the points made by Meinong in the course of defending it.

It is unclear, says Meinong, to speak merely of the time of the presentation in contrast with the time of the content. "If a presentation occurs at time T", he explains, "the content, which is ultimately nothing but a part of the presentation, is also at time T".[2] Husserl underlines the words "nothing but a part of the presentation" and writes in the margin: "confusion between content and object".[3] This charge could indeed be applied to the entire *Beiträge* as well as all of Meinong's previous writings, for he does not come to distinguish between content and object until 1899 in *Über Gegenstände höherer Ordnung*.

Instead of speaking of the time of the presentation Meinong prefers to speak of outer time; instead of speaking of the time of the content he prefers to speak of inner time.[4] One might expect the terms "inner" and "outer" to be used in precisely the opposite way, but Meinong's usage of them is perhaps made somewhat more intelligible if one keeps in mind that the content is *in* the presentation and its time is accordingly *inner* time. In any case it may be suggested that the inner time of a *perceptual* presentation is always determined as the present. In reply to such a suggestion Meinong says: "I do not doubt that wherever the perceptual presentation is

---

[1] This thesis had been stated in Herbart, *Psychologie als Wissenschaft*, § 115 (*Sämtliche Werke*, VI, p. 107): "[...] the presentation of the temporal as such is like that of the spatial in that *a stretch of it must be given all at once, as inclosed between its starting and end point* [die Vorstellung des Zeitlichen als eines solchen kommt darin mit der des Räumlichen überein, dass *eine Strecke desselben auf einaml vorliegen muss, wie sie eingeschlossen ist zwischen ihrem Anfangs- und Endpunkte*]". In his early treatment of sensations and their contrast with other presentations Meinong already accepted a Herbartian view which Brentano had emphatically rejected, namely the view that the act of presenting has an intensity in addition to the intensity of its content. Sensations are thereby distinguished from other presentations by virtue of being acts of greater intensity. See "Über Begriff und Empfindung der Empfindung", *Vierteljahrsschrift für wissenschaftliche Philosophie* 13 (1889): 1-31.

[2] *Beiträge zur Theorie der psychischen Analyse*, p. 67.

[3] "Verwechslung von Inhalt und Gegenstand".

[4] *Beiträge zur Theorie der psychischen Analyse*, pp. 67 f.

joined by a perceptual judgment this consciousness of presentness is not lacking or it is at least to be easily summoned up on request. What experience does not tell me, however, is that I *could* not have the perceptual judgment without including the 'now' in the content of the judgment".[1] This passage is partly underlined by Husserl, who writes a question mark and comments in the margin: "Not quite intelligible".[2] While he is thus uncertain about Meinong's attempt to deny the necessity of the determination of inner time as regards the contents of perceptual presentations, he agrees with Meinong concerning the timelessness of certain "contents", e.g., the difference between red and green or that 2 is smaller than 3.[3] In the margin next to this passage Husserl writes: "Yes, *general* states of affairs".[4] Here we see a very important agreement between Meinong and Husserl, namely that our cognition of such states of affairs cannot be accounted for unless we accept the notion of timeless objects.

If it is accordingly granted that, in spite of the fact that outer time always has a temporal determination, there are cases where the inner temporal determination is lacking, the question remains whether the remaining cases, where inner time *is* temporally determined, also involve the temporal *extension* of inner time. While Meinong's attempt to argue for this thesis by means of a diagram is not commented on in great detail by Husserl and therefore does not require exposition here, the following statement is subject to attack from Husserl: "For the inner determination t, which is, after all, itself something co-presented only as a constituent part of x, it turns out that, during the relevant outer or objective time, it must remain unchanged or likewise continually change".[5] This passage is partly underlined by Husserl, who writes alongside it the following: "Content-time and object-time are always mixed up. What is meant here is the phenomenological content-time. This, however, cannot remain unchanged!?"[6] This confusion between content-time and object-time is of course the result of the confusion between content and object.

This latter confusion, according to Husserl, also arises again in the following pas-

---

[1] *Ibid.*, p. 70.

[2] "Nicht recht verständlich".

[3] *Beiträge zur Theorie der psychischen Analyse*, p. 71.

[4] "Ja, *generelle* Sachverhalte".

[5] *Beiträge zur Theorie der psychischen Analyse*, p. 72.

[6] "Es wird immer vermengt Inhaltszeit und Gegenstandszeit. Gemeint ist hier die phänomenologische Inhaltszeit. Die aber kann doch nicht unverändert bleiben!?"

sage where Meinong distinguishes between cases where the object immediately presented and those where it is mediately presented:

> I present 'something' if I grasp through my presenting an actuality independent of myself, a landscape, a building, an apparatus; but I also present 'something' if I have a phantasy image in mind. [...] If that which is presented is called the object, as is the convention, then something characteristic of this difference lies in the fact that in the second case the object is immediately presented vis-à-vis the presentation, but not in the first case, so that one can speak of immediate objects of presentation in contrast with mediate ones without being prejudiced in favor of other differences.[1]

Husserl partly underlines this passage and writes the following alongside it: "Thus I present a centaur immediately and my friend Hans mediately. Fundamentally wrong."[2] We have of course already seen that as early as 1894 Husserl rejected the thesis that wherever the object of a presentation does not exist in actuality it nonetheless exists immanently. If, however, one does maintain that the object exists immanently, it is easy to see why Meinong's claim that such an object is likewise *immediate*. As the presentation is accessible to inner perception, which allegedly has immediate access to its objects, everything immanent to the presentation must likewise be immediate in the same sense. If, however, we push this way of thinking to its logical conclusion, we would have to say that the centaur is no less immediate than the presentation of it.[3]

While Meinong finds it difficult to concede that a perceptually presented object is always temporally determined (namely, as present), he is absolutely certain that such an object cannot as such be temporally extended. "I have no *perceptual* presentation of motion, for motion cannot take place in a single point of time [...]".[4] Next to this passage Husserl raises the question: "= intuitively self-present in a single point of

---

[1] *Beiträge zur Theorie der psychsichen Analyse*, p. 75.

[2] "Also einen Zentauren stelle ich *un*mittelbar und meinen Freund Hans mittelbar vor. Grundfalsch."

[3] The passage just cited from *Beiträge zur Theorie der psychischen Analyse* (p. 75) continues: "If an mediate object, i.e., the grasping of an actuality, is under consideration, it certainly makes good sense to say that I grasp the whole as soon as I present one part after the other". Husserl underlines "mittelbares Objekt, also um das Erfassen einer Wirklichkeit" and writes in one margin next to it "?!", while he writes in the other margin: "Obviously the 'immanent object' [is] confused with the phenomenological content [Offenbar [wird] das 'immanente Objekt' verwechselt mit phänomenologischem Inhalt]". Meinong continues: "[...] if, however, the immediate object under consideration, what is presented is not at all a whole of which only one part after the other is presented." Husserl underlines the entire independent clause of this passage and writes alongside it: "NB??".

[4] *Ibid.*, p. 76.

time?".[1] Here Husserl expresses misgivings about the obviously Brentanian theory of perception which Meinong conveys. It has been seen that for Brentano motions and other temporally extended objects are not perceivable since perception is restricted to the present. Contrary to this theory, Husserl prefers to say that whatever is "intuitively self-present" not only can, but must be temporally extended. Meinong later came to the same conclusion in *Über Gegenstände höherer Ordnung*, as Husserl notes next to the passage just cited.

4. PSYCHOLOGISCH-ETHISCHE UNTERSUCHUNGEN ZUR WERTH-THEORIE (1894)

Husserl thanks the author for a copy of this work in letter of 22 November 1894 (*Briefwechsel* I, 133), wherein he also expresses his regret that the second volume of *Philosophie der Arithmetik* demands his full attention for some time to come, leaving no time for the study of Meinong's value theory. On 5 April 1902, however, Husserl writes: "On this Easter holiday I worked on a total re-shaping of my ethical lecture and studied your *Psychologisch-ethische Untersuchungen zur Werth-Theorie* with the *greatest profit*" (*Briefwechsel* I, 145). The lecture to which Husserl is referring here is the one given in SS 1902 on basic questions of ethics. Unfortunately the notes of this lecture are for the most part no longer extant. The 1902 texts on value which are extant (Hua XXVIII, 384-418) contain no references to Meinong. In Husserl's lectures on value theory, which were given in 1908 and 1914 (Hua XXVIII), Meinong is not mentioned at all. The only data available for discerning Husserl's response to Meinong early value theory are to be found in the few annotations which he wrote in his copy of the work under consideration.

As the title of this work indicates, Meinong's approach to value theory is psychological in character. While this is of course to be expected from a pupil of Brentano, value is construed by Meinong as completely dependent on valuing subjects. As we may recall, Brentano insists on an analogy between judgments and acts of love and hate and therefore ascribes correctness and incorrectness in some sense to acts of the latter kinds. As the truth or falsity of judgments is determined by something independent of the judging subject, the same can be said for the correctness or incorrectness of loving and hating. Meinong's position is somewhat more subjectivist, for he characterizes value in the following way:

---

[1] "= anschaulich selbstgegenwärtig in einem Zeitpunkt?"

[...] value is not tied to actual valuing, but rather to possible valuing, and to be taken into consideration for this are also favorable circumstances, more precisely, sufficient orientation, also a normal intellectual and emotional state. Value accordingly consists not in being-valued, but rather in being-able-to-be-valued under the presupposition of the required favorable circumstances. An object has value insofar as it has the ability to provide the factual basis for a value-feeling for the sufficiently oriented person, provided that he is normally predisposed.[1]

This passage alone, which is marked "NB" by Husserl, may leave doubts about how value is here conceived. On the one hand, the possible valuing which comes into play here may be construed as presupposing that there is a subject which could value. On the other hand, it may be suggested that, even if there were no subject, valuing would be possible in the sense that a valuing subject nonetheless *could* exist. Depending on how possible valuing is understood, Meinong's position is more subjectivist in the former case, more objectivist in the latter. The following passage, again marked "NB" by Husserl, leaves no room for doubt:

Whatever the properties or abilities of a thing, these in themselves do not yet make up its value as long as a subject does not exist in whose feeling-life the thing has a particular place. Without the least bit of change, a thing which just had value can lose this when the subject ceases to exist to which it had referred. To ascribe value to a thing therefore means not only to ascribe a certain ability to it, but at the same time to claim the existence of a subject to which this ability can, as it were, be transferred in reality.[2]

Since the possible valuing which is involved in the ascription of value to a thing presupposes the existence of a subject, Meinong's theory of values is subjectivist. Husserl, however, takes issue with this position, for he prefers the more objectivist orientation which had been suggested by Brentano in *Vom Ursprung sittlicher Erkenntnis*. One may therefore doubt his "greatest profit".

It should be pointed out that the acts of valuing to which Meinong refers are acts of *feeling*. The subject on which values depend is according first and foremost a *feeling* subject and not a *willing* subject. We have of course already noted that Brentano, on the one hand, challenged the old Kantian classification of psychical phenomena into thinking, feeling, and willing by dividing thinking into presenting and judging and by regarding feeling and willing as belonging in one and the same class with each other. We have also seen that Husserl to some extent challenges Brentano's view on this matter by considering acts of willing as the ones relevant to ethics and acts of feeling as the ones relevant to aesthetics and thus by seeing a clear-cut division between these

---

[1] *Psychologisch-ethische Untersuchungen zur Werth-Theorie*, p. 25. This passage is partly underlined by Husserl.

[2] *Ibid.*, p. 28. This passage is partly underlined by Husserl.

two classes of acts. While this alternative to orthodox Brentanism is clearly reminiscent of a Kantian view on the matter, it should be noted that the division between feeling and desire (including wishing and striving as well as desire) had already been adopted by Meinong and his pupil, von Ehrenfels, and made central to their investigations concerning values.[1] Whereas Meinong characterizes valuing primarily in terms of feeling, von Ehrenfels does so primarily in terms of desiring.[2] Though Husserl's very limited interest in both of these theories of value indicates that his own division between feeling and willing is more likely a borrowing from Kant than from the two Brentanists in question, we must not regard his already-mentioned departure from Brentano on the matter under consideration as a departure from the *school* of Brentano. Moreover, Husserl's value-objectivism is indeed much more in line with orthodoxy than the more subjectivist views of Meinong and von Ehrenfels.

Meinong's early theory of values and the closely related one which was worked out by Christian von Ehrenfels have been treated many decades ago, together with Brentano's, as belonging to the "second Austrian school of value theory".[3] The question naturally arises whether Husserl should also be considered as a member of this school. Insofar as his theory of values is influenced by Brentano, he may indeed be so considered. Yet, we must be reminded that this theory and the one which Marty put forward differ from those found in the work of von Ehrenfels and the early Meinong not only as regards the question of the objective status of values, but also in their relation to the "first Austrian school of value theory". This is the school which had been founded by Carl Menger and continued in the work of Eugen von Böhm-Bawerk and Friedrich von Wieser. While the concern of this school was primarily the *economic* theory of value, von Ehrenfels and the early Meinong drew upon these economic theories in their own attempts to establish the concept of value in application to both

---

[1]Though von Ehrenfels had already launched the publication of his series of articles, "Werth-Theorie und Ethik", *Vierteljahrsschrift für wissenschaftliche Philosophie* 17 (1893): 76-110, 200-266, 321-363, 413-475; (1894): 77-97, before Meinong's *Psychologisch-ethische Untersuchungen zur Werth-Theorie* was published, the latter book is nevertheless based on earlier lectures which von Ehrenfels attended and whose influence he acknowledges.

[2]The views of von Ehrenfels concerning values were first worked out in the above-mentioned series of articles and given their mature statement in his *System der Werth-Theorie* (Leipzig: O.R. Reisland, 1897/98). Husserl's copy of this book and the series of articles bear only a few markings and annotations.

[3]H.O. Eaton, *The Austrian Philosophy of Value of Value* (Norman: University of Oklahoma Press, 1930.

economic and non-economic domains.[1] Husserl and Marty, however, do not exhibit the influence of Menger's school. This is not to say that these two Brentanists completely agree on matters of value, for it will be seen in the following chapter that they certainly do not. Their disagreement on these matters is however not as extensive as the one between Husserl and the early Meinong.

5. ÜBER GEGENSTÄNDE HÖHERER ORDNUNG UND DEREN VERHÄLTNIS ZUR INNEREN WAHRNEHMUNG (1899)

On 27 August 1900 Husserl wrote to Meinong in order to thank him for the reception of "Abstrahieren und Vergleichen"[2] and in the same letter refers to "your fine and instructive essay, unfortunately only just now more closely familiar to me, 'concerning objects of higher order'" (*Briefwechsel* I, 136). References to Cornelius in both of these texts, says Husserl, could be inserted in the *Logische Untersuchungen* during the summer 1900. While it is thus clear that at this time Husserl had some familiarity with *Über Gegenstände höherer Ordnung*, it is also clear that he read some or all of it a few years later. In his copy of it he writes at the beginning of the third part (on the presenting and perceiving of temporally distributed objects): "Read September 1904".[3] This reading was done in preparation for his 1905 lecture on time-consciousness, where the work under consideration is discussed (Hua X, 216-228). Even in a part which precedes the final one, however, Husserl writes next to a footnote: "Probably 1901?"[4] It thus appears that there were at least two (if not three) readings, one in the summer 1899 and the other in autumn of 1904.

---

[1] Smith, *Austrian Philosophy*, pp. 281-197. See also Wolfgang Grassl, "Christian von Ehrenfels als Werttheoretiker", in von Ehrenfels, *Philosophische Schriften* I. edited by Reinard Fabian (Munich: Philosophia, 1982), pp. 1-22.

[2] Husserl's copy of this text, published in *Zeitschrift für Psychologie und Physiologie der Sinnesorgane* 24 (1900), bears only a few markings and no annotations.

[3] "Gelesen Sept. 1904".

[4] "Wohl 1901?" This footnote (p. 203) is a reference to "Zur Psychologie der Komplexionen und Relationen" which had of course been published in 1891.

5.1. Founding

We have already seen how Meinong spoke of founded contents in his early writings and regarded figures and melodies as outstanding examples of such contents. In 1899, however, he begins to refer to these as "objects of higher order". This shift in terminology is in large measure motivated by the content-object distinction which he adopts. If, for instance, a melody is presented, this is the *object* and not the *content* of the presentation. How is the notion of the content to be understood?

We may here be reminded of the notion of the immanent object. If the object of a presentation is a golden mountain, then this object does not actually exist, though it does exist as an immanent object. Meinong says, however, "that this presumptive existence deserves at best to be called a *pseudo-existence*".[1] While the merely presented object, e.g., the golden mountain, at best pseudo-exists, the content, according to Meinong, is something that actually exists wherever the presentation occurs, namely as that "wherein presentations with different objects are different from each other, regardless of their agreement in act".[2] Insofar as this concept of the content comes close to anything in Husserl's theory of consciousness, it is best compared to the matter of an act. For this, too, is what differs wherever the direction to an object differs, whether or not the quality of the remains the same. It is accordingly clear why Meinong can no longer speak of melodies and figures as founded contents, for these do not in any sense exist in the acts. Even if they pseudo-exist, this is not the same as existing in the act.

Objects of higher order are objects which are in a very special sense dependent on others. Meinong asks us to consider the notion of *difference* as an example of such an object and says:

> I can simply not think this thought without reference to objects to which it is attached, as it were, whereas it would make very good sense to adopt the view that in the thought of blue or yellow there is still no hint at all of spatiality, although it is impossible to think of color without thinking of extension.[3]

If two objects differ, the difference between them has an *intrinsic* dependence on these objects, whereas the dependence of color on extension is an *extrinsic* one. An intrinsic dependence is to be found in the case of all objects of higher order, whether these be

---

[1] *Über Gegenstände höherer Ordnung*, pp. 186 ff.

[2] *Ibid.*, p. 188. This passage is underlined by Husserl.

[3] *Ibid.*, p. 28. This passage is partly underlined by Husserl.

differences, similarities, melodies, figures, etc. The object of higher order may also in each case be called the "superius", the objects on which it intrinsically depends the "inferiora". It may of course be difficult for us to accept the distinction between an intrinsic and an extrinsic dependence, for Meinong takes for granted that it is intuitively clear. We shall see below that one of Husserl's criticisms of Meinong's theory of objects of higher order is aimed in principle at the failure to make this distinction plausible.

According to Meinong, there are two classes of objects of higher order: the real and the ideal. An example of an ideal object of higher order is similarity. "Similarity does not exist, but it obtains; and precisely that which can obtain, but which cannot, strictly speaking, exist, is indeed what is here to be regarded as ideal in contrast with the real".[1] This ontological contrast is comparable to Husserl's contrast between the real and the ideal, for (as we shall see) Meinong later comes to the more precise characterization of what obtains (the ideal) as timeless. While similarity is viewed as an example of an ideal object of higher order, the relation between a quality and its location is regarded as a real object of higher order.[2] Another real object of higher order is, as Husserl notes in the margin of page 199 of *Über Gegenstände höherer Ordnung*, "the relation between phenomena of love und the underlying presentations".[3] While the ontological contrast between the real and the ideal is certainly acceptable to Husserl, he nonetheless finds difficulties in Meinong's attempt to describe this contrast in psychological and epistemological terms. Let us now consider this description.

Though Meinong no longer speaks of founded contents, the terms "foundation" (*Fundament*), "founding" (*Fundiering*), and "founded" (*fundiert*) nonetheless still play a role in his investigations concerning objects of higher order. The context in which this notion is utilized by Meinong is precisely his attempt to examine the psychological and epistemological side of the topic under consideration. Ideal objects of higher order, he maintains, cannot be perceived. His reason for saying this is partly based on his acceptance of the Brentanian doctrine that any judgment, and therefore any perception,

---

[1] *Ibid.*, p. 199.

[2] *Ibid.* Husserl writes in the margin: "Thus quality and location make up a real complexion or relation [Also Qualität und Ort bilden eine reale Komplexion bzw. Relation]". The disjunction "complexion or relation" here refers to Meinong's claim in the text under consideration that complexions and relations are the only objects of higher order familiar to him, but also to his claim that there is a principle whereby relations and complexions "co-incide" (see *ibid.*, pp. 193 ff.) While it remains obscure how relations and complexions differ and also how they co-incide, I shall not enter into these matters here since Husserl does not enter into them.

[3] "Das Verhältnis zwischen Phänomenen der Liebe und den zugrundeliegenden Vorstellungen = real".

is in each case founded on a presentation. While the presentations which underlie perceptions, e.g., the sensations which underlie outer perceptions, are passive, the presentations which underlie our cognition of ideal objects of higher order are active. "There is here not only an action in the judgment: also the material of presentation with which judging here has to operate on, as it were, must be worked for. It is quite a trivial matter that whoever wants to get clear about equality or inequality of two things must compare them with each other".[1] The comparing activity, says Meinong, brings two presentations (namely those of the compared objects) into a real relation and thereby produces a new presentation, e.g., the presentation of a difference. Now let us consider the more particularly epistemological side of the matter at hand.

"This difference", he significantly adds, "is moreover as a rule (perhaps without exception) not only presented, but at the same time cognized by means of a judgment in whose evidence a typical case of cognition, quite characteristically different at first from inner perception, makes itself felt".[2] The evident judgment in question is moreover one in which logical necessity is cognized. In this vein Meinong continues: "if A and B are different, they are so at all times, for they *must* be so, this word understood here in the sense of 'logical necessity'".[3] Accordingly, it is justifiable to call A and B not only members, but also still in particular *foundations* of the relation of difference".[4] Alongside the last sentence of this passage Husserl raises the question: "Thus, *not* every relation has 'foundations' in this sense?"[5] What Husserl here surmises seems to be correct. A quality and the place in which it exists are not called "foundations". But it is not merely a terminological question at stake here, for Meinong clearly maintains that ideal objects of higher order are *necessarily* founded on their inferiora and real objects of higher order are not. If, accordingly, logical necessity makes such a crucial difference between the two cases, then we may ask whether it is not correct to say that the extension of a color is founded on the color, for the color is, after all, necessarily extended.

The question just raised occurs to Husserl when he writes the following in the top margin of the same page (202) of *Über Gegenstände höherer Ordnung*: "The relation

---

[1] *Über Gegenstände höherer Ordnung*, p. 201. Husserl underlines "vergleichen".

[2] *Ibid.*, p. 202. Most of this passage is underlined by Husserl.

[3] This sentence is partly underlined by Husserl.

[4] *Ibid.*

[5] "Also *nicht* jede Relation hat in diesem Sinne 'Fundamente'?"

of *my* 'founded' and Meinong's needs an exact investigation. To be considered: *Psychologische Studien zur elementaren Logik*".[1] Though he by no means investigates the matter at hand exactly (if "exactly" means the same as "at length"), he still indicates the result of such an investigation when he writes in the left margin of the following page: "Cf. *Psychologische Studien zur elementaren Logik*. There I have already called the Gestalt qualities 'founded', not in this but in a related sense, but used the concept of 'founded' in reference to all dependent moments."[2] While Husserl's concern may here be more to stress the priority in time of his investigations in comparison with Meinong's, the comparison in question suggests a legitimate criticism of Meinong's notion of founding. It is unclear why this notion is limited to ideal objects of higher order in relation to their inferiora and not extended to other dependent moments, such as extension in relation to color, for the logical necessity which figures so prominently in Meinong's investigations is to be found in all such cases. This point is moreover related to the above-mentioned obscurity of Meinong's distinction between intrinsic and extrinsic dependence, for in either case the dependence seems to be a logically necessary one.

It is also peculiar that Meinong makes the following claim: "Most of what in particular already forces itself on extra-psychological thinking as 'relation' is ideal in nature and therefore founded".[3] Next to this passage Husserl writes a large question mark and raises the question: "Ideal and founded, do they co-incide?"[4] The claim just cited by Meinong clearly indicates that they do co-incide. The implication is of course that all ideal objects are objects of higher order, but there is no consideration of possible counter-examples. Perhaps numbers could be construed as ideal on the hand and not as objects of higher order on the other.

---

[1] "Verhältnis *meines* 'fundiert' und Meinongs bedarf einer genauen Untersuchung. Zu beachten: *Psychologische Studien zur elementaren Logik*".

[2] "Vergleich *Psychologische Studien zur elementaren Logik*. Dort habe ich die Gestaltqualitäten schon als nicht in diesem, aber verwandtem Sinne 'fundiert' bezeichnet, aber den Begriff des 'Fundierten' auf alle unselbständigen Momente bezogen."

[3] *Über Gegenstände höherer Ordnung*, p. 204. This passage is partly underlined by Husserl.

[4] "Ideal und fundiert, deckt sich das?"

5.2. *Temporally Distributed Objects and Perception*

Now let us consider Meinong's views on the presentation and perception of temporally distributed objects and Husserl's reaction to these views. Crucial to them is the contrast between temporally distributed and temporally undistributed objects. "The core of the contrast under discussion," says Meinong, "is not to be sought in whether the object occupies a stretch of time, for this is always occupied by it, but in whether and how the object is *distributed* in this stretch of time. Color, tone as such lack such a distribution: in a certain way it belongs to melody, change of color".[1] In reference to the words "as such" Husserl raises the question in the margin: "What does that mean?"[2] Of course, understanding the contrast in question turns on deciding what this means.

In the 1905 lecture on time-consciousness Husserl says that we can speak of certain moments in abstraction from their temporal determinations (Hua X, 228, 220). Here we may think of a red-moment in abstraction from its temporal determination. While this is what might be meant by "temporally undistributed objects", Husserl maintains that we can also take this expression to mean "objects which have the character of 'nonchanges'" (Hua X, 222). Here we may of course think again of a red-moment, but this time we do not abstract from its temporal determination; rather, the red-moment remains unchanged for a certain stretch of time. It is accordingly temporally undistributed in this sense insofar as the red at one time is qualitatively indistinguishable from the red at a later time. Whether the expression in question is used in the one sense or the other, however, it turns out that objects such as melodies, i.e., objects which cannot be what they are without change, would have to count as temporally distributed.

Now Meinong raises the following question concerning the presentation of temporally distributed objects: "if a temporally distributed object is to be presented, can or must a succession of the content correspond to the succession of the object".[3] Husserl takes this question to be a query into whether the presentation of a change must itself involve change (Hua X, 222 f.), but he also is quite aware of Meinong's particular concern with the *content* of the presentation. Meinong is, after all, asking not whether the act of presenting itself is a change, but rather whether there is a change in the content which corresponds to a change in the object. As we have seen, the content of an

---

[1] *Über Gegenstände höherer Ordnung*, p. 248. This passage is partly underlined by Husserl.

[2] "Was heisst das?"

[3] *Über Gegenstände höherer Ordnung*, p. 248.

act in Meinongian terms is more or less the same as the matter of an act in Husserlian terms. But Husserl takes the notion of content in Meinong's question as equivalent to his notion of phenomenological contents, e.g., sensations in the case of an outer perception. If there are such contents in the latter sense, we may, to be sure, ask whether these must change in a way that corresponds with the changing object. This is however not what Meinong is asking.

Meinong answers his question by saying "that there are so many difficulties in the way of the initially so obvious assumption, that a distributed presentation must belong to the distributed object, that one [...] may not at all concede that this is possible".[1] The reply is accordingly that there must not be any change at all in the content of the presentation. The basic consideration which leads Meinong to this conclusion is this: if a temporally distributed object, e.g., the motion of a ball, is presented for one stretch of time and also presented for an immediately succeeding stretch of time, the two presentations together do not make up the presentation of the entire motion of the ball. If a motion is presented, the presentation in which the final phase of the motion is presented must have a content which corresponds to all the preceding phases of the motion. The presentation of this final phase is the presentation of the entire motion, if indeed the entire motion is presented.

While Meinong painstakingly argues for this claim by means of a diagram, Husserl writes the following in the bottom margin of the page of *Über Gegenstände höherer Ordnung* (p. 250) where this diagram is presented

The long-winded discussion is rather superfluous. Briefly: the perception of the single phases of the moving object in succession is not yet - and this is at once clear - the perception of the motion. Meinong should have simply distinguished: the act in which the perception of the entire motion ot-o't' unitarily comes to perceptual consciousness and the continuously changing act of perception which terminates and culminates in this consciousness. Thus everything becomes clear through the double meaning of "perception of motion". .[2]

---

[1] *Ibid.*, p. 251. This passage is partly underlined by Husserl. He also writes underneath it: "The 'perception of motion' can be understood in two senses. In one sense we have distribution, in the other not. [Die 'Wahrnehmung der Bewegung' oder Vorstellung der Bewegung kann in doppeltem Sinne verstanden werden. Im einen Sinn haben wir Distribution, im anderen nicht. Cf. vorige Seite Fortsetzung]".

[2] "Die langatmige Erörterung ist ziemlich überflüssig: kurzum: die Wahrnehmung der einzelnen Phasen des Beweglichen im Nacheinander ist noch nicht, und das ist ohne weiteres klar, die Wahrnehmung der Bewegung. Meinong hätte einfach scheiden sollen: den Akt, in dem die Wahrnehmung der ganzen Bewegung ot - o't' einheitlich zum Wahrnehmungsbewusstsein kommt und den sich fortgesetzt ändernden Akt der Wahrnehmung, der in diesem Bewusstsein terminiert und kulminiert. Also klar wird alles durch den Doppelsinn von 'Wahrnehmung der Bewegung'."

Now Meinong clearly maintains that "perception of motion", or "presentation of motion", cannot be understood as merely consisting of the perceptions of the different phases of the motion; thus, he denies that we may speak of perception in the second sense designated by Husserl. More precisely, he calls into question whether we can properly speak of one "continuously changing act" unless this act "terminates and culminates" in the final act whereby all the previous phases of the motion are presented. Thus we may ask: Why does Husserl make so much fuss about the alleged double meaning of "perception of motion"? Why cannot Meinong be defended by simply embracing the first meaning and dismissing the second one as inappropriate?

The answer to these questions is to be found in the lecture on time-consciousness where Husserl says the following (Hua X, 227):

He [Meinong] believes that he is able to infer: Since the perception of the time-object [e.g., the motion] does not consist of the continuous succession of momentary perceptions [...], insofar as each of these gives only its now, there must be an act which embraces the entire time-object beyond the now. The object is completed for perception in the end-point: thus the act must take place and must, embracing the entire object, make up the perception of the object. Thus distributed objects are presented only means of undistributed 'contents' [...]. But that is false or true depending on how it is understood, and false as Meinong seems to understand it. Certainly, consciousness must reach beyond the now. It must do so in every momentary act, but this act is not the perception of the time-object, but rather an *abstractum*. In order for perception of the time-object to be possible, not only the end-act, but rather every momentary act must be an overlapping one; perception, which is itself extended, *distributed*, consists in the fusion of these overlapping acts. None of these acts has a right to be called 'perception'.[1]

Thus, instead of speaking of the perception of the final phase of a motion as the perception of the motion, Husserl maintains that it is better to regard the whole continuously changing act as the perception of the whole motion. Otherwise we are talking of a mere *abstractum*, i.e., a moment of the perceptual act rather than the concrete act itself.

As already indicated, both Meinong and Husserl deal with the problem of time-consciousness by assimilating the memory of the immediate past as much as possible to perception. We have nonetheless seen that there are still important differences in their respective views on this matter. It should moreover be pointed out that Husserl shows greater enthusiasm for this position. To be sure, Meinong comes to the conclusion that the perceivability of an unextended present as such is impossible and therefore rhetorically asks, "why could one not designate as 'perceptual judgments' what is closest to

---

[1] The following quotation is taken from a text which had not been included in the 1928 publication of Husserl's 1905 lecture of time-consciousness. As it turns out, the original manuscript of this lecture included a critical treatment of Meinong's theory of time-consciousness (Hua X, 216-228). The original lecture is indeed different from the published text in many other important respects.

this ideal in attainability, i.e., the memory judgments, which are still sufficiently certain and assured for all practical needs, about the span of time measured with sufficient brevity and immediately prior to the time of judgment?"[1] But Husserl writes alongside this passage: "Only designate?".[2] The point of Husserl's rhetorical question is of course that the concrete act which includes primary memory turns out to be the only act which can in the last analysis be called "perception" in the strict and proper sense and is not merely something given this name as some sort of consolation.

6. *ÜBER ANNAHMEN* (1902)[3]

Husserl received a copy of Meinong's *Über Annahmen* (1902) on 26 of March 1902 (*Husserl-Chronik*, 71). Just a little more than a week later (5 April 1902) he wrote a letter in which he conveyed his first reaction to Meinong (*Briefwechsel* I, 139 ff.). In this letter Husserl expresses his disappointment that his *Logische Untersuchungen*, especially the second volume, were for the most part ignored or, where not ignored, misunderstood in *Über Annahmen*. Much of the territory which, according to Meinong, is explored for the first time in this latter work had already been investigated quite extensively, says Husserl, in the *Logische Untersuchungen*.[4] Husserl also refers to earlier manuscripts of his in which related issues had been treated. Some of this manuscript material was offered to Meinong.

It is of course clear, as Husserl himself acknowledges, why Meinong had not been able to make a thorough-going study of the second volume of the *Logische Untersuchungen*. When he received a copy of this volume, he was already in the process of writing *Über Annahmen*. As he explains in his letter to Husserl (10 April, 1902 in *Briefwechsel* I, 145 ff.), he was striving to be finished with writing by the winter semester of 1901 and naturally had little time to study a newly published and volu-

---

[1] *Über Gegenstände höherer Ordnung*, pp. 261 f. This passage is partly marked by Husserl.

[2] "Bloss bezeichnen?"

[3] This section was presented as a lecture in Trento, Italy at the conference on Meinong and his school, December 1994. This lecture has already appeared in *Axiomathes* 7 (1996): 89-102. The version of it which appears in the following pages is the result of only slight revisions.

[4] As a matter of fact, Meinong himself does not take full credit for the discovery of assumptions, for he says in the preface of *Über Annahmen*, vii, that M. Radakovic introduced this notion to him in June 1899. At that time, of course, none of Husserl's *Logische Untersuchungen* was published.

minous work.[1] In response to Husserl's charge that the references in *Über Annahmen* to the *Logische Untersuchungen* exhibit misunderstandings, Meinong writes that it might have been better if he had given Husserl's work the same silent treatment that Husserl was inclined to give the works from the Graz School. In the same letter Meinong declines the offer to read Husserl's manuscripts. One reason for declining this offer lies in his occupation with other problems at the time. The other reason lies in his uneasiness regarding Husserl's obvious concern about plagiarism. Meinong fears that one day he might express thoughts which are similar to the ones expressed in Husserl's manuscripts and fail to remember that he had already come upon them there. At a later date he would be willing to read this material provided that Husserl in the meantime becomes more light-hearted about intellectual possessions.

Such are the highlights from the less than friendly exchange between Husserl and Meinong which ensued upon the publication of the first edition of *Über Annahmen*. This exchange is indeed climactic in a correspondence which had never been particularly warm and which was soon to be broken off completely. Moreover, Husserl did not have much to say about Meinong or the Graz School in later writings.[2] Nor did Meinong have much to say about Husserl.[3] But Husserl's recognition of parallels and contrasts between *Über Annahmen* and the *Logische Untersuchungen* is a matter which

---

[1] Two other important facts may be mentioned here. First of all, Meinong was blind at this time. Thus if he was interested in a newly published scientific work, it had to be read aloud to him. This was of course very time-consuming.

Secondly, in letter to E. Heinrich (25 July 1910) he says: "I do not know to what extent it is the fault of my peculiar intellectual traits: the fact of the matter is that the manner of investigation and exposition in the second volume of the *Logische Untersuchungen* made it at all times quite exceptionally difficult for me to work out the leading thoughts and results in it - and almost even more to hold on to them also for further use once they were worked out, or at least to maintain the ability to find again the relevant discussions when necessary [Ich weiss nicht, inwieweit meine intellektuelle Eigenart es verschuldet hat: Tatsache ist, dass die Untersuchungs- und Darstellungsart im II. Band der *Logischen Untersuchung* es mir jederzeit ganz ausnehmend schwer gemacht hat, die leitenden Gedanken und Ergebnisse darin herauszuarbeiten -und fast noch mehr sie, wenn sie herausgearbeitet, auch für weiteren Gebrauch festzuhalten, oder wenigstens die Fähigkeit zu bewahren, die massgebenden Ausführungen im Bedarfsfall wieder herauszufinden]." Heinrich had written his dissertation (*Untersuchung zur Lehre vom Begriff*, 1909) under Husserl and sent a copy to Meinong. The passage just cited is taken from Husserl's copy of the letter from Meinong to Heinrich (K III 33/18).

[2] Wherever Meinong is mentioned in Husserl's later work, what is said is never flattering and usually derogatory. See, for example, his remark in Hua XXVI, 6 f., and his explanation in Hua III/1, 254 n, why he does not take into consideration comparable views of Meinong. See also his hostile outburst in a letter to Alois Fischer (27 February 1914) in *Briefwechsel* II, 83 f.

[3] This is not to say that Meinong altogether ignored developments in Husserl's philosophy, for Meinong did read and criticize *Ideen* I in notes which have been published posthumously in the *Ergänzungsband* of Meinong's collected writings.

demands our attention. Moreover, the fact that he saw his 1894 text on intentional objects (one of the manuscripts offered to Meinong, already discussed in connection with Twardowski)[1] as relevant to the contents of *Über Annahmen* is also a matter worth discussing.

I should now like to examine these matters. I shall draw on the above-mentioned texts: the first editions of both *Üb er Annahmen* and the *Logische Untersuchungen* and the 1894 text just mentioned. Also to be taken into account here are some of the annotations which Husserl wrote in his copy of the first edition of *Über Annahmen*.[2] The focus here is on the concept of assumptions. There will moreover be more extensive exposition of Meinong's views here than there has been in the case of other works by him, since the matters now under consideration are of particular importance for understanding the Husserl-Meinong relation.

I shall discuss three arguments which Meinong puts forward in favor of his theory of assumptions. The discussion of each argument is followed by a consideration of relevant parallels and contrasts in Husserl's views or actual responses on his part. Closely related to the topic of assumptions is another concept which is used in *Über Annahmen*, namely the concept of objectives. This concept and its relevance to Husserl cannot be ignored here.

6.1. The Argument from Convictionless Negation

The theory of assumptions is the view that certain psychical phenomena, called "assumptions", have something in common with both presentations and also with judgments. Acts of presenting and judging, as we have already seen, are important topics in the psychology of Brentano. The only other basic class of acts which had been acknowledged in this psychology are phenomena of love and hate, which were by no means regarded as belonging "between" presentations and judgments, as Meinong regards assumptions. While Brentano regarded presentations as the acts on which all others are founded, he maintained that affirmation and negation was possible only in judgments. I can merely present a unicorn on the one hand, such as when I imagine it, but affirmation and negation do not come into question until I judge whether the

---

[1] The other manuscript which Husserl offered to Meinong (K I 57), concerning the origin of modal concepts, has not been published.

[2] Some of these annotations could have come from Husserl's initial reading of the text, others from his reading of it in September 1906 (Hua XXIV, 442). It is difficult and perhaps impossible to discern whether a given annotation comes from one of these readings or possibly from another one.

unicorn which I present exists or not.¹

The first argument which Meinong puts forward in support of his theory of assumptions is particularly important because it establishes this class of acts as one that belongs between presentations and judgments.² Two features, namely position (i.e., being affirmative or negative) and conviction (*Überzeugtheit*), are ascribed to judgments. Presentations lack both of these features. Certain phenomena, however, are observed which have position and lack conviction. If, for example, I am asked to "suppose" or "assume" that the boers were *not* defeated by the British, the ensuing act has position (for it is negative) and lacks conviction, since I know quite well that what I am assuming is not the case. Granted that such a convictionless phenomenon is not a judgment, it might be objected by the opponents of the theory of assumptions that the act under consideration is a presentation. Since the particular example which is used here is obviously negative, the theory of assumptions could be opposed only be introducing the notion of negative presentations. Therefore, Meinong painstakingly argues against the possibility of negative presentations. However, since this part of his first argument in favor of the theory of assumptions is of little interest to Husserl, we shall not dwell on it here. For the sake of brevity the argument just exposited can be called "the argument from convictionless negation".

This argument is put forward in the first chapter of *Über Annahmen*. In Husserl's copy of this work the first chapter bears few annotations. However, in the margin next to the passage where Meinong formulates the concept of assumptions in terms of their place between presentations and judgments, Husserl writes "LU". We are left on our

---

[1] The challenge that Meinong thus makes against the descriptive psychology of Brentano was taken up by Marty, who defended the orthodox classification of psychical phenomena in "Über Annahmen (Ein kritischer Beitrag zur Psychologie, namentlich der deskriptiven)", *Zeitschrift für Psychologie und Physiologie der Sinnesorgane* 40 (1906): 1-54. Meinong replied to Marty in "In Sachen der Annahmen", *Zeitschrift für Psychologie und Physiologie der Sinnesorgane* 41 (1906). In Marty's *Untersuchung zur Grundlegung der allgemeinen Grammatik und Sprachphilosophie* (Halle: Max Niemeyer, 1908) the theory of assumptions is again attacked. It is once again defended by Meinong in the second edition of *Über Annamen* (1910). Against Meinong's proposal to insert the class of assumptions between those of presentations and judgments, Marty insists that this would violate the Aristotelian principle of classification, according to which a given generic class can be divided only by properties that are shared by no other generic class. Since the generic class of judgments is divided into affirmations and negations, it is accordingly impermissible to divide any other generic class into affirmations and negations. It is of course not surprising to find that Meinong does not feel compelled to embrace the Aristotelian principle in question. As far as Husserl's views are concerned, it should be abundantly clear in the above text that he stands closer to Meinong than he does to Marty on the issue of assumptions, in spite of the fact that Marty himself is under the contrary impression because he fails understand Husserl's revised concept of presentations. See *Untersuchung zur Grundlegung der allgemeinen Grammatik und Sprachphilosophie*, p. 245 n.

[2] *Über Annahmen*, 1 ff.

own to find the parallel in the *Logische Untersuchungen* which Husserl has in mind, but the only place in this work where it could be found would be the fifth "Logical Investigation". There the distinction between acts which have the character of belief and those which lack belief comes into play. The acts which lack belief are called "mere presentations" (*blosse Vorstellungen*) (Hua XIX/1, 381, 444, 457, 463 f., 471 f., 504 n., 521). While this class of acts might at least partly co-incide with the class "assumptions", as indeed some of Husserl's annotations suggest, we must be cautious to note that the character of position, as understood by Meinong, is nowhere identified by Husserl as a feature which differentiates some mere presentations from others.

From a consideration of Meinong's second argument for the theory of assumptions and from the views of Husserl which are relevant to this argument it will indeed be seen that certain mere presentations are precisely phenomena which Meinong regards as assumptions. It will also be seen that certain *other* mere presentations cannot be Meinongian assumptions. This will again be apparent in our consideration of Husserl's views in relation to the third argument for the theory of assumptions.

6.2. The Argument from Linguistic Considerations

The second argument which is used in support of the theory of assumptions is based on linguistic considerations.[1] Words, says Meinong, are signs (*Zeichen*) insofar as they allow us to make certain inferences. A sign is the sign of something (X) in the sense that the existence of X can be inferred from the sign. In this sense words are signs of certain psychical phenomena. These phenomena, Meinong prefers to say, are expressed (*ausgedrückt*) by the words. What words express, however, has to be distinguished from what they *mean*, or simply their meaning (*Bedeutung*), and also from the understanding of them in the hearer's consciousness.

While the notion of meaning which is discussed in the present context is not directly relevant to the argument under consideration, this notion must briefly be touched upon here since it proves to be of considerable interest to Husserl. The meaning of a word or complex of words is identified by Meinong as the object of the expressed phenomenon. If I use the words "the sun", it is my *presentation* of the sun which is thereby expressed. The meaning of these words, however, is the sun itself, i.e.,

---

[1] *Ibid.*, 16 ff.

the presented *object*.[1] The identification of the meaning with the object of the presentation, Meinong adds in a footnote,[2] is opposed to the Husserlian conception of meaning due to a narrower concept of an object on Husserl's part. While it is quite understandable that Husserl writes a question mark next to this footnote, what Meinong apparently has in mind here is Husserl's stated preference for the term "objectivity" (*Gegenständlichkeit*) instead of "object" (*Gegenstand*) (Hua XIX/1, 45 n). While Husserl prefers the former term because the latter may suggest a concept which is indeed too *narrow*, this turns out to be irrelevant to his distinction between the sense of an expression and that to which the expression refers. Later on I shall return to this topic of the differing views of meaning which are found in *Über Annahmen* and the *Logische Untersuchungen*. Now let us continue to discuss how Meinong argues for the theory of assumptions on the basis of linguistic considerations.

It is the expression and understanding of sentences (*Sätze*) which, according to Meinong, cannot be accounted for unless we adopt the theory of assumptions. If it is claimed that sentences express judgments, he points out that this is obviously not so in the case of certain whole sentences which can stand on their own, e.g., questions. Moreover, certain dependent clauses are obviously not expressions of judgments. More important here, however, is Meinong's insistence that the *understanding* of sentences, on the part of the person who hears or reads them, cannot be construed as a judging or a presenting of judgments.

First let us consider how he argues against the view that the understanding of a sentence lies in the presentation of the judgment which the sentence in question expresses (if indeed the sentence expresses a judgment). In reply to this view Meinong maintains that the speaker often lies in the background when we understand what he says. This is especially obvious when the speaker is a writer of some printed work. Only if the expressed psychical phenomena are *emotional* ones rather than judgments, says Meinong, is the presentation of them essential to understanding the words of the

---

[1]This is the "Fido"-Fido theory of meaning which Gilbert Ryle ("Intentionality-Theory and the Nature of Thinking", in Rudolf Haller (ed.), *Jenseits von Sein und Nichtsein*, pp. 7-14) not only attributed to Meinong, but also held to be the motivating factor behind Meinong's theory of objects. It has been correctly pointed out by Peter Simons, in "Meinong's Theory of Sense and Reference", *Grazer Philosophische Studien* 50 (1995): 171-186, that this theory of meaning, though indeed at one time espoused by Meinong, is to be completely dissociated from the theory of objects and was later to be abandoned by Meinong and replaced with a much more sophisticated theory. Unfortunately, Husserl had such a low opinion of Meinong after the first edition of *Über Annahmen* that he gave no attention at all to the new theory, as this is found in the second edition (1910) and also in *Über Möglichkeit und Wahrscheinlichkeit* (Leipzig: Johan Ambrosius Barth, 1915). (An exposition of this theory is to be found in the article by Simons just cited.)

[2]*Über Annahmen*, 20 n.

speaker. It is somewhat inappropriate that Husserl marks "LU" next to the passage where the presentation of emotions is singled out as peculiar case of understanding. For even though Husserl briefly touches on the presentation of someone else's psychical phenomena, so-called *Kundnahme*, as part of the communication process (Hua XIX/1, 39 ff.), he does not indicate that such presentations are essential in the case where emotions are expressed. Indeed, he does not even maintain explicitly, as Meinong does, that judgments of the other need not be presented in communication. He only claims that expressions need not function as signs insofar as they can be used in solitary thinking.

Now after Meinong establishes to his own satisfaction that expressed judgments need not be presented in order to understand a sentence, he proceeds to consider whether such understanding is reducible to a duplicate judging on the part of the hearer or reader. Even if it is granted that the sentence in question expresses a judgment, Meinong insists that the hearer or reader need not judge as the speaker or writer does. "I understand the report which is made in good faith by someone notoriously credulous or superstitious, even though I by no means let myself be convinced by him".[1] Since this understanding lacks conviction it cannot be a judgment. Thus Meinong concludes "that where the judgment fails to be of service in this matter, the assumption comes into consideration in its place".[2] Thus, when I understand the report of the credulous or superstitious person, what this brings about in me is an assumption rather than a judgment.

Next to the passage where Meinong points out the possibility of understanding without conviction Husserl marks "LU". Though he does not identify the passage from the *Logische Untersuchungen* which he has in mind here, parallel passages from the "5th Investigation", as already mentioned, are not difficult to find. "That there is for every judgment a presentation which [...] presents the same thing in the same way as the judgment judges," says Husserl, "no one will doubt. For example, corresponding to the judgment 'the earth's mass is roughly 1/325,000 of the sun's mass' is [...] the act which someone performs who hears and understands this expression, but who finds no motive for deciding judgingly" (Hua XIX/1, 462). A presentation of the sort identified by Husserl here is of course precisely an example of a Meinongian assumption. Perhaps this parallel is not so easily seen because Husserl prefers to call phenomena of the kind in question "mere presentations". In this case it may seem as though Husserl stands closer to Brentano than to Meinong. Wherever Husserl cannot identify an

---

[1] *Ibid.*, p. 33.

[2] *Ibid.*, p. 34.

intellectual phenomenon as a judgment, one may think, he feels compelled to regard it as a presentation. However, the context of the passage just cited from the *Logische Untersuchungen* is precisely an argument against Brentano's claim that mere presentations are the foundations of other acts. As it turns out, Husserl does work out a conception of presentations which assigns to them a fundamental status in psychical life. But presentations in this sense differ from presentations in the Brentanian sense. Some presentations, according to Husserl, are themselves judgments insofar as they have the character of belief, whereas others are mere presentations which do not serve as the foundations for judgments and include at least some of the phenomena called "assumptions" by Meinong.

Some mere presentations in the Husserlian sense, on the other hand, cannot fit into Meinong's class of assumptions. In this regard we may consider another example of a mere presentation, namely the presentation which is left over after one realizes that one has been deceived (Hua XIX/1, 458 f.). Already in the first chapter we have encountered Husserl's view on this matter. In a wax museum, we may recall, one may see what looks like a smiling young lady. Initially one may even greet her, only soon to find out that this was only a wax figure. While one may continue to present the young lady, this presentation does not have the character of belief which belonged to the preceding presentation of the same object. From the standpoint of the arguments for the theory of assumptions which have been considered thus far, the convictionless presentation of the young lady need not be an assumption. This presentation is neither negative nor a case of understanding a sentence. Moreover, as will soon be discussed further, both assumptions and judgments, according to Meinong, always have objects of a special type, called "objectives".[1] Objects of this type can be picked out by applying expressions of the form "that such and such is the case". While the convictionless understanding of a sentence may certainly be construed as a phenomenon that has an objective as its object, this is not the case when the object in question is simply and straightforwardly *a young lady*.

It is therefore apparent that Husserl's class of mere presentations include phenomena which are not Meinongian assumptions. It will now be seen that certain Meinongian assumptions are likewise *excluded* from Husserl's class of mere presentations.

---

[1] *Ibid.*, 155 ff.

6.3. The Argument from the Grasp of Formal Validity

The third argument is made from the fact that we can grasp the formal validity of an inference without actually accepting the premises or the conclusion.[1] In this case the inference cannot be construed as the derivation of one judgment from other. Indeed, we may even grasp formal validity where the premises and the conclusion actually contradict our judgments. Accordingly Meinong prefers to speak of a "quasi-inference" here. It might be suggested that such quasi-inferences are reducible to hypothetical judgments, but it must be asked how such judgments are to be described. If they are actual judgments, then they cannot be expressed by the antecedent or by the consequent; rather, the judgment must be about a special if-then connection. But Meinong finds it impossible in most cases to identify the members which are thus connected. It cannot be a connection between the judgment expressed in the antecedent and the one expressed in the consequent, for these, he insists, do not exist and are often not even presented.[2] The only feasible alternative which he sees here is to construe quasi-inferences and most instances of so-called hypothetical judgments as *assumptive* inferences (*Annahmeschlüsse*). Where the premise (or antecedent) and conclusion (or consequent) could not reasonably be regarded as judgments or as presentations of judgments, there is no difficulty in considering them to be assumptions. Just as one judgment can motivate another, one assumption can motivate another. The evidence which obtains in the grasp of formal validity is accordingly attributed by Meinong to an assumptive inference. In this way he further departs from Brentanian orthodoxy in which evidence in the strict sense is attributed only to judgments.

Now if we look at Husserl's criticism of the argument just exposited, it is seen that certain instances of Meinongian assumptions are viewed very differently by Husserl. This is especially true with regard to so-called quasi-inferences. According to Husserl, the grasp of formal validity has absolutely nothing to do with an inference, either genuine or "quasi", for this grasping is simply an evident general judgment. In the margin of one of the passages from *Über Annahmen* (p. 78) where Meinong speaks of the quasi-inference Husserl thus writes the following: "In the mode *Barbara* etc. we have

---

[1] *Ibid.*, 61 ff.

[2] Missing here is the consideration of the alternative that objectives are the connected members. This alternative is adopted later by Meinong in *Über die Stellung der Gegenstandstheorie im System der Wissenschaften* (1907), p. 44, where he concedes in a footnote that in *Über Annahmen* he had been insufficiently confident in the notion of the objective. The observation that Meinong must have discovered the objective in the course of writing *Über Annahmen* is made in Grossmann, *Meinong* (London: Routledge, 1974), 79 ff.

no premises, but premise-forms. There is no inference or quasi-inference (under assumption), but rather a general law of inference. That, however, is no hypothetical, but rather a general judgment".[1] When we grasp formal validity, on Husserl's view, we see that *all* premises of a certain form yield conclusions of a certain form. This logical insight is therefore by no means an assumption of any kind, but rather a judgment, more particularly a general judgment. What such a judgment is *about*, on Husserl's view, will be discussed briefly soon.

The fact that Husserl regards the grasp of formal validity as explained above must not be taken to mean that he does not allow for quasi-inferences (or assumptive inferences). This much is clear not only from certain annotations in his copy of *Über Annahmen* and from the above-cited letter to Meinong, but also from the 1894 text on intentional objects. According to his position in this text, we often state claims categorically without expressing certain assumptions or hypotheses on which they are based.[2] We say, for instance, that Zeus is the highest Olympian god without adding "according to Greek mythology". This is often the case when we speak from the standpoint of myth, fiction, religion, and even a good part of science, especially mathematics. While Husserl accordingly seems to allow for assumptive inferences in a sense which could not be alien to Meinong, it is also worth pointing out that in the above-cited letter to Meinong he claims quite explicitly (*Briefwechsel* I, 142 f.):

The assumptions [*Assumptionen*], i.e., the assumptions in the *proper* sense [*die eigentlichen Annahmen*], and the belief-acts which are performed *under* assumption I quite deliberately separate from the merely propositional presentations [...], the cases of straightforwardly understanding sentences - since I believe that I here find a descriptive difference.

Here Husserl clearly differentiates certain instances of Meinongian assumptions, including at least assumptive inferences, from the convictionless understanding of sentences as highlighted in Meinong's second argument for the theory of assumptions.

It is difficult to know what to make of this differentiation. Since objectifying acts are divided into those which have the character of belief on the one hand and mere presentations on the other, according to Husserl's view in the *Logische Untersuchungen*, we would expect that the only other acts would be emotions, desires, and the like, i.e., the ones *founded* on objectifying acts (presentations in the broad Husserlian sense).

---

[1] "Im Modus Barbara u.dgl. haben wir keine Prämissen, sondern Prämissenformen. Es liegt kein Schluss oder Quasischluss vor (unter Annahme), sondern ein generelles Schlussgesetz. Das aber ist kein hypothetisches Urteil, sondern eben ein generelles".

[2] Husserl, "Intentionale Gegenstände", 151 ff.

But the assumptive inferences would be excluded from both classes. Part of the difficulty here lies in the fact Husserl never managed to work the results of his 1894 text into the *Logische Untersuchungen*. In the above-cited letter to Meinong he says that he plans to work on the phenomenology of hypothetical judgment further. From the texts available to us within the present scope, however, the separation between assumptive inference and the convictionless understanding of sentences must remain an unsettled matter.

6.4. Objectives and Meanings

We have thus far examined three arguments for the Meinongian theory of assumptions and the views of Husserl which are relevant to these arguments. We have also seen important divergences in their attempts to describe many of the same phenomena. Before closing this discussion regarding Meinong and Husserl on assumptions, I should like to explore this matter further from the objective side.

It has already been mentioned above that the objects of assumptions and judgments, according Meinong, are objectives (*Objektive*) rather than objects in the narrow sense (*Objekte*). While Husserl speaks of states of affairs (*Sachlagen, Sachverhalte*)[1] rather than of objectives, he also identifies objects of this kind as the correlates of judging and the convictionless understanding of sentences (Hua XIX/1, 416, 453, 462, 477 ff.). But there is at least one important difference in their views on the intentional reference to states of affairs. According to Meinong, this reference can only be found in judgments and assumptions and in certain feelings and desires based on them. If we view sentences as the linguistic expressions which convey judgments and assumptions, as indeed suggested by Meinong, it can be said that on his view objectives are the objects which sentences *mean*. In this case, however, the question inevitably arises whether objectives (or states of affairs) cannot also be the objects of *names*. According to Husserl, they can (Hua XIX/1, 490 ff.). Our propositional presentations, he maintains, can be *nominalized*. We can, for instance, regard a state of affairs as a subject of certain predications. We might say, for example: "The fact that it has rained will please the farmer". The subject of the judgment here is *the fact that it has rained*. While Meinong certainly acknowledges the possibility of one objective being included in another, as it were, he fails to see the relevance of this to the question whether objectives can be named. His allocation of objectives to every kind of act *but*

---

[1] In Hua XXVI, 29 f., a distinction is made between *Sachverhalt* and *Sachlage*, but these terms are used synonymously in the *Logische Untersuchungen*.

a presentation and his concomitant identification of objects in the narrow sense as the proper correlates of presentations are clear indications that nominalization has no place in his theory of acts. In this regard he clearly differs from Husserl.

In *Über Annahmen* Meinong claims to have clarified a good deal under the heading "objective", a good deal which his predecessors had allegedly left unclear. Among the properties which he ascribes to states of affairs are truth, possibility, necessity, and probability, all of which prove to be of crucial importance for logic and epistemology. In this connection he says that Husserl's defence of a pure logic seems to arise from "insights which concur with what has been said here about the objective in quite essential points".[1] Accordingly, Meinong thinks that his ascription of truth and of the modal properties to the objective, instead of the judgment or indeed mental acts of any kind, is the way out of psychologism. In a footnote he adds that in the *Logische Untersuchungen* Husserl "did not mark off the concept of the objective terminologically" and "repeatedly avails himself [...] of the figurative meaning of the word 'proposition', through which, if I am right, language has already for the longest time given testimony, though long unnoticed, for the objective."[2] Next to this footnote Husserl wrote a large question mark in his copy of *Über Annahmen*.

Though the reasons for his objection to Meinong's charge are not stated, they are clear enough to those familiar with Husserl's views in the *Logische Untersuchungen*. As we have already noted, Husserl calls the objects which may be referred to by that-clauses "states of affairs". Hence, he is exonerated from the charge of failing to mark off the objective terminologically. Moreover, Meinong's suggestion that Husserl was groping towards the notion of the objective under the heading "proposition" may also be dismissed, once it is recognized that propositions are characterized in the *Logische Untersuchungen* as meanings (*Bedeutungen*) of a certain type and therefore distinguishable from states of affairs. Meanings as such, says Husserl, are to be differentiated from the objects of reference, as this is made clear from cases where meanings differ while the object remains the same and vice-versa. A case in point is of course Husserl's famous example of the expressions "victor at Jena" and "vanquished

---

[1] *Über Annahmen*, p. 197: "Insbesondere darf ich hier nicht unerwähnt lassen, dass mir E. Husserls Eintreten für die 'reine Logik' Einsichten zu entspringen scheint, die mit dem hier über das Objektiv Dargelegten in ganz wesentlichen Punkten zusammenstimmen [...]". Husserl underlines this passage beginning with his name, with particular emphasis on the word "scheint".

[2] *Ibid.*, p. 197 n.: "Ohne dass übrigens der genannte Autor den Begriff des Objektivs terminologisch ausgeprägt hätte. Er bedient sich wiederholt [...] der übertragenen Bedeutung des Wortes 'Satz', durch die, wenn ich recht sehe, die Sprache längst schon für das Objektiv ein nur lange unbeachtet gebliebenes Zeugnis abgelegt hat". Here Meinong refers to pages of the first edition of the *Logische Untersuchungen* I which can be found in Hua XVIII, 180 f. n., XIX, pp. 99 ff.

at Waterloo" which both refer to the same object, but differ in meaning (Hua XIX/1, 53). While this example illustrates the difference between meaning and object in connection with *names*, the same difference is to be found in *sentences*.

The object of a sentence, according to Husserl, is a state of affairs, whereas the meaning thereof is a proposition. To stress once again what this amounts to according to Husserl: the sentence is an expression which is given meaning by an act, e.g., an act of judging, which *intends* the state of affairs, whereas the meaning is the species which this act (or part thereof) *instantiates*. Moreover, it must be noted that Husserl ascribes truth and falsity to propositions, not to states of affairs. Accordingly, when logic treats inferences and their validity or invalidity, what is under consideration here is how certain propositions relate to each other. In this connection we can make sense of Husserl's claim that the laws of inference are generalizations. If the mode Barbara, for instance, is seen to be a valid form of inference, this is a generalization about the relations which obtain among certain propositions or, better, propositional forms.

In *Über Annahmen* we find nothing like Husserl's distinction between propositions and states of affairs. This failure to make such a distinction can moreover be attributed to the failure to make the more general distinction between the meaning of an expression and its object.[1] While we may have misgivings about the way in which Husserl regards this distinction, namely as one between the species of an act (or part thereof) and the object which the act intends, it should be conceded that this distinction should in some way be accepted. Since Meinong allows only for states of affairs (objectives) and not for corresponding propositions, it is difficult to see how he can account for cases where the meaning of a sentence can vary while the object remains the same, e.g., in the case of the following two sentences: "the sum of the angles of an equiangular triangle is equal to the sum of two right angles" and "the sum of the angles of an equilateral triangle is equal to the sum of two right angles".

Should we then say that Meinong made no progress at all in his investigations of the objective and that Husserl had already advanced far beyond him in this regard? I do not think so, for we must remember that Meinong attributes not only truth and falsity, but also possibility, necessity, and probability, to objectives. While it may be left open whether this aspect of his theory of the objective is acceptable, it must at least be said that he thereby offers a suggestion on an issue which Husserl leaves untouched. The notions of possibility, necessity, and probability are, after all, hardly thematized in the *Logische Untersuchungen*. Thus, we must not let Husserl give us the impression that he

---

[1] Given Husserl's peculiar conception of meanings as species, it may be said that the difference between him and Meinong which is observed in the text is closely related to another difference between them: Husserl's Platonistic realism vs. Meinong's conceptualism.

had more adequately dealt with all the problems which are addressed in *Über Annahmen*, for some of these problems had not even been mentioned in the *Logische Untersuchungen*.

6.5. Conclusion

We have examined three arguments for Meinong's theory of assumptions. In our consideration of Husserlian views which are relevant to these arguments it has been seen that their descriptions of the phenomena under consideration overlap only to some extent. Such a partial overlap is again seen when we turn to the objective side of acts. Since Husserl has emerged as the more prominent and influential philosopher, it is only natural for us to prefer his views where there is no overlap. I would suggest however that we proceed cautiously in this respect. For Husserl's views on assumptions are still in need of considerable clarification and perhaps revision. This is especially seen in his separation between the convictionless understanding of sentences and so-called proper assumptions. Such a remark indicates that his views are by no means finished and complete while Meinong is left toiling behind. Moreover, we must not let Meinong's deficient views on meaning, as these are found in the first edition of *Über Annahmen*, prevent us from appreciating his description of acts. His failure to distinguish meaning from object (or reference) occurs in a context where little damage is done to his psychological position. And if one prefers an austere ontology, then Husserl's views on this matter are hardly palatable, since they commit us to *species* as objects in their own right. Above all, however, it must be said that Meinong's theory of assumptions, as unsatisfactory as it is, could have met with a more friendly reception from Husserl. A fruitful exchange of ideas could have then come about. As matters stand, it is up to Meinongians, Husserlians, and those who sympathize with both to continue thinking through the topic of assumptions and related matters without falling prey to petty concerns about who was the more original.

7. *ÜBER GEGENSTANDSTHEORIE* (1904)

All the works by Meinong considered thus far have been concerned in one way or another with psychological matters. What Meinong is famous for nowadays, however, is not his psychology, but rather his theory of objects. This theory was fully announced as a program in 1904 in "Über Gegenstandstheorie".[1] Meinong sent a copy of this work along with a letter to Husserl on 6 December 1904 (*Briefwechsel* I, 147 f.), to which Husserl responded in a perfunctory way in 11 December 1904 (*Briefwechsel* I, 149). Nevertheless, Husserl read the text, as the underlinings and annototations in his copy and substantial excerpts bear witness.[2] As he was convinced that he had pioneered the notion of assumptions in the *Logische Untersuchungen*, he was also convinced that he had stated the basic program of a theory of objects (under the heading "pure logic") in the *Prolegomena* and made a substantial contribution to this discipline in the third "Logical Investigation".

7.1. Comparison with the Logischen Untersuchungen

The question which is posed at the outset of "Über Gegenstandstheorie" is:

where the scientific treatment of the object as such and in its generality, properly speaking, has its, so to speak, justifiable place, i.e., the question whether there is among the sciences accredited by the scientific tradition one in which the attempt could be made to deal with the object as such or from which this could at least be required.[3]

While it might be suggested that metaphysics is the "science" sought after here, it is construed by Meinong as a discipline concerned "with the totality of that which exists".[4] From this it follows, however, that it cannot be the science which deals with the object as such, for some objects do not exist at all. Here we must keep in mind that existence for Meinong is the same as actuality, i.e., restricted to the temporally determinate. Ideal objects, such as equality and difference, are altogether timeless and therefore excluded from the purview of metaphysics. The objects of mathematics, for

---

[1]This essay was first published in volume edited by Meinong himself, *Untersuchung zur Gegenstandstheorie und Psychologie* (Leipzig: Johan Ambrosius Barth, 1904). As far as contributions to the theory of objects are concerned, the volume contains two others by pupils of Meinong in addition to his own essay. An offprint of one of these contributions, namely "Untersuchung zur Gegenstandstheorie des Messens" by Ernst Mally (pp. 121-262), is to be found in Husserl's private library. Though the first twenty pages of it bear markings and annotations, these are not substantial enough to warrent a discussion of Husserl's reaction to Mally's early contribution to the theory of objects.

[2]The excerpts are to be found K III 33/35-46.

[3]"Über Gegenstandstheorie", p. 3. This passage is for the most part marked in Husserl's copy.

[4]*Ibid.*, 5. "was existiert" is underlined in Husserl's copy.

instance, are ideal. But Meinong adds that the objects which do not exist need not be ideal. Our "prejudice in favor of the actual" (*Vorurteil zugunsten des Wirklichen*) keeps us from taking into consideration not only ideal objects, but also objects which neither real nor ideal, e.g., the golden mountain or the round square.[1]

Before we enter into Husserl's opposition against Meinongianism as such (i.e., the view that some objects do not have being of any kind), remarks on a few other points are appropriate. It may be observed, first of all, that metaphysics had already been restricted to considerations of the real in the *Prolegomena zur reinen Logik* (Hua XVIII, 26 f.). This is however no surprise when we take into account that Husserl had learned from Stumpf the following: "Metaphysics is the science of the universal determinations and laws of the actual, the real".[2] As it turns out, this is the conception of metaphysics which Stumpf had learned from Lotze, who had presented his system of philosophy in metaphysics and logic as two distinct parts. The consideration of ideal objects is saved for the second of these parts.[3] Given the immense influence of Lotze, it is no wonder that Meinong, too, exhibits this in his conception of a theory of objects.

We may further take notice of Husserl's reaction to Höfler's review of the volume in which "Über Gegenstandstheorie" was first published.[4] From Husserl's *Nachlass* it is evident that he resents not only Höfler's characterization of Meinong's own contribution to this volume as "a theoretical grounding of 'antipsychologism'",[5] but also the following reminiscences:

From personal memories and impressions I add that, when Husserl orally characterized for me the contents of his *Logische Untersuchungen* prior to their appearance by saying that he aimed at a universalized mathematics (and thereby also stressed the antipsychologistic aim), I could by no means at once get away from the prejudice that the mathematical method fits only the mathematical content. In fact still even now that content of Husserl's embracing work which again sounds psychological [i.e., most of the second volume] does not make it easy also for the antipsychologistically inclined reader to find alongside this

---

[1] *Ibid.*, pp. 3 ff.

[2] Q 10: "Metaphysik ist die Wissenschaft von den allgemeinen Bestimmungen und Gesetzen des Wirklichen, des Realen". This statement comes from Husserl's notes from Stumpf's lecture on metaphysics (undated, but no doubt from c. 1886/87), which are included in a notebook together with notes from Marty's lecture on genetic psychology (1889) and fragmentary notes from Brentano's lecture on descriptive psychology (1887). The pages of this notebook are unnumbered.

[3] Lotze, *Logik*, §§ 313-321.

[4] The review is published in *Zeitschrift für Psychologie und Physiologie der Sinnesorgane* 42 (1906): 192-207.

[5] *Ibid.*, p. 192.

negation the positive unifying element of what is offered and to see it especially as expanded mathematics, perhaps as a system of relations especially made free from quatitative considerations.[1]

The misgivings which Höfler expresses here, namely that the apparently psychological investigations in the second volume of the *Logische Untersuchungen* seem to be inconsistent with the anti-psychologism of the first volume, were shared by others. In this regard it is understandable why Meinong is given credit by Höfler for the theoretical grounding of anti-psychologism, for the discipline projected in "Über Gegenstandstheorie" does not contain any psychological remnants at all.

However we regard the two volumes of the *Logische Untersuchungen* in relation to each other, the characterization which Höfler had claimed to hear from the author is one that Husserl emphatically denies:[2]"Everyone who knows this work immediately sees the *nonsense* in this characterization and will therefore never be able to believe that I have ever given this characterization orally. And of course I have never given it". While it may be granted that it was not Husserl's aim to work out an expanded mathematics, we may nonetheless ask whether the pure logic which Husserl projected should be regarded in this way. The answer to this question is that it should not. Whereas mathematics can include a good deal of the material *a priori*, pure logic in both of its branches, i.e., the one concerned with meaning-categories and the other concerned with object-categories, is to be a purely formal discipline. The latter branch of logic, which comes closest to Meinong's theory of objects, is indeed called "formal ontology" in the second edition of the *Logische Untersuchungen* (Hua XIX/1, 228) and later writings (Hua III/1, 26 f., 37, 126 f., 274, 312, 337, 342 f.; Hua XVII, 16, 50, 80, 82 ff., 88 ff., 92, 111, 115 f., 124 f., 148 ff., 153, 157, 183, 188, 231, 277 f.). Meinong's theory of objects, by contrast, is to encompass all *a priori* disciplines and is therefore to include a good deal more than statements about the object *as such*. In this regard it may be said that Husserl's division between material and formal disciplines is

---

[1]*Ibid.*, p. 194: "Aus persönlichen Erinnerungen und Eindrücken füge ich bei, dass, als mir Husserl vor dem Erscheinen seiner 'Logischen Untersuchungen' deren Inhalt mündlich dahin charakterisierte, dass er eine verallgemeinerte Mathematik beabsichtige (und dabei auch die antipsychologische Absicht hervorhob), ich keineswegs sogleich loskommen konnte von dem Vorurteil, die mathematische Methode passe eben nur auf den hergebrachten mathematischen Inhalt. In der Tat macht es auch jetzt noch der zu so grossem Teile geradezu doch wieder psychologisch anmutende Inhalt von Husserls umfassenden Werk auch dem dem antipsychologistisch gestimmten Leser nicht leicht, neben dieser Negation das positive Einheitliche des Gebotenen zu verspüren und es insbesondere als erweiterte Mathematik, ewa als ein speziell von Quantitativem frei gemachtes Relationssystem zu erkennen".

[2]K III 33/12 a: "Jeder Kenner dieses Werkes sieht unmittelbar den *Unsinn* dieser Charakteristik ein und wird daher nie glauben können, dass *ich* diese Charakteristik jemals mündlich gegeben hätte. Und selbstverständlich habe ich sie nicht gegeben."

sadly missing from Meinong's philosophy.

7.2. The Principle of Independence

While Husserl in some sense allows for a theory of objects, he has misgivings about Meinong's attempt to overcome the prejudice in favor of the actual. The claim that objects as such need not have any being at all, not even ideal being, is regarded as unacceptable by Husserl. In this regard he criticizes Meinong's celebrated principle of independence (*Unabhängigkeitsprinzip*), according to which an object can have being-thus without having being of any kind.[1] The classic example is to be found in the being-golden of the golden mountain. The golden mountain has being-thus, i.e., being-golden, but it neither exists nor subsists.

In this connection we may be reminded of Twardowski's rejection of the Bolzanian doctrine of objectless presentations. We may recall that a presentation such as "round square", on Twardowski's view, has an object and that this object must moreover not be identified with the *content* of the presentation. The reason why it cannot be identified with the content lies in the fact that the content *exists* whereas that which is both round and square does not (and cannot) exist. Perhaps the only differences between Meinong and Twardowski are to be found in 1) the fact that Twardowski considers the matter primarily from the psychological side (thereby claiming that all presentations have objects) whereas Meinong does not do so (thereby claiming that some objects do not exist), and 2) the fact that Twardowski fails to give an adequate formulation of the objective from Meinong's standpoint. If, however, we look at the matter from the objective side and also formulate the concept of the objective as Meinong proposes (thereby dissociating it from the content), the move from Twardowski's proto-Meinongianism to full-blown Meinongianism is hardly avoidable.

As Husserl had opposed the former, he accordingly opposes the latter. But the argument which he uses against Meinong's principle of independence in the following previously unpublished text differs from the argument which had been used against Twardowski:

> What now should the principle say? That something can in truth be such and such without this something being? That the predicative state of affairs can in truth have subsistence without its subject truly being? This is certainly fundamentally wrong.
> The example of the geometrical figure of course means nothing here. For a geometrical state of affairs subsists only if the figures in question exist in the geometrical sense, if they "are", just as the geometer and

---

[1] "Über Gegenstandstheorie", pp. 8 f.

the mathematician as such never utters - and may never utter - a sentence without having first conducted the existential proof for the subject or the subjects thereof.

If, however, it is said that the figure does not exist really, and if the "principle" is interpreted as independence of the being-thus from being in the sense of "existence", that is all the more wrong: for of course every categorical judgment includes the being of *that* subject which it *has*. And if the subject is a real one, then the being is a being of the real, i.e., in the Meinongian sense "existence"; if an ideal one, then being of the ideal, and thus not "existence". If Meinong would try to explain away the being of the figures somehow, or believe that he escapes it through the interpretation of the being of figures as possibility, or in any other way whatever, the new sentence, which has arisen from the interpretation, provided that it still has categorical form, would have again its subjects, and these would have to *be* in order to be able to be *thus*. E.g. also regarding possibility I can make only categorical assertions, but in truth only if the possibility *is*.

Being-thus can itself again be subject of predications. If these are to be true, that which functions as subject must subsist. The assertion "the golden Mont Blanc is golden" is either true and the golden Mont Blanc in this case *is*, or the assertion is false. Likewise with the example of the round square. If I say "the round square is round" in the sense such as "the triangle has as the sum of its angles ...", there lies in this as an implication that there is a figure "round square" (in the specific and geometrical sense). At all events it could be said that the sense of the categorical judgment implies the positing of the subject, and indeed essentially, and accordingly the claim "A is B" implies the view that A is. Likewise the truth that A is B [implies] the truth of "A is". Now the objection of falsehood is directed as a rule against that which the sentence means to say in a special sense, i.e., newly, and not against that which it merely presupposes. And accordingly, in retaining the normal sense of this form of speech, only the one who believes that there "are" round squares (of course in the geometrical sense, which says nothing of the existence of real things in world space) can express himself in this way. So much regarding the newly discovered principle.[1]

---

[1] K III 33/46: "Was sollte nun das Prinzip sagen? Es könne in Wahrheit irgendetwas so und so beschaffen sein, ohne dass dieses Etwas ist? Es könne der prädikative katoregorische Sachverhalt in Wahrheit Bestand haben, ohne dass sein Subjekt wahrhaft ist? Das ist sicher grundfalsch.

"Das Beispiel der geometrischen Figur besagt hier natürlich nichts. Denn ein geometrischer Sachverhalt besteht nur, wenn die betreffenden Figuren im geometrischen Sinne existieren, wenn sie 'sind', wie denn der Geometer und der Mathematiker überhaupt niemals einen Satz ausspricht und aussprechen darf, ohne dass er den Existentialbeweis für das Subjekt oder die Subjekte desselben geführt hat.

"Sagt man aber, die Figur existiert nicht real, und interpretiert man das 'Prinzip' als Unabhängigkeit des Soseins vom Sein im Sinne der 'Existenz', so ist das erst recht verkehrt: denn natürlich schliesst jedes kategorische Urteil das Sein *des* Subjekts ein, das es *hat*. Und ist das Subjekt ein Reales, so ist das Sein Sein des Realen, also im Meinong'schen Sinne 'Existenz'; ist es ein Ideales [instead of 'Sein eines Idealen'], so eben Sein des Idealen, und dann eben nicht 'Existenz'. Würde Meinong das Sein der Figuren irgendwie wegzudeuten suchen, oder glauben ihm zu entgehen durch Interpretation des Seins der Figuren als Möglichkeit, und wie immer, so hätte der neue Satz, der aus Interpretation hervorgegangen ist, wenn er noch kategorische Form hat, wieder seine Subjekte, und diese müssten sein, um so sein zu können. Z.B. auch über Möglichkeit kann ich nur kategorisch aussagen, aber in Wahrheit nur, wenn die Möglichkeit eben ist.

"Das Sosein kann selbst wieder Subjekt von Prädikationen sein. Sollen diese wahr sein, so muss das als Subjekt Fungierende bestehen. Die Aussage: 'der goldene Mont Blanc ist aus Gold' ist entweder wahr, dann ist der goldene Mont Blanc, oder sie ist falsch. Ebenso mit dem runden Viereck-Beispiel. Sage ich: 'Das runde Viereck ist rund' in dem Sinne wie 'Das Dreieck hat zur Winkelsumme...', so liegt darin als Implikation, dass es eine Figur 'rundes Viereck' gibt (im spezifischen, und geometrischen Sinne). Allenfalls wäre zu sagen, dass der Sinn des kategorischen Urteils die Subjektsetzung impliziert, und zwar wesentlich, und dass demgemäss die Behauptung, A sei B, die Meinung, es sei A, impliziert. Ebenso die Wahrheit, es sei A B, die Wahrheit des: es sei A. Nun richtet sich der Einwand der Falschheit in der Regel gegen das, was der Satz im besonderen Sinn, nämlich neu sagen will, und nicht gegen das, was er bloss voraussetzt. Und demgemäss kann, bei Erhaltung des normalen Sinnes dieser Redeform, nur derjenige, der glaubt, es 'gebe'

Now let us consider the gist of this argument, especially in contrast with the one used against Twardowski in "Intentionale Gegenstände". As we may recall, Husserl argued that not every presentation, strictly and properly speaking, has an object because otherwise a division would have to be made between existent and nonexistent objects. This division, however, can be made only in an improper sense, namely insofar as it is derived from the division between objectual and objectless presentations. By contrast with this argument, the above-cited passage involves a particular conception of being. According to this conception, an object *is* simply insofar as it is the subject of a true categorical affirmation. This is indeed the Lotzean conception of being (i.e., being as *Geltung*) which lies behind the Platonism of the *Logische Untersuchungen*.

It is of course obvious that from this standpoint the principle of independence is unacceptable. If "the golden mountain is golden" is true and accordingly the *being-golden* of the golden mountain obtains, it follows the golden mountain has *being simpliciter*. It is moreover clear why Husserl needs this theory of being or, in any case, additional artillery against Meinong. While he could argue against Twardowski that the *presentation* of the golden mountain need not in any way be construed as objectual in the proper sense, Meinong shifts the whole matter to a consideration of objectives and the acts to which these objectives correspond. As we may recall, the acts in question cannot be presentations, for objectives are characteristically correlated with *judgments* and *assumptions*. These acts are of course expressed (or "manifested") in declarative sentences. Meinong comes up with sentences such as the "the golden mountain is golden" in order to support his principle or, in any case, to make it more palatable than it would otherwise be. In this light, however, Husserl's appeal to the Lotzean conception of being is somewhat unsatisfactory, because it allows for no clear-cut account of the apparent tautological nature of such a sentence. If, however, we here apply the argument which had been used against Twardowski, things look much more promising. What we are to "assume" in this case is that the golden mountain exists. If this assumption were correct, then it would necessarily follow that the golden mountain is golden. If, by contrast, the assumption from which we start is Greek mythology, it does not necessarily follow that Zeus is the highest Olympian god. Greek mythology, after all, could have been different. It is impossible, however, for the golden mountain not to be golden if it exists. In this way the tautological nature of this case can be preserved while full-blown Meinongianism is nonetheless rejected along with Twardowski's weak immanentism. Moreover, this approach does not involve Platonism.

---

runde Vierecke (natürlich im geometrischen Sinn, der nicht von der Existenz realer Dinge im Weltraum spricht) sich so ausdrücken. Soviel über das neu entdeckte Prinzip."

It is also worth adding here that the standpoint of 1894 was developed a decade prior to the transcendental turn. This is stressed here in light of a tendency to regard Husserl's transcendentalism, with its so-called *epoché*, as both an actual cure for certain (if not all) philosophical ills and as already implicit in Husserl's early work. If Meinongianism is considered to be a philosophical ill (as it indeed usually is), those who are affected by this tendency might accordingly believe that the ill in question can be avoided by means of the *epoché*.[1] From the foregoing it should be clear that it can be effectively dealt with by pursuing the line of argument taken in "Intentionale Gegenstände" and thus from a psychological point of view, not a transcendental one.

8. *ÜBER DIE STELLUNG DER GEGENSTANDSTHEORIE IM SYSTEM DER WISSENSCHAFTEN* (1907)

Though Husserl has very little to say in connection with this text, it is interesting to note that one of the objections which Meiong raises against Ernst Mach is adopted in *Ideen* I without any mention at all of either Meinong or Mach.

The objection in question concerns the notion of the "thought-experiment" (*Gedankenexperiment*) which plays a central role in Mach's conception of the sciences as essentially unified.[2] In opposition to any attempt to see a sharp division between *a priori* sciences, such as mathematics, and *a posteriori* ones, such as physics, Mach insists that, while not all sciences do not involve experiments in the laboratory, all of them require us to perform experiments in thought. In geometry, for instance, we often picture various figures and changes thereof in order to obtain insight into the matter at hand. Meinong however objects that the talk of thought-experiments is equivocal, for it can refer to experiments *on* thought, as these occur in psychology, or it can be used to modify the term "experiment". In the latter sense a thought-experiment is no more than an *imagined* experiment, which is in fact not an experiment at all.[3] Since Mach is by no means inclined to regard thought-experiments as psychological experiments in the proper sense, he is, according to Meinong, left with no choice but to say that the

---

[1]This is in fact suggested in David Carr, *Interpreting Husserl: Critical and Comparative Studies* (Dordrecht: Martinus Nijhoff, 1987), pp. 161 ff. Carr also says, "While the *epoché* as a methodological tool is explicitly formulated in the *Ideas*, it is already at work in the *Logical Investigations*. Only on this assumption can we make sense of what Husserl says there about perception and related topics" (*ibid.*, p. 133). Hopefully one of the results of the present study is the refutation of this claim.

[2]See Mach, *Erkenntnis und Irrtum* (Leipzig, 1905), pp. 180 ff.

[3]*Über die Stellung der Gegenstandstheorie im System der Wissenschaften*, pp. 67-77.

alleged experiments which are conducted in mathematics are in fact not experiments in the proper sense. Accordingly the division between the *a priori* and the *a posteriori* must remain as sharp as ever.

Now we may recall that this very division is of great importance to Husserl in *Ideen* I under the title "sciences of essence and sciences of fact". It is moreover widely known that the sciences of essence on his view involve exercises in imagination for the sake of grasping *a priori* truths. The question whether "we owed geometrical insights [for instance] to 'phantasy experience', [whether] we performed them as *inductions from phantasy experiments*" is asked in this connection, as if it were raised by an opponent, and answered as follows by Husserl (Hua III/1, 52):

But why, according to our counter-question, does the physicist make no use of such wonderful phantasy experience? Certainly because experience in the imagination would be imagined experiments, just as figures, motions, sets in phantasy would be imagined rather than actual ones.

The opponent here seems to be Mach and the response nothing more than Meinong's response to Mach regarding the matter under discussion.[1] This is not to say that Husserl deliberately plagiarized, for the passage just quoted was, after all, written years later than 1907.[2] It is nonetheless important here to note how much Husserl and Meinong have in common in their sharp division between *a apriori* and *a posteriori* sciences in opposition against empiricists and positivists such as John Stuart Mill and Ernst Mach.

9. CONCLUDING REMARKS

From the above considerations of the Husserl-Meinong relation it is obvious to see why Husserl said the following in 1906: "We are like two travellers in one and the same dark region of the world. Of course, we often see the same thing and describe it, but differently in accordance with our respectively different masses of apperception" (Hua XXIV, 444). This is seen time and again, from their early attempts to come to grips with the notion of indirect presentations to their conflicting views regarding the theory of objects. What had been said in the conclusion of the discussion regarding Meinong's *Über Annahmen* and Husserl's reaction to this work applies in general to the Husserl-

---

[1] The same point is observed by Meinong (*Alexius Meinong. Ergänzungsband zur Gesamtausgabe*, p. 295) in his notes on *Ideen* I, but without the slightest accusation of plagiarism.

[2] The same can be said about Husserl's usage of the contrast between being (*Sein*) and being-thus (*So-Sein*), which crops up in *Ideen* I (Hua III/1, 100) and is again used in later writings (Hua VI, 160, 188; Hua VII, 80) without any reference to its Meinongian origins.

Meinong relation. Their pioneering journeys into the same dark region of the world could have been more instructive if they had only shared their observations more readily. In any case the ultimate results of their investigations do culminate in genuine disagreements, most notably on whether an objective (or state of affairs) can be named and on whether an object can have being-thus without having being. Regarding the former issue, Husserl seems to adopt the more plausible position. The evidence given by our linguistic practices compells us to conclude that we can indeed name a states of affairs. Moreover, while Husserl's actual attempt to refute the principle of independence leaves much to be desired, the position which he had already worked out in his 1894 essay on intentional objects can nonetheless be developed in a way which effectively deals with this principle without succumbing to immanentism, Platonism, or (what is worse) transcendentalism.

CHAPTER SEVEN

HUSSERL AND MARTY

While Husserl, more than any other pupil of Brentano and more than Brentano himself, has become one of the outstanding philosophical celebraties of the twentieth century, and while Meinong has achieved some sort of shady presence within analytical philosophy, the name of Anton Marty seldom arises in contemporary philosophical literature, whether this be systematic or historical.[1] Nevertheless, Marty was of considerable importance to Husserl. Much of Husserl's early thought, culminating in the *Logische Untersuchungen*, becomes more understandable if it is seen in relation to Marty's philosophical investigations.

Marty was without a doubt Brentano's closest pupil, as regards both their personal and their philosophical relation.[2] Already in 1867, before Marty came to Würzburg, he had received a prize for *Die Lehre des hl. Thomas über die Abstraktion der übersinnlichen Ideen aus den sinnlichen Bildern nebst Darstellung und Kritik der übrigen Erkenntnistheorien* in which he referred to Brentano's dissertation on the Aristotelian doctrine of the different meanings of "being" and criticized Kant, Fichte, and Schelling. Marty's reading of Brentano's dissertation is indeed what prompted him to go to Würzburg where he could attend the lectures of the young priestly *Privatdozent*. Once he began attending these lectures he experienced a transformation. "A new world is opening up to me", he wrote in his diary at the time.[3] Though Marty had already decided to become a Catholic priest, his devotion to Brentano proved stronger than his devotion to the church. He was ordained in 1870, without any awareness of the profound doubts which his mentor was entertaining about the Catholic faith. When he found out that Brentano had left the faith, this was of course a dramatic event for him. As a result, he too left the faith and decided to pursue a philosophical career. This he did by writing a dissertation, *Kritik der Theorien über den Sprachursprung* (1875), under the direction of Lotze and subsequently, thanks to a recommendation of Brentano who had in the meantime become a professor in Vienna,

---

[1]This situation has recently been somewhat rectified in Kevin Mulligan (ed.), *Mind, Meaning and Metaphysics: The Philosophy and Theory of Language of Anton Marty* (Dordrecht: Kluwer, 1990).

[2]The biographical data here are primarily drawn from Oskar Kraus, "Martys Leben und Werke. Eine Skizze", in *Anton Marty. Gesammelte Schriften* I (Halle a.S.: Max Niemeyer, 1918).

[3]*Ibid.*, p. 4: "Eine neue Welt geht mir auf".

obtaining a position at the newly founded university in Czernowitz, where he was made full professor in 1879. In 1880 he was called to Prague, where he stayed for the remainder of his academic career. He was the teacher of Oskar Kraus, Alfred Kastil, and Hugo Bergmann, all of whom played a role in defending the doctrines of Brentano against the heterodoxies of Meinong and Husserl. Though he preferred the earlier teachings of his mentor and accordingly resisted some of the innovations which Brentano introduced in later years, he was always eager to defend these earlier teachings against all attacks.

As already mentioned in the first chapter, Husserl must have met Marty during the summer of 1886 in St. Gilgen. They were also soon to correspond with each other, beginning as early as January 1887, when Husserl was at Halle with Stumpf. As a good Brentanist, Husserl was interested in obtaining lecture notes from Marty, who however wrote that nothing could be learned from them which could not be learned from the lectures of Brentano and Stumpf (*Briefwechsel* I, 70). Nevertheless, Husserl was persitent in his efforts to obtain notes from Marty, for among Husserl's literary remains the notes from Marty's 1889 lecture on genetic psychology can be found.[1] They were not taken from Marty directly, for they are were copied out by Husserl's wife from C. Deetjen. Little is known about Deetjen, except that he was a doctor at Bad Nassau in 1904, when he attended the psychology congress at Giessen, and later at Wilhelmshöhe bei Kassel in 1914, when he attended the psychology congress at Göttingen. In any case he functioned as a liaison between Marty and Husserl.

There are two works by Marty which are of the utmost importance for understanding his relation with Husserl.[2] The first of these is the series of articles called "Über subjectlose Sätze" (1884/94-95). The fact that Husserl had his copies of these articles bound together in a single volume shows how important they were to him. The many marks and annotations in this volume also indicate that he read them quite thoroughly. This is also is indicated by his report of the fourth and fifth articles (Hua XXII, 135 f.) and again his report of the sixth and seventh articles (Hua XXII, 236-258). While the first of these reports is perfunctory in character (in spite of the friendly attitude which it conveys), the second one contains some critical remarks which will prove to be of some significance here. Moreover, in the back of the volume in which

---

[1] These notes are to be found in are in Q 10.

[2] Besides the writings by Marty mentioned in the text, there is one other to which Husserl refers in the *Logische Untersuchungen* (Hua XIX/1, 61n): "Über das Verhältnis von Grammatik und Logik", *Symbolae Pragenses* (Vienna/Prague: Tempsky; Leipzig: G. Freytag, 1893), pp. 99-126. There is however no copy of this work extant in the remains of Husserl's personal library.

Husserl's copies are bound he had written out a rather detailed table of contents in shorthand. It should finally be mentioned that Husserl gave this volume to Heidegger in 1927. All this underlines the importance of these articles for Husserl.

The other work by Marty which is of considerable importance here is his *Untersuchung zur Grundlegung der allgemeinen Grammatik und Sprachphilosophie* (1908),[1] which contains many criticisms of Husserlian positions. Though Husserl reviewed this work in 1910 (Hua XXII, 261-265), it is most unfortunate that his review had to be a rather brief one for its publication in *Deutsche Literaturzeitung*. Husserl's copy of the work also bears markings and annotations. Some of these are clearly responses to criticisms from Marty.

Of some importance here, though much less than the two works just mentioned, is also Marty's extensive review of James' *Principles of Psychology*.[2] Husserl had an offprint of this review which bears some markings and a few annotations.

1. INTENTIONAL REFERENCE

Here we shall examine the difference between Husserl and Marty on the topic of intentional reference. As far as Husserl's views are concerned, the focus here will be on the *Logische Untersuchungen* here, whereas we shall see that Marty changed his views on this matter. Early in the twentieth century, after both Husserl and Meinong denounced the immanentism which they had learned from Brentano, Marty continued to defend this doctrine against Husserl in particular. In his *Untersuchung* of 1908, however, he rejected it too and preferred another theory which will be discussed in detail below. In his defence of this later theory he nonetheless still continued to attack Husserl's views on intentional reference.

1.1. Marty's Early Immanentism

We have already seen that the concept of intentional reference was not only central to the psychological investigations of the Brentanists, but also a matter of controversy

---

[1] This work is dedicated to "Franz Brentano, teacher and friend, on his 70th birthday (16 January 1908) [Franz Brentano, dem Lehrer und Freund, zum 70. Geburtstag (16. Januar 1908)]".

[2] The review in question, published in *Zeitschrift für Psychologie und Physiologie der Sinnesorgane* 3 (1892): 297-333, will henceforth be referred to as "James review".

among them. Though Brentano had construed intentional reference as an "inexistence of the object" and accordingly used the terms "content" and "object" as synonyms, some of his pupils insisted upon a distinction between the content and object of a psychical phenomenon. Husserl, too, followed suit and developed from 1894 onward a theory in which the phenomenological contents, e.g., sensations, are distinguished from the object which is intended through the apprehension of these contents. Within the act there is also a distinction to be made between the quality and the matter. While the latter is the moment of the act which is responsible for its reference to this or that object under this or that conception, the object itself is not identified with the matter, the phenomenological content, or anything else immanent in the act.

This theory of intentional reference was of course espoused in the second volume of the *Logische Untersuchungen*. In 7 June 1901 Marty writes to Husserl: "With great interest I have read through the imposing second volume of your *Logische Untersuchungen*, partly superficially, partly (and not for a small part) thoroughly" (*Briefwechsel* I, 71). In this letter Marty also expresses his misgivings about some of Husserl's views. While he is content with Husserl's attack against nominalism and also against the related theory which Cornelius had defended, he adds that he takes issue with Husserl's own views regarding universals (*Briefwechsel* I, 71). "You protest here against a 'psychological hypostatization of the universal' [title of the second chapter of the second "Logical Investigation"], i.e., against the view, if I understand correctly, that the universal is thought as an immanent object of presentation. Your view is therefore related to James', who indeed also emphatically says of thoughts that 'they are not what they mean'".[1] Marty, by contrast, maintains that every presentation and every act, including those which are "general" or "universal", has an immanent object.

In the James review Marty argued that a failure to appreciate the immanence of the object leads to a failure to appreciate the analyzability of consciousness:

An intentional object is given in every psychical act. It is the inseparable correlate of consciousness, a side of it without which this consciousness itself would not be. No presenting without something presented, and this is something that in some manner inheres in the presenting entity, and likewise no loving without something loved. An actual object, however, i.e., something which corresponds to the intentional object in actuality and independently of it, is not always given, as in the example of the presentation of blue or red [or the presentation of a centaur]. [...] However many parts can be differentiated in the whole of the inherent

---

[1] See William James, *Principles of Psychology* I, p. 471, where J.S. Mill and others are attacked for holding "that a thought must *be* what it means, and mean what it *is*".

object, there are as many inherencies also to be distinguished, i.e., as many sub-references in the whole reference of the subject to its part.[1]

As we distinguish the sound and color of a seen and heard object, for instance, we can likewise distinguish seeing and hearing as parts of presenting the object in question. We have of course already seen that the correspondence between the whole-part structure of the presented object and the act of presenting has been an issue for Bolzano and Twardowski, as well as for Husserl, though Marty's treatment of it here is specifically related to the issue of the intentional object.

One of the motivating factors behind James' denial of the intentional object, according to Marty, lies in the recognition of symbolic or inauthentic presentations. Such presentations, after all, are nothing like the objects which are allegedly presented by them. If, however, we allow for the analyzability of the intentional object and, by implication, of the act of consciousness, it becomes understandable, on Marty's view, how even inauthentic presentations have objects which are immanent in them. These are presentations in which an object is presented by means of a sign, whether this be a sign in the strict sense or an image which is only remotely similar to the inauthentically presented object. The sign functions as a surrogate. Hence, the presentation can be called a "surrogate presentation". "It is this in the sense that in truth it has a content completely different from what the name of its so-called object signifies, a content which stands to the one designated by the name merely in some relation. This other content, however, is now fully and authentically presented. It is impossible for a presentation to be represented always again only by a sign. Rather, the means of presenting

---

[1] James Review, pp. 321 f.: "Ein *intentionales Objekt* ist bei jedem psychischen Akt gegeben. Es ist das untrennbare Korrelat des Bewusstseins, eine Seite desselben, ohne welche dieses selbst nicht wäre. Kein Vorstellen ohne Vorgestelltes, und dieses wohnt in gewisser Weise dem Vorstellenden inne, und ebenso kein Lieben ohne Geliebtes. Ein *wirkliches* Objekt dagegen, d.h. etwas, was dem intentionalen Objekte in *Wirklichkeit* und unabhängig von ihm entspricht, ist nicht immer gegeben, so z.B. bei der Vorstellung von blau oder rot nicht. [...] So viele Teile in dem Ganzen des innewohnenden Objektes sich auseinanderhalten lassen, so viele Innewohnungen sind auch zu unterscheiden, d.h. so viele Teilbeziehungen in der Gesamtbeziehung des Subjekts zu seinem Inhalt". This passage is partly underlined by Husserl. Marty again speaks in favor of the immanentist theory of intentional reference in "Über subjeklose Sätze" (1894): 443 ff. On the cover of the particular article in question Husserl writes "immanent object" (*immanenter Gegenstand*) and notes the relevant pages. Much of the text on these pages is moreover underlined. There are also markings in the margins, indicating that Husserl read it with great interest. One notable point which Marty makes there (p. 445) is this: "[...] of our own psychical acts and their immanent contents we have 'perception' in the strict sense, we grasp them with immediate certainty [von unseren eigenen psychischen Akten und ihren immanenten Inhalten habe wir im strengen Sinne eine 'Wahrnehmung', wir erfassen sie mit unmittelbarer Sicherheit]". Alongside this passage Husserl writes "inner perception" (*innere Wahrnehmung*).

X inauthentically is at once, considered in itself, an authentic presentation. That is to say, it authentically presents something which stands in relation to that X, but not that X itself [...]".[1] We may of course be reminded here of Meinong's conception of indirect presentations, which were also said to be achieved by means of relations of the content to something else, e.g., "the joiner who made my desk". Though Marty does not refer to Meinong in his discussion of inauthentic presentations, it nonetheless appears that he conceives of them in much the same way. The advantage of this view for Marty's purposes is in any case that it allows him to adhere to the thesis that all presentations have immanent objects.

What is authentically presented via relations in inauthentic presentations is not only one of the terms of the relation in question, but also the relation itself. Besides the authentic presentations of relations, other authentic presentations, on Marty's views, can function as surrogate presentations. The other authentic presentations which he has in mind here are *concepts*, i.e., the presentations of universals. By analyzing these into parts, he tells us, we can have inauthentic presentations, though he does not illustrate this claim by means of examples.

In the above mentioned letter to Husserl Marty briefly repeats all this, insisting "that there can be no 'intending' without an object immanent in the presentation" (*Briefwechsel* I, 73). This holds good, on his view, for "meaning something" in any acceptable sense, whether this indicates the intention to communicate or merely presenting as such. The presentation can moreover be authentic or inauthentic; in either case there inheres an object in it. As already mentioned, Marty sees the analysis of the immanent object and its relations to other objects as the key to understanding how we have inauthentic presentations.

If for the moment we leave aside the issue of objectless presentations, it is obvious that it can be said from Husserl's standpoint that presentations do have objects; these objects, however, need not at all be immanent. Against this view Marty argues that 1) there must always *exist* an object which is presented, for both of the members of a relation, including the relation of intentional reference, exist, and 2) this object must exist in the presentation, since it is possible for there to be no actual object. It may of

---

[1]*Ibid.*, p. 327: "Es ist dies in dem Sinne, dass es in Wahrheit einen ganz anderen Inhalt hat, als der Name seines sogenannten Objektes besagt, einen Inhalt, der zu dem durch den Namen bezeichneten bloss in irgend einer Beziehung steht. Dieser andere Inhalt aber wird nun voll und eigentlich vorgestellt. *Es kann nicht ins Unendliche eine Vorstellung immer wieder bloss durch ein Zeichen vertreten sein.* Vielmehr ist sofort das Mittel, ein X uneigentlich vorzustellen, *in sich betrachtet* eine eigentliche Vorstellung, d.h. sie stellt irgend etwas, was zu jenem X in Beziehung steht, nur nicht jenes X selbst, *eigentlich* vor [...]." This passage is partly underlined by Husserl.

course be pointed out that in some cases there *is* an actual object. Even in this case, however, "an immanent one, it seems to me, belongs to the essence of consciousness and is indispensable, for what is under consideration here is a being-for-me of something" (*Briefwechsel* I, 74). Given this argument, Marty sees no difficulty in psychologically hypostasizing the universal as something which exists in consciousness and is therefore temporal, though not real. While both the real and the non-real, according to Marty, are temporal, the distinguishing feature of the real is that it enters into causal relations. Universals, he says, come into being and go out of existence with consciousness. But they do not enter causal relations. Their coming-into-being is merely "co-genesis" (*Mitwerden*), namely in conjunction with certain acts of consciousness.

Another one of Marty's misgivings about Husserl's theory of consciousness is relevant here, namely about the view that sensations are contents which are interpreted in outer perception. Following Brentano once again, Marty maintains that sensations are themselves presentations with their own immanent objects. On this view the intentional reference of sensations is not dependent on interpretations or apprehensions as is the case with Husserl in the fifth "Logical Investigation".

In Husserl's draft of a response to Marty (7 July 1901) there is some consideration of the contrast between authentic and inauthentic presentations. Among the points in Marty's conception of inauthentic presentations which receive attention from Husserl is the claim that even certain phantasy presentations can be inauthentic. This claim had been made by Marty because of the lack of actual resemblance in many cases between the phantasy image and the actual object. If we now consider the phantasy image as immanent in the act of imagining, as Marty apparently does, inauthentic presentations which make use of an image would seem to support Marty's thesis that a presentation always has an immanent object. Against any attempt to argue in this manner, however, Husserl insists that the phantasy image is not at all the object of a phantasy presentation (*Briefwechsel* I, 77). We have of course already seen that Husserl had insisted on this point in "Intentionale Gegenstände".

As regards Marty's claim that an inauthentic presentation can be achieved by means of analysis, Husserl claims that, while the parts of a presentation can indeed have objects of their own, these may not, properly speaking, be regarded as objects of the entire presentation (*Briefwechsel* I, 78). If, for example, the entire presentation is one of the knife on the table, the table is presented only insofar as the knife is presented as on it. Thus, even if an inauthentic presentation can be analyzed into authentic presentations and immanent objects are found in these, this will not allow us to say that the entire inauthentic presentation has these immanent objects as their proper objects.

To this argument Husserl adds that it is nonetheless wrong to regard the objects of the partial presentations as necessarily immanent. To regard them in this way, he maintains, is to confuse the contents which are to be apprehended in order to present an object with the presented object itself.

Against the conception of inauthentic presentations as presentations which are achieved via the authentic presentation of relations, Husserl raises the following doubts (*Briefwechsel* I, 82): "But can I present the relation with only one foundation? The other one must also be presented. How is it presented? If I present another object, as a surrogate, the question arises how is the being-a-surrogate presented. Surely, once again, by means of a relation, and thus we would arrive at an infinite regress".

In Marty's response (17 August 1901) three objections from Husserl are identified: 1) that, if every presentation would require an object, this would entail the necessary existence of an actual object for every presentation, 2) that the object of a presentation is, according to Marty, the *presented* object, 3) that Marty's conception of inauthentic presentations leads to an infinite regress. Marty answers the first objection by saying that only an *immanent* object is required for each presentation while anything *transcendent* makes no difference as far as the presentation is concerned. He answers the second objection by saying that the *presented blue*, for instance, is not the primary object of the presentation of blue, for this object is simply *blue*; the presented blue is rather only the object of secondary consciousness. Finally, he answers that his conception of inauthentic presentations does not involve an infinite regress, for involves a distinction between internal and external properties which had not been mentioned in the James review. An atom, for instance, is one of the terms of an external relation, e.g., to our sensations. "If I present it only as a correlate of such an external relation," says Marty, "it is - insofar as I, speaking of the atom, nonetheless *intend* not merely these external relations, but rather the sum of its determinations, also its internal ones - inauthentically presented" (*Briefwechsel* I, 85). Perhaps this point becomes clearer by an example which Marty does not use, namely "the carpenter who made my desk". While this relation between the carpenter and the desk is an external one, by designating the carpenter as the term of this relation I also mean this person, including all of his internal properties.

1.2. Idea-Dependent Similarity

Though Marty defended immanentism as late as 1901, this notion was to be abandoned in his *Untersuchung zur Grundlegung der allegemeinen Grammatik und Sprachphilosophie*, where the following alternative theory of intentional reference is offered. "Presenting [...] is a real process in the soul, to which there is joined as a non-real consequence that - provided that what is called 'presented' therein exists - the presenting soul enters into a peculiar relation to it, a relation which can perhaps be designated as an idea-dependent similarity or adequacy with it".[1] Husserl's dismay at this theory is expressed by the large question mark in the margin alongside this passage. The question is of course whether any sense at all can be attached to the suggestion that the act of presenting or the presenting entity is somehow *similar* to the presented object.

Marty calls the similarity in question "idea-dependent" (*ideell*) to distinguish it from similarity in the ordinary sense and explains as follows:

Idea-dependent similarity, after all, means nothing but a similarity as it obtains between the "idea" or the presenting on the one hand and its object on the other, and mental adequation as nothing but an adequation as it alone can be given in the case of the mind vis-à-vis its objects. But it is important for me to stress in any case that there is at stake - provided that both correlates are given - a correlation which, in spite of the fact that it by no means co-incides with that which is usually called similarity or equality, can nonetheless most suitably be given this name [i.e., similarity or equality].[2]

---

[1]*Untersuchung zur Grundlegung der allgemeinen Grammatik und Sprachphilosophie*, p. 406: "Das Vorstellen [...] ist ein realer Vorgang in der Seele, an welchen sich als nicht-reale Folge knüpft, dass - falls *dasjenige, was man das darin Vorgestellte nennt, existiert* - die vorstellende Seele zu ihm in eine eigentümliche Relation tritt, die sich etwa als eine ideelle Ähnlichkeit oder Adäquatheit mit demselben bezeichnen kann." This passage is partly underlined by Husserl.

The term *ideell* is translated in the text as "idea-dependent" and not "ideal". In this way the impression is avoided that the relation called "idea-dependent similarity" is ideal in the sense of being timeless, nor should this notion be taken to suggest anything like something to be hoped for or aspired to (contrary to Barry Smith's suggestion in *Austrian Philosophy*, p. 110). This relation, as is made clear especially in the next passage to be cited, is idea-dependent in the sense that one of its terms *must* be an idea, i.e., a presentation or a psychical act of some other kind.

[2]*Ibid.*, pp. 406 f.: "Ideelle Ähnlichkeit heisst ja wieder nichts anderes, als eine solche, wie sie eben zwischen der "Idee" oder dem Vorstellen einerseits und ihrem Gegenstand andererseits besteht und mentale Adäquation nichts, als eine solche, wie sie allein beim Geiste gegenüber seinen Objekten gegeben sein kann. Aber worauf es mir ankommt, ist doch, zu betonen, dass es sich - falls beide Korrelate gegeben sind - um eine solche Korrelation handelt, die, wiewohl sie durchaus nicht mit dem zusammenfällt, was man gewöhnlich Ähnlichkeit oder Gleichheit oder Übereinstimmung nennt, doch am *ehesten mit diesem Namen* belegt werden kann." Much of this passage is underlined by Husserl.

Next to the qualification "provided that both correlates are given" Husserl writes: "Given how?"[1] Moreover, next to the claim that idea-dependent similarity does not coincide with similarity in the ordinary sense Husserl again writes a very large question mark. His dismay at this point is of course quite understandable, for Marty so far gives us almost nothing positive to illuminate his new theory of intentional reference. Nonetheless, he explains further that similarity is "to be understood here [...] in a modified and only somehow analogous sense".[2]

In order to clarify the difference between similarity proper and idea-dependent similarity, Marty distinguishes two types of similarity in the former sense and points out "that idea-dependent similarity is not an equality of the genus [of the related terms] while the difference between the species remains small [one type of similarity proper] [...]; but also not properly an equality of certain parts or moments while others differ [the other type of similarity proper]".[3] However, when Marty repeats himself by saying: "Idea-dependent equality between consciousness and that which it is consciousness *of* obtains by no means by virtue of the fact that both fall under the same concept, whether this be a genus or species concept",[4] Husserl writes in the margin next to this passage: "Even if consciousness is directed at consciousness as its object?"[5] Here, then, is a case, according to Husserl, where a similarity in the proper sense occurs between consciousness and its object. Nonetheless, it may be said in defence of Marty that this similarity *as such* is not what makes the relation in question (if one may speak of a relation here) an intentional one.

While there is not one genus to which idea-dependent similarity and similarity proper belong, Marty further explains that both relations have one thing in common, as emphasized in the following passage which is marked "NB" by Husserl: "What is especially at stake in either case is a grounded or conditioned relation and in both cases

---

[1] "Wie *gegeben?*"

[2] *Untersuchungen.*, p. 407: "in einem modifizierten und nur irgendwie analogen Sinn zu verstehen".

[3] *Ibid.*: "dass die ideelle Ähnlichkeit nicht eine Gleichheit der Gattung bei geringer Verschiedenheit der Spezies ist [...]; aber auch nicht eigentlich eine Gleichheit gewisser Teile oder Momente bei Verschiedenheit anderer". Most of this passage is underlined by Husserl.

[4] *Ibid.*, p. 408: "Aber die *ideelle* Gleichheit zwischen dem Bewusstsein und dem, wovon es ein Bewusstsein ist, besteht durchaus nicht darin, dass beide unter denselben Begriff, sei es Gattungs-, sei es Artbegriff, fallen".

[5] "Auch wenn Bewusstsein sich auf Bewusstsein als seinen Gegenstand richtet?"

it turns out that instead of the actual correlation something is sometimes given which we want to call a relative determination".[1]

If a conditioned relation occurs, says Marty, it is conditioned by what has traditionally been called the foundation of the relation. "A founded [i.e., conditioned] relation", he explains, "is e.g., equality of color. It is based on [i.e., conditioned by] the fact that belonging to two or several things are certain absolute color-determinations, and it would not be possible without these latter, which is for this very reason called the foundation or that which founds that relation".[2] An idea-dependent relation is "above all grounded in a certain real process in the soul, which differs if I present red or if I present blue or a sound".[3] Such a relation, however, may fail to occur altogether, namely when there is no object corresponding to the real process in the soul. This is what Marty means by "relative determination". It is comparable to the case where a picture is said to be an excellent likeness of a deceased person. Since the person in question no longer exists, it would be wrong to speak of an actual relation here. It may be noted here that Marty thus in effect agrees with Bolzano that there are objectless presentations and thereby comes closer to Husserl's position on intentionality than he had been with his earlier view.[4] Still, the thesis that, whenever the presented object

---

[1] *Untersuchungen*, p. 408: "Vor allem handelt es sich hier wie dort um eine *begründete* oder bedingte Relation und kommt es beidemal vor, dass statt der wirklichen Korrelation unter Umständen etwas gegeben ist, was wir eine relative Bestimmung nennen wollen". This passage is partly underlined by Husserl.

[2] *Ibid.*, p. 409: "Eine fundierte Relation ist z.B. die Gleichfarbigkeit. Sie beruht darauf, dass zwei oder mehreren Dingen gewisse absolute Farbenbestimmungen zukommen und wäre ohne diese letzteren, die eben darum das Fundament oder das jene Relation Fundierende heissen, nicht möglich". This passage is partly underlined by Husserl.

[3] *Ibid.*, p. 413: "vor allem begründet in einem gewissen realen Vorgang in der Seele, der ein anderer ist, wenn ich Rot, ein anderer, wenn ich Blau oder einen Ton vorstelle". This passage is partly underlined by Husserl.

[4] This is not to say that Marty draws from Bolzano in any significant way. Indeed, he exhibits misunderstandings of Bolzano. For instance, he writes that Husserl follows Bolzano in allowing for affirming and denying without belief, but also in considering them "as something belonging to the realm of presenting [als etwas dem Gebiete des Vorstellens angehörendes]" (*ibid.*, p. 245 n). This passage is partly underlined by Husserl. In one of the margins next to it he writes "?!", while in the other margin he correctly writes: "None of this can be found in Bolzano [Davon findet sich bei Bolzano nichts]". Also Marty attributes to Bolzano "the erroneous doctrine that all thinking can be resolved into presentations [die irrtümliche Lehre, dass alles Denken sich in Vorstellungen auflösen lasse]". This passage is partly underlined by Husserl. In the margin next to it he writes a large question mark and exclaims: "Presentations in the Bolzanian sense [Vorstellungen in Bolzanoschem Sinne]!"

exists, there obtains an idea-dependent similarity between it and the presentation is not accepted by Husserl, as his markings and annotations indicate.

Though idea-dependent similarity is like similarity proper insofar as both are founded relations (or relative determinations), the comparison breaks down when it is noted that, wherever the idea-dependent similarity does occur, the presentation and the presented object are not on an equal footing. Objects which are similar to each other in the proper sense, however, are so. This difference between the two cases is discernible as far as both the cognition and the being of similarity is concerned. While each of the properly similar objects can be cognized independently, this is not the case wherever an idea-dependent similarity occurs. In a passage marked "NB" by Husserl Marty explains: "It is a peculiarity of idea-dependent adequation that it is only cognized insofar as in and with the cognition of one foundation (namely of consciousness) also the other and adequation of both members is grasped".[1]

The conception of intentional reference as idea-dependent similarity, says Marty, explains how it is possible to present universals. In the following passage he elaborates on this point:

A universal cannot exist either mentally or really, if this means a true being, i.e., a possibility of correct affirmation, of it. Every hypostasization of something intrinsically indeterminate is contradictory, both an immanent and a transcendent one. And if there is an immanent object, what is inseparable in actuality is therefore so in thoughts too. The matter is different if the general thought is nothing else but an indeterminate assimilation with many objects, if therefore what is claimed in the affirmation of this thought is only the existence of a *presenting entity*, which is - as far as it is concerned - in agreement with many individuals or concreta in the same way. It can quite well be essential to the idea-dependent assimilation that it is possible also in such indeterminacy and incompleteness and in this way alone the fact of abstraction becomes understandable.[2]

---

[1]*Ibid.*, p. 414: "Es ist eine Eigentümlichkeit der ideellen Adäquation, dass sie nur erkannt wird, indem unter Umständen in und mit der Erkenntnis des einen Fundaments (nämlich des Bewusstseins) auch das andere und die Adäquatheit beider Glieder erfasst wird".

[2]*Ibid.*, pp. 416 f.: "Ein *Universale* kann so wenig mental existieren als real, wenn damit überhaupt ein wahres Sein, d.h. ein mit Recht Anerkanntwerdenkönnen, desselben gemeint ist. Jede Hypostatierung eines in sich Unbestimmten ist widerspruchsvoll, eine immanente so gut wie eine transzendente. Und wenn es einen immanenten Gegenstand gibt, ist darum, was in Wirklichkeit nicht trennbar ist, dies auch in Gedanken nicht. Anders wenn der allgemeine Gedanke nichts anderes ist als eine unbestimmte Verähnlichung mit vielem, wenn also mit seiner Anerkennung nur die Existenz eines *Vorstellenden* behauptet ist, welches - soviel an ihm liegt - unzählig vielen Individuen oder Konkreta in derselben Weise konform ist. Es kann sehr wohl im Wesen der ideellen Verähnlichung liegen, dass sie auch in solcher Unbestimmtheit und Unvollständigkeit möglich ist und dies ist überhaupt das einzige, woraus die Tatsache der Abstraktion begreiflich wird". This passage is partly underlined by Husserl.

In this manner Marty eliminates the universal as an *object* and at the same time avoids an extreme nominalism. Husserl's question marks and exclamation marks alongside the just-cited passage express profound dissatisfaction. Since Marty considers only two alternatives here, namely either the existence of the universal as an indeterminate object or the idea-dependent similarity between a presentation and many individuals, it is obvious why Husserl has misgivings here. For his rather Platonistic theory of universals is a third alternative. On his view, they are no less determinate than any other objects. To be sure, they are said to be timeless. But this lack of temporality is an indeterminacy in the proper sense; it is comparable not to the triangle which is not scalene, isosceles, or equilateral, but rather to the color which lacks pitch and volume. It is indeed arguable in favor of Husserl's theory of universals that it avoids both the inconsistencies of the immanent object and the obscurity of idea-dependent similarity. Making room for the timeless is, on the other hand, an ontologically high price for the understanding of how a presentation can be general. We shall have more to say below about the differences between Husserl and Marty on the topic of universals.

In connection with conceptual presentations Marty maintains that, if they are not in any sense held to be similar with objects, the consequence is "an extreme nominalism or semanticism, which would make all presentations into something which would in no way be similar or in conformity with the presented object, but would rather be a merely dissimilar and in this sense arbitrary sign thereof".[1] Sensations, according to him, are indeed not instances in which an actual idea-dependent similarity with the objects obtains. Since colors and sounds do not exist, our sensations "of" them are only relative determinations. Thus, the similarity between presentation and object would not be maintained "with any show of plausibility" even in the case of sensations. If none of our conceptual presentations is in any sense similar to external objects, e.g., light and sound waves, the question arises whether it would be correct to say that physical reality is knowable. "Indeed, if our thoughts were in no sense similar to actuality, how could one then speak of them at all as signs of it? In order for this even to be the case, something must at least be given in actuality such as presentations and their being signs for something else, i.e., a possibility of inferring correctly from the existence of one to

---

[1] *Ibid.*, p. 422: "[...] wir ständen also vor einem extremen Nominalismus oder Semantizismus, der die Vorstellungen insgesamt zu etwas machte, was dem Vorgestellten in keiner Weise ähnlich oder konform sondern ein bloss unähnliches und in diesem Sinne willkürliches Zeichen desselben wäre". This passage is marked in the margin by Husserl.

the existence of the other".[1] Here we may be reminded of Husserl's remark, cited above, that a case of similarity in the proper sense is to be found where consciousness is directed at itself. While Marty has eliminated the possibility of a similarity obtaining between sensations and external objects and accordingly warns that it would be a much too far-reaching semanticism to regard conceptual presentations too as merely symbolic, there is still one type of presentation which is left to be considered, namely the presentation of consciousness itself. While Husserl's remark that similarity in the proper sense occurs in precisely this case may accordingly be kept in mind as a safeguard against an extreme semanticism, this will hardly save Husserl against the charge that his view cannot do justice to the cognition of *physical* reality. We shall soon see, however, that even this charge is not applicable to Husserl.

There can indeed be no doubt that Husserl in particular is to be regarded by Marty as a semanticist. In a footnote Marty insists that the opposition to the thesis of the immanent object must not be confused or identified "with the doctrine that presenting is not at all similar or in conformity with the presented object, but rather a mere 'intending' thereof".[2] Next to this footnote Husserl writes a large question mark. He also indicates that there is an important postscript to this passage, one which is moreover specifically directed against him.[3] This postscript indeed makes clear that Husserl is the one who Marty has in mind here. The words "similar or in conformity" (*ähnlich oder konform*) are underlined in the passage just cited, for they indicate a crucial point for Husserl, who, after all, maintains that some presentations, namely fulfilling ones or "intuitions", are in some manner *in conformity* with their objects.

---

[1]*Ibid.*: "Ja, wenn unsere Gedanken in keinem Sinne der Wirklichkeit ähnlich wären, könnte man dann auch nur davon sprechen, dass sie Zeichen derselben seien? Damit auch nur dies der Fall sei, muss zum mindesten doch in Wirklichkeit etwas gegeben sein wie Vorstellungen und etwas wie ein Zeichensein derselben für etwas anderes, d.h. eine Möglichkeit, aus dem Dasein des Einen richtig Dasein des Anderen zu entnehmen." Most of this passage is underlined by Husserl.

As pointed out by Barry Smith (*Austrian Philosophy*, p. 112), the view that signs are in some sense similar to what they signify was later taken up by Wittgenstein.

[2]*Ibid.*, p. 423 n: "[...] mit der Lehre, dass das Vorstellen dem Vorgestellten überhaupt nicht ähnlich oder konform sondern ein blosses 'Meinen' desselben sei [...]".

[3]Husserl refers to page 732, but the remark which he has in mind is to be found on page 762. Next to this remark Husserl writes a question mark.

1.3. Husserl's Alternative

In this light we may consider what one commentator has recently said on this matter, namely that Husserl had already clarified that towards which Marty was groping under the heading "idea-dependent" similarity.[1] What this commentator has in mind is that the empty intentions (in Husserl's terms) are the phenomena in which something is merely meant by signs, whereas the fulfillments are the phenomena in which "signs have been substituted by intuitions of the relevant objects".[2] We may here ask whether what takes place in such fulfillments is anything like the idea-dependent similarity suggested by Marty. The comparison between Husserl and Marty on this point breaks down when we consider that the idea-dependent similarity obtains wherever the correlate of consciousness actually does exist and not only in cases where it is given *with evidence*. What Husserl means by "fulfilment", however, is restricted to instances where the object is given with evidence.

Nevertheless, it may be observed that a kind of similarity *does* take place, according to Husserl, when an object is intuited: "As an intuitive representative of an object only a content which is similar or equal to it can serve" (Hua XIX/2, 623). An outer perception, for instance, contains various sensations, e.g., color-sensations, which are "similar or equal" to the outwardly perceived object. This similarity, however, would not be a similarity only by analogy, as Marty's idea-dependent similarity, but rather a similarity in the proper sense. We may of course ask whether this position is actually preferable to Marty's. But it must first be born in mind that Husserl does not mean to say that the alleged *similarity itself* between the phenomenological contents and the moments of the object is cognized or presented in any way, as if we compared our sensations, for instance, with external objects. In this regard one may consider his warnings against construing consciousness in terms of pictures or signs which represent objects (Hua XIX/1, 436 ff.). Though a picture must of course to some degree be similar to the pictured object, similarity is not a sufficient condition for being a picture; something is not a picture of an object (however similar it may be to this object) unless it is *regarded as a picture*. Since the apprehension of the phenomenological contents

---

[1] Barry Smith, *Austrian Philosophy*, pp. 112 f.

[2] *Ibid.*

is not in any sense a presentation of them, there is no question here of a pictorial representation.[1]

In light of such considerations it may be said that Marty comes closer to a radical semanticism than Husserl, since Marty does not allow for an idea-dependent similarity between outer perception and physical reality. But this is not to say that Husserl's views on these matters are preferable to Marty's. Though it must be conceded without hesitation that Marty's notion of an idea-dependent similarity is obscure, perhaps hopelessly so, the Husserlian conception of consciousness in terms of the apprehension of phenomenological contents is by no means a model of clarity. Nowhere does Husserl illuminate the nature of this apprehension. We know of course that it is not an act in the proper sense, for the apprehended contents are not objects in the proper sense. But if it is not act, what is it? Part of an act? Perhaps so, but not just *any* part. It is related to the phenomenological contents, which are themselves parts, in a peculiar way, but this *sui generis* relation is only *asserted* by Husserl and never sufficiently *clarified*.

Even if we leave aside these difficulties in Husserl's views, it may also be pointed out that the above-characterization of intuition, in terms of an alleged similarity between its phenomenological contents and its object, is made in the sixth "Logical Investigation" prior to his attempt to expand the notion of intuition in order to allow for the intuition of states of affairs (Hua XIX/2, 670 ff.), collectives (Hua XIX/2, 688 f.), and general objects (Hua XIX/2, 690 ff.). These alleged cases of so-called "categorial intuition" are particularly difficult to account for by means of the notion of similarity. Husserl's own example of seeing that this paper *is* white (a state of affairs) may be considered here. According to him, this instance of seeing is not to be equated with simply seeing *this white paper*. The addition of the "is" makes the intuition in question a categorial one as opposed to a straightforward one. However, even if we are willing to allow for color-sensations and the like which are similar to the white paper, it can still be asked whether it is possible to discern sensations or phenomenological contents of any kind which are similar to the *being* of the white paper (or to the *being* white of the paper).

Here it must be stressed that we should be very careful about construing being as something which is *added* to the object of a straightforward intuition. It is not as though we had the categorial intuition that the paper is white by putting together, as it were, different objects, namely the ones named by the words "the", "paper", "is", and

---

[1] In this regard it is understandable why Husserl is considered a naive realist by Kevin Mulligan, "Perception", in *The Cambridge Companion to Husserl*, pp. 168-238. However, given Husserl's characterization of intuitions in terms of similarity between their phenomenological contents and the intuited object, it can also be said that in this sense he espouses a crude representative realism.

"white". If the categorial intuition took place in this manner, and if we moreover accepted the characterization of intuition in terms of a similarity between the phenomenological content and the object, then it would not be unreasonable for us to consider whether there is a special phenomenological content which is similar to being (named by "is" in the above example) as the white-sensation is allegedly similar to the white-moment of the paper. As it turns out, Husserl is unfortunately inclined to construe being as an added element. This is clear from his denial that the concept of being is not derived from inner perception. "Being", he says, "is no judgment and no real constituent part of a judgment. [...] In the judgment [...] there occurs the 'is' as a moment of meaning. The 'is' itself, however, does not occur in it [...]" (Hua XIX/2, 668). The very mention here of the "is" itself suggests that this is something besides the meaning of "is", just as white itself is something besides the meaning of "white". To be sure, being is not a *real* constituent part of the intuited state of affairs, but it is nonetheless regarded as a constituent part of another kind, an "ideal" one. Thus Husserl is prompted to go searching for phenomenological contents which are peculiar to categorial intuition.[1]

This search, however, can only be made in vain, for it is obvious that we can account for acts (whether or not they be called "intuitions") of the kind under consideration without positing additional elements in the object. Consider, for instance, an act which has a collective, e.g., A and B, as an object. As Husserl had already convincingly argued in *Philosophie der Arithmetik*, being a collective is not reducible to being presented by the same consciousness at the same time or in succession. If, for instance, I am thinking of A and also thinking of B, this is not the same as thinking of A and B together as a collective. Yet, the collective is not presented by adding a third element, called "and", to the others, for we would then be compelled to ask what makes this threesome a collective. Surely not by adding a second "and", for the presentation of a collective would then be an infinite task which no entity of any kind, finite or infinite, could ever accomplish. Instead of viewing the presentation of a collective in such a way, it is clearly better to go in the direction espoused by Husserl in *Philosophie der Arithmetik*, namely to characterize the collective only in terms of a collective combination which is peculiar to certain acts. If we do this, then we may do the same for a number of other acts, namely all of those which Husserl calls "categorial

---

[1] The search in question makes up an entire chapter of the sixth "Logical Investigation" (Hua XIX/2, 694-709). In the preface to the second edition of this "Logical Investigation" Husserl says that he no longer approves of the chapter in question, although he did not remove it and moreover still considers it be "worth an exacting reflection" (Hua XIX/2, 535). A discussion of it here, however, would take us much too far afield.

intuitions". We should therefore avoid any suggestion that being is to be found in certain *objects* and, instead of this, account for the distinction between the intuition of *this white paper* and the intuition *that this paper is white* purely in terms of some new peculiarity in the latter act.

In light of such misgivings it turns out that both Husserl and Marty, in spite of their rejection of immanentism, do not work out an alternative theory which will allow them to make a convincing escape from semanticism. While Marty's notion of an idea-dependent similarity is obscure, Husserl's notion of apprehension is no less so. Husserl's concept of categorial intuition, moreover, complicates his theory with additional difficulties.

2. EXISTENCE

Marty follows Brentano in both conceiving of existential judgments as affirmations or denials of existence and construing all judgments as existential. In this way he deals with the problem of subjectless sentences, e.g., "it is raining". This problem arises only for those who conceive of judgments as combinations of presentations. Once it is recognized that a judgment is the affirmation or denial of a presented object, he claims that subjectless sentences no longer pose a problem.

2.1. The Concept of Existence and its Origin

On page 172 of the second article on subjectless sentences, where the concept of existence is again under consideration, the following passage from Brentano's lecture on elementary logic is cited by Husserl in the left margin: "Belonging to existence is not necessarily a factual correspondence with a true affirmative judgment, but rather only that, insofar as the object is concerned, the precondition is fulfilled for the correspondence between the affirmative judgment and the thing".[1] In the adjacent passage Marty makes the same point, but with emphasis on the claims that the concept of existence differs from the concept of reality and is derived from reflection. We have already indicated that for Marty both the real and the non-real exist. What must be explained here is how, on his view, the concept of existence has its origin in reflection

---

[1]"Zur Existenz gehört nicht notwendig die faktische Übereinstimmung mit einem wahren anerkennenden Urteil, sondern nur dass, soweit es auf das Objekt ankommt, die Vorbedingung für die Übereinstimmung zwischen anerkennendem Urteil und Sache erfüllt ist."

In an unpublished anuscript (1895) Husserl says the following, with reference to Marty in particular, regarding this concept of existence:

We must give this definition credit for at least offering a concept which is equal in extension to the one which is to be defined. The matter of every correct affirmative judgment is certainly an existent one, and by converse we can also say that, wherever with regard to a presented object a judgment is possible which affirms this object and is correct, the object also exists. There is no undue restriction here to real objects, to effective ones, to perceived ones or those capable of being perceived, etc. And the concept of the object is taken in the broadest sense, according to which a state of affairs just as well as a horse is an object.[1]

Thus to a certain extent Husserl approves of Marty's definition of "existence". It is at least broad enough to include the non-real as well as the real. However, we must note that Husserl regards the concept which is thus defined as only *equivalent* to the concept of existence.

In order to see what is inadequate, according to Husserl, in Marty's definition of "existence" we must turn our attention not to the extension of this concept, but rather to the claim that existence in this sense is derived from reflection. This claim is of course only natural for a Brentanist, who maintains that all concepts are derived from either outer or inner intuition. Husserl, however, came to adopt the view that there is yet another source of our concepts, i.e., categorial intuition. This is moreover the source of our concept of existence. We have this concept and know what it means to speak of existence "only if some existence is, either actually or pictorially, put before our eyes" (Hua XIX/2, 670), i.e., only insofar as we intuit that this or that is the case. Such an intuition of a state of affairs (*Sachverhaltsanschauung*) is of course not reducible to a straightforward inner or outer intuition.

As we know what "existence" in general means from such intuition, the same goes in particular for knowing what subjectless sentences, so-called impersonalia, mean: this is known from intuiting the relevant state of affairs. Thus Husserl writes the following in his copy of the fourth article (p. 339, right margin) on subjectless sentences:

---

[1] K I 23/25: "Wir müssen es dieser Bestimmung nachrühmen, dass sie zum mindesten einen dem zu bestimmenden umfangsgleichen Begriff darstellt. Sicher ist die Materie eines jeden richtigen anerkennenden Urteils eine existierende, und umgekehrt können wir auch sagen, dass, wo in Ansehung eines vorgestellten Gegenstandes ein Urteil möglich ist, das ihn anerkennt und richtig ist, er auch existiere. Hier fehlt jede unzulässige Beschränkung auf reale Gegenstände, auf wirkende, auf wahrgenommene oder wahrnehmungsfähige usw. Under der Begrif des Gegenstandes ist im weitesten Sinn genommen, wonach ein Sachverhalt ebenso gut ein Gegenstand ist wie ein Pferd."

To be distinguished is the "origin" of the impersonal judgment and its meaning. In the case of origin we ask: where is the state of affairs of the impersonal *given*? In the relevant act of the intuition of the state of affairs we find the intuitive sense, towards which the symbolic sense is then directed.[1]

In the bottom margin of the same page Husserl again makes a similar point:

Sense of the impersonal: what does it mean, what is the "matter", the sense, is it an articulated one or not, what are its constituent parts, its sub-meanings? The sense must come to light in cases where we see in the impersonal also the state of affairs thereof, and thus we resort to its origin.[2]

While Husserl thus differs with Marty regarding the origin of the concept of existence, the question remains how Husserl regards Marty's claim "that the presentation of an object A is simply neither enriched nor otherwise changed in its content by adding the thought that A is".[3] This claim, according to Marty, compels us "either to teach that the existential sentence is an analytical one in the narrowest (Kantian) sense, i.e., one where the predicate overtly or covertly already lies in the subject-concept, or to admit that the simple belief in the existence of an object A does not at all consist in predicating of the concept of this object some other one".[4] At the bottom of the page

---

[1] "Es ist zu unterscheiden der 'Ursprung' der impersonalen Urteile und ihrer Bedeutung. Beim Ursprung fragen wir: wo ist uns der Sachverhalt des Impersonalen *gegeben*? In dem betreffenden Akte der Sachverhaltsanschauung finden wir den intuitiven Sinn, nach dem sich dann der symbolische Sinn richtet." Both this annotation and the following one are directed against Sigwart, rather than Marty, for they are clearly written in response to a passage from Sigwart's *Impersonalien* quoted and also challenged by Marty.

[2] "Sinn des Impersonale: was meint es, was ist die 'Materie', der Sinn, ist er ein gegliederter oder nicht, welches sind seine Bestandstücke, seine Teilbedeutungen. Der Sinn muss zutage treten in Fällen, wo wir im Impersonale zugleich den Sachverhalt desselben erschauen, desher Rekurs auf den Ursprung."

[3] "Über subjectlose Sätze" (1895): 20: "[...] dass die Vorstellung eines Gegenstandes, dass A sei, in ihrem Inhalt schlechterdings weder bereichert noch sonst irgendwie verändert werde." This passage is partly underlined by Husserl.

[4] *Ibid.*, p. 21: "[...] entweder zu lehren, dass der Existentialsatz ein analytischer im engsten (Kant'schen) Sinne sei, d.h. ein solcher, wo das Prädikat offen oder versteckt schon im Subjektbegriffe liegt, oder aber zuzugeben, dass der einfache Glaube an die Existenz eines Gegenstandes A überhaupt *nicht darin bestehe, dass von dem Begriff dieses Gegenstandes irgend ein anderer prädiziert wird.*" This passage is partly underlined by Husserl, who writes next to it: "But what is called 'content', what is called 'concept' [Aber was heisst 'Inhalt', was heisst 'Begriff']?" Moreover, immediately after the above-cited disjunctive claim Marty gives in parentheses his reason for making it: "For by every such connection with a concept which is not already included in it [the subject-concept A] A would necessarily have to be changed somehow in its content [Denn durch jede solche Verknüpfung mit einem Begriffe, der nicht schon in ihm enthalten ist, müsste A notwendig irgendwie in seinem Inhalt verändert werden]". Next to this passage Husserl comments: "In its content certainly, but not in its 'material' [In seinem Inhalt wohl, aber nicht in seinem

where Marty makes this disjunctive claim Husserl says the following: "But if we take the equivalent sentence 'A is something', is not 'something' here a predicate, and yet neither analytically contained in A, nor adding to A a new 'concept'? Content as 'matter'. Something is not a matter, and the 'concept' of something is not a feature-concept".[1] While Husserl thus raises doubts about the disjunction "either a predicate adds to a concept or the sentence in which this predicate occurs is analytic" and suggests that an existential sentence is a counter-example to this disjunction, this objection turns on whether the sentence "A is something" is equivalent to "A exists". As we have seen above, Bolzano had maintained that "something" is the highest genus, even higher than "being" or "reality". We have also seen that Meinong also allows for objects, for *somethings* one might say, which do not exist. If, however, we have to choose between Husserl's position on this matter and the position of Bolzano and Meinong, this dilemma might seem to eliminate the possibility of the orthodox Brentanian position which Marty defends. Perhaps the only way of saving this position is by denying another one of Husserl's presuppositions, namely that "something" is a predicate.

2.2. The Real and the Non-Real

Marty's division of existing objects into the real and the non-real is different from Husserl's. According to Marty, the concept of the real is illustrated "in every physical quality such as color, tone, etc., intensity, extension, but just as well in physical processes too, such as presenting, judging, fearing, hoping, wishing, etc.", whereas the nonreal is to be found in "the lack of something real, such as a hole, a boundary, the past, the future, the merely possible and the impossible, the presented, loved as such, etc."[2] He is content to give such examples without defining the concept of the real and

---

"Stoff"]". It is uncertain what Husserl means here by "material".

[1] "Aber wenn wir den äquivalenten Satz nehmen 'A ist etwas', ist da nicht 'etwas' Prädikat, und doch weder analytisch in A enthalten, noch zu A einen neuen 'Begriff' hinzubringend? Inhalt als 'Materie'. Etwas ist keine Materie, und der 'Begriff' Etwas ist kein Merkmalbegriff."

[2] "Über subjectlose Sätze" (1894), p. 171: "Den Begriff des Realen erfassen wir in jeder physischen Qualität wie Farbe, Ton u.s.w., Intensität, Ausdehnung, aber ebenso auch in psychischen Vorgängen wie Vorstellen, Urteilen, Fürchten, Hoffen, Wünschen u.s.w. [...] Den Gegensatz des Realen bildet: der Mangel eines Realen, wie ein Loch, eine Grenze, das Vergangene, das Zukünftige, das bloss Mögliche als solches und das Unmögliche, das Vorgestellte, Geliebte als solches u.s.w."

its opposite, for he claims that such a definition is impossible. The reason for this, he claims, lies in the fact that every concept either directly or indirectly includes the concept of the real.

Now we have already seen in previous chapters that for Husserl the contrast between the real and the ideal plays an important role in the *Logische Untersuchungen*. Like Marty, Husserl does not *define* the concept of the real, but he finds its equivalent in the notion of the temporal. Ideal objects are accordingly timeless objects, such as meanings (including propositions), numbers, states of affairs, and specific unities. The nonreal which Marty speaks of, however, includes a good deal of temporally determined objects, the objects of the past and the future being outstanding examples. Thus, in spite of the fact that in 1895 Husserl was willing to say that Marty's (and of course Brentano's) characterization of existence was correct in its *extension*, i.e., insofar as it included the non-real as well as the real, Husserl later came to the view that ontology must embrace more than just the real and the so-called non-real.

In the *Untersuchung zur Grundlegung der allgemeinen Grammatik und Sprachphilosophie* Marty returns to the topics of existence and reality, this time with a *criterion* for distinguishing between the real and the non-real: "It is true of the real that there belongs to it an effecting and being-effected and, in this sense, an independent coming-about and passing-away, whereas the non-real has a mere co-genesis, i.e., becomes and passes away in that the real is effected and passes away".[1] We may of course be reminded of the above-cited list of non-real objects which Marty had provided in "Über subjectlose Sätze", but now the examples of collectives and also relations of equality, similarity, and differences are used to illustrate the concept of the non-real.[2]

---

[1]*Untersuchungen zur Grundlegung der allgemeinen Grammatik und Sprachphilosophie*, p. 320: "Vom Realen gelte, dass ihm ein Wirken und Gewirktwerden und in diesem Sinne ein selbständiges Entstehen und Vergehen zukomme, während das Nichtreale ein blosses Mitwerden habe, d.h. werde und vergehe, indem das Reale gewirkt wird und vergeht".

[2]Marty also adds another example, namely "remotely related to equality, the intentional relation, the idea-dependent equality or adequation between the psychical occurrence and its content [die, der Relation der Gleichheit entfernt verwandte, intentionale Relation, die eigentümliche ideelle Gleichheit oder Adäquation zwischen dem psychischen Vorgang und seinem Inhalt]" (*Ibid.*, p. 333). In Husserl's copy of Marty's *Untersuchung* the words "der Gleichheit entfernt verwandte, intentionale Relation" are underlined. Moreover, Marty adds that, if such a relation were real, it would have to be decided "whether it sould be included in the class of the physical or in that of the psychical [ob [sie] zu der des Physischen oder zu der des Psychischen [zu rechnen wäre]]". Husserl underlines this passage and writes in the margin "Philosophie der Arithmetik". In this work he had of course spoken of psychical relations (Hua XXII, 71 & 75), but Marty's

One apple and another apple, for instance, make up a pair, but this pair cannot be a reality in addition to the two realities; "otherwise", says Marty, "we would inevitably be led to an infinite multiplication of realities".[1] If the pair of apples were an additional reality, then this pair and the apples would together make up a new reality, i.e., the foursome, and so on *ad infinitum*. Marty adds also that, if a collective were real, it would have to have the unitary accidents which are ascribed to the collected members. But there is no such thing, for instance, as one collective will or one collected motion. Many people, in a state for example, may will the same thing. Likewise, many bullets may move in the same direction and at the same time (at the same velocity, one might add). Still, the willing in the first case is reducible to the willings of the individual human beings, just as the motion in the second case is reducible to the motions of the individual bullets.

Given Marty's characterization of the non-real in the above quotation, it is however somewhat more instructive to consider the example of the already mentioned relations. If, for instance, two horses are white, their similarity in color is not an additional reality. To be sure, the color of one of the horses could change and thereby the similarity of color would cease to be. But this is precisely what Marty means when he says, "the non-real, if it comes into being and passes away, arises and passes away as a consequence of the coming-into-being and passing-away of the real".[2] Similarities, differences, and equalities may come to be and pass away only insofar as real objects undergo changes.

If we now take into consideration Marty's characterization of the non-real in his *Untersuchung*, it is all the more apparent that his concept of the non-real, which includes temporally determinate objects, is not co-existensive with Husserl's concept of the ideal. Thus Marty writes: "In the *Logische Untersuchungen* Husserl ascribes a *timeless* existence to that which he distinguishes as ideal from the real, whereas the real is allegedly temporal. I cannot regard a distinction of *this* kind as justified".[3] Next

---

point is precisely that the intentional *relation* is no more psychical than it is physical.

[1] *Ibid.*, p. 331: "[...] sonst würden wir unweigerlich zu einer unendlichen Vervielfältigung der Realitäten geführt".

[2] *Ibid.*, p. 333: "[...] dass das Nichtreale, wenn es entsteht und vergeht, als Folge des Entstehens und Vergehens von Realem auftritt und vergeht".

[3] *Ibid.*, p. 328: "In den 'logischen Untersuchung' schreibt Husserl dem, was er als Ideales vom Realen unterscheidet, eine *zeitlose* Existenz zu, während das Reale zeitlich sei. Ich kann auch eine Unterscheidung *dieser* Art nicht berechtigt finden".

to this passage Husserl writes in his copy of Marty's *Untersuchung*: "Of course, the concept which I thereby have, after all, is not Marty's concept of the real",[1] as if there were only a verbal dispute under consideration here. But it is clear enough that for Marty the matter is not so easily settled, for he emphatically claims, in opposition to both Husserl and Meinong, that timeless objects cannot exist.[2] While he admits that we may present a given object and leave out of consideration its temporal determination or that we may regard an object as existing at *all* times, neither of these manners of presentation or judgment allow us to characterize the object in question as timeless. Moreover, he claims that his denial of timeless objects does not entail the denial of "eternal truths", e.g., that a triangular rectangle is impossible. These are eternal, says Marty, only in the sense that the contents of judgment in question "obtain at any time as something present as well as past and future, not that they obtain timelessly".[3]

In the second "Logical Investigation" Husserl argues that species are to be regarded as timeless objects. Meanings are construed as species and thus regarded as timeless as red in general and all the other species. Since Marty denies that there are timeless objects, he also of course denies that there are species, including meanings, in the Husserlian sense. The Aristotelian arguments whereby the Platonistic theory of Ideas is refuted, says Marty, also suffice for the refutation of Husserl's theory.[4] Husserl replies, however, "that 'ideal' objects and Platonic Ideas (in the sense of the Aristotelian conception) are totally different" (Hua XXII, 263). While Husserl does not say here what the difference consists in, we may of course bear in mind warnings in the *Logische Untersuchungen* against confusing his theory of ideal objects with traditional Platonism (Hua XIX/1, 116 f.). According to his view, these objects have being only in the sense that they have "validity" (*Geltung*), i.e., only in the sense that true propositions regarding them hold good. Whether or not all the Aristotelian criticisms of Platonism are applicable to this Lotzean Platonism, it is at least clear that

---

[1] "Ja dabei habe ich doch nicht Martys Begriff des Realen". A question mark and an exclamation mark, to express Husserl's outrage, are written underneath this remark.

[2] *Ibid.* Husserl writes in the margin: "Timelessness of the ideal disputed [Zeitlosigkeit des Idealen bestritten]", but it would be more accurate to say that it is *timelessness as such* which Marty disputes. Again Husserl somewhat trivializes the dispute.

[3] *Ibid.*, p. 329: "... von *solchen* Urteilsinhalten gilt, dass sie zu jeder Zeit als etwas Gegenwärtiges wie Vergangenes und Zukünftiges bestehen, nicht dass sie zeitlos bestehen". Next to this passage Husserl writes "NB".

[4] *Ibid.*, pp. 337 ff.

on Husserl's view there is an undeniable "separation" (*chorismos*) between ideal objects and their corresponding particulars. This is already clear from the alleged timelessness of the former and the temporal character of the latter. Marty's attack on Husserl's theory of ideal objects is thus not as far-fetched as Husserl suggests.

It is moreover arguable, though necessarily not from an Aristotelian standpoint, that Husserl fails to make a convincing case in favor of his Platonism. Whether the allegedly ideal objects under consideration are meanings or those of some other kind (e.g., the species which are instantiated by quality-moments), it is crucial to Husserl's Platonism to maintain that similarity or equality among individuals would be impossible if there were not one identical species which they instantiate. Meanings, for instance, are construed by Husserl as ideal objects, not only because he thinks (erroneously, as we have seen in Chapter One) that relativism and scepticism would otherwise prevail, but also because there is no other way to account for the fact that an expression can be used by different people and even by the same person at different times and yet have the *same* meaning. If, for instance, we state the Pythagorean theorem in modern English it has exactly the same meaning which it had when stated in ancient Greek two thousand years ago. It will not suffice here to appeal to the same state of affairs as that which accounts for the identical meaning, for as we have seen, Husserl maintains that the object, including the state of affairs which is meant in a judgment, is not the same as the meaning. He therefore sees no recourse but to say that there is here in the strict and proper sense one single meaning which is instantiated by all the acts of judging which give meaning to the expressions in question.

Here we may object that it is permissible to speak of the "same" meaning here only in a derived sense, as we say that two people are wearing the "same" hat. The expression which I use now has the "same" meaning as the expression which someone else uses, or which I use at another time, only in the sense that the different acts of judging are equal to each other. The same can indeed be said about any of the cases where we are allegedly compelled to posit a species as one single object distinct from the individuals which it instantiates. Two objects have the "same" color only in the sense that the color, the color-moment to be precise, is equal to that of the other object. In response to such an objection against Platonism, however, Husserl maintains that equality is reducible to identity and not vice-versa. For if we say that two individual moments are equal, this can be the case only if they are equal *in some respect*. It is this talk of "some respect", according to Husserl, which shows that we are really thinking of an identity in the strict and proper sense (Hua XIX/1, 117 f.).

If, however, Husserl argument here is a sound one, then it must be the case that we can never speak of equality without admitting that there is some respect in which the objects under consideration are equal. One stripe of the American flag is equal to another *with respect to color*. One color is equal to another *with respect to hue, to brightness, or to saturation*. But suppose that we say the brightness of one color is equal to the brightness of another. Would we then feel compelled to say in what respect the brightnesses in question are equal? Certainly not. It would indeed be absurd to talk of such a respect. And so it is in all cases of equality. One can go on "specifying" the respects in which the objects are equal until it no longer makes any sense at all to do so. It therefore follows that equality is not reducible to identity. In light of this argument it would seem advisable to prefer Marty's anti-Platonism over Husserl's Platonism.

2.3. Double Judgments and Positing Names

In the first chapter of this study we discussed Brentano's view that all judgments are existential. In this regard he opposes the theory according to which judgments are syntheses of presentations. If we affirm the existence of something (S) we do not thereby combine the presentation of S with the presentation of existence. The affirmative judgment in this case, namely the judgment that S exists, has only the presentation of S as its foundation. Besides the view, favored by Kant and his followers, that a judgment is a synthesis of presentations, it might be also held that some judgments, so-called "categorical judgments", are to be construed in this way, whereas existential judgments make up a special class and are not as such to be regarded as syntheses. While this latter view had been held by some, most notably by Herbart, Brentano opposes it too. He insists that *all* judgments are reducible to existential ones. The challenge for such a view is of course to show how certain judgments which are apparently categorical, at least as far as their expression in sentences are concerned, are in truth existential.

According to Marty, judgments of the kind just mentioned are to be characterized as "double judgments", as elaborated on in the following passage:

The categorical or two-membered form of statement has arisen as an appropriate expression for double judgments, and a double judgment is what we unquestionably have before us in sentences such as "this is red", "this flower is blue", "I am well", "my brother has departed", "some of my fields are mortgaged", "some flowers of your garden have suffered from frost", and so forth. In these cases and all similar ones the meaning of the sentence is a peculiarly composed affirmative judgment which cannot be resolved into a sum of simple acknowledgments. Already by saying "I" or "this flower", the acknowledgment of an object is given; but built on this basis is now a second acknowledging which would not be conceivable without the first one. This second acknowledging in some manner involves the first one; the former is necessary foundation from which it is inseparable. In the so-called complex judgment a subjectual and predicating part can be distinguished, it being also possible to speak of a subjectual and a predicating judgment or sub-judgment. For in truth there are not just two concepts, but rather two judgments, whereby however the second, predicating one is such that it involves the first one in way similar to that in which the thought of red includes the thought of color, so that - as this is indeed here the case - there is only a one-sided detachability between the two elements.[1]

The old Brentanian theory of judgment is therefore still upheld insofar as Marty maintains that the purely predicative aspect of a judgment is at best a dependent part of an existential judgment. Husserl, however, has misgivings about the doctrine of double judgment.

Most importantly Husserl insists on his theory of positing which had been put forward in the *Logische Untersuchungen*. As we may recall, this is the view that there are positing nominal acts just as well as judgments in the strict and proper sense. However much acts of these two types are qualitatively equal, i.e., to the extent that they are indeed both positing, there is nonetheless a difference between them in *matter*. Thus Husserl says the following in opposition to Marty and Brentano (Hua XXII, 245 f.):

It is now certainly important what Brentano and Marty call attention to, that in the context of judgments nominal presentations can arise which are borne by a special belief. If the essence of judgment is seen in this "belief", "validity consciousness", or however it may otherwise be called, we may justly regard such nominal acts as judgments and Marty's examples of categorical judgments as double and multiple judgments. But names are not sentences, the meaning-content of nominal acts does not have the character of sentences in the logical sense. As long as the concepts of sentence and judgment are brought into essential relation and that which is judged (as the identical sense) in the "judgment" is taken as a sentence - for which very weighty logical reasons nonetheless speak -, the nominal positings must be excluded from

---

[1] "Über subjectlose Sätze" (1895): 63: "Die kategorische oder zweigliedrige Aussageform ist entstanden als angemessener Ausdruck für Doppelurteile, und ein Doppelurteil haben wir unfraglich vor uns in Sätzen wie: Dies ist rot; diese Blume ist blau; Ich bin wohl; mein Bruder ist abgereist; einige meiner Felder sind verpfändet; einige Bäume deines Gartens haben vom Frost gelitten u.s.w. In disen Fällen und allen ähnlichen ist die Bedeutung des Satzes ein eigentümlich zusammengesetztes bejahendes Urteil, welches nicht in eine Summe einfacher Anerkennungen aufgelöst werden kann. Schon indem gesagt wird: Ich oder "diese Blume", ist die Anerkennung eines Gegenstandes gegeben; aber auf diese Basis ist nun ein zweites Anerkennen gebaut, welches ohne das erste nicht denkbar wäre. Dieses zweite Anerkennen involviert gewissermassen das erste; letzteres ist sein notwendiges Fundament, von dem es unlöslich ist. Man mag an dem so zusammengesetzten Urteil einen subjektischen und einen prädizierenden Teil unterscheiden oder auch von einem subjektischen und einem prädizierenden Urteil oder Teilurteil sprechen. Denn es liegen in Wahrheit eben nicht zwei blosse Begriffe, sondern zwei Urteile vor, wobei nur das zweite, prädizierende von der Art ist, dass es das erste in ähnlicher Weise involviert, wie etwa der Gedanke Röte den Gedanken Farbe einschliesst, so dass - wie dies ja hier der Fall ist - zwischen den beiden Elementen nur eine einseitige Abtrennbarkeit besteht". This passage is partly underlined by Husserl.

the sphere of judgment. "The emperor", "this house", and the like are not existential sentences, for they are not sentences at all, not grammatically, not logically. They posit objects as names do and do not assertively posit states of affairs. There corresponds logical-ideally with every positing name a possible equivalent existential sentence - which however must inevitably contain the same or another positing name.

Here it may be added that what the positing nominal act posits need not be an object in the narrow sense, e.g., the emperor or the Kaiser, since it is possible that a judgment is nominalized. In this case there occurs a nominal act, e.g., "that it has rained", which posits a state of affairs. An act of this kind, however, is no more a judgment than any other positing nominal act.

As already mentioned in the concluding remarks of the preceding chapter, Husserl's views on nominalization are certainly to be preferred to Meinong's denial that an objective can correspond to a nominal act. We may moreover grant that the resulting names, but also names of other kinds, are no less positing than certain sentences or the psychical acts which they manifest. It however becomes very difficult to distinguish Husserl's views on these matters from Marty's. Their differences seem to be purely verbal. While Marty says that in double judgments the subject terms manifest judgments, Husserl says that in these cases the subject terms manifest positing nominal acts. What is the difference here? We have seen in the first chapter that Husserl, in his attempt to make a case for the distinction between positing and non-positing names, regards these acts as "one-rayed" and the corresponding judgments as "two-rayed". But here we are, once again, given only metaphors, "stones instead of bread".

3. MEANING

The dominant theme of most of Marty's investigations is language. The concept of meaning of an expression, e.g., of a name or a sentence, is of course one of the central concerns in any philosophical treatment of language. It is no less a concern for Marty, who is careful not to confuse meanings with other functions which expressions perform. In the first "Logical Investigation" we also find a treatment of meaning, but it differs considerably from Marty's.

3.1. Meaning and Manifestation

The following passage, quoted from "Über subjectlose Sätze", concerns meaning and its distinction from manifestation (*Kundgabe*):

what we in every case refer to as the *meaning* of an expression is that content of the soul whose arousal *in the addressee* is the proper job, the final goal of the expression (whether by nature or by habit) if it is at the same time able to reach this goal as a rule. However, it never reaches it immediately, but only by being also a sign of psychical processes *in the speaker*. Every linguistic utterance is therefore a sign in two senses. If, for instance, I express a name, this is (at least as a rule and disregarding the case of thoughtless distraction) a sign that I am presenting something and arouses in the listener the awareness of this state of my psyché. This function of the name may be called the *manifestation* which is peculiar to it. Only by manifesting my presenting, i.e., arousing in the listener the conviction that I am presenting something, does it at the same time stimulate him to summon up within himself this same presentation which I have, and *this* is what I want to achieve, properly speaking, by expressing the name; this is *its meaning*.[1]

This passage highlights an important distinction, namely between meaning and manifestation, which is taken up by Husserl in the first "Logical Investigation", even though he fails to give Marty credit there. But for Husserl the manifestation of an expression is purely accidental, merely something which occurs when one talks with other people, but which can also be absent, namely when expressions are used in solitary thought. He does not assign it any special task, whereas Marty plainly says that *by manifesting* a presentation, for instance, an expression causes the same (or "equal") presentation to arise in the listener and *thereby* has meaning. Here we see an enormous difference in the concepts of meaning which are put forward by Marty and Husserl. While the former construes meaning as a function of communication, the latter does not.

As the meaning of a name is to be found in evoking a presentation in the listener,

---

[1] "Über subjectlose Sätze (1884): 300: "in jedem Falle bezeichnen wir als *die Bedeutung* eines Ausdruckes denjenigen Seeleninhalt, den *im Angeredeten* zu erwecken sein eigentlicher Beruf, sein Endziel ist (sei es von Natur, sei es durch Gewohnheit), falls er zugleich die Fähigkeit hat, dieses Ziel in der Regel zu erreichen. Allein er erreicht es niemals unmittelbar, sondern nur, indem er zugleich Zeichen der psychischen Vorgänge *in dem Redenden* ist. Jede sprachliche Äusserung ist also Zeichen in doppeltem Sinne. Spreche ich z.B. einen Namen aus, so ist dies (in der Regel wenigstens und den Fall gedankenloser Zerstreuung abgerechnet) Zeichen, dass ich etwas vorstelle, und erweckt in dem Hörenden die Erkenntnis dieses meines Seelenzustandes. Man mag diese Funktion des Namens die *Kundgabe* nennen, die ihm eigentümlich ist. Allein indem der Name mein Vorstellen kundgibt, d.h. in dem Hörenden die Überzeugung erweckt, dass ich etwas vorstelle, regt er ihn zugleich an, diese selbe Vorstellung, die ich habe, gleichfalls in sich zu erwecken, und *dies* will ich eigentlich erreichen, indem ich den Namen ausspreche, dies ist *seine Bedeutung*". This passage is partly underlined by Husserl.

more particularly the same presentation which the speaker manifests by uttering the name, the meaning of an assertion (*Aussage*), says Marty, is to be found in evoking the same judgment in the listener which is manifested by the assertion. The manifestation in this case is the "subjective fact that I judge thus, e.g., that a is equal to b; the meaning however is that a is equal to b objectively".[1] Next to this passage Husserl writes in his copy: "But this is something new".[2] What he has in mind here is perhaps the notion of a state of affairs as this is presented in the *Logische Untersuchungen*. According to Husserl, two different assertions can differ in meaning and yet refer to the same state of affairs. Thus he is accusing Marty of confusing the meaning of an assertion with the state of affairs to which this assertion refers.

3.2. Meaninglessness

As the topic of meaning is central to any philosophical treatment of language, the topic of meaninglessness is also not to be ignored. Everyone grants that not every combination of words constitutes a meaningful expression, but there is often considerable disagreement about what expressions are meaningless. According to some, contradictory expressions, e.g., "round square", are meaningless. Marty however says the following:

If the words were without sense, how could we understand the question, whether there were such a thing [e.g., a round square], and reply negatively? Even in order to reject it, we must still somehow present such a contradictory matter.[3]

"If such absurdities are called absurd," Marty further explains in a footnote, "this can mean only that they obviously have no *acceptable* sense.[4]

---

[1] "Über subjectlose Sätze" (1884): 301: "[...] subjektive Tatsache [...], dass ich so urteile, z.B. a sei b; die Bedeutung aber ist, dass objektiv a = b sei".

[2] "Das ist aber etwas Neues".

[3] "Über subjectlose Sätze" (1894): 80: "Wären die Worte ohne Sinn, wie könnten wir die Frage verstehen, ob es etwas Derartiges gebe, und sie vermeinen? Selbst um sie zu verwerfen, müssen wir eine solche wiederstreitende Materie doch irgendwie vorstellen". The opponents under attack here are Sigwart and Erdmann.

[4] "Über subjectlose Sätze" (1894): 81 n.: "Wenn man solche Absurditäten sinnlos nennt, so kann dies nur heissen, sie hätten offenbar keinen *vernünftigen* Sinn".

Husserl cites these passages with approval in the first "Logical Investigation" (Hua XIX/1, 61). The failure of contradictory expressions to have a "acceptable sense" is construed by him in terms of the "*a priori* impossibility of a fulfilling sense". While meaning is given to expressions such as "round square", it is impossible for fulfilment to occur here as it can in the case of certain other expressions. While the name "Cologne", for instance, is given meaning, it is also possible for this name to have a fulfilling sense insofar as one can actually perceive Cologne. But such a fulfilling sense is *a priori* impossible in the case of contradictory expressions.

While Marty's claim that contradictory expressions are meaningful is not referred to in the fourth "Logical Investigation" (concerning pure grammar), this claim plays an important role there, where Husserl distinguishes between nonsense (*Unsinn*) and counter-sense (*Widersinn*). He maintains that in some cases the combination of meanings does not amount to one unitary meaning. These are cases of nonsense, whereas the combination of meanings in the case of "round" and "square" is indeed a unitary meaning, albeit a case of counter-sense.

There is however one aspect of Marty's thought which is explicitly referred to in the fourth "Logical Investigation". This is Marty's distinction between categorematic and syncategorematic signs.[1] The former are names, which are characterized in terms of their manifestations of presentations, whereas the latter consist of signs which do not alone manifest presentations or acts of any other kind. Those signs or combinations of signs which manifest acts besides presentations are accordingly not classified as categorematic or syncategorematic. According to Husserl (Hua XIX/1, 311 f.), "it would have been more consistent, properly speaking, if they [Marty and others] had taken the concept of a categorematic expression with a suitable breadth and consequently extended it to *all independently significant* or complete expressions of any psychical phenomena, in order then to differentiate categorematic expressions of presentations or names, categorematic expressions of judgments or assertions, and so forth". This is in any case the way in which Husserl prefers to speak of the distinction between categorematic and syncategorematic expressions. Corresponding to the signs in question he identifies respectively independent and independent meanings (Hua XIX/1, 312 ff.). The distinction in question is accordingly given a significance which goes beyond the grammar which varies from language to language. A word such as "and" has a meaning, but one which depends on the meaning of names or sentences and cannot stand alone. It is to be contrasted with certain parts of words,

---

[1] "Über subjectlose Sätze" (1884): 293 n. See also Marty, "Über das Verhältnis von Grammatik und Logik", *Symbolae Pragenses* (1893): 121 n.

which cannot in any sense be construed as intrinsically meaningful. In spite of Marty's failure to emphasize this point, Husserl sympathetically attributes it to him (Hua XIX/1, 313).[1]

Both the distinction between categorematic and syncategorematic expressions, more particularly the distinction between *meanings* which correspond to these expressions, and the distinctions between nonsense (*Unsinn*) and counter-sense (*Widersinn*) play an important role in Husserl's notion of a pure grammar, as presented in the fourth "Logical Investigation". Before leaving this discussion of language it should be pointed out that, while Marty is in favor of investigations concerning *universal* grammar, he refrains from calling it "pure".[2] As he understands Husserl (and his understanding is indeed correct), "pure" here means the same as *a priori*. Though Marty is willing to allow for *a priori* claims in universal grammar, especially those derived from Brentanian descriptive psychology, this discipline is also to include empirical generalizations. A pure grammar, according to Marty, would not be rich enough to be a discipline in its own right. While it may here be left undecided whether his view on this matter is correct, it may at least be said that what we are offered in the fourth "Logical Investigation" hardly amounts to an entire discipline.

4. VALUE

The three different classes of psychical phenomena, according to the later Marty, are but three types of idea-dependent similarity between such phenomena and their objects. "While presenting is essentially an adequation with the differences of the what of an object, judging is a conformation to its being or non-being, or being this or that and its necessity or impossibility [...]".[3] What the correct judgment is an adequation of is called the "content of judgment" (*Urteilsinhalt*) and is comparable to the state of affairs (in the terminology of Stumpf and Husserl) or the objective (in the terminology of Meinong). Any of the remaining psychical phenomena, which Marty refers to as

---

[1] While it is commendable of Husserl to do this, he does not always give credit where credit is due. For instance, his discussion of the *suppositio materialis* (Hua XIX/1, 330 ff.) is taken from Mill, *A System of Logic*, I.ii.2.

[2] *Untersuchungen*, pp. 56 ff., 63 ff.

[3] *Ibid.*, p. 425: "Während das Vorstellen wesentlich eine Adäquation mit den Unterschieden des *Was* eines Objektes ist, ist das Urteilen eine Konformation zu dessen Sein oder Nichtsein, resp. Dies- oder Jenessein und Notwendigkeit oder Unmöglichkeit [...]". This passage is partly underlined by Husserl.

"phenomena of interest", likewise has "something which we can analogously call *its* content: namely, if it is loving and hating under consideration, the value and disvalue of the object, if preferring and considering inferior, the greater or less value of it".[1] The usage of term "content", however, must not be construed as a relapse into the old theory of the immanent object, for Marty insists that it is meaningful to speak of the content of a false judgment, for instance, "only with regard to the fact that the harmony or conformity with a possible content belongs to it in the sense of a relative determination".[2] The same goes for the phenomena of interest in relation to value. Indeed, Marty even says "that only [...] because value is an analogue of being and truth, and consequently something objective and universally valid, the states of interest are a consciousness in a truly analogous sense, as are judging and presenting".[3] That is to say, the status of such phenomena *as intentional* is only to be granted if value has an objective status.

This last point is of considerable interest because, as we have seen, there had been a controversy as to whether feelings are to count among intentional experiences. Like Brentano, Marty regards feelings as belonging to the same class as volitions and insists upon an analogy between this class with the class of judgments. As judgments 1) have contents, 2) are affirmative or negative, 3) are true or false, depending on whether the judgment has an idea-dependent similarity with its content, 4) are in some cases evident, phenomena of interest are exactly analogous with judgments on all four counts. In this manner Marty upholds the objectivity of ethics. This view is referred to in Husserl's 1908/09 lectures on the fundamental problems of ethics, where he upholds the analogy between the objectifying and the non-objectifying acts and appeals to Brentano as the one who first discovered this analogy and attempted to make use of it for ethics (Hua XXVIII, 344 f.): "No greater tasks here await analytic investigation. Only when they are completed, shall we have a true critique of valuative reason. The paths, I think, are however clearly marked off, and I am certain that they will fulfill our hopes". Here Husserl refers to Marty as someone who has related views,

---

[1] *Ibid.*, pp. 425 f.: "[...] etwas, was wir in analoger Weise *seinen* Inhalt nennen können: nämlich, wenn es sich um Lieben und Hassen handelt, der Wert und Unwert des Objekts, wenn um Vorziehen und Nachsetzen, der Mehr- und Minderwert desselben". This passage is partly underlined by Husserl.

[2] *Ibid.*, p. 426 f: "[...] nur mit Rücksicht darauf, dass ihm die Harmonie oder Konformität mit einem eventuellen Inhalt *im Sinne einer relativen Bestimmung* zukommt".

[3] *Ibid.*, p. 427: "[...] dass, nur [...] weil der Wert ein Analogon des Seienden und der Wahrheit und somit etwas Objektives und allgemein Giltiges ist, *die Zustände des Interesses in wahrhaft analogem Sinne ein Bewusstsein sind*, wie das Urteilen und Vorstellen".

but he adds: "Of course, what he further says about presentations shows that he is not completely clear" (Hua XXVIII, 345 n.). Let us now consider what Husserl has mind here.

In what way, one may ask, do phenomena of interest have the analogue of evidence? Evidence, after all, can be apodictic, as in the case of logical and mathematical truths, or assertoric, as in the case of empirical truth. Marty answers as follows:

> The manner in which correctness manifests itself to us is especially analogous to the manner in which the impossibility of the non-being of something manifests itself in the negative apodictic judgment. As we know, this knowledge is caused or motivated by the *presentation* of the impossible, and it belongs to apodictic judging that this relation of motivation is grasped. By analogy it sometimes occurs that, if in the presentation something offers itself to us which, if it would *be*, would be valuable, love is caused by that presentation and we grasp also here this peculiar relation of motivation. Insofar as we grasp it, however, we say, 'the relevant object can not be without being justifiably loved' and call it good or valuable. In short: we have before us here an analogue of the apodictic, not of the merely assertoric evidences.[1]

Husserl expresses his misgivings about this claim with a question mark and an exclamation mark, and again with another question mark, in the margin next to this passage.[2] The doubts which he expressed in his 1908/09 lectures on the fundamental problems of ethics (Hua XXVIII, 345n) were clearly meant in reference to the above-quoted claim about the relation between the presentation of an object and the resulting act of love which is analogous to an apodictic judgment. While Husserl thus wants to avoid this formulation of the foundations of ethics, he nonetheless insists upon an objectively oriented theory of values which is analogous to logic. In this regard both

---

[1] *Ibid.*, p. 429: "Die Weise, wie die Richtigkeit sich uns kundgibt, ist speziell ein Analogon der Weise, wie sich uns im negativen apodiktischen Urteil die Unmöglichkeit des Nichtseins von etwas kundgibt. Wie wir wissen, wird diese Erkenntnis durch die *Vorstellung* des Unmöglichen kausiert oder motiviert, und zum Wesen des apodiktischen Urteilens gehört, dass dieses Verhältnis der Motivation erfasst werde. In analoger Weise geschieht es unter Umständen, dass, wenn sich uns in der Vorstellung etwas bietet, was, wenn es wäre, wertvoll wäre, durch jene Vorstellung selbst die Liebe verursacht wird und wir auch hier dieses eigentümliche Verhältnis der Motivation erfassen. Indem wir es aber erfassen, sagen wir: der betreffende Gegenstand könne nicht sein ohne *mit Recht* geliebt zu werden und nennen ihn gut oder wertvoll. Kurz: wir haben hier ein Analogon der apodiktischen, nicht der bloss assertorischen Evidenzen vor uns". This passage is partly underlined by Husserl.

[2] A couple of pages later (*ibid.*, p. 431) Marty repeats the claim by saying "that there is in the realm of loving and hating no analogue of assertoric Evidence [dass es auf dem [Gebiet] des Liebens und Hassens kein Analogon assertorischer Evidenz gibt]". This passage is underlined by Husserl. In the margin next to it here writes "NB !?" and "No [Nein]", again manifesting his profound disagreement on this point.

he and Marty show themselves to be faithful pupils of Brentano, as opposed to Meinong and von Ehrenfels.

One final point about the concept of value must be made here. Given Marty's characterization of value as the content of an interest-phenomenon by analogy to the content of a judgment, it is no surprise that he maintains that our concept of value is derived from the inner perception of interest-phenomena as our concepts of being and truth are derived from the inner perception of judgments. The concept of value is accordingly referred to as a concept of reflection (*reflexer Begriff*). It is of course granted by Marty that not all interest-phenomena enjoy the analogues of either evidence or truth. "In such cases", he says, "the concepts of reflection which are and can be drawn are not identical with what is worthy of love (or worthy of preference), but they are rather concepts of that which is in fact taken as agreeable (or what is preferred) and of the *loveable* as such, i.e., what can actually somehow compel us to love and recommend itself to us".[1] In reply to this claim Husserl raises the following question: "Is the 'reflection' which offers this concept actually the same as the reflection which offers the concept of value and being?"[2] As we have seen, Husserl maintains that the concept of being is not derived from reflection at all. Likewise, he feels compelled to defend the objectivity of value by denying such an origin of the concept of value. Whether he has anything better to offer is another question.

5. CONCLUDING REMARKS

We have seen in this chapter how Husserl and Marty confront each other on fundamental issues. Most fundamental is of course the issue of intentional reference. True to the spirit of the 1894 text on intentional objects, Husserl opposes the immanentism of the early Marty. While Husserl argues effectively against this position and Marty is also right to abandon it, the positions which they develop leave much to be desired. While Marty leaves us with obscure talk about an idea-dependent

---

[1] *Ibid.*, p. 373: "Dann sind die reflexen Begriffe, die man daraus schöpft und schöpfen kann, nicht identisch mit dem des Liebenswürdigen (resp. Vorzugswürdigen), sondern es sind die Begriffe des tatsächlich Genehmgehaltenen (resp. Vorzogenen) und des überhaupt *Liebbaren* d.h. dessen, was uns tatsächlich irgendwie die Liebe abzunötigen und sich uns zu empfehlen vermag". This passage is partly underlined by Husserl.

[2] "Ist die 'Reflexion', welche diesen Begriff offeriert, wirklich dieselbe wie *die* Reflexion, welche den Begriff des Wertes und Seins offeriert?"

similarity, Husserl's conception of consciousness in terms of the apprehension of phenomenological contents is no less obscure.

As regards their views on existence, the main difference is to be found in their stance for or against Platonism. Though Marty's attack on Husserl from an Aristotelian perspective may be somewhat amiss, it is nonetheless clear that there are grave difficulties in Husserl's Platonism, most notably in his attempt to reduce equality to identity. The Platonism which is introduced into Husserl's theory of meaning, accordingly, makes this theory a rather a dubious one. This Platonism is of course primarily motivated in the service of pure logic. Here it can be said that this point of view, though not an ontologically acceptable one, is at least *understandable*. For logic is ultimately concerned with the validity of arguments and therefore, at least formally, with the truth-value of judgments. Since truth-value is in no way determined by who makes the judgment or by when, where, how, or why (causally speaking) the judgment is made, it is convenient to speak of propositions *as if* these were objects distinct and, at least in some cases, even separate from the acts of judging. But we must not be misled into ontological excess by notions which are concocted purely for the sake of convenience. This is indeed the lesson of Husserl's 1894 text on intentional objects.

Even if Platonism is left aside, however, there is much to be said in favor of Marty's theory of meaning as opposed to Husserl's. While Marty construes the meaning as a function of manifestation, Husserl allows for a conception of meaning which would allow for expressions to be meaningful in solitary speech. A theory of meaning should, to be sure, be able to account for the occurrence of such speech. But a theory which would allow for the possibility of an entire language involving no manifestation of the speaker's intention at all is unacceptable. Unfortunately, this possibility is apparently acceptable from Husserl's perspective.

Regarding the theory of values, we have seen that both Marty and Husserl, though they differ somewhat, take the objectivist route which had already been taken by their common mentor. It is however to be regretted that neither of them seriously comes to grips with the opposing views which had arisen in the school of Brentano, namely the more subjectivist views of von Ehrenfels and Meinong.

CONCLUSION

We have initially characterized the school of Brentano in terms of its psychological orientation. The orthodox position involves the thesis that psychology is the central philosophical discipline. The psychology in question is however neither the old associationism of the British empiricists nor the psycho-physiology of Wundt, but rather one in which intentional reference is made the prominent theme. The description of those phenomena which intentionally refer to objects is moreover regarded as a task which precedes the identification of their causes. In Husserl's early work (1887-1893) we find no considerable divergence from this path of orthodoxy. We also find other ways in which he adhered to the teachings of his mentor, e.g., to immanentism, the division of presentations into concrete and abstract ones, also into authentic and inauthentic ones.

At this stage of his development one can to some extent juxtapose his philosophical orientation vis-à-vis other Brentanists. We have, for instance, seen that there is a contrast with Kerry, insofar as Husserl maintains that there are authentic presentations at the foundations of mathematics. We have also seen that in his early work he enhances his psychological descriptions with the concept of fusion which is drawn from Stumpf, but which is also not exactly the same as the one Stumpf had used. As regards Husserl's relation with Meinong at this stage, it has been seen that for both Brentanists the distinction between authentic and inauthentic presentations was of great importance, although Husserl is critical of Meinong's attempt to characterize inauthentic ("indirect") presentations in terms of relations. Husserl is also critical of Meinong's challenge to Brentanian orthodoxy concerning whether instances of causation are inwardly perceivable.

While such contrasts and parallels are certainly to be seen, it must also be added that Husserl at this orthodox stage does not give a great deal of attention to the work of his fellow Brentanists, and moreover that he was not a sufficiently outstanding presence in the school in order to receive much attention himself. The *Logische Untersuchungen*, however, made Husserl a force to be reckoned with not only in the school, but also in the larger arena of philosophical discussion. While he was developing the views which were stated in this work, he was moreover examining what other Brentanists had to say on central issues. If we now attempt to decide on Husserl's position in the school of Brentano at this stage we accordingly have two primary tasks: 1) to examine parallels and contrasts with Husserl's rejection of psychologism, 2) to consider how his peculiar theory of intentional reference stands vis-à-vis the theories which other Brentanists had put forward in order to describe this allegedly characteristic feature of psychical phenomena.

As regards the rejection of psychologism, we may at once set aside lengthy considerations of his relation to Kerry or Twardowski. Kerry was already dead by the time the issue in question arose in the school, whereas Twardowski's only significant work, as far as his relation to Husserl is concerned, is his habilitation thesis which, in spite of hints at a theory of objects, is explicitly meant to be a psychological investigation. It is far more appropriate to contrast Husserl's position in this regard with those of Stumpf, Marty, and Meinong.

The issue of psychologism was of course well known to Stumpf. As we have seen, he was by no means convinced that there should be a pure logic completely independent of all psychology. While he allowed for disciplines such as phenomenology (concerned primarily with the contents of sensations), eidology (concerned with psychical formations), and the theory of relations, he also maintained that these disciplines are ultimately dependent on psychology, more particularly on *descriptive* psychology. We moreover find not the slightest hint of an acceptance of relativism as a consequence of the orthodox psychological orientation in philosophy. As far as *truth* as a property is concerned, the charge that the ascription of this to judgments leads to relativism makes no particular impression on Stumpf (and for good reason).

Just as Stumpf accordingly turns out to be the more orthodox Brentanist as regards the issue of psychologism, it is clear that Marty is likewise no less orthodox in this regard. Once he was aware of Husserl's espousal of a pure logic, he subjected this espousal to an attack which focused on Husserl's ontological commitment to Platonism. Moreover, Marty is by no means willing to embrace relativism as a consequence of psychologism and still continues, as does Stumpf, to regard judgments as the proper bearers of truth. But his adherence to Brentanian psychologism is unlike Stumpf's, insofar as he gives up the old immanentism.

It therefore turns out that Husserl looks rather unorthodox in his rejection of psychologism as long as he is contrasted with Stumpf and Marty, but when we consider his relation to Meinong we confront a rather striking parallel. Independently of Husserl, Meinong had been developing a philosophical program in favor of a theory of objects which is in large measure comparable to Husserl's pure logic. Even the Platonism which Husserl advocated has a parallel in Meinong's philosophical work, which allows for objects which are ideal in the sense that they are said to lack temporal determinations. To the degree that we confront parallels of this kind it can be said that Husserl's rejection of psychologism is still not a move beyond the *school* of Brentano.

The inclusion of Husserl as the author of the *Logische Untersuchungen* in this school is in addition confirmed by Stumpf's respect for this work in contrast with his ruthless attack on *Ideen* I.

There are however important differences between the anti-psychologistic tendencies of Husserl and Meinong. While Husserl identifies meanings of a certain kind, namely the species of propositional acts, as the proper bearers of truth, Meinong adopts a more economical view in this regard, claiming that objectives (states of affairs) are to serve this function. Moreover, Meinong's claim that the theory of objects can concern itself with objects which have no being of any kind whatever is, by contrast, decisively rejected by Husserl. In this regard, however, Meinong turns out to be a less orthodox Brentanist than Husserl. The closest parallel to Meinong's espousal of a scientific treatment of objects without being is to be found in Twardowski's claim that a presentation can have an object which does not exist, but this claim was made about presentations and was thus still a psychological thesis as far as Twardowski was concerned.

These comparisons accordingly yield the result that Husserl, in his rejection of psychologism and his concomitant stance in favor of a pure logic, adopts a position which is less orthodox than the views held by Stumpf and Marty, but still more so than the one held by Meinong. At the heart of this issue, however, is no doubt the question of how intentional reference is to be understood. Let us now look at the contrasts and parallels between his views on this matter, as found in Husserl's 1894 essay on intentional reference and subsequent writings (but of course prior to the introduction of the noema into his descriptions). Here we shall be concerned with Husserl's relation with Twardowski as well as the ones with Meinong, Marty, and Stumpf.

While Brentano had characterized intentional reference as the inexistence of objects, we have seen an ambiguity in this characterization. On the one hand, he warns us against construing the inexistence of objects as an existence in the proper sense. If, on the other hand, the appeal to Aristotle is to be taken seriously, at least part of the object (the form) can be said properly to exist in the relevant psychical phenomenon. Thus we may distinguish between strong immanentism (according to which the object actually, albeit partly, exists in consciousness) and weak immanentism (according to which the object exists only in a modified sense). We have also seen that in the early work of Marty and also in the work of Stumpf, there is a tendency to embrace strong immanentism, whereas Twardowski was a proponent of weak immanentism. Both forms of immanentism were in any case rejected by Husserl.

Against strong immanentism he argued that it could not account for the fact that there is an identity between the object rejected and the object presented whenever an object is rejected, i.e., whenever it is judged that the object does not exist. He also argued that this view would allow for round squares and other absurdities as objects which exist in consciousness. Though Husserl saw no difficulties in admitting the *meaningfulness* of expressions such as "round square", he insisted that there cannot be *objects*, either outside or inside consciousness, corresponding to these meanings. Finally, against Marty's early attempt to argue in favor of strong immanentism Husserl tried to show various flaws in these arguments, which were moreover later abandoned by Marty himself.

Against the weak immanentism of Twardowski Husserl argued that such a view, which is, after all, adopted only in order to uphold the thesis that all presentations have objects, involves construing the division between existent and non-existent objects as a proper one. This division - just like the division of objects into determinate and indeterminate ones and also the division of them into possible and impossible ones - is however derived from a division among presentations.

Accordingly, Husserl is willing to concede to Bolzano and say that some presentations are objectless in the strict and proper sense. Once this is acknowledged, there is no longer any temptation to embrace either strong or weak immanentism. Yet, Husserl is willing to say also that, when there is no reference to an object in the proper sense, there is nonetheless such a reference in the improper sense, namely insofar as we make certain judgments under assumption. It is, for instance, true in an improper sense that our presentation of Zeus refers to an object, insofar as we judge under assumption ("according to Greek mythology") that Zeus is the highest Olympian God. In this regard Husserl's position in the school of Brentano is a less orthodox one than that of Stumpf, Twardowski, and the early Marty, though it is still in large measure a psychologically oriented one.

When we ask how he stands on this matter vis-à-vis the later Marty and Meinong, it turns out that their positions are no less unorthodox than Husserl's. While Marty construes intentional reference as an idea-dependent similarity and maintains that there is no such similarity, but only a relative determination, wherever there is no object corresponding to a presentation, Meinong carries on in the vein first suggested by Twardowski and strips away the last vestiges of immanentism.

Besides the disputes about immanentism, other aspects of theories of intentional reference must not be forgotten. Here we may be reminded that Husserl attributes the intentional reference of an act to one of its moments, namely the *matter* which is contrasted with the *quality* on the one hand and with the phenomenological contents on the other. While the notion of matter had already been suggested by Brentano in application to judgments, it was still not extended to all acts of consciousness. Though such an extension is to found in Twardowski's habilitation thesis and then again in the subsequent work of Meinong under the heading "content", neither of these Brentanists had sufficiently thematized the quality of the act. They contrast the content with the object and with the act, without explicitly identifying it with a *moment* of an act. Husserl's matter-quality distinction, applied not only to judgments but to acts of *all* kinds, accordingly turns out to be a peculiar development in descriptive psychology. The same might of course be said regarding his notion of phenomenological contents and its correlative notion of apprehension, though we have seen that these notions are very dubious ones.

Closely related to the theme of intentional reference, including the matter-quality distinction, are the classification of acts and the thesis that every act is either a presentation or founded on a presentation. In the *Logische Untersuchungen* Husserl formulated this latter theme in such a way that acts were divided into two classes instead of three. The founding class is said to consist of objectifying acts, while the remaining class of non-objectifying acts is sub-divided into feelings and desires. While the resulting classification is accordingly antithetical to orthodox Brentanism, it should also be kept in mind that Meinong and von Ehrenfels also distinguished between feelings and desires. More important, however, is the fact that between the class of presentations and that of judgments Meinong inserted the class of assumptions. Husserl was indeed right to insist that he had already accommodated the notion of assumptions as non-positing presentations, but it is in any case clear that, as far as the present issue is concerned, both Meinong and Husserl again turn out to be the heretics in the school of Brentano.

Regarding most of the above topics, namely psychologism, intentional reference, and the classification of acts, the conclusion is unavoidable that Meinong takes a position in the school of Brentano which is at least as unorthodox as Husserl's and sometimes more so. It should be added here that on the topic of values Husserl adopted the extreme objectivist view of his mentor. This view had indeed been adopted by him at an early stage and continued to be held at later stages as well. In this regard he agrees for the most part with Marty too, whereas he is opposed to the value-subjectivism which Meinong had espoused in 1894. Here we find Meinong (even before von Ehrenfels) to be less orthodox than Husserl.

Thus it turns out that Husserl's departure from the doctrines of Brentano, as this departure is to be found in the *Logische Untersuchungen* and closely related works, is not to be construed as more radical than Meinong's. While this is perhaps the most concise statement which can be made about Husserl's position in the school of Brentano, we have also said in the introduction that the present study is to help us to evaluate Husserl's pre-transcendental philosophical work. This has to some extent been done in the course of the foregoing. We have seen that Husserl's 1894 essay on intentional objects has much in its favor, including a possible escape from Platonism, in spite of the fact that Husserl himself did not pursue this avenue. Instead, his Platonism became all the more pronounced in the *Logische Untersuchungen*, which also exhibit other weaknesses, especially to be found in the obscure talk about the apprehension of phenomenological contents.

This work, however, also has its strengths, most notably the division between matter and quality and the resulting classification of acts, but also the development of the theory of wholes and parts in certain respects beyond the horizons within which Brentano and Stumpf had operated. Mention should also be made of his conception of outer perception, already put forward in 1898, which allows for the perception of things in the ordinary sense and not the hypothetical constructs of natural science. If these strengths are taken together with that which the 1894 essay has to offer, Husserl's philosophical contributions may well be developed in a direction which would be very promising - certainly more promising than the direction which Husserl actually took in his later work - for the goal of a scientific philosophy. In spite of the fact that the *Logische Untersuchungen* may be ranked among the classics of philosophy, together with Hume's *Treatise of Human Nature* or Kant's *Kritik der reinen Vernunft*, it must be kept in mind that he never intended to write a work of this kind. His intention was to make a contribution to scientific philosophy. Though his contribution in this regard is at best only a modest one, such contributions seldom, if ever, occur in philosophical literature. We must, after all, be extremely cautious about what is to be called a "breakthrough".

APPENDIX ONE

INTENTIONAL OBJECTS
Edmund Husserl

[142] [...] If, according to these considerations, we may assume that a meaning-content belongs to every presentation, there now remains the incomparably more difficult question: whether every presentation also refers to objects. Here, too, opinions are divided, although the prevailing tendency undeniably leans towards the affirmative decision. It is considered obvious that every presentation refers, either determinately or indeterminately, to some object, to the very one which is said to be presented by it. But curious difficulties are attached to this view. *If every presentation presents an object*, then there *is* an object for every presentation, and therefore: *Every presentation has a corresponding object.* On the other hand, it is considered to be indubitably true that *not* every presentation has a corresponding object; there are, to speak with Bolzano, "objectless presentations". It is indeed evident, for instance, that an object does not correspond to the presentation "a round square"; we are certain of this also in the case of presentations such as "present French emperor", etc. Therefore it seems that we may, to be sure, ascribe to every presentation a meaning, but not a reference to something objective. This tendency is however counterbalanced by a new consideration. It is still meaningful and no doubt correct for us to say: "'a round square' presents an object which is at the same time round and square, but that there is certainly no such object". And the same goes for other cases. We speak of "imaginary" numbers such as the square root of -1, of the fictional object of mythology such as "Lernaic lion". In the [143] relevant presentations the impossible or fictional objects are presented, but they do not exist. It must be explicitly observed that such misgivings are effective not only regarding presentations in the ordinary and narrower sense of the word, which excludes statements, but also regarding statements themselves, i.e., regarding the entire extension of that more comprehensive concept of presentation which we prefer. Every statement, also the false and even the absurd statement, presents - one might say - a state of affairs (as its "object"), and yet not every statement has a corresponding state of affairs. An invalid statement presents a state of affairs which does not exist, does not obtain.

It is curious that these difficulties, the solution of which was already candidly vexing to scholasticism, are still not removed; at least we are nowhere near unanimity about what is considered to be the correct solution.

Neither scruple nor doubt trouble the broad masses here; they are soon ready to decide. Of course we can present an object, even if it does not at all exist; for "presenting it" means having a mental picture corresponding to it, and as any picture can exist while the pictured object does not exist, so here too. The content of the presentation is not affected by the being or non-being of the object. The phantasy picture is inside the presentation and the object is, or is not, outside. In either case the presentation is not at all affected by whether or not the object is, will be, or has been.

The popular appearance of this solution could lure us - if only the same problem which is first to be solved were not hidden in the metaphor, and if it were not still subject to other objections which are so decisive. First we must raise the objection that one plays with the facts (with regard to a few arbitrarily preferred and favorable examples) in accordance with the theory, instead of fitting the theory to an unbiased and comprehensive discernment of the facts. That every presentation refers to its objects by means of a "mental picture", we take to be a theoretical fiction. There are countless presentations in which a pictorial representation does not in fact occur, countless ones in which it cannot at all occur. I would like to know what "mental pictures" supposedly inhere in the concepts "art", "literature", "science", and the like. Or does it still make sense to designate the fleeting phantasm of a golden frame (which I now come across) as a picture of art, the mental reproduction of my book case as a picture of literature and science? I would also like to know the mental pictures of objects conceived in absurd presentations and also those which the mathematician has in mind while reading a treatise filled with complicated formulae. Veritable whirlwinds of phantasms would have to occur in his consciousness. Just consider the enormous complex storage of concepts [144] which are contained in a single formula in the theory of functions and often explicable only by means of pages of definitional statements, and now try to hold on to the assumption that to every such constituent concept a corresponding (hence, not just any) intuition must be offered in the form of phantasy images which lend concretion to the relevant abstract moments. I still repeat what has already been argued earlier; in a word, experience has never verified these adventurous assumptions, and if one resorts to unconscious or unnoticed items, then one uses these always available hypotheses rather immodestly, without concern for the rules of healthy probability theory.

The violence that this theory does to the facts, however, is totally futile. This does not help it; this explains nothing. The images are supposedly the presented objects of which it is truly said that every presentation presents an object. The corresponding things, on the other hand, are the presented objects of which it is in turn validly said that not every presentation has a corresponding object. But does not the sense of the apparently or really contradictory statements discussed above imply that it is in each case the *same* object which is presented and exists or does not exist? The same Berlin that I present also exists, and the same would no longer exist if judgment were brought down as in the case of Sodom and Gomorrha. The same centaur Cheiron, of which I now speak and which I consequently present, does not exist. And it is similar in every case where the presentation is univalent, and we can also restrict ourselves to such cases for the sake of simplicity. Hence, what is intended cannot in every case be the phantasm, which does indeed exist, but is altogether of no interest to us in objective thinking - except insofar as we are psychologists, and in that case it is of interest in *new* presentations which are especially directed at these phantasms. The difficulty therefore remains unabated; when presentations are spoken of in the two cases, it is not the same object referred to, and the whole appearance of solution arises because "picturing something" is occasionally what we have in mind as presenting, but it is not what is meant here.

Against this view it has also been justly objected that it pretends that the phenomenon which we call the "presentation of the object by means of an image" is exhausted with the existence of the image in consciousness. When we have the image (this subjective content) in the presenting act, what we intend is nonetheless the corresponding "outer" object, which often plays the trick on us of not existing, and not the image. It is the object itself which we present, about which we judge, to which joy and sadness, wish and will are attached. One overlooks that the phantasy content must first become the representative image of something, and that this pointing-beyond-itself of the image, which is what first makes it an image and what differentiates it from the mere content that we take intuitively as it is, is something additional which must essentially be noted. And this pointing-beyond-itself of course does not mean a certain [145] reflection which, starting from the content, relates it (in thinking) to objects. The reflection, after all, would also consist of presentations which could not themselves be absorbed in present image-contents, and thus an infinite regress would be inevitable. With mere dispositions, however, it is likewise impossible to make headway. They are unconscious real possibilities, and therefore their differences cannot constitute the differences of lived actualities. They can at best have the value of causal moments on which the phenomenal differences depend. Whether we take a content as that which it is, or whether we "apprehend", "understand", it as an image - this is a difference in immediate lived-experience; in the latter case there is quite simply a peculiarly new act-moment which lends (dispositionally conditioned, of course, by effects of earlier lived-experiences) to the present content a new mental *habitus* which we (circumscriptively) express in the form: the present content represents something; it is not that which we intend; by means of it we present a certain object.

Some investigators have adopted the scholastic distinction between intentional and real existence and have conceived the situation in the following way: Every presentation has an object, even the presentation of what is absurd. We understand what "round square" means, and consequently have a presentation; now by our denial of the existence of a round square we have not denied the content of the presentation, for we have immediate knowledge of it. (This obviously holds good both for the content in the sense of the subjective content of the presentation and for the content as objective meaning.) The denial can therefore concern only the object presented in the presentation and would be altogether meaningless if the presentation would be without an object, if an object on which the rejection operated did not "appear as given" to it. Hence, there *is* for every presentation an object (presented by it). But this existence is not "true", but "merely intentional" existence, consisting in "merely being presented". "True" existence comes into play only in the affirmative existential judgment and already presupposes "intentional" existence. Recently Twardowski,[1] for example, has proposed this view (in close connection with Brentano).

It can at first be understood in such a way that it is a mere repetition of the difficulty, only in other words. Every presentation has an object; a truth is no doubt expressed by this statement. What this having presupposes we call "intentional" existence. And again: Not every presentation has a corresponding object; not every one founds an affirmative, but many a presentation founds a negative existential judgment. This, too, is undeniable, and what is here presupposed by the mention of existence we call "true" existence. But from this we notice nothing about how the apparent conflict

---

1. Twardowski, *Über den Inhalt und Gegenstand der Vorstellungen*, 1894. In order to establish the statement that every presentation has its object Twardowski uses an additional argument which I was not inclined to state above: To what, he asks, do the incompatible features in the case of a contradictory presentation belong? They certainly do not belong to the content of presentation, for in this case this content would not exist; hence they belong to the object of presentation: this is the bearer of those features which, to be sure, does not exist, but is nevertheless presented as such. One may well object here: The contradictory properties likewise do not belong to the presented object, since what does not exist also cannot have properties; they are only presented as belonging to an object. This is, to be sure, given some consideration in the argument, by speaking of the 'non-existent, merely presented bearer'; but in a manner which robs it of all consistency. One could say with some plausibility only: In the contradictory presentation something is presented as the unitary subject of contradictory or conflicting features, as round and square, and the like. This something cannot be the content which exists, while at the same time such a subject cannot exist. On the other hand, it is still something. If it were nothing, how could it be presented as a bearer of features, etc.? In this version the argument is very closely connected with the one in the text.

of the two truths is to be solved. Only a terminological distinction has been created. And it is now questionable what actually lurks behind it.

[146] Nevertheless, one believes to have a solution, and one believes oneself able to give this distinction such a content that to every presentation there is granted an immanent object, but not a true object. Thus I have no choice: Here I see again the false duplication which became fatal to the picture theory: The immanent object (assuming again the case of univalence) cannot be anything but the true object wherever truth corresponds to the presentation. The same object which is merely presented in the presentation is posited in the relevant affirmative judgment as truly existing. Whether we merely present Berlin or judge it as existing, it is still Berlin itself. Whoever merely presents that gold is yellow means identically the same state of affairs which someone else affirms as obtaining in the judgment "gold is yellow". And of course in the very same way the objects of the presentations "Cerberus", "2 x 2 = 5", etc. are identical with the objects which are posited as non-existent in the judgments: "Cerberus does not exist", "It is not the case that 2 x 2 = 5", etc.

Perhaps the opposition agrees with the identities which are emphasized here and tries to escape from the objection of duplication in the following way: The objects are in both cases the same, but the object which is at first merely presented receives from the affirmative or negative existential judgment the seal of validity or invalidity which marks it as the true or false object. In this sense the true existence must be separated from the merely "intentional", merely "modified" existence. One therefore insists upon conceiving the presented object as something that inheres in the proper sense in the presentation. Presenting and judging are still, one says to oneself, activities which refer to objects; in them objects are either merely presented or also accepted or rejected. How would this be possible if the objects on which mental activities could operate, precisely in a presenting, accepting, or rejecting manner, did not inhere in these activities?

I need hardly say that I regard this position as an untenable one. If the "immanent" object (as is said flatly, instead of the "intentional" object) of the presentation is immanent in the proper sense, then its existence is just as real and genuine as that of the presentation itself, and it becomes totally unintelligible why we should degrade it and allow it to count as merely modified. It becomes unintelligible also what the meaning and purpose of "modification" is here. There are no doubt cases of genuine immanence, but they are *eo ipso* also cases of genuine existence. If I present a color to which I am *intuitively* directed, then this color is something that exists just as genuinely as any other thing in the world. If it is true that there is no colored real *thing*, then this truth takes away none of the existence from the intuited color. It is no more a thing than the whole presentation in which it is an immanent constituent. But now whether it be a thing or a non-thing, it exists as this part of the presentation, and [147] nevertheless it occurs to no one to degrade its existence. Whether it is psychologically (hence in the real and causal sense) possible that rejection refers to the intuited colour, we need not consider. What is evident is the logical impossibility. What is evident is that a negative existential judgment would here be false - here and therefore in every case of genuine immanence of that which is presented: so in every case if the opposing view were correct. The unbridgeable gulf which separates presentations in that class just illustrated by example from those others, for which "figure with a million angles", "ten-headed serpent", "an unequilateral right triangle" provide examples, does not make itself felt. One distinguishes intuitive and non-intuitive presentations, but exerts oneself in vain to grasp the distinction correctly, for it is overlooked that the case of (i.e., total and strict) intuition coincides with that of the immanence of the (or a) presentational object, while in the other case immanence cannot truly be spoken of. What absurdity we would have to accept otherwise! If a round square is immanent in the presentation in the same sense as the intuited color, then there would be a round square in the presentation. The truth "there is no round square" would no longer have strictly universal validity and would be taken incorrectly in the expression. It would be only outside the presentations where round squares did not exist; in (i.e., as constituent parts of) presentations there would very well be such things. Hence, there would be round squares as often as "they" were presented. Since the presentations really exist, then the existence of each and every absurdity also would have to be fully and completely admitted. The realm of the objects and states of affairs immanent in the presentations would not be subject to mathematical and logical laws. But is it not more reasonable to judge that the evident incompatibilities of logic and mathematics, as intended in the strictest generality, are thus valid with evidence in the entire extent of their intention? That they know of no distinction between that which occurs and obtains in the subjective experiences of human beings and whatever else occurs and obtains in the world? In any case, before we decide in favor of such grave consequences, it is worth considering whether it cannot be understood as improper to speak of "immanent" objects of presentations and judgments, i.e., improper in the sense that in the acts themselves in general there inheres nothing, that in them there is in the proper sense nothing which could be said to be the object which the act presents or also accepts or rejects; that therefore the acts, if they require, in the manner of operations, an existing material on which they operate, could not have in the objects "to which they refer" the material that they require; that rather the talk of inherence and the whole distinction between true and intentional is reduced to certain peculiarities and distinctions of logical function of presentations, i.e., of forms of possible objective connections into which the presentations, considered exclusively in terms of their objective content, can enter. It would quite well suit such a conception in this case **[148]** to speak of the modifying power of the attribute "being presented". For everywhere the modification indicates an *impropriety* of the expression which essentially alters the normal meaning of a grammatical attribute in any connection. We are compelled towards such a conception from the outset also by the distinction of the ideal from the psychological content of the presentational acts. The former indicates, after all, certain networks of identifications in which we grasp the identity of the intention (perhaps with evidence), whereas the individual presentations would not have any psychological-identical constituent in common. From the outset we ascribed the objective reference of presentations to their ideal content, though presentations with identically the same meaning could still exhibit objective difference, while presentations with different meanings could still exhibit identity. The basis for speaking of presentations which present the same object was here nothing but the synthesis in the judgment or in cognition. Upon close inspection, the posited connection is in this case concerned directly with the objective contents of the relevant presentative acts; objectively this connection has a different sense (the identification proceeds in a different "direction"), depending on whether meaning or objective reference is spoken of. But now the question remains how the paradox under consideration is to be solved, how on closer inspection those networks of judgments look which reconcile the apparently contradictory assertions "every presentation presents an object" and "not every presentation has a corresponding object" with each other, and which unfold in detail the distinction, so easily understandable and still in need of explanation, between merely intentional and true objects.

First[1] we must concede to a comfortable restriction which is indeed in a certain respect indispensable. According to this restriction, presentations *simpliciter* are to be understood only as that distinguished class of presentations which correspond to "names" (in the broad sense à la J. St. Mill). In the dispute concerning the questions treated here this restriction is everywhere, albeit tacitly, at work. For the rest it may here at once be observed that, as regards method and results, our investigation is applicable to presentations of all kinds, i.e., to propositional presentations also (original presentations of states of affairs), albeit with certain modifications, including the following: what is understood as "reference to the object" exhibits very essential varieties which simply determine the modes of presentation.

---

1. *The following paragraph is a relatively late addition (probably about 1900) to the original manuscript. It must have originated at the same time with the unpaginated paragraph at the end of this chapter ("As the main result...") which is expressed in the same spirit.*

In order to clarify the essential improprieties at work here, let us first look at related cases. Analogous to the quasi-division of objects into true and intentional ones is that division of objects into determinate and indeterminate ones. Presentations such as "Charles V", "the brightest fixed star", etc. present determinate objects, whereas presentations such as "a lion" present indeterminate ones. If we understand the expression "a lion" or if we judge "there is a lion", then we do in fact present a lion [149] -but one that is not individually determinate, and it is what the judgment concerns. Accordingly one might divide objects into determinate and indeterminate ones. But are there, in addition to determinate lions, also indeterminate ones running about in the world? Does the extension of the concept "lion" accordingly fall into these two types? In the extension there belongs, after all, everything that exists as a lion, consequently also that indeterminate lion spoken of in the above judgment. One will of course reply: Every object is intrinsically determinate. The division of lions into determinate and indeterminate ones is no division of lions - such as the division into African and Asiatic ones - but rather a division of presentations (of objective presentations, of course) into those whose objective reference is a determinate one and those in which it is an indeterminate one (something, an A).

It is quite similar in the case of the division of objects into possible and impossible ones (of numbers, e.g., into real and imaginary ones). Here there obtains not a division of objects, but rather a division of presentations, in each case based on the valid compatibility or incompatibility judgments into which they enter. A number which yields the result -1 when it is squared: this cannot exist. The presentation which is indicated in front of the colon unites conflicting features; that it does so and that for this reason its corresponding object does not exist, is precisely what the judgment says, and taking into account that it is a constituent in such a valid judgment, it is itself called "impossible presentation", and again its object is called an "impossible" one.

Obviously the matter is likewise the same in the case of the division of objects into existent and non-existent ones; it is merely a division of presentations into presentations A, which fit into valid existential judgments of the form "A exists", and again into presentations B, which fit into valid existential judgments of the correlate form "B does not exist". We do know, after all, according to the law of contradiction and so forth, that every presentation P belongs either in the class A or in the class B and can never at the same time belong in both. The presentations here continue to exist, whether they enter the one or the other judgment-synthesis.

One must of course be on guard here against misunderstandings which can be involved in speaking of presentations A, which fit into judgments of the form "A exists". If I say "God exists", then obviously the presentation "God", but by no means the presentation "the presentation 'God'", is a constituent of the judgment (or the statement-presentation). The statement does not say "the presentation 'God' exists". In one case we say that it is God, in the other case that it is the presentation "God" that is judged about. In the former case it is the presentation "God", in the latter case it is the presentation "the presentation 'God'" that enters into the judgment. The obvious confusion of the two thoughts "every judgment combines presentations" and "every judgment judges about presentations" was surely the source of the error, wide-spread in the old logic, [150] that only presentations, instead of presented things, are judged about. And in this way the division of presentations according to the forms of judgments or of truths in which they "enter" must not in our case be misunderstood.

In the case of the quasi-divisions involved here, behind which divisions of presentations were actually concealed, the subjective acts of presentation did not at all come into consideration, rather only their possible objective content, i.e., presentations in the objective sense in such and such objective networks. If now we want to reduce the division of objects into true and intentional ones to the realm of presentations and here to take only objective presentations into account, it is clear that we come back to the just-discussed division of objects into non-existent and existent ones, provided that we understand "intentional objects" as *merely* intentional objects. A merely intentional object is a non-existent one, a true object an existent one: the concepts surely have the same extension. The exclusion of existence is expressed in the first case by the word "merely". If we omit it, then the attribute "intentional" no longer "modifies" the object into a non-existent object, but rather an object is now meant in the sense in which it supposedly belongs to every presentation, valid as well as invalid, or an object in the sense in which the existential question concerning it is totally disregarded. Since the extension of the concept "intentional" includes also true objects, a division can now no longer be spoken of.

Of the two assertions which apparently contradict each other, one of them is already completely clear from the reflection thus far: "Not for every presentation P is there a corresponding object", i.e., not every presentation P justifies the truth of the statement "A exists", not every presentation is a "valid" presentation, not every one has a "true", "existing" object, or to say this concisely and *properly*: Not every presentation has an object. The fact of the matter is that the expressions "an object" and "an existent, true, real, proper object" are fully equivalent, and if the meaning of the word "have" also remains unmodified, then it entails the being of that which is had. Objects in the proper sense are referred to by every genuine identity: it combines two presentations and identifies their object. For being-identical (and likewise: being-different) presupposes the being of the identical (or different). It is similar in the case of every genuine truth of relations, for the being of the relation entails the being of the members of the relation. Referring to objects rests in all cases upon the validity of presentations which enter into such judgment-combinations. We observe here still that the distinction of the statements "the presentation 'P' is valid" and "its object exists" or - in order to introduce the direct expression in accordance with the guiding intention - "P exists" lies only in the fact that, in an equivalent exchange for the [151] presentation of the presentation, the straightforward presentation is substituted in the judgment and thus the reflexive judgment "concerned with the presentation" is carried over into the correlate one directly "concerned with the object".

The other one of the repeatedly mentioned assertions which apparently contradict each other, namely "every presentation presents an object", refers to "intentional" objects, as the first refers to true ones. In its sense "a round square" supposedly presents an object just as "a square", "Cerberus" and likewise "Bismarck's Tyras" do. If now the possibility exists of speaking everywhere of "the" object of the presentation, then it must, above all, also be possible to identify and distinguish these "intentional" objects. If it is now asked what it means here, in the sense in question, to say that two presentations - disregarding their existence or non-existence - present the same object, then it is seen at once that identity can be meant here only under hypothesis. Unconditionally posited identity, after all, implies the existence of the identified objects. "Disregarding existence and non-existence" can here therefore mean only that no decision about this is necessary, that what is at stake in such identification is in each case a relation of presentations which is not biased in favor of validity or invalidity, and this is indeed correct where we posit objective identity under hypothesis, while it is incorrect if the identity is posited absolutely. If it is therefore said that the presentations P and P' present the same object, that they have the same intentional object, then it is meant only that under an assumption, which is obvious in the circumstance at hand and is to be added, they have the same object; for example (to select the simplest case), that if they have any object at all this is the same. "The" object which "might be" is the same, and "it" is perhaps the questionable, doubtful, falsely believed, non-existent, impossible object - nothing but improprieties of speech in attribution and identification. The presentations "Zeus" and "the highest of the Olympian Gods" have the same intentional object; that is to say, Zeus is the highest of the Olympian gods - according to Greek mythology. As a rule we omit this addendum and do not miss it where it is absent. It goes without saying that whoever judges about mythical objects puts himself on the foundations of myth, but without truly accepting it. If truth corresponded to the myth of the ancient Greeks, i.e., if the two presentations were valid ones, the posited identity would obtain. This is the sense of the apparently absolute identity claim which would not be valid if understood as absolute. Or the sense lies in an assertion equivalent to this hypothetical one: The ancient Greeks believed that there was a god Zeus; the same god is the highest of the Olympian gods which are likewise accepted by them, etc. And in like manner the grammatical assertion "the two names name the same object" is understood. Literally and properly speaking, it is false, but its natural function lies in the [152] impropriety in which it is generally understood. A name names something; that is to say, belonging to it is a presentation whose object is precisely that which it names. Hence, as regards propriety or impropriety in speaking of identity of the named object, this corresponds exactly with speaking of the identity of the presented object, and in both cases the improper usage prevails.

Our view fits not only particular presentations, to which our last examples belonged, but also the common presentations of traditional logic which were often defined as presentations that present several objects. Of course, if the objects belonging to the extension of the common presentation are thus designated as ones which are presented by it, this is not done without force. Speaking of several presented objects in this way, however, would much better fit the presentations of totalities and collectives, which are generally distinguished from common presentations. Depending on the context, the same common presentation "human being" or "a human being" refers now to a determinate individual human being, such as Socrates ("Socrates is a human being"), now to an indeterminate plurality of human beings ("there are human beings"), now to all human beings (as in this very expression "all human beings"). But if the extension is defined as the sum total of the objects which can be subsumed under the general presentation, then it still seems unnatural to say that the common presentation presents the objects of its extension, as if a ubiquitously identical reference to this sum total is peculiar to it, just as a ubiquitously identical meaning content is. However, we find in the reference to the extension the same equivocation or impropriety of speech which allows both assertions to be advocated: "every presentation (more precisely at first: every general presentation) has an extension" - "not every presentation has an extension". Analogously one might speak here of true and merely intentional extensions: the former, where the relevant context presupposes the existence of an extension, i.e., where it must be understood as proper to speak of "the" extension; the latter, by contrast, where the existence of an extension is left undecided, due to an unexpressed assumption which is to be added from the intention of the whole context of thought. This improper manner of speaking is obviously the one that almost exclusively dominates wherever the extensional relations of presentations (or concepts) are treated. The assertion that the extensions of presentations A and B are identical (that both presentations refer to the same objects, etc.), as regards its meaning, is equal in value to the assertion that the two presentations have, if any extension at all, the same extension or in equivalent reformulation: If something is A, then it is B, and if something is B, then it is A; in other words, the two presentations are equivalent. If the existential statement "there is an A" is added, then the intentional extensions pass over into true ones. [153] Nothing essential changes in these relations if we consider indeterminately attributive presentations to which only one object corresponds or can correspond, i.e., presentations of the form "an A", for which the truth obtains that only one object, if any at all, exists which is an A. For example: "smallest prime number", "power of rational numbers", "root of a (that is, given) linear equation", etc. The essential logical character of the indeterminately attributive presentation does not change if the number of objects to which it is predicatively attached is reduced to one. The concept of extension retains here, too, its normal application; the "general" presentations, defined as presentations which refer to several objects, simply form no natural class.

It is different in the case of presentations which are particular in the sense that justifies an exclusive contrast with the indeterminately attributive ones. Examples of particular presentations in this sense are provided by those which are represented by proper names (perhaps joined together with attributive determinations), but especially provided by perceptual presentations. As they are essentially different in character, a natural usage of the notion of extension is no longer guaranteed when their extension is spoken of, though it is generally customary to speak in this manner. Indeterminately attributive presentations have reference to objects only indirectly. They point to certain predications, to statements of the form "X is an A", "Y is an A", etc., where the symbols $X, Y, \ldots$ indicate presentations of other groups which present an object in a direct and proper manner without such mediation of attributes and propositional thoughts. In perception, however, the object itself is presented; of course it has therein the attributes which are allotted to it. But its having them does not belong to the content of the presentation. The presentation itself does not have the form "something which is a, β ..."; rather, it does no more than present the object straightforwardly and simply "as that which it is". The objective-logical syntheses bridge these essential differences in certain respects. They link direct and indirect presentations and allow concepts which were stamped for one group to be expanded to the other. Wherever no attributes appear in the presentation (meaning), the concept of extension also loses its support, as is at once evident from the definition of this concept. Nevertheless, in the case of direct presentations, as already observed, one speaks of an extension to which one assigns the one object they present. They are, after all, called "individual presentations" also in the same way as those indirect presentations of one-membered extension. In spite of the essentially different meaning which the vague expression "reference to the object" bears in both cases, it is the same way in which one speaks of presentations which present only one object. Along with the concept of extension, the sense of whatever is the case regarding extension is of course also expanded: The formula of the two-way hypothetical judgment "if something is A, then it is B, and vice-versa" **[154]** [fixes] the objective content of the identity assertion [and] gives, in the simplest manner, the equivalent for extensional identity in the expanded area. But now the so-called copula "is" does of course acquire an equivocal sense which, due to certain uniformities of formal contexts, is not disruptive, which rather arises from them naturally; as the most essential impulses for the practically useful transferences at work here lie in these very uniformities of formal lawfulness. If we substitute for "A", for instance, "Socrates", then the hypothetical antecedent is "if something is Socrates". We cannot, however, say "something is Socrates" in the same sense as "something is red" or "something is a tree". "Socrates" is no attribute which might be allotted to an object in precisely the manner of an attribute. Again, the presentation of Socrates is not a connecting presentation such as "a tree", that it could serve in the manner of such presentations to connect a "concept" to a "concept-object". In contrast to these meanings of the copula (usually not distinguished by logicians) there obviously arises a new one here: "something is Socrates" can after all mean only that something is identical with Socrates.[1] It must therefore remain open in our hypothetical formula for the word "is" to function in either sense or, what comes down to the same thing: The meaning of the copula in our formula, in disjunctive conceptual expansion, encompasses the differentiated single meanings. The reason why this expansion, this "remaining open" is permissible is the fact that within the laws of hypothetical networks the disjunctively expanded concept of references corresponding to "is" functions formally just as the narrower concepts do. For the "is" of identity and likewise for the "is" of attribution and subsumption the law of transitivity holds good: If the statements "if something is A, it is B" and "if something is B, it is C" both hold good, then the statement "if something is A, it is C" holds good. And not only that: Also for the disjunctively expanded "is" the law remains valid, insofar as the combination of hypothetical premises of the stated form -even if the meaning of the copula varies - yields an appropriate conclusion in which the copula possesses one or another of these meanings. Something similar holds good also for the

---

1. It must by no means be denied here that all meanings of the copula are based on something identical which, fused with different items, grounds the multiple meaning of "is" in categorical assertions. Hence, even the concept of existence, the "is" of the existential statement, is after all ambiguous, depending on whether the concept of the real (being as, or in, real actuality) is linked to the "pure position" or not.

other logical laws which come into consideration for the propositional forms that arise here.

Accordingly we can establish the unitary hypothetical form as the criterion of extensional identity (or non-identity) for all forms of presentations as such and in like manner arrange the other objective or, what is the same, other extensional relations among whatever presentations we please.

The claim that every presentation has an extension, that every one presents objects, would therefore have to be interpreted as a merely improper way of speaking. Its proper intention would be expressed or indirectly indicated in the statement: "Every presentation, assuming that for it the appropriate existential affirmative judgment were to hold good, would have an extension, i.e., would present one or several [155] objects". The purpose and support of this impropriety could lie only in its practical usefulness, i.e., in the fact that every presentation can enter into hypothetical relations of the mentioned forms; that one can work, in a broad and strictly delimited group, with the extensions by assuming such existential judgments as one can do so with real extensions. More precisely, that equivalence has exactly the formal properties of an equality relation, subordination the formal properties of an inclusion relation, etc., so that, provided only that the area of hypothetical connections is not exceeded, i.e., if all judging concerning the existence or non-existence of the relevant objects and extensions is omitted, it will suffice to speak of extensions and extensional relations, just as if it were proper and absolute. And this is also connected to the fact, for instance, that images from the intuitive sphere may be employed as characteristic symbols and technical aids for the formation of judgments. Obviously in this situation (I do not mean the recognition thereof *in abstracto*) there lie very effective motives for the natural emergence and persistence of the improper mode of speaking, both inside and outside of logic.

It can moreover be tied to deeper and universal logical reasons. If, within a web of thought of the sort considered here, we think of the existential statements, which would be necessary for lending propriety to the improper turns of speech and thought, as conjunctively combined in a unitary assumption, we can make a connection with a logical law which holds good quite universally and is of extraordinary importance for the understanding of scientific method: namely, that the formal laws which regulate thinking under a fixed assumption are just the same as those which are valid for thinking which is, so to speak, free, i.e., restricted by no conditions. From a psychological viewpoint, an assumption which we have fixed "once and for all" - or which is "obviously" the basis, without explicitly being fixed, for our further exercises of thought (this points to dispositions towards subsequent considerations and restrictions) - can often be completely ignored by us during these exercises, and we likewise actually do so. Every manner in which the relevant judgments under an assumption are shaped according to purely logical laws, or every manner of inferring from them consequences which would be justified if these judgments were unconditional, is also valid in the present case of dependence on the hidden or tacit assumption: only that the derived judgments themselves are again dependent on it. Or from a logical viewpoint: The consequents of one and the same assumption are subject to the same laws of deduction that hold good for independent statements; every conclusion which would hold good in itself from such consequents would also hold good under the assumption, and indeed as one that stands under it. Connected with this is the fact that all conditional talk of truth and falsity, existence and non-existence, consequence and non-consequence, real and fictional [156] objects, etc., can be treated completely as unconditioned, as long as one is assured that the framework of the prevailing assumption is not exceeded. This has significant consequences especially in the systems of deductions of so-called "formal arithmetic", where hypothetical configurations of basic formal concepts and related axioms based on them serve for the constitution of a closed mathematical region, an "algebra" whose content is the infinitely ramified system of formal consequences which can be derived in pure deduction from those foundations. Here one not only speaks but also judges as if the deduced truths, existences, relations, incompatibilities were absolutely valid ones.

In view of the (useless) intellectual work which must otherwise be performed, it would simply be unfeasible to speak and judge in another, more proper manner. The validity of the statements is controlled and the bounds of free logical movement are practically determined by the unimpeachable rule - alive in the well-developed investigator as a complex of active dispositions - of judging nothing which does not follow purely from the axioms. If, however, an investigator - something not without example - misinterprets the hypothetical character of the foundations and perhaps believes that the definition (which creates "the" region) has in all seriousness the power to posit existences, to create entities, then this has no influence on the inner correctness of the mathematical system. If one misconstrues the character of the foundations, if one conceives the deduced truths as in fact absolutely judged, likewise as absolutely independent in their objective validity, the only necessary correction is the mere subordination of them under the conditioning assumption. And something similar holds good universally: to a considerable extent we may trust in improper speech and the improper thinking that usually goes with it. To the degree that logical thinking is active in it, we may do so on the basis of the above-discussed law, and in other cases, where combinations of judgments with each other and with the assumptions are of a purely factual nature, we may do so on the basis of reliability of our memory, which is activated also in the former cases insofar as it makes possible the connection of the results to the assumptions. These improprieties of thinking, this fact that we pass countless judgments which we nonetheless do not mean "fundamentally", that there is a substitutive judging as well as a substitutive presenting, inseparable from each other, is a major part of the "economy of thinking". Science as an intellectual achievement of human beings cannot be understood without it.

Mathematics is precisely where we have found a support for our view, and yet one will want to draw counter-arguments from this very science.

One might find it objectionable that, on our view, the distinction between mathematical existence and non-existence (i.e., the distinction between real and imaginary in the sense of old mathematics [157] and logic) does not come into its own. The question whether objects do in fact correspond to the ideal concepts of geometry, it will be said, lies entirely outside the realm of geometrical investigation. And yet geometers distinguish valid and invalid concepts, they speak accordingly of the existence and non-existence of geometrical formations and often conduct the most involved proofs or constructions for one or the other. Hence, in the case of presentations to which objects need not correspond in actuality and likewise, on the view of most, do not exist at all, there seems to obtain an essential distinction, entirely analogous to the one usually made between valid and invalid presentations: The former present geometrical objects, while the latter do not. The judgment of identity "two presentations have the same objects" cannot here depend on the hypothesis "assuming that objects correspond to them"; for it is mathematical rather than concrete objects which are referred to by the judging comparison, and such objects do actually exist in the case of "real" concepts. Thus, to base the concept of the presented object on the merely hypothetical relations of judgments seems to be dubious, or it seems appropriate only if one wants to speak of objects in the case of all presentations as such, hence also in the case of "round squares". But one will still not put concepts of this sort on a par with the genuine geometrical concepts, whose "reality" might be demonstrated by construction, while we thereby move on the foundations of mathematical rather than true reality.

If we appealed above to formal mathematics, then our opponents appeal to real mathematics. The former is a *raisonnement* cut loose from all intuition, considering the pure forms of mathematical connections and systems in the most general generality, investigating their diversely possible variations and thus, with the deepest insight into the technique of mathematical concatenations, effecting a greater methodical mastery over the mathematical objects, a greater methodical freedom and skill. Real mathematics, however, has support in intuition; herein lies the basis for its concepts, and from this they receive also their peculiar reality.

In this way a new attempt might therefore be made to salvage a sort of existence for the intentional objects at least in the area of mathematics; here too, however, the deceptive appearance dissolves by making note of several layers of improprieties. There are not different modes of existence and validity. And where we believe them to be found, *either* speech is improper, *or* the differences concern the extension of application, which seems narrowed by habitual reference to a prevailing sphere of interests, while the concept at the same time undergoes a tacit enrichment.

[158] Often the term "existence" is used in the sense of concrete being, i.e., existence within real actuality. Here the primitive and more general concept of existence is enriched in content and the extension is narrowed to real objects. Truths, statements, concepts are also objects; in their case, too, existence is spoken of in the full and proper sense, but they are nothing which could be encountered in real actuality. The extent to which the expression "there is an A" can claim meaning and truth is likewise the extent to which the domain of the concept of existence reaches. Accordingly, the claim that objects which correspond to mathematical concepts do not exist is ambiguous, depending on whether one thinks of real actuality or not. If we had, as some believe, adequate intuition of the geometrical forms in the imagination, then there would correspond to their presentations truth and still perhaps no actuality, as when the assumption of an actual world, for instance, would be a deceptive appearance. It would be as it is in the case of concepts of sensory qualities: In the phantasm of a red object the red color and that which is red truly exist, even if in *actuality* a red thing and consequently also the red that individually inheres in the thing did not exist. The representative reference of the intuitive image to a non-intuited actuality certainly allows us to say: a merely imagined object is no object. But that means only that the phantasm is not what it presents. It is however taken for itself, including all abstract moments which constitute it and which we see in it. To be sure, one may doubt whether intuition of the geometrical objects is in truth possible, or rather it is certain that this is not the case. Intuition and the empirical-spatial apprehension contain starting points and leading motives for the formation of geometrical concepts, but the abstract objects which belong to the concepts and their attributes are not simply to be obtained through "abstraction" (in the now customary sense of attentive emphasis of particular characteristics) from intuitions; they are not embedded in these like the visual shape in the visual "plane". The triangle as intuited *abstractum* is no geometrical figure; it serves the geometer as a mere symbol whose characteristic type has in his mind a dispositional connection with the corresponding pure concept and with its ideal and merely

"thought" object. The intuited shape has genuine existence as does the intuition itself; it therefore provides the basis for the evident possibility of the presentation of objects of this sort as such. The geometrical shape has, on the contrary, merely presented existence, the existence by means of the definition and valid deduction from the axiomatic foundations. The possibility of geometrical shapes, i.e., the compatibility of the determinations which are unified in the presentations of them, is not guaranteed by the intuition of these shapes (for, after all, we lack such intuition), but rather by the compatibility of the elementary determinations, which are ordered together in the axiomatic foundations, and by the pure deduction which provides the [159] "proof of existence". The foundations of a complete and pure geometrical system are nothing but the definition analyzed into a series of individual assertions or the hypothetical positing of the manifold which has to count as geometrical space. These assertions are of a two-fold nature: existential assertions and universal (nomological) assertions relevant to the objects of the former. "We posit, presuppose (or simply 'think') a manifold which we call space and whose elements we call points with the following properties: Every two points determine a 'straight line'. Every two lines intersect at one point. Etc." The system of pure consequences (considered in connection with space, the totality of its consecutive features) makes up the content of geometry. In space every shape "exists" whose existence is a pure consequence of the foundations, i.e., of the definition or positing of space. All statements of geometry, both existential and nomological, stand under one - never uttered because obvious - general assumption: Provided that there is a space, a manifold of such and such a determinate kind (exactly defined in the foundations), then such and such shapes exist in it, such and such statements are true about these, and so forth. Mathematical existence and non-existence is therefore existence and non-existence under hypothetical postulation of the relevant foundations. The existential statements, like all mathematical theorems, are all together incomplete, are mere consequents of hypothetical statements, always with the same antecedent. Only the existences which are posited in the foundations constitute an exception; they are not existences under hypothesis; rather, they are the hypothesis and therefore, once again, improper existence. Geometrical truth and existence, therefore, do not signify possibility or compatibility, whether it be without qualification or under presupposition of the foundations. A red square is not a geometrical existence, a square that is red and black (over the entire surface) is not a geometrical existence. Rather, it is a matter of purely deductively conditioned existence or non-existence (which follows by logical necessity) under a hypothesis of the foundations, if not a matter of the explicitly *assumed* existential content of these as such. "In the (defined) space" there exists a square, but not a round square, and a triangle, but not an equilateral right triangle, and so forth. Similarly we say, after all, that "in Greek mythology" there are nymphs, "in the German fairy tale" a Little Red Riding Hood, and so forth: only here we are not concerned with scientific hypotheses and pure deductions. Hence, we shall not approve of the unclear talk of different realms of existence, universes of discourse, of different "worlds", which have the existence and non-existence of the same object at their disposal in different ways. The "world" of myth, the world of poetry, the world of geometry, the actual world are not "worlds" with equal rights. There is only one truth and one single world, but various presentations, religious or mythical convictions, hypotheses, fictions, and the whole distinction comes down to the fact that we often, perhaps for reasons of practical convenience, spaeak as [160] if the judgments which we pass were conditional, that we avail ourselves of absolute existential assertions, while their correct expression would demand hypothetical statements with these existential assertions as their consequents (or also other propositional forms which are equivalently reducible to hypothetical statements of this kind). This naturally occurs where a comprehensive manifold of assertions stands under one assumption, whether it be fictional (arbitrary, poetic, mythological) or scientific, and this is not only unuttered, but usually not actually thought; it thus often remains in dispositional excitation and gives the conditional judgments a subjective mental character whereby we can recognize them as conditional. But also this often does not occur; the judgments are made unconditionally, while the necessity of understanding them as only conditionally valid does not arise until they are considered together with judgments of other groups. The geometer does not pass conditional judgments. Only critical reflection on their value leads him, if ever, to the knowledge of the correct situation.

After discussing the talk of presented objects as it is related to matters of extension, we shall still look at those cases where a series of judgments which concern their possibly non-existing object are expressed as an "unfolding of the content of a presentation". We explicate the content of the presentation "a lion" by saying: this presentation presents an object, and more particularly let it be an animal, of the feline family, etc. What is meant here by "content" is obviously the meaning-content of the presentation; we explicate what we mean by "a lion", what we want to know to be designated and understood as "lion". In precisely this manner we also explicate "objectless" concepts, such as "squaring the circle", "continuously curved polygon", etc. They, too, present objects, and these non-existent [objects] appear as subjects of judgments, whose predicates are the features which constitute the content. Here begins a fallacious argument for the assumption of "intentional objects" in the case of these attributive presentations. For one might say: In the valid presentation something is presented as the unitary subject of incompatible, perhaps even *a priori* contradictory features, e.g., as constantly curved and angular. This something cannot be the very presentation's "content", which does exist, whereas a subject of incompatible features does not exist. On the other hand, it is not simply nothing - how could it otherwise be presented as an identical bearer of features and judged in that chain of explicative judgments? It is therefore "a something" thought of in the presentation, a something which the presentation bears in itself in a certain manner, albeit not in the manner of the content, and to which only nothing in reality corresponds.

The argument obviously succumbs to the repeatedly stressed objection of the identity of the presented and of [the] true object. It is moreover wrong insofar as the same reason, which rules out the possibility **[161]** that the content is a valid judgment-subject of the contradictory features, would also go for every other something that is immanent in the presentation, whether it inheres therein as the content or not. Strictly and truly speaking, the presented object of invalid presentations is therefore nothing; that is to say, it is not something. Something and something-which -*is* are equivalent concepts; "not something" is "something which is not". But what is the status of those judgmetns which explicate the content of such presentations? If they may claim absolute, i.e., unconditional validity, then their subjects also exist; for what *is not* can in fact have no properties, either. And conversely, since their subjects cannot truly exist, we shall conclude that they lay claim to conditional validity alone and are permitted nothing else. This is confirmed by the closer consideration of the sense of those content-articulations. If we assume, for the sake of simplicity, that the expression "a lion" is a mere abbreviation for a definitional formula of fixed content, then it would be an articulation or unfolding if we analytically indicated the individual parts of this objective presentation - if, for example, we indicated the presentation "a" (= something), the presentation "animal", and so forth. It is obviously not an articulation in this most proper sense that is encountered here; rather, we "dissolve" the unitary attribution into a chain of predications, and it is beyond doubt that these latter are not true meaning-parts of the given presentation, that the transition from attribution to predication represents a change in meaning, though of course this is apparently a transformation from equivalent to equivalent. By "explicating the content of a presentation" we therefore produce a *new* presentation which is immediately equivalent to the original and constituted in its content more advantageously for certain logical purposes. What is now the status of the predications which are newly formed here and make up the explication? Explicatively we judge: "a lion is an animal, is of the feline family, etc." or: "a lion is something, of which it is true that it is an animal, of the feline family, etc." It is clear that these judgments have no existential character, as if they co-judged the existence of lions. They say only: "by lion we understand or conceive something of such and such a nature"; or: The presentation (i.e., the objective presentation = meaning) is the presentation of something which etc. By starting with this thought, however, we execute the "presentative positing" of something as such or of an animal, and the predications connected thereto ("it is of the feline family", etc.) are subject to this positing; they are conditioned by it. The terms "understand", "imagine", "conceive" are modifying ones; they bring the judgments down to the level of merely conditionally valid ones. Hence, many will not hesitate to put the true sense of these explications into the hypothetical assertions: "A lion as such is an animal", that is to say: "If something is a lion, then it necessarily has the relevant features". However, this interpretation would be no mere indication of the sense, only altered in the mode of expression, but rather an indirect limitation of this sense through a statement of an [162] immediate equivalent presentation. After all, it is obvious that the statements "Being a, b ... belongs to the presentation (= meaning) of A" and "If something is A, then it is an a, b ..." are not identical in meaning, but only equivalent. In the former an explicit judgment is made about meanings, but not in the latter. And the former is more complicated, insofar as it includes (might as well include) the latter: It belongs to the meaning "an A" that it (or that an A) as such is a, b ...

Of course, it will not seldom occur that someone who wants to explicate a meaning to himself will execute the simpler hypothetical judgment which is familar to him as equivalent and not the more complicated one. And again, it will not seldom occur that the explicative singular predications are occasionally worked out much as absolute ones are, although the judging person certainly "knows" that they cannot be claimed as straight-forwardly valid ones. If someone, for example, has intuitively presented a lion and now links to the phantasy image the unconditional judgments, this person does not fall into error; for he is disposed in such a way that he will claim the (revived) judgments in the wider contexts of thought only as conditional ones.

From these reflections we see that here too, in speaking of presented objects, we are not taken beyond the presentation's meaning-content, and that this way of presenting is determined by certain valid networks of judgment which incorporate the meaning. What the presentation itself contains is at best the presentation "object" (it is the "one" or "something" in the attribute-presentation), and if the "something" is missing as an explicit part in the presentation, then this presentation includes it implicitly, namely in the logical sense. Of each and everything we can say that it is something. A lion is something. A statement is something. Socrates is something. And so forth. These are assertions which should of course be interpreted not in the existential, but rather in the hypothetical sense (or in a sense equivalent to this). In this regard the statements "a presentative experience has a content" and "it presents an object", or objectively phrased, "something is an (objective) presentation" and "it presents an object" are equivalent. For every presentation (= content, meaning) fits in validly with the formula "if something is A, then it is something". Here we are concerned with one of those primitive axioms in which the essence of the objective presentation (of the "content") is stamped.

Finally, it is hardly necessary to remark that all cases where presented objects are spoken of without consideration of their existence or non-existence lead to networks which are distinguished only by logical equivalence. Whether we say that every presentation presents an object, each one has an extension, each and everything is something, etc., it "comes down to the same thing", although the different forms of assertion do not merely have different psychological geneses, but are also not identical as regards the meaning-content.

We must still add something. We have related the distinction between true and intentional objects exclusively to the objective [163] content of the presentations. Though it may also be psychological motives which determine the so easily misleading expressions, their meaning contains none of these motives and none of the psychological peculiarities of presentations as such. A presentation has a genuine object. That is to say, an object corresponds to it. A presentation has an intentional object. That is to say, it has no true object and merely presents. Normally objective presentations are spoken of here. Whoever says here that the presentation "a tree" has true objects, the presentation "dragon" merely intentional ones, certainly does not speak of his subjective and momentary presentations.

The distinction can however be related also to subjective presentations, and more particularly in such a way that their meaning undergoes an essential alteration. "A presentation 'merely' presents an object" must now mean: The object "itself" or "as such" is not given in the presentation, rather only the thought-of object or the object as thought-of. "The presentation has a (not merely intentional, but also) true object" means that it bears its object "itself" in itself. It not merely presents the object; rather, the object exists in it.

This distinction presents itself primarily in the case of presentations to which objects actually correspond. But it has been extended also to invalid presentations, since in their case one likewise speaks of objects which they present. If we look at its solid core, the distinction separates: the subjective presentations into those which are related to adequate intuition and thus made one with their objects, and into those which lack adequate intuition, perhaps because the objects do not actually exist. Everything beyond this is false and misleading.

It is objectionable in the sense and context under discussion to speak of merely intentional objects, of "presented objects as such". It sounds as if the presented object as something in its own right were present in the non-intuitive presentation (as subjective experience), albeit only in the form of a ghostly shadow-image whose "true" existence is justifiably disputed. But the presented object and the true one are identically the same, and however shadowy the delineation of the intentional object is, it is only all the more separated from the true one; if it is an object in the presentation, then it is no longer identical with the object outside.

The subjective presentation presents an object. This assertion must be interpreted precisely in accordance with the corresponding assertion regarding the objective presentation. It is artificial anyway to go back to the subjective presentation: In thought we are always turned towards the objective content, directly and properly towards the meaning, and [164] cognition, which is directed at objective connections, is achieved through the meaning. But this claim concerns the mere function of presentation and does not say that object and objective connection leads a peculiar "mental existence" in presentation and judgment. If the mental activity (e.g., of presenting) upon the intentional object, of the presentation's being-directed at its object, etc. are spoken of, this is inappropriate wherever the object is not intuitively present, or they have only an improper or figurative meaning. What has mostly contributed to the confusion and the form of expressions themselves is the circumstance that the most original and widespread presentations, those of sensory objects, are usually accompanied by representative image-presentations. In this case cognitive activity is often directed at the images as it is directed to the matters at hand in the case of intuition in the proper sense. It seems as if these mental images, which are present to us as substitutes of the matters at hand, have been regarded as the presented objects, just as one confused them in other connections once more with the "content" of the presentations, their meaning-content.

As[1] the main result of the reflections of the last chapter we may designate the realization that in fact, as we had suspected, the meaning alone is the inner and essential determination of the presentation while the objective reference indicates certain connections of truths into which the meaning is incorporated. To be sure, our reflections were limited to a certain class of presentations which was preferred from the outset, externally characterized by the linguistic form of expression which we call

---

1. *The following paragraph is a late addition (1900?) which does not fit organically into the present context. Like the paragraph "At first we must" below (cf. the note there), it has the function of claiming that the discussions hold good not only for nominal, but also for propositional presentations.*

"names". But whoever has placed himself on the foundations of our view will see at once that our result and - *mutatis mutandis* also the justification are applicable to all meaning-forms which can be designated, in a sense ever so broad, as presentations of certain objects, even though their function in connection with cognition or truth may be totally different from the function that fits those nominal presentations. If, for example, we assign to a statement an object as that which is presented by means of its meaning-content, and more particularly by means of its total meaning-content (if it is therefore not only the object of the subject term, the property corresponding to the predicate, etc., which we mean), then we thereby fix the "state of affairs", which obtains if the statement is valid and does not obtain if it is invalid. If, in the case of nominal presentations, the question regarding the difference between true and intentional objects has led us to existential affirmations in which these presentations function as subject-presentations, and which were understood either as absolutely posited or only conditionally, then this is all applicable by analogy to the case here at hand only by substituting validity affirmations ("A is valid") for existential affirmations; these, too, can be meant now straightforwardly, now under a hypothesis. The circumstance that in connection with any statement one can find an equivalent existential statement, [165] which - however its meaning-content may be altered -presents the same state of affairs as the originally given statement, reduces the present case in a certain way to the earlier one that includes only nominal presentations, and thus one may in both cases speak of intentional and true objects in an analogous way. For example, belonging to the statement "A is similar to B" is the nominal presentation "a similarity between A and B", or also the other one "validity of the statement 'A is similar to B'", and the objectivity of the latter presentation can, as a matter of fact, define the first one.

After these detailed considerations, the impropriety hidden in the distinction between intentional and true objects we may regard as clarified. Likewise, the apparent contradictions into which the evasive talk of presented objects entangles us we may regard as solved. Since it is practically unavoidable to speak in this way, even where objects do not actually exist or where their being or non-being must be held in suspension, it is best to differentiate manners of expression in such a way that speaking of corresponding objects is fixed as proper, and speaking of presented objects as improper. The statement "every presentation has a corresponding object" is in this case false, the statement "every presentation presents an object" true. The correct counterpart of the former says: "Not in connection with every presentation 'P' is the relevant existential judgment 'P is' valid". The latter statement, on the other hand, says: "Every presentation can function under an assumption as if it were, as far as objects are concerned, an unconditional one; it can be a subject-presentation in various valid (i.e., hypothetically valid) categorical statements, and such and such features can be ascribed to its (hypothetically assumed) objects while others cannot", just as if the presentation were an unconditionally valid one, except that all these predications would exist themselves as merely conditional ones or demoted in subsequent critical reflection to the status of merely conditional ones. Judging about objects whose existence is left in suspension is nothing but a conditional judging on the basis of presentations whose validity is left in suspension and therefore remains under hypothesis. What influences our manner of expression to a special degree here is, as shown, the circumstance that we usually follow the natural tendency of our thought-economy and thus lapse from conditional into unconditional judging. In this case the means of correction lies in the disposition to enact the required restrictions, wherever necessary, and to claim the acquired judgments in other contexts of thought, for which the relevant assumptions no longer form the obvious basis, merely as conditional ones.

Whatever the psychological motives which make us speak now properly, now improperly of presented objects, it is in any case clear that only the meaning is an irrevocable and primary [166] determination of the subjective presentation, while the reference to objects indicates various networks of truths which incorporate the meanings. The object itself, if it exists at all, may occasionally be immanent in a subjective presentation. But whether it is or is not so, its objective content thereby undergoes no alteration; it is precisely determined by the "content" alone. One person may see Bismarck, and someone else may merely present him; objectively both are presenting the same thing, and this would also hold good if we were to regard the seeing as adequate intuition. Both have in their subjective acts the same meaning and refer to the same object. That one of them perceives and is able to utter an evident existential judgment gives him an important advantage in matters of cognition, but it is a difference which exceeds the framework of the objective aspect of the presentation as such.

The meaning is the essence of the presentation as such; it is that which distinguishes presentation and presentation in objective thinking, "the" presentation of a tree from "the" presentation of the North Pole, etc. Indeed, it is precisely what we commonly designate in objective networks as "the" presentation. For this reason we did not find the Bolzanian term "objective presentation" inappropriate. In a certain sense, to be sure, reference to objects is also allotted to every presentation; but this concerns only an external feature of meaning with regard to certain *a priori* truths which are for all presentations validly grounded in the "essence" of the presentation, in the meaning.

A closer discussion of the relation between the meaning and the subjective presentation in which it "inheres" will now be desired.

[...]¹

Of course, such a view is possible only for those who get the image-presentations, which may arise together with the subjective presentation and provide the corresponding intuition for the meaning-content, either completely or only as regards parts, mixed up with the presented objects on the one hand and with the meaning on the other hand. The ideality of the meanings, the existence of objectless meanings, the possibility of referring in the meaning-consciousness to each and everything without its having to be present - these are the familiar arguments which show it to be impossible for meaning and object to merge - in general, in particular cases, or as regards particular moments - into one identity. If the only alternative is therefore that the meanings or objective presentations refer, after all, to the object presentatively, this is however not to say that this relation provides no starting points for further investigations. On the contrary, difficult problems arise here. From the side of psychology the question has already been considered whether the manner of presentative reference is in all cases the same, or whether instead essentially different modes of this reference would not [167] have to be assumed. Behind the subjective-psychological question, however, there lies hidden a problem regarding the objective presentations: whether there are essentially different "presentative forms" in which the thinker can refer now in this, now in that way to any object. In other words, which are the essentially different meaning-forms, not grounded in the mere peculiarity of the objects? Many a difference regarding their objective reference arises especially in the case of the complex presentations and complexes of presentations. But also many a doubt arises: Is there for every part of the presentation a corresponding part or moment of the object, presented as belonging to the object? Indeed, can objective reference be spoken of in the case of all distinguishable parts of the presentation at all and in the same sense? Is it therefore appropriate to allow them all to count equally as "presentations"?

And this very same doubt, about what is and what is not to count as "presentation", arises in the case of the unitary-significant complexions of presentations which we call statements. Some play their role as parts of presentations, such as the relative clauses, and are to be subsumed under the previous question. However, others appear as independent meaning-forms and it is no easy matter to decide whether they are presentations completely in the same sense or have reference to objects as do the meanings which are indicated by names (and which are the natural starting point for a

---

1. *A page is missing from the manuscript here.*

delimitation of the term "presentation"), or whether in the concept of meaning a unitary genus-concept is given which branches off here into essentially distinguished species.

We shall now discuss these and similar, obviously intimately relevant problems.

First we make clear with few words that composite of presentation and composite of object do not run parallel. Composite presentations can present simple objects and simple presentations can present composite objects. For the former case the presentation "simple object" already provides an obvious example, as does the presentation "something" for the latter case. This also shows that parts of the presentation need not correspond to parts of the object. Other examples are of course abundantly available: "The son of Phainarete" is a composite presentation; but certainly no part of the object of the total presentation corresponds to the part "Phainarete". Likewise: "a country without mountains", "nothing"[1] in the sense of "something which is not", etc. In this question one must of course avoid the confusion of psychological and logical concepts. We are speaking of presentations as meanings, not of presentations as phenomena. The presentative experience in the understanding of the word "something" is certainly composite, while the meaning is a straightforwardly simple one. Whoever has grasped the difference between the subjective and objective content is safe from the error [168] of lumping together, in composites such as "country without mountains", the parts of the objective meaning with subjective moments of the experience, with the etymon or other auxiliary presentations. Through such confusions of psychological and objective intentions Twardowski falls into contradiction with Bolzano's indubitably correct and obvious doctrine.

Once again, and from another side, the incorrectness of the view in question comes to light if we look at the peculiarities of attributive and indirect presentations. In the case of direct presentations which refer without articulating forms to an intuitively existing object (such as "this" - which I am seeing right now, "John" - who is standing right in front of me), it is very tempting to assume that the object itself is the meaning or the intuition of the meaning; however, the impossibility of the same view comes to light as soon as we look at articulated presentations or at ones which are simple, but refer to their objects completely indeterminately. If someone says "a white surface", "a red square", then we can intuit such things; but what we have thus intuited is their object (more precisely: an object to which the attributes are allotted) and not the meaning, and between the two there is an unbridgeable chasm. This, which I have in my imagination, is a red square. Intuitively I grasp in the object the moment of red and

---

1. Bolzano's examples.

that of the square-extension; but even if now these moments and the constituent presentations of our meaning-whole which are represented by the words "red square" were identical, then there would still be left much that likewise belongs to this whole, while one must not speak of its intuition in the object. To begin with, what about the meaning of the indefinite article? The intuited square is a this, not something indeterminate. The indeterminacy which the "a" expresses cannot be intuited as a moment in the object, as its part. There are in the proper sense no indeterminate objects, but only presentations which relate to objects in indeterminate ways, and what this means can be clarified in no other way but by pointing to the indeterminate presentations and to the possible judgments in which they gain reference to directly presented objects.

It is much more difficult to get clear about the function of the various parts of a composite presentation, about how they make their own contribution to the unitary objective reference of the whole presentation, and to what extent they may themselves lay claim to objective reference in a single or multiple sense. Not always can one decide so unhesitatingly, as in the above examples, whether a part of the presentation also presents a part of its object, even though we readily concede to expanding the concept "part", as is at present often the custom, by including both pieces and dependent ("abstract") moments of the object. Thus, in the presentation "this tree with [169] green leaves" or also in the statement-presentation "this tree has green leaves", which presents in a certain way the same object, something presented in the object, a part, certainly corresponds to the statement's part "green" insofar as the color is - albeit not in the manner of a piece, but in the manner of a positive feature - a genuine constituent of the object. But what about the explicit relation of having in either the attributive or predicative form? Certainly the pieces and positive moments of the object make up its real unity. But is having, i.e., the relation of whole and part, also present as a positive moment in the objective unity? If we answer "yes", then we must consequently keep linking all the single parts of relations and the relations of these relations with each other and to the whole and so on *ad infinitum* - everything attached to the infinite chain of logical networks - to parts of the object. Another example: A simple spatial relation "a adjacent to b" is presented in such a way that a is to the left of b. If we may allow the intuitive connection in the adjacency count as an objective unity, then it can be doubted whether the two correlative presentations "a to the left of b" and "b to the right of a" indicate the same objective unity in different ways or whether they present two sides, two positive moments which are present in it and, as it were, overlap. Whoever decides for the latter alternative would consequently have to interpret this unity-relation of the two as a moment of the whole under consideration and keep adding to this all the new relations mentioned, to be recognized in reference to a, b and their relations of first, second ... level, likewise in reference to the parts and moments of these parts and relations *ad infinitum*. As atrocious as these consequences may seem, they have been drawn in all seriousness and advocated. In the view that insight into the depths of the concept of the object is thereby gained, Twardowski has untiringly followed the complications of multi-layered part-relations, as he is likewise, in another direction, not deterred from linking all external determinations of objects, their relative attributes as well as purely formal ones such as identity and unity, to their presumptive parts.

A different view, closer to natural thinking, would in any case be worth considering here. Instead of assigning a new part of the object to every member from the infinite manifold of semantically different determinations and relations valid for it, one might disregard all external determinations and allow for only so many internal ones as are assertable in non-analytic and analytically independent judgments. There are, it will be said, diverse viewpoints of apprehending the object or state of affairs presentatively and cognitively. In other words, there are many different meanings in reference to the same objectivity, and grounded in them are many truths which give expression in their diversity to no inner wealth in [170] properly objective moments, but rather to the wealth in forms of reference, in viewpoints and turns of cognition. To practical thinking they allow the indispensable ladders for bringing about the necessary connection of objectively different instances of cognition; they make possible the analytical transformations of given instances of cognition and networks whereby the states of affairs which are hidden in implications can arrive at explicit cognition, whereby one can know equivalent states of affairs as equivalent, incompatible ones as incompatible, and so forth.

One might object here: How are the different presentations to present the same object if they do not find different aspects of it, different parts or moments, by means of which they refer to it pictorially, by means of which they can provide an image that is projected from different viewpoints of this object? Where there are no distinctions in the subject-matter, the presentation can likewise make no distinctions; otherwise, it falsifies the cognition of the object and brings into it what is not in it. Furthermore: How could we truly add determinacies to the object, while it does not have something it itself corresponding to them? Therefore, we do not avoid co-ordinating special parts or moments of the object with external, relative determinations, too.

Here it is important to keep clearly in mind, first, that presentation is not picturing. According to our earlier analyses, this does not fit the subjective and still less the objective presentations. The recourse to the concept of the image contributes nothing at all, we have seen, to stripping the fact of presenting of its peculiarity and uniqueness. One may not confuse the objective similarity between picture and subject-matter, which functions merely as the presupposition of the pictorial relation, with the proper essence of this relation, and therefore one may not deceive oneself in thinking that the peculiarity of the presenting reference has been reduced to the content of a mere similarity relation and that the number of primitive facts has thus been decreased. The similarity between two objects, however great it may be, is not sufficient to make one the picture of the other. A presenting entity's ability to use something as a representative for something similar to it, to have only one of these consciously present and to mean not this one, but the other one - in a word, the ability to present - is the only means whereby the picture becomes a picture. And the subject-matter does not become more understandable if pictorial similarity is increased at random, nor less if it is decreased at random and is eventually eliminated. It is certain that the similarity is often a small one and is altogether lacking in innumerable cases: not all representations, after all, are pictorial representations. Consequently, also the thought which lies at the foundation of the argument - that the presentation must at least mirror some parts or moments of the subject-matter in order to be able to function at all still as a depiction - loses its strength as a proof.

[171] We have however conceded far too much to the disputed view insofar as we have drawn into discussion only the subjective presentations and not the objective ones which are the sole concern here. Of course, in the case of meanings a pictorial relation to the subject-matters cannot at all be spoken of, unless they are confused in the manner discussed repeatedly with consituent pieces of the subjective phenomena, or unless the term "depiction" is used in a sense as improper as in the mathematical disciplines for the sake of designating a mutual correspondence, in this case between parts of the meaning and relevant intended parts of the subject-matter. But if it is required that, at least corresponding to individual parts of the meaning, there must in turn be parts or positive moments of the subject-matter which the parts of the meaning especially make contact with, or - more precisely speaking - which they intend directly, this can nonetheless be put forward as an *a priori* requirement only by someone who is still inwardly guided by the idea of the relation of depiction in the more proper sense and therefore keeps giving into the above argument. Why does one not otherwise make the requirement that the meaning or presentation must always make contact with its object itself, so to speak, as regards all its parts and moments? Is it obvious that it, fixing something particular about the object, becomes able to present the whole object? Of course, the requirement was not made, for it is evident that meanings of a totally different content can present one and the same object, and thus it seemed to be ruled out that meanings absolutely mirrored their objects in that manner. Should it not also be evident that meanings gain objective reference by means of a content which possibly

has no special and direct reference to anything at all that can be called "part of the object" in the proper sense? This will be confirmed by examples. They will also show that different meanings can refer to the same objects without the difference having an effect on the special reference to the parts and aspects of the subject-matter itself.

If we say, "This human being is something, is a person, is identical or not identical with a person whom I met in Italy", etc., the predicates certainly do not mark positive moments of the object, as when we would say that he has body and limbs, pale complexion, and so forth.

If we further compare meaning-forms such as "the night is calm" and "the calm night", something identical, i.e., the calm night, is presented in both the predicative and attributive form. Though there may otherwise be something more or something distinct in the subject-matter's content in one of these forms in contrast to the other one, we nevertheless find in both cases the same thing presented, but via a difference of meanings which certainly show no hint of difference as regards what they make contact with in this same thing. Likewise, when we compare: "the similarity of a and b", [172] "a is similar to b", "b is similar to a", and consequently correlative relations as such: "the number a + b - the number b + a".

For the sake of clarifying the disputed issue as to what is to count as constituent part of the object and what is to count as form of apprehension, it is however necessary to be clear especially about the fact that it is not implicit, say, in the concept of the determination that there corresponds to it a "part" of the object. If one says, "Every determination is allotted to its object; the object has it", then this is obviously correct. But it is a tautological statement which means only that a determination which is allotted to an object is, after all, allotted to it. It is however not at all obvious that the being-allotted is a having in the sense which ascribes to the whole the having of the parts. We shall further admit that there corresponds to every determination a special object, i.e., the (subjective) feature which subjectively presents that which is allotted to the object. We shall therefore allow unity, difference, identity, etc. to count as objects, but of course not as those which inhere as parts in the object to which they are predicatively allotted. The general object which we designate as "unity" is not part of the object "this tree" which we designate as one. Part of the object is everything which constitutes it genuinely, i.e., what can - if it is a real object - also count as real itself, consequently its pieces as well as its positive features and, if need be, the real connections which give unity to it. Ideal determinations, which are allotted to all objects as such, independently of their matter, of their individual and specific determinacies, do not belong to their content. But other determinations, more closely related to content, are also to be excluded. The object receives from the more comprehensive contexts in which it "participates", or from the ideal relations of comparison, various "external" determinations which "adhere" to it, but do not internally inhere in it and therefore do not constitute it in the true sense. The non-being of the part eliminates the whole, and nothing is a part, whose elimination leaves the being of the whole unaffected: this principle must guide us. If, for example, the parsonage is next to the church, the church is not a part of the parsonage; consequently, the determination "next to the church" does not indicate a part the parsonage, though the church essentially belongs to the corresponding subject-matter of this determination.

In the last paragraph we have seen that the whole object or a part (perhaps a dependent moment) of it does not always correspond to parts of the meaning. But in a certain manner every part of the meaning nonetheless presents something, as indeed it has in turn the character of a meaning itself. Suppose that we say "the linden in front of the gate". To be sure, the determination "in front of the gate" presents nothing that intrinsically inheres in the linden and makes up its own content. But it is nevertheless a determination of this linden and presents something related to it. And thus we can in a certain manner say of all parts of the meaning - as they belong to the individual words and connections of words which fit together in the articulated expression - [173] that they have reference to the object of the whole meaning, whether this be only by virtue of the fact that they primarily mark parts or relations of this object or contribute to their being-marked or to their connection. But already in the urgency of such additions as we have just now used them, the fundamental difference is conspicuous in the way in which the different meanings or meaning-parts conduct themselves presentatively. Some meaning-parts refer to the object of the whole meaning in the same way in which the whole meaning itself does: it is the reference which we mean by "presenting of the object" in normal speech. For example, the linden -the linden in front of the gate. Others refer in this manner to a totally different object (the meaning "gate" in our example does not present the linden), but still contribute in the unity of the total meaning also to the presentation of its object and consequently have also a reference to it. Here an essential difference in the sense of "reference to the object" therefore obtains. The case of other meaning-parts is again different. It is only the second sense in which they show, as it seems, reference to the object presented in the total meaning, while they themselves "present" nothing properly. In the case of meaning-parts such as "in front of", "next to", and "is", but also "in front of the gate", "similar to B", etc., we would find it completely inappropriate if one were to say that they presented objects. Only as constituents of other meanings do they contribute to the presentation of objects, and only through these relations to the more comprehensive meanings, to which alone the presenting of objects in the correct and proper sense may be ascribed, do they themselves obtain a mediate reference to objects. In fact, wherever one speaks of what such meaning-parts present, what one has in mind is inevitably a network of meanings in which they find their complement to a unity of meaning that is closed and, properly speaking, presentative for the first time. If this network is overlooked, if such meanings are grasped in isolation, then it also becomes completely meaningless to speak of the object which they present.

[...]

In[1] contrast to this, the composite presentation then presents its object with regard to such and such parts or features. But this is not to say that to every part of the presentation a part or a feature of the object, as that which is presented, is to be assigned (consider formal elements of the above-stressed kind such as "a", "is", etc.). Rather, it is only said that there are always such parts in the presentation. At least this holds good if we disregard tautological unities of presentation, such as "Socrates is Socrates".

Simple and composite presentations, one sees, may not be defined also as presentations of simple and composite objects. Simple presentations can have composite [174] objects, while simple objects can have composite presentations; for the simple object, too, has infinitely many relations and therefore infinitely many (external) features, in which infinitely many composite presentations of this same object are grounded.

The non-attributive presentations are now very similar to the simple ones. They themselves are often, but not always simple. The presentation of Socrates is a simple one, while the presentation "Socrates and Plato" is a composite and yet non-attributive presentation. As the simple presentations are to all parts and features of their objects, the non-attributive ones are to the features alone. The object has its features, but the presentation does not present it as a bearer of these features. That is to say, it contains no meaning-part which means any feature as such. The opposite goes for the attributive presentations, which are consequently *eo ipso* composite. If they are objectively determined, as "Protagoras, the Sophist", for example, is, then they contain a presentative part which presents the object non-attributively; to this there are added other presentative parts which present at the same time features as belonging to the object. These are likewise added to the indeterminate object-presentation "a" if the presentation refers indeterminately to objects. As a rule, adding is mediate, in that to the presentation of something determined as A there is added the further determination B: An A,

---

1. *The insertion of this unpaginated single sheet is unclear; Husserl himself marked it (probably for this reason) with a question mark. The appeal to elements "of the above-stressed kind such as 'a', 'is', etc.", however, could in the context of the present manuscript refer only to the preceding sheet. Hence, it is inserted after this.*

which is B, a presentation which can likewise once more provide the basis for a further attribution. These distinctions of course run parallel to the analogous predicative ones (this or something is A, an A is B, something which is B is C, etc.) whose psychological priority is familiar; the meaning-content, however is in both cases different and in a [...]

APPENDIX TWO

SYLLABUS FOR PSYCHOLOGY
Carl Stumpf

Translator's Preface

Translated here is the syllabus which Stumpf made available to his students in order to facilitate the understanding of his lectures on psychology (WS 1886/87). In the Husserl Archives (Louvain) this syllabus is to be found among Husserl's own notes of these lecutures (Q 13 1-2) and also in a lithographed text provided by Stumpf himself (Q 12). The titles of the sections, however, are in both cases written out by Husserl. This translation is taken from Q 12, which for the most part differs only slightly from the syllabus in Q 13 1-2. Wherever significant differences occur, these will be indicated in angular brackets.

These sketches are certainly *not* meant to make the taking of notes dispensable. Their only purpose is to formulate precisely with extreme brevity the main points, but they must be difficult to understand without the memory of the procedure of proof, the examples, and other elaborations. They therefore demand in these connections an essential supplementation by students' own notes during the lectures.

INTRODUCTION

§ 1. Definition

Psychology is the science of psychical states, i.e., presentations, judgments, feelings.

§ 2. Method. Direct Discernment of Facts

1. The facts of psychology are known to us primarily through inner perception. Outer perception would provide us only with concepts of colors, sounds, etc., not of hearing and seeing as states of sensation, not to mention the other states connected to them.

To its advantage inner perception is distinguished from outer perception through its immediate evidence; for while the assertions of the latter (outer) permit doubt and error (sensory deceptions), inner perception bears the guarantee of its truth in itself. One cannot doubt that the inner states one is conscious of at a given moment are real, and indeed just as they appear. But of course in our naming and description of them errors may slip in, but errors which concern the theoretical processing of perception, not perception as such. Also, immediate evidence extends only to the momentary states. Facts of memory must here too be certified through the vivacity of their appearance, their cohesion with present ones, etc.

2. It is a great disadvantage for psychology that only perception - not observation, i.e., attentive fixing of the momentary states - is possible. In such attempts attention is fixed on the objects of thinking or feeling instead of this itself. Feelings are even necessarily changed when attention is directed at them. The observation of the present must therefore be replaced in psychology with the observation of what has just passed, and herein lies the reason for the main difficulty of psychological investigation and the importance of continuous practice in this kind of observing.

§ 3. Indirect Discernment of Facts

Another drawback, the restriction of psychological observation to states of a single individual, of the observer himself, must be counterbalanced by indirect acquaintance with the psychical life of others, as conveyed by language and other expressions of animate entities. Deserving special attention are the less complex psychical life of children and animals, pathological appearances, cases of single activities in the extreme, e.g., in ingenious individuals, finally the comparative study of peoples. Obviously, however, this so-called objective method presupposes the subjective one.

§4. Discernment of Laws

As this is done in all empirical sciences, it is done in psychology too: not by induction alone, but by a combination of this with deduction. On the basis of the analysis and comparison of single cases laws as general as possible will be inferred with probability and confirmed or perhaps corrected by drawing from them conclusions, which can again be tested by observation or by already familiar, more special laws.

§ 5. Auxiliaries of Exactness

1. The experiment in its purely psychical form is constantly used in our science; that is to say, psychical acts are voluntarily produced under certain circumstances for the sake of observation. But external experiments can also lead to psychological cognition if the inner states which are aroused by them are psychologically observed.

2. Measurements are in principle possible in the psychical sphere concerning temporal duration, but not concerning intensity. A feeling, for instance, can certainly be stronger or weaker, but the difference cannot be presented separately. Concerning measurements of the forcefulness of sensations cf. below.

3. As far as mathematics is concerned, Herbart's attempt to inititate higher analysis on the basis of a general measurement of intensity is, already for the reasons just mentioned, illusory. Cf. also § 19. Some success is promised by statistical countings.

4. Obviously, psychology cannot at first be based on anatomy and physiology. But their co-operation is indispensable in the boundary questions (psycho-physics) and especially every advance of neurology is welcome. Of course, neurology supports its hypotheses partly by facts of psychology.

PART ONE: GENERAL CHARACTERIZATION OF PSYCHICAL STATES

§ 6. Psychical states have temporal duration, but not spatial extension

Ordinary observation teaches that complicated functions require temporal duration. This however entails the same also for their constituent parts, the simpler functions. For some of them (apprehension and distinction of sensory impressions, choice between simple movements) the average duration is explored (small fractions of a second in the case of the utmost attention) by way of experiment. No psychical state appears to us, on the other hand, as endowed with length and breadth. It is also not to be assumed that there is extension without being perceived, for it, like time, is by its very nature co-perceived wherever it is.

§ 7. Every Psychical State is a Consciousness of a Content[1]

Whether I merely present or judge or feel or will, always something is present to me to which the act is directed. Certain sensations, moods, drives, whose content can be stated by language only deficiently, are only apparently exceptional

This content is not identical with the psychical act itself; e.g., the sensation of green is not itself green. The relation co-incides with no other empirically given relation and must be simply acknowledged as something undefineable.

At the same time there is an essential difference here between the phenomena of inner and outer perception. The latter are characterized by the fact that they are contents of a state, but do not again include a content in the manner mentioned.

§ 8. There are Three Different Basic Types of Consciousness, and Accordingly the Psychical States are Divided into Presentations, Judgments, Feelings

The division of psychical phenomena into presentation, feeling, and willing - current for a century in German psychology - must be corrected in two respects. First: Judging cannot be dissolved into mere presentations or relations between them. A combination or separation of presentations is not in itself already a judgment, but only if affirmation or negation, assent or rejection is added. There are also judgments with a simple

---

1. Concerning §§ 7-10 cf. Brentano, *Psychologie* I (1874).

content of presentation, without any combination or separation: e.g., it is raining. Although judging therefore includes presenting, it is nonetheless added as an essentially different function. Accordingly, the judgments follow also completely different special laws from the mere presentations as regards their origination and combination. Secondly: Between purely passive feelings and willing there exists a series of mediate states, such as longing, hope, wish, courage and the like, which can be designated both as feeling and as striving and are indeed differently classified by different psychologists. This already makes clear that willing is not different from feeling to the degree in which this is different from presenting. At stake is only the modification of a state which can be designated with the general expression "love or hate". <Always, in the case of both willing and feeling, something appears to us as a good or evil; also the predicates of morality and freedom are applicable to both purely passive feelings and the will.> The laws of origination, finally, are common to both states. We therefore include the will among the feelings in the broader sense of this word.

§ 9. Of every presenting, judging, and feeling there is consciousness, i.e., each one not only has a content, but is at the same time itself a content of a consciousness, of so-called "inner consciousness"

1. As regards the existence of unconscious presentations, judgments, etc. the following items are brought to bear:
   a) Sensations during sleep,
   b) forgotten presentations which arise once again,
   c) unnoticed co-sensations (like the ticking of the clock, the overtones),
   d) so-called "unconscious inferences" in sensory perception,
   e) the manner of production of the genius,
   f) instinctive and habitual actions.

But in all these cases there are confusions. Lumped together as unconscious are: that which is no longer remembered (a) and e)); that which is not perceived singly, although it forms a constituent part of the entire content of consciousness (c)); that which is executed without presenting a goal or without deliberation, but not purely and simply without consciousness (e) and f)). Associations of conscious presentations are moreover confused with "unconscious inferences" (d)) and unknown dispositions to revive presentations with unconscious presentations (b)).

2. Inner consciousness supervenes on its contents, the psychical states, not as a new independent act. For example, the consciousness of hearing is not a second state

besides the hearing itself; otherwise, after all, we would have to have the content of the latter, the tone, twice in ourselves. Inner consciousness is therefore only a peculiarity which is immanent to the psychical states and, as it were, interpenetrates them. This directly entails that there cannot be an unconscious presenting and so forth. At the same time it explains the evidence of inner perception.

3. Consciousness is immediately directed towards the outer content and only secondarily towards itself. Hence, inner perception cannot become observation. The observation of a psychical state that has just passed, however, is possible, for the present act of observation, as new and independent, stands in contrast with that state.

§ 10. All Simultaneously Conscious Presentations, Judgments and Feelings are Parts of a Whole State. (Unity of Consciousness)

Proof: They are perceived as simultaneous. This, however, can occur only in one and the same act of perception, and this act is, according to § 9,2, immanent to the perceived acts. Consequently these are also only partial states of one whole unitary state.

§ 11. Psychical States Leave Behind a Disposition towards the Emergence of Similar States under Similar Inward Circumstances even without the Involvement of Primary Causes. (Law of Habit)

In the realm of presenting this is memory, in the realm of judging "expectation of similar cases", the formation of prejudices etc., in the realm of feeling the development of passions and the like. It is often ascribed to habit not only that it makes more sensitive and able, but also that it deadens. The facts of the latter kind, such as becoming accustomed to coldness or warmth, the deadening of sorrows or joys, are nonetheless explained by other counteractive circumstances, e.g., the alteration of outer organs, exhaustion, exhaustion, the diversion of attention.

§ 12. On the Presumed Relativity of the Psychical States

1. It is often claimed that a psychical state is possible only in combination with an opposing state. Thus heat could be sensed or presented only in contrast with cold, motion in contrast with rest; but this is false regarding the sensations for the simple

reason that not all classes of sensations contain such contrasts. Among presentations as such it is correct only in the case of one class, the concepts of relations (near and far, father and son, cause and effect).

In the case of judgments, every affirmation is by no means combined with the negation of the contrary, even though the latter can be inferred from the former. Likewise, where there is joy concerning an object, the sadness concerning the earlier or future lack thereof is not always connected to this joy, for precisely the negative presentation itself is not necessarily connected with the positive one. The only correct thing to say is that feelings increase in intensity through contrast.

2. In another form the so-called law of relativity is expressed also to the effect that every psychical act presupposes a change; but since it is absurd that a psychical act would arise only if another one is already there, the claim would have to be restricted to the effect that a psychical act comes to consciousness only through change; but also this claim can be put forward only if consciousness is identified with attention or with discrimination. The fact of the matter is simply that changes are especially suited for arousing the attention. Sensations, which change very little or not at all over a long period of time, still do not for this reason vanish altogether from consciousness, but rather enter into the mass of unanalyzed presentations which form the background of the soul's life.

PART TWO: THE DIFFERENT CLASSES OF PSYCHICAL PHENOMENA

SECTION ONE: PRESENTATIONS

CHAPTER ONE: SENSATIONS

§ 13. Preliminary Determination of the Sphere

Those presentations which are aroused from outside by mediation of external organs are in everyday life called "sensations"; but since also presentations of a related kind arise through muscle activity, these too have been designated as sensations (muscle sensations) and the concept expanded to all presentations which have their immediate cause in neural processes, whether these themselves be produced again by the external world or by occurrences in the organism (after-sensations, co-sensations, organic sensations, subjective sensations, hallucinations).

§ 14. Classification

This can be grounded on the differences in the origin of the sensations (with which principle also the old discrimination of five senses goes together), but psychologically more important is the division according to the main differences of the contents of sensation, and more precisely of the sensory qualities. Within the so-called fifth sense a distinction is to be made between sensations of temperature and touch, and sensations of pressure and muscle sensations are also to be included among the sensations of touch. A special group is made up of sensations of feeling which arise in violent stimulation of every outer sensory organ and also as a consequence of inner processes and which are related with each other not only by the intense pleasure or displeasure linked to them, but also by their sensory quality; still, all so-called lower senses are less different from each other than the two higher ones. Recently so-called sensations of innervation, too, are affirmed which are said to be distinguished from the usual muscle sensations insofar as they allegedly occur already in merely intended motion; however, as long as there is not the slightest twitch, nothing is given in consciousness besides the will and the underlying memory image of an earlier muscle activity. These, however, are not sensations which properly belong to the senses.

§ 15. Sensations of Tone and Color in Particular

1. The tones are ordered into a qualitative series in which each one takes its inalterable place. The division into octaves and other intervals is based on the peculiarity that the so-called consonant tones in simultaneous hearing or presenting approximate the impression of one single tone. The degree of this approximation determines the degree of consonance.

2. The colors do not form such a one-dimensional series. They can be put into a qualitative order only by assuming certain so-called "primary colors", about which, however, there is still not total agreement. Here it is essential to abstract from the merely physical and physiological facts which however do not concern the quality of sensations, but rather their manner of origination. Hence, for instance, white may not be defined as a composite sensation and black as the negation of a sensation. Both are simple and positive as sensations.

§ 16. Specific Energies

A sensory nerve can be aroused in other ways, e.g., through pressure or electricity, besides the way of the so-called adequate stimulus, for whose reception the organ is especially suited. But in this case too the optical nerve always gives only light sensations, the auditory nerve only sensations of sound. This is called the specific energy of the nerve. It is probably due to the peculiarity of the ganglia cells, rather than that of the neural fibres; but it is to be taken as an ultimate inexplicable fact that a particular agitation in the brain produces just tone-sensations, another agitation produces color-sensations.

§ 17. Forcefulness of Sensations and the Psycho-Physical Law

What is loud and soft is not hearing, but rather a tone, and thus there is absolutely not a forcefulness of the act of sensation, but only of the content. This so-called forcefulness of sensation differs from the physical intensities through the impossibility of a direct measurement. A tone can be discerned as more intense than another, but the difference cannot be stated in unities of sensations, in tone-intensities. A measuring comparison of differences in forcefulness with each other is however possible. One can judge whether an intensity a is as distant from b as b is from c. Consequently, it is permissible to speak also of a double, triple, etc. distance. If the resulting scale of sensations is taken together with the corresponding scale of stimuli, it turns out that the greater the given sensation, the greater the increase of the stimulus necessary for the production of an equal increase of a sensation. Fechner expressed this more specifically in the thesis that, while the stimulus increases geometrically, the sensation does so only arithmetically. This formula has however been proved to be sufficiently exact only in single areas.

The forcefulness of the stimulus where a sensation is just noticeable is called "threshold", the just noticeable difference of stimulus "threshold of difference".

CHAPTER TWO: PHANTASY PRESENTATIONS OF SENSORY CONTENTS

§ 18. Difference from Sensations

Presentations whose immediate cause lies wholly or partly in other presentations or other psychical states we call phantasy presentations in the broadest sense of the word. But the question arises whether they are also distinguished from other presentations by their inner nature. If we restrict ourselves at first to phantasy presentations of sensory contents (which are often designated also as presentations in the narrow sense), we find two main differences between them and sensations.

1. The intensity of the presented object is extremely small, not only in comparison with the sensations with the same name, but also in comparison with sensations as such. A presented fortissimo, for instance, is fainter than a sensed pianissimo. The fact that in spite of this we do not apprehend it as a pianissimo and indeed put it on a par with a currently sensed fortissimo is explained partly from the equal proportion of intensity to other presented contents (e.g., if it occurs in the memory image of a melody), partly from the co-presented effects, the concomitant feelings etc.

2. Presentations possess a smaller fullness of immanent or concomitant features in comparison with sensations with the same name.

Two further differences supervene which are connected with the manner of origination, but which can nonetheless be taken as differences of the inner nature:

1. Presentations possess a smaller durability; they are extremely volatile and changeable; longer duration must constantly be replaced with voluntary renewal. Sensations can steadily endure at least through corresponding stimulating effects.

2. We can usually within certain limits voluntarily produce or change presentations without any bodily motion, especially as regards space. We can voluntarily modify sensations, disregarding very isolated cases, only by means of motions.

Finally there are two differences with regard to psychological consequences which depend on the already mentioned peculiarities.

1. It is usually only on the basis of reasons that presented objects are taken as real by adults, whereas sensed objects are so taken immediately.

2. In ordinary cases presentations are bearers of fainter feelings than are sensations with equal content.

All these differences, however, can vanish under special circumstances. In that case the presentation or at least a part thereof is replaced by a sensation (involuntary or voluntary hallucinations, etc.). In such cases, however, either an intense feeling linked to presenting or to extremely enhanced voluntary attention in all probability at first produces a neural process of the sort which is otherwise the basis of sensation, and consequently there is no need to give up defining the two classes of presentation by means of their different manners of origination.

§ 19. Of Intensity, Clarity, Vivacity and the Contrast of Presentations

1. The concept of intensity is no more applicable to phantasy presentations as states than it is to sensations. All differences belonging here concern only the content.

2. The differences regarding "clarity and distinctness" co-incide with those of completeness of the content.

3. We call a presentation "livelier" if it approximates sensation more than another one does, i.e., possess greater forcefulness and fullness of content.

4. There are likewise no contrasts between the states of presentation, but rather only between the contents. Since the presentation of black is not black, neither is the contrast between black and white a contrast of presenting.

5. This entails the untenability of the Herbartian mechanics of presentations which is allegedly based on the contrast and the degrees of intensity of presentations.

§ 20. Law of Memory

This can be derived from the law of habit and can thus be expressed: If a presentation has once taken place, this results in a disposition whereby a similar presentation recurs under similar circumstances. What is meant here by circumstances is psychical states of all kinds. These are designated as the reproductive moments. The disposition or habit itself is called association or, in case a presentation itself works as a reproductive moment, an association of ideas. This word, however, does not yield any knowledge about the mechanism of reproduction. We know nothing about the force whereby one presentation instead of another was picked out from the unconsciousness; rather, we must content ourselves for the time being <or forever> with the mere fact as we do in the case of the physical law of attraction. Even the attempts to explain this by brain processes are primarily altogether hypothetical and bound up with immeasurable difficulties.

Remark: Often two basic laws are formulated. 1) The law of supplementation or contiguity, according to which the part reproduces the whole or that with which it was earlier presented simultaneously or in immediate succession. 2) That of similarity, according to which similar presentations reproduce each other.

But the first law does not consider reproduction via feelings, and the second one is included in the general law that the similar traits of two presentations make up that required similarity of circumstances whereby the earlier presentation is reproduced.

§ 21. Conditions for the Certainty of a Reproduction

Reproduction will all the more certainly occur,

1. the more frequently we had the presentation which is to be reproduced under similar conditions, or the longer it stayed each time in consciousness (which is conditioned by attention and pleasure in it as well as by other things)

2. the more similar the present circumstances are to the earlier ones (for which reason especially perception of external unchanging objects works reproductively)

3. the greater the number of independently reproductive moments, i.e., of those present states with each of which the relevant presentation was earlier connected on different occasions (law of complex associations)

4. the more attention is directed at the reproductive moments; for if they continue for this reason in consciousness, the course of psychical life easily in the meanwhile brings new moments, through which the similarity of the present state with the earlier one is heightened (auxiliaries).

Only in this way does the will, too, gain influence. By means of voluntary attention we can retain a presentation from which we hope that it will reproduce the one which is sought (e.g., the name of a person). If one is not offered, the will is powerless.

§ 22. Centralization and Abbreviation of Associations

1. From the law of complex associations there results an important inference. If attention is uninterruptedly directed at a dominant idea A for some time, it reproduces various other ones: a b c. Each of these is associated with further presentations: a with a b c, b with a_1 b_1 g_1... etc., of which however those which are at the same time associated with A by preference arrive at reproduction in accordance with the mentioned law. Thereby a certain unity of the train of thought is preserved and the materials are presented to artistic and scientific invention concerning a certain object.

2. If a series of presentations of more than two members a b c d ... is formed by association, it often happens that single members are less and less attended to and ultimately drop out, so that a and c or a and d now directly reproduce each other.

§ 23. Influence of the Bodily Condition and of the Course of Time. Amnesia and Hypermnesia

1. It is well known that memory depends on momentary states of the nervous system and on certain physical agencies whereby the ease of reproduction is heightened or decreased. This influence is certainly not to be conceived as a direct one, but rather as mediated by the bodily common feeling and the mood tied to it.

2. The influence of the course of time on memory. The more difficult reproduction of the longer past can presumably likewise be reduced to the common feeling which is changeable with time, whereby the psychical circumstances become more and more dissimilar to the earlier ones.

3. Also the cases of an extraordinarily diminished or heightened memory during some diseases and in old age, the forgetting of most dreams, "double consciousness" and the like are sufficiently grasped, psychologically speaking, from an unusual similarity or dissimilarity of the common feeling due to the special neural state. Only the latter itself, i.e., the physiological cause of the changed common feeling, is still often enigmatic.

Concerning direct bodily conditions of memory, see Part Three.

§ 24. Individual Differences. Productive Imagination

1. Under otherwise equal circumstances tones are better stamped on one person's memory, while colors and shapes are better stamped on another person's memory. These individual differences are partly based on the perfection of the relevant sense which makes possible a more detailed grasping, mostly however on an originally different strength of the feeling of pleasure which is linked to the relevant sensations and pushes towards a more attentive grasping.

2. Some learn and forget quickly, others slowly. Sometimes also quick and lasting memory are found together.

3. Complex associations are more effective for one person, less so for another, depending on the ability of concentration on a certain idea.

4. In some people very similar presentations are predominantly reproduced, while less similar ones are reproduced in others.

In this way the reproductive talents in the narrower sense differ from the productive ones.

The so-called productive imagination is not essentially, but only gradually different from faithful memory. Strictly speaking, an equal presentation is presumably never reproduced. It is also certain that differences 2-4 are mainly based on peculiarities of the life of feeling whose more precise investigation is however still hardly advanced.

CHAPTER THREE: PRESENTATION OF TIME AND SPACE

§ 25. Emergence of the Presentation of Time through Original Association

Although every sensation lasts a certain time, duration itself however cannot be sensed. For the perception of a temporal duration it is essential not only that we are conscious of a content throughout a certain time, but also that it appears to us at the same time as a temporally receding, more and more past content. It is of no help to point to the duration of the external stimulus or to the after-sensations. This would explain only the first fact; rather, it is necessary to ascribe to every presentation the peculiarity to bring about a presentation which is otherwise equal in content, but continually changing with regard to the time-moment (Brentano). This process, however, has its limits which essentially depend on attention, and since this attention is continually attracted by new presentations, no presentation is incessantly retained for consciousness.

In the described manner only the presentation of the past initially arises; that of the future we then form by analogy when we think of a temporal slipping away in the opposite direction.

§ 26. Presentation of Space through the Sense of Sight

1. According to the so-called nativist doctrine certain spatial intuitions are given to us through the optic nerve simultaneously with the color-sensations. According to the empiricist doctrine, on the other hand, the spatial intuitions arise initially through the combination of color-sensations with each other or with other sensations, especially with those of the muscle sense. In favor of this theory it is mainly put forward that we come to know the size, shape, and distance of bodies only gradually, and indeed with the help of movements of the eye or of the whole body.

Against the empiricist thesis it can however be objected

a) that through the combination of several presentations, as experience testifies, a new presentation which is completely different from them never arises in consciousness

b) that even specific muscle sensations can be excluded (e.g., through instantaneous illumination of an object with the electrical flash), and still even then spatial perceptions are possible. We must therefore in principle return to the nativist view. This is also the only way of grasping the absolute impossibility of presenting a color without any extension. Just like intensity, extensity is an integral moment of the sensory impression.

2. It would however be wrong to reduce all differences of shape and distance to differences of the optic space-sensation. With regard to the differences of depth, which we present in the stimulation of one and the same retinal point, this is even evidently impossible. Hence, there must be ascribed a tremendous effect to the experiences which the individual has by means of movements and through the sense of touch, the associations of ideas which thereby arise, and the judgments based on them. The coloring, the phenomenal size of a familiar object, the muscle sensation in convergence and accommodation and other features are utilized by us with increasing certainty as criteria of distance, the sensed shape as a criterion of the true three-dimensionally determined shape, i.e., the one familiar to us through earlier experiences thanks to the muscle sense, and so forth. We especially learn also to attribute the double images which arise through both eyes to unitary objects; finally, the presentation of a unitary unlimited space in which the things are moved arises through the experience of the continuous connection of all spatial images.

§ 27. Presentation of Space through other Senses

It can be shown in an analogous way that spatiality must also be ascribed to the sensations of touch; but here, too, the influence of experience is powerful. Especially the consciousness of the form of our body and of the momentary position of our members comes about only with the assistance of the muscle sense. In the case of hearing, the discrimination of impressions of the right and left ear can be explained only by a spatial difference of the auditory impressions themselves; everything else, however, is merely associated. And thus a spatial moment seems peculiar to all sensations. Although the special presentations and judgments of an adult are therefore to a far greater degree based on acquired associations, these are themselves nonetheless again based on sensations of space.

CHAPTER FOUR: ABSTRACT AND SYMBOLIC PRESENTATIONS

§ 28. Abstract Presentations

1. The metaphysical question whether the universal has separate existence (Plato's realism and related currents in the middle ages) will nowadays be answered negatively everywhere, whereas the psychological question whether the abstract presentations form a special class alongside the concrete ones is not yet unanimously answered. According to nominalism, only names are general, insofar as they allegedly designate a sum of singular presentations. But in the case of "dog" we by no means think of a pack of dogs, but only of one or a few, and these according to only a few of their features and not all of them. On the other hand, it is also false that these features would be presented in isolation in abstract thinking while a concrete presentation would only perhaps run alongside them, accompanying or supporting them (Aristotle). Rather, we have exclusively concrete singular presentations in consciousness. But we are able especially to notice inseparable parts and also to grasp their equality in different singular presentations. Such parts of a presentational content, which can be noticed apart, but not presented apart, we call *abstracta*.

2. In this vein the question concerning the origin of our concepts is to be answered in its most general form. All concepts are, as mentioned, abstracted from singular presentations. But these themselves, with the exception of the time-moment, come partly from outer, partly from inner perception. The difficulty lies now in the precise demonstration of those singular presentations from which a concept can be abstracted. E.g., regarding the concept of cause, outer perception offers no phenomena in which more than mere succession could be noticed (Hume). The observation of the logical process of inference, on the other hand, shows us not only the succession of judgments, but the being-conditioned of the concluding judgment by means of the premises. In this way, too, the concepts of existence, necessity, possibility are abstracted from judgment-phenomena (cf. § 31 & § 33) and most of the so-called categories of Kant come from the realm of inner perception.

3. It has been denied that animals have the capacity for abstraction (Aristotle, Locke, Leibniz, Johannes Müller et al.) In fact, the unsuitability of even the higher classes of animals for the acquisition of scientific knowledge can certainly not be reduced to the mere lack of linguistic understanding. For this very lack cannot be easily explained by any other reason but by the lack of universal concepts which are expressed in language.

§ 29. Symbolic Presentations

By this we mean those presentations which occur only as signs for others by replacing them for the usage of judgment. Seldom is that which a name expresses completely thought; usually however a certain part of it. Sometimes, as in the case of larger numbers, the adequate presentation is altogether impossible for us and we think, instead of it, the indeterminate concept of a large number together with certain relations of the number we mean to other numbers. E.g., 1000 = 10·100, 100 = 10·10. Often the mere presentation of the phonetic or written sign also stands in for the content which is thereby designated. It is easy to see the inestimable advantages of these symbols, especially of the symbol system of language and of the digits, for the quickness, indeed for the executability of complicated operations of thought; on the other hand, also the disadvantages, when a changed meaning is imputed on a symbol without being noticed, as this is especially the case in the names of very abstract concepts.

CHAPTER FIVE

§ 30. Presentations of Psychical States

1. Given together with and in psychical states are the presentations of them (§ 9). They are analogous to sensations insofar as they are the presupposition of all other presentations of psychical states, just as sensations are the presupposition of all presentations of sensory contents.

2. Through original association the presentations of the momentary states are joined by those of one's own states just past, as something analogous occurs regarding sensory contents (§ 25). These presentations already essentially differ from those indicated under 1) with respect to their completeness, and if presentations of feelings are concerned, also regarding the intensity of that which is presented.

3. Finally presentations of earlier and future psychical states, as well as those of others, arise through reproduction. Directly, however, only the objects or causes of the relevant acts are reproduced, e.g., the cause of a pain. Thereby this pain itself is brought about again and together with it also the immanent presentation of it. The difference from the presentations indicated under 1) lies primarily in the fact that the pain etc. here is interpreted precisely as a past or future one or the pain of someone else, for we have

the cause in mind as something past etc. However, the presentations which belong here are further also only symbolic ones insofar as the psychical act to which the presentation is referred is usually not in consciousness with the same completeness or intensity, often not even in consciousness at all. If I want to imagine, for instance, a violent pain from an earlier time or one belonging to someone else, then I try to bring about a beginning of that feeling by presenting the painful object and grasp this smaller pain in combination with the presentation of the object itself, of the concomitant gestures and other external circumstances as a surrogate for the presentation of that violent pain. Often even only the object and the manner of expression are presented instead of the feeling itself.

(A consequence of this is that only the presentations indicated under 2) are suitable as the foundations for inner observation, for in this case alone we habe authentic presentations of psychical states, but without having these states themselves - something that would be incompatible with observing as described in § 2.)

SECTION TWO: JUDGMENTS

§ 31. Of the Linguistic Expression of Judgments

Presentations are generally expressed by names, judgments by those sentences or items of speech which we designate as assertions, while feelings (e.g., wishes, commands) are expressed in other sentences. The simplest form of assertion is offered by the existential sentences "A is" and "A is not". The name A here means the content of the presentation which is judged. The expressions "is" and "is not" mean the affirmative or negative judgment itself.[1] Here, too, is where to put the impersonal and subjectless sentences, e.g., it is raining = a raining is. More complicated forms of assertion are the categorical, hypothetical, and disjunctive ones. They can all however be transformed, as logic more closely shows, into the existential form and therefore do not express different types of judgment and have arisen only through linguistic and practical needs. Thus, e.g., by placing a part of the judged content in front as the subject, attention is primarily directed to that moment from whose vantage point the judgment is most easily made evident.

---

1. Cf. Brentano, *Psychologie* I, pp. 279 f.

§ 32. Of the Inner Differences of Judgments

The judgments divide

1. in terms of quality into affirmative and negative ones,

2. in terms of quantity

a) into general and particular ones, depending on whether the judgment refers to all individuals falling under a concept (= to the entire extension) or only to an indeterminate part thereof. E.g., no human being is happy (general); there are happy human beings (particular).

b) into collective and distributive, depending on whether the judgment refers to the content of a presentation taken as a whole or also to each single part thereof. E.g., in the judgment "there are millions of white flowers" it is not merely this complex of contents, but also implicitly each one which is affirmed. On the other hand, in the judgment "there is no white raven" the two features are negated only as a whole, but not each single one.

3. in terms of scientific value

a) into true and false ones, depending on whether a content to be affirmed is affirmed or one to be negated is negated or vice-versa. Thus, though truth and falsity are properties of the judgment, they are grounded in the judged content.

b) into evident and non-evident ones, depending on whether the judgment results with or without insight into the matter.

c) into certain and probable ones.

This difference, too, is grounded in the judged content.

d) into judgments which assert a law and ones which assert a mere fact. E.g., "2 x 2 = 4" in contrast with "It has just rained" (cf. the following §).

The affirmation of a present fact on the occasion of sensation or inner consciousness is called perception. The affirmation of certain relations is designated as distinguishing, comparing, analyzing, counting, etc.

§ 33. Of the Origin of Judgments

1. An evident judgment (judgment of the understanding) is either immediately or mediately evident. In the former case the causes lie in certain presentations, and indeed a) the axioms are grounded in the relevant abstract presentations included in them, b) inner perceptions in the concrete presentations included in them. Mediate cognition arises from immediate cognition through inference. The axioms and the instances of

cognition inferred from axioms alone are called *a priori* truths, while any other cognition, even if only one perception is among its premises, is designated as *a posteriori* truth or as experience.

From the *a priori* truths we abstract the concept of law or necessity. This is then also transferred to general *a posteriori* judgments, of which we assume with reason that they would be evident to us in a manner similar to the *a priori* truths if adequate concepts of the essence of things were available to us (natural laws in contrast with logical laws). What does not contradict a logical or physical law we therefore call "possible". Finally, every truth which is neither a logical nor a physical law is called "mere fact".

2. Blind judgments can arise from different causes:

a) from an original drive whereby everything presented is affirmed as long as consideration and critique have no counter-effect (instinctive judgments). This explains, among other things, the naive belief in the external world as it appears to the senses. Only experiences of sensory deceptions cause doubts, which are partly confirmed and partly corrected by thinking. Even the first abstractions, discriminations, comparisons, etc. come about instinctively; no less does the "expectation of similar cases" (on the basis of the assent to reproduced presentations) which, confirmed more and more through repetition, determine our action, but certainly not to be confused with scientific inferences by induction.

b) From feelings, too, blind judgments arise. There is in general the tendency to believe that which is suited to nurture a prevalent feeling.

c) Finally, habit is a source of blind judgments. If a judgment has already somehow emerged earlier, it emerges once again under similar circumstances more and more easily and reliably in accordance with the general law of habit. This is how most prejudices and pseudo-axioms arise.

PART THREE: FEELINGS

CHAPTER ONE

§ 34. Classification of Feelings

Feelings are infinitely diverse in terms of their quality. Nonetheless the following differences can be picked out.

1. Positive and negative ones, such as pleasure and displeasure, love and hate.

2. Active and passive ones. By the active ones we mean those whose content is presented as something to be realized by the feeling itself. In the case of passive feelings this causal presentation is not there. The active ones already include the wish to perform some action, even if it is seen as impossible, as long as the presentation of that causal connection is there. If the wish is joined by a judgment in which the realization is seen as not impossible, other active feelings (hope, courage) arise; these feelings pass over into a willing as the probability of success increases. The latter occurs in the case of moral certainty in success.

3. Feelings concerning physical and psychical contents. The first class includes every feeling which is directed at color, motion, etc. as such, whether these properties be presented singly or as complexes (physical things, entities). The second class includes every feeling which is directed at psychical states as such, whether they be presented, once again, singly or as complexes (characters, persons).

4. Value feelings and blind feelings. Certain contents of feeling are worth loving, others worth hating, and this is ultimately revealed to us through feeling itself, rather than cognition. Positive feelings with regard to that which is worth loving (good) and negative ones with regard to that which is worth hating (bad) we call value feelings. These are contrasted with blind ones, in which something is loved or hated not because it is valuable in itself, but rather due to instinctive desire or habit, and quite generally from "heterogeneous" motives. The distinction corresponds to that of evident and blind judgments and is the foundation of ethics, as the latter distinction is the foundation of logic.

CHAPTER TWO: OF THE CAUSES AND EFFECTS OF FEELINGS

§ 35. Primary Modes of Origination

1. Every content of presentation is joined together with a positive or negative feeling which can however differ infinitely in strength. It is in general more intense in the case of the lower senses than in the case of the higher ones. It varies also among individuals as regards intensity and often even as regards quality.

2. It can be assumed as probable that whatever is beneficial for the physical or psychical life of the individual or of the species is at the same time pleasant or leads to pleasant states, while that which unbeneficial makes itself felt in the opposite way. But

a more definite form and a general proof of this hypothesis is thus far impossible. Only the facts of instinct and the feelings of pain in the case of excessive sensory impressions give examples of this.

§ 36. Secondary Modes of Origination

This is what we call every origination of a feeling in which the present or earlier givenness of a feeling is presupposed.

1. Mixture. While presentations remain unchanged even in the case of the most firm association, there arises a mixed feeling by the combination of two feelings ("chemistry of feelings"). This feeling, however, is not completely different from the elements, but similar to them with respect to their strength.

2. Habit. The more often a feeling is joined to a content, the more easily and more forcefully it is aroused again under similar circumstances by the stimulus. This is the basis of the origination of the passions.

3. Expansion. Every feeling is expanded from its original content to all contents simultaneously present in consciousness, insofar as it is not hindered in this by opposite feelings or other effects (rational reflection). Thus, hate of a property of a person expands to the whole person, and so forth. If such an expansion from A to B has often taken place, the feeling is later immediately joined by habit to B, even though A is not present in consciousness.

4. Origination of feelings through relational judgments. If a feeling is joined to the content A, and if B is seen as a cause or effect of A or as a part thereof, B is loved or hated for the due to A. The outstanding case is the willing of means towards ends, where B is judged as a cause of A. In such cases, just as under 3), habit gradually transforms the secondary feeling into a primary one; what was first striven for only as a means, later becomes the end in itself, if reflection does not thwart it. Thus irrational passions arise (avarice, glory seeking). According to Hartley and others, this is also how the altruistic feelings arise, in that the good of others first is striven for only as a means, later habitually as an end in itself. However, while the origination of those passions is especially made easy by the fact that a means (e.g., money) serves many ends and therefore arises more and more in consciousness as opposed to these, the many other persons would here, by converse, serve as a means to the single end of one's own welfare. This end must therefore arise in consciousness with greater and greater force. Thus from egoism there can arise by habit more and more forceful egoism, but not altruism.

§ 37. Of the Causes and Effects of Attention

1. Attention or interest is a feeling. Its quality can no more be defined than that of any other feeling. It can be characterized only by concomitant features, especially by causes and effects.

2. The causes of attention can hardly be fully classified; nonetheless, especially every change has a chance - and the more significant the change, all the more chance - to arouse attention, while it quickly decreases vis-à-vis evenly proportioned, not too strong, not too unpleasant, impressions. Among the simultaneous contents of consciousness, the most forceful, the most pleasant, the one connected with a dominant feeling, further the one that reproduces presentations which had already earlier won our interest, is *ceteris paribus* the most powerful stimulus for attention.

3. So-called voluntary attention is not an attention which is brought about by the will, but rather the will itself, insofar as it is directed at the perception of relations (to a distinguishing, comparing) which can then also become the starting point of actions. The highest attainable degree of voluntary attention is by no means always the same, but rather depends on exercise, on the momentary state of the central organs and on an individual talent. The latter is at the same time the main root of intellectual ability.

4. The most proximate effect of attention consists not so much in a strengthening of that which is presented (which is sometimes observed in the case of weak sensations) as it is in a longer retention of the presentation in consciousness (§ 25). In this way attention is favorable for the reliability of the memory.

5. Full attention cannot be directed at the same time towards any number of presentations, however large, but only to very few ("narrowness of consciousness"). The more it is therefore directed towards a few or one, the more it is drawn away from the others for which the reversed effects then occur (quick disappearance from consciousness, etc.).

§ 38. Of the Causes and Effects of the Will

1. If the previously mentioned effects of involuntary attention on psychical life have become the object of an experience, the expectation of a similar outcome will by habit occur under similar circumstances. On the basis of this experience a feeling can therefore at first arise which is directed at the continuation of a presentation and connected with the expectation that this outcome will occur as an effect of the feeling itself, i.e., the will of the retention of a presentation in consciousness. On the basis of

further experiences of consequences which follow from the longer duration of a presentation the will can then direct itself to these too. Thus the realm and dominion of the will is more and more extended over memory, the function of judgment (regulated thinking), and the life of feeling itself (control of the affects by guiding presentations and deliberations).

2. The origination of voluntary motions presupposes the presence of certain involuntary ones. Linked to lively muscle feelings are certain corresponding motions due to an innate psycho-physical connection. By retaining or reproducing the relevant muscle-presentations those motions too can therefore also be voluntarily brought about. If these motions have been pleasant, either intrinsically or as regards their further consequences, the will directs itself in the future towards them, e.g., towards the enjoyment of a food, etc. The presentation of this will reproduce the corresponding muscle-presentations and thus bring about the motion in actuality.

If in the case of more complicated causal series the means have been found by inferences rather than by mere reproduction of presentations, the deliberated action arises, whose expansion and certainty increases without limit with the advancement of knowledge. The middle members of the associated series of presentations or of deliberation can again drop out due to the influence of habit (§ 22, 2), but not the muscle-presentations which make up the indispensable psychical antecedent of voluntary motions. Still, as a consequence of practice while receiving little attention, these are later reproduced with sufficient liveliness and distinctness. Hence, the attention of the orator, for instance, can be turned to the ideas to be expressed and still every motion of the head and of the body occur with the utmost precision.

By habit, voluntary actions can also pass over into involuntary ones, in that motions which have come about at first on certain occasions, under the influence of deliberation and will, later occur without any volitional operation already due to the acquired associations of the relevant presentations with muscle-feelings.

§ 39. Origination of Involuntary Motions

Some of the so-called involuntary motions have purely physiological causes (reflex motions in the narrower sense, e.g., that of the pupils). The remaining ones are linked partly to muscle-feelings such as the motions of imitation, partly to lively feelings of another kind such as the motions of expression, some defensive motions, and the instinctive motions of animals. This connection is partly innate, partly acquired (cf. § 38, 2). In the former case the possibility does of course remain that what is at present innate has been acquired from earlier generations (Darwin), but in every such explanation certain psycho-physical connections must nevertheless be presupposed as given.

APPENDIX THREE

SYLLABUS FOR LOGIC
by Carl Stumpf

INTRODUCTION

§ 1. Definition

By "logic" we mean the practical doctrine of cognition or the guide to correct judging. We include it in philosophy, for it draws its presuppositions for the most part from a philosophical science, psychology.

§ 2. Value

Although natural talent and practice cannot be replaced by logic, these factors still do not suffice, as experience shows, for the prevention of mistakes or for the recognition of ones already committed. There are disputes about many current hypotheses not only with regard to the actual material, but also as regards the formal provability of this material. Numerous statements are regarded by some as obvious, by others as in need of proof. Logic provides the criteria for the necessity and the requirements of a proof. It teaches not only testing, however, but also finding by bringing to full awareness the most universal maxims of asking questions, forming hypotheses, and working out proofs.

PART ONE: OF THOUGHTS AND THEIR EXPRESSION IN LANGUAGE

SECTION ONE: PREPARATORY PSYCHOLOGICAL REMARKS

§ 3. Speaking and Thinking

1. Between words and thoughts there is not a mythical unity, but merely an association. The child learns to connect sound-presentations with other sensory presentations, later also with general concepts, and this connection, like every association, becomes more and more fixed by habit. Thus words and complexes of words become signs of thoughts. But this system of signs is not merely determined by the need for expressing thoughts, but also by motives of convenience and beauty, by physiological and incidental historical causes. Logic can thus indeed take many clues from language, but can by no means use it as the definitive guide in the analysis of thought-processes and for establishing its rules.

2. The associated sound-presentations exert on thinking an influence which is in the main advantageous, but also in some details disadvantageous. Language has an *advantageous* effect by a) more distinctly separating abstract thoughts by means of the features of sound which are evident to the senses, b) supporting memory by means of these very features, c) abbreviating the thought-operations through the simple designation of complicated thoughts, d) mainly facilitating communication and learning. It can be said regarding these achievements that without language or a system of signs equivalent to it a considerable development of thinking would not be possible.

On the other hand, language has a *harmful* effect a) by like designations of unlike thoughts (homonymity or equivocation) especially in the case of very abstract concepts, b) by unlike expressions for like thoughts (source of verbal disputes).

Due to all of these influences logic has to be concerned at different places with the investigation of linguistic expression.

§ 4. Presentation and Judgment

Every judgment is founded by an object (*matter*), i.e., one or several presentations. But judgment is not a mere combination or separation of presentations or any other relation between them. Even if a relation, e.g., the equality of 4 and 2 + 2, is the object of judgment, we can still present this relation without affirming or denying it. These acts are first and foremost what makes up the essence of the judgment. It therefore supervenes on presentations, relations of presentations or presented relations, just like pleasure and displeasure, for instance, which are linked to these.[1]

From the matter of a judgment we distinguish its *content* or the state of affairs expressed in the judgment. E.g., "God is" has God as its matter, the being of God as its content. "There is no God" has the same matter, but "nonbeing of God" as the content.

§ 5. Names and Assertions

As names we designate here every simple or complex linguistic expression which means a presentation. So-called syncategorematic expressions, such as "not", "but", "is", "of", which mean something only in combination with others, are thus excluded here.

From names we separate sentences as the proper form of linguistic communication. Among sentences in general, however, including also optative and interrogative sentences etc., only the assertions constitute the linguistic expression of judgments.

SECTION TWO: OF THE PRESENTATIONS IN THEIR LOGICAL REGARD

§ 6. Differences between Presentations

1. With respect to *content* we distinguish

a) *simple and complex* presentations. The parts of a complex presentation can be of four kinds: a) *collective* parts (members of a sum), b) *physical* parts, i.e., those which border on each other, such as spatial and temporal sections, g) *metaphysical* ones, i.e., properties or moments, such as direction and velocity of a motion, intensity and quality of a tone, d) *logical* ones, i.e., genera and differences, such as color and red. In the last two cases the parts or features are also called "abstracta", for they interpenetrate each

---

[1] The essentials of this theory of judgment and some of its most important consequences for logic can be found in Brentano's *Psychology* I. They have been developed into a system of logic by this investigator in oral lectures which are often used in the present sketch.

other and are distinguished from each other only by a peculiar concentration of consciousness (abstraction). By far most names designate abstracta.

Remark. To be well distinguished from features in the proper sense are the "modifying" features which do not add to the concept to which they are attached, but rather change it. A "presumptive", "painted", "future" horse is not a horse, but simply the thought, the picture, the wish or the possibility of a horse. The fact that language treats such features as epithets like others may therefore not mislead us to co-ordinate them logically as parts of a concept with that to which they are attached.

b) *substantial and accidental* presentations. The former we find regulary connected with an unlimited number of other features. Thus, linked to the content of the presentation "chemical element of the combination weight 31" (phosphorus) are all the relationships of phosphorus to other substances, its modifications in the case of different temperatures, its effects on organisms, and so forth - properties whose number increases continually with the growth of knowledge. Analogously in the case of "insect", "organic". On the other hand there is nothing, or only very little, regularly linked, e.g., with "white", "yesterday", "four years old". In language this distinction has not sufficiently been marked.

2. As regards *extension*, i.e., as regards the number of objects which fall under a presentation or in which they occur as a logical part, we distinguish *individual* and more or less *general presentations (concepts)*. All abstract presentations are at the same time general presentations. Not to be confused with the general presentation is the collective one, in which a sum of individuals is presented, although the same expression is sometimes used for this (e.g., "humanity"). Nominalism wrongly teaches that general names always designate only a sum of individuals. They designate rather one or several abstract features which are already fully contained in one individual, but also occur elsewhere in the same way.

§ 7. Relations between Presentations

1. With regard to *content* two presentations are completely or partly *equal* or fully *unequal* (disparate, heterogenous). Concrete presentations always contain equal abstract features. However, the most general concepts are disparate, e.g., color and velocity.

Presentations which, as regards their content, cannot be thought without each other, insofar as they are members of a relation, e.g., cause and effect, are *correlative*.

Presentations which are extremes within a common concept are *opposite*. In the strict sense there are therefore such presentations only where there are series; e.g., absolute black and absolute white, between which the gradations of grey lie. Still, in the broader sense an opposition is spoken of also where only two presentations within a concept are possbile, e.g., hot and cold, love and hate.

(Usually a distinction is made between contrary and contradictory opposition and the former defined as it just was, the latter however as mere negation of a concept, e.g., human being - non-human being. But non-human being is as such not a presentation or concept in the proper sense. Everything which does not fall under "human being" would fall under it, triangle, fork, dog, God, possibility - for these there is however certainly no common concept. Such expressions therefore have sense only if there is a basic positive concept which is then denied a feature by a negative *judgment*; e.g., non-smoker = *passenger* who does not smoke. Sometimes the negation is also only a linguistic form of a completely positive concept.

N.B. a/b means from now on: a not-b in the sense explained = an a which is not b.)

The presentations which are equal in *extension* are called "equipollent", reciprocal or convertible ("human being" and "able to speak"), those with a fully different extension *disjunctive*.

Those with partly equal extension *overlap* or one is *subordinate* to the other (species - genus). If the distinguishing feature of a species (the specific difference) is a substantial feature, the species is called a natural one.

3. The rule "the greater the content, the smaller the extension and vice-versa" holds good with exactness only regarding the logical parts of a presentation. However, the concept does not necessarily become more general through a metaphysical abstraction. The same is of course true if the physical content is simplified.

4. There are highest or *most general generic concepts* (categories such as "space", "color", "judgment"). There are however in general no lowest *species*, for the extension of each concept can be infinitely narrowed by adding new features. Only if the features are to lie within a definite category or if they are to be substantial, does this process receive a limit.

SECTION THREE: OF THE JUDGMENTS IN THEIR LOGICAL REGARD

§ 8. Distinctions in the Form of Assertion

If we designate an affirmation with +, negation with -, and the matter of a judgment, however complex, with A, we obtain as schema of every judgment: + A or - A. Language has however created a great diversity of forms of assertion in which the matter and the judging of it are often not distinctly separated.

1. The "existential" sentence "A is" or "is not" is closest to the schema. "Is" ("obtains", "exists") expresses nothing but affirmation, positing in the most general sense, no matter what kind of matter is under consideration. The being of a thing is nothing different from that of a law, a property, a relation. However it must be admitted that in most cases, according to ordinary linguistic usage, a thing is not only quite generally affirmed by adding "is", but is affirmed as a substance independent of my consciousness (external thing). But this "as a substance ..." must be especially mentioned in logically exact analysis and then included within the *matter*.

Furthermore *time* determinations which likewise always belong to the matter are linked by language with the "is": "A was, will be". Reduced to the schema: +(past, future A).

The existential sentence undergoes a slight transformation in the *impersonal sentence*. It is raining = there is raining. Here the "is" is united with the name which expresses the matter into a verb. This form of assertion will preferably be applied when the object of the judgment is not things, but rather events. (Of course this does not preclude that sometimes a so-called subject, namely the cause of the event, is co-presented or at least easily found; e.g., in the case of "it is ringing". But the bells here still do not belong to the matter of the judgment, as it is expressed in the assertion; and in numerous cases the cause of the event is not at all, not even indeterminately, co-presented.)

2. The *categorical* form of assertion is in the main motivated by the need to express the relation of thing and property within the judged matter. Hence "subject" and "predicate" (S and P) are distinguished and the designation for the judgment is put in the middle as the so-called copula. That substance relation has nothing to do with the essence of judgment; it can, after all, also be merely presented (green tree). Hence the distinction between S and P is likewise not absolutely required for the judgment. In the reduction to the schema it drops out: some a are b = +(ab) = +A. No a is b = -(ab) = -A. (For more about the reduction, see § 11.)

Also the categorical form is subject to many kinds of transformation by introducing the verb with its inflexion and conjugation. a has bloomed = is having bloomed (withered). I sit = I is sitting. And so forth. Thus, only the least assertions can be fit to the categorical pattern without violation of linguistic habits.

It is of great importance to distinguish those categorical sentences which are only to state the meaning of a name from those which are to give substantive insight. The sentence "God is an infinitely perfect being" gives first and foremost a definition in which no assertion is even made about the possibility, let alone the existence of the matter. The corresponding schema goes: "+ a name 'God', meaning infinitely etc."

3. The *hypothetical* form of assertion originates from the consideration of the relation of condition and consequence within the matter. The reduction is accomplished by transforming the content of the consequent into its contradictory and negating its conjunction with the antecdent, e.g., "if a is, then b is" = "-(being of a and non-being of b)".

4. *Disjunctive* assertions take place where we affirm of a state of affairs only an indefinite part. Hence reduction e.g., "either a or b is" = +(one of the two: being of a and being of b)".

Disjunctive assertions according to current linguistic usage, however, usually mean not only that *at least* one of the members, but also that *only* one is true. In this case the above affirmation must still be supplemented by the negation: "-(one member together with the others)". Such exclusive-disjunctive assertions therefore no longer express one, but several judgments.

5. The *remaining forms of assertion* partly express a plurality of mutually separable judgments ("both - and" and the like), to a larger extent however complex judgments, i.e., those which include certain judgments, but without being completely dissolvable into a sum of independent judgments (After ..., Although ..., Because ... and the like). The reduction of the latter always yields affirmation of a determinate relation of two states of affairs which are thereby co-affirmed.

§ 9. Distinctions between Judgments

We distinguish 1. *simple* and *complex* judgments. The latter include, besides those just mentioned, the so-called indirect or modal judgments, wherein a state of affairs is judged with regard to its logical nature (with regard to the judgment whose content it is): "it is true, false, necessary, probable etc. that a is". Furthermore, every judgment is complex in which a so-called negative concept occurs (consequence of § 7, parenthesis). Finally, every inference is a complex judgment, for at stake here is not a mere sum of judgments, but a unitary act of cognition which encompasses premises and conclusion.

2. *affirmative* and *negative*. This so-called quality of the judgment is not always apparent in the form of assertion; only through reduction is it made doubtless. See § 8 and 11.

3. *universal* and *particular* (so-called quantity), depending on whether the judgment refers to the whole extension of the matter or to an indeterminate part of this extension. "-immortal human beings" negates every instance, "+happy human beings" does not affirm every instance of the concept. Judgments with concrete matter are of course universal; if the matter is abstract, the affirmation is always particular, the negation universal.

4. *comprehensive* and *distributive*, depending on whether the judgment holds good for the matter only as a whole or also for every part thereof. (Here it is thus not the extension, but rather the content of the judged presentation, which comes into consideration.) "-red swans" negates this complex of features, not "something red" and "swans". "+black swans" affirms implicitly also "something black" and "swans". Judgments with a simple matter are of course distributive; in the case of complex matter the affirmation is always distributive, the negation comprehensive. (Here modifying features are to be taken into account in accordance with § 6.)

5. *true* and *false*. Truth is not agreement of our presentation with a reality (hypothetical sentences, mathematical truths), but agreement of the judgment with the matter, i.e., affirmation of a matter which is to be a
ffirmed, negation of one which is to be negated. *When* a matter is to be affirmed or negated, see Part Two.

6. *evident* judgments (=cognition) and *non-evident* (blind ones), depending on whether the judgment is made with or without insight. The essence of evidence can be grasped only in examples. It is a) a *mediate* or *immediate* evidence, depending on whether or not the judgment, in order to be seen, presupposes other judgments; b) an *a posteriori* or *a priori* evidence, depending on whether it requires perceptions or not. Perception = noticing (affirming) of contents of sensation or of inner consciounsess. Example: "2 + 2 = 4" in contrast with "oil stays on top of water". In the first case the presentations can nonetheless be based on perception; but the judgment itself arises from the presentations and does not in addition need a special perception.

7. *certain* and *probable* ones. A matter, as it is given to me including all leads, can permit a certain judgment (relation of 2 to 4) or a more or less probable one. Hence, these properties, too, have their basis in the matter, just as truth and falsehood do. An

infinite probability $(1 - 1/\infty)$ (so-called physical certainty) will justly be equated with absolute or mathematical certainty.

8. Judgments which have a *law* and which have a *mere fact* as their content. The former include a) the general judgments which are evident from the presentations (*a priori* or logical laws), b) certain general judgments which are inferred with probability on the basis of perceptions, but of which we must assume that they would be evident to us as those under a) if we had adequate concepts of the essence of the things (*a posteriori* or natural laws). Only for this reason we call them laws. Correspondingly: logical - physical (natural) necessity. Possible means: what does not contradict a law (logically - physically possible). Logically impossible = absurd, inconceivable.

Every truth which is not a law is called a mere fact (in contrast with fact in the broader sense = any truth at all); e.g., "I am" (difference between evidence and necessity).

The most general and hence simplest *a priori* laws are called "axioms" or "principles", the most general and simplest *a posteriori* laws are called primary or basic laws. Natural laws which can presumably still be reduced to a basic law are called "merely empirical laws".

§ 10. Relations between Judgments

1. *Opposition.* Judgments equal in matter and unequal in quality are opposite, e.g., +spirits, -spirits.

2. *Equivalence.* Certain judgments can be used for each other in the practice of thought without being identical. Thus every affirmation is equivalent to the negation of the contradictory state of affairs ("+a" equivalent to "-nonbeing of a"), every direct judgment is equivalent to an indirect one (cf. above), further judgments about correlatives ("a ist the cause of b" equivalent to "b is the effect of a") and so forth.

3. *Inclusion.* Acually included in every complex judgment is one or several simple ones. Virtually included is the affirmation of the part in that of the whole, the negation of the whole in that of the part. Thus the matter of an affirmative judgment can be randomly reduced, that of a negative one randomly enlarged without detriment to the truth of the judgment.

4. *Entailment.* By two or several judgments another one can be entailed in terms of content. The relation is an irreducible one. E.g., by "+a" and "-ab" there is entailed "+a/b". By "-ab" and "-a/b" there is entailed "-a".

§ 11. Older Theory of the Differences, Relations and the so-called Transformation of Judgments

1. Main division of Aristotelian-scholastic logic: a e i o (*affirmo*, n*ego*).

Kant's division: *quality*: affirmative, negative, limitative; *quantity*: universal, particular, singular; *modality*: apodictic, assertoric, problematic; *relation*: categorical, hypothetical, disjunctive.

The limitative and the singular judgment are nowadays given up by most; in this case the criss-crossing of the qualitative and quantiative viewpoint yields the old division.

2. Accordingly there is also devised a *three or fourfold opposition* of judgment: a subaltern i, contradictory o, contrary e; e contrary a, contradictory i, subaltern o; i subaltern a, contradicory e, subcontrary o; o subcontrary i, contradictory a, subaltern e, where the contradictory judgments can neither be true nor false together, the contrary ones not true together, the subcontrary ones not false together.

3. Finally the theory of *conversion* and *contraposition* is tied to this. Conversion = exchange of S and P. It is called *coversio simplex* if the quantity can remain unchanged, *conversio per accidens* if a universal judgment must be transformed into a particular one in order to remain true in the conversion. Rules: e and i allow for simple conversion, a only *per accidens*, o not at all.

Contraposition = conversion with change of the quality of the predicate and of the judgment itself (Every human being is mortal - Nothing immortal is a human being). It also occurs *per accidens* or *simpliciter*, depending on whether quantitative change takes place at the same time or not. a and o allow for *contrapositio simplex*, e only *per accidens*, i not at all.

Critique

All of these theories are to be corrected in accordance with § 8 - 10. Especially: *ad. 1.* There is a quantity of a judgment not merely with regard to the extension, but also of the content of the judged matter (§ 9, 3 and 4). "Modality" is not a general feature of judgments, but rather a certain class of complex judgments, which however by no means includes only those 3 members (§ 9, 1). The table of "relation" contains no distinctions of judgments, but rather of forms of assertion and is also very incomplete (§ 8).

Reduction of the four older classes: (a) All a are b = -a/b. (e) No a is b = -ab. (i) Some a are b = +ab. (o) Some a is not b = +a/b.

Negation is therefore always universal, affirmation particular, there is only e and i (in the case of abstract and complex matter, which is also presupposed by the old fourfold division). § 9, 3. The linguistic schema a is, to be sure, used not only for general sentences with abstract matter (in which the existence of the subject is not claimed: "all a are b" = "if something is a, it is b" = "-a/b"), but also occasionally for sentences which have a *collectivum* of individuals as their object. These can express affirmations, e.g., "All (50) passengers are men" = "+(50) passengers, each of the male gender". Cf. § 6, 2.

ad 2. All oppositions besides the contradictory one between e and i are abolished, for a and o themselves are abolished. So-called contrary judgments can in fact be true together, subcontrary ones false together, if the subject does not at all exist.

ad 3. Switching of S and P is in all cases and without qualification possible as soon as only the true quality of the judgment and of the singular features is in advance made clear in the assertion. The only reason why the conversion of o, for instance, is supposedly impossible is because the "not" is first put with the copula and is then, in the conversion, put with the predicate. As soon as it is assigned to the latter: "Some a is not-b", nothing stands in the way of conversion.

(Also through Hamilton's "quantification of the predicate" conversion becomes everywhere possible. But this is based on the erroneous view that judgment consists in a comparison of the extension of two concepts. Attempts of Boole, de Morgan, Jevons to express judgments in equations. Consistent development of the old logic: "most a are b, 50% a are b" etc. Logic, however, is not an application of arithmetic, but rather vice-versa.)

§ 12. Origin of Judgments

The psychological causes of judgments must be known in order to guard against sources of error.

1. Immediate *cognition* originates directly from its matter if this is attentively presented for the sake of judgment. In mediate cognition the cause co-incides with the logical reason, the premises, if they are thought in a unitary act of consciousness with attention to the features essential to the cognition of the conclusion.

2. *Blind* judgments originate a) from an original *drive* by which everything presented is at once affirmed as long as consideration does not counter-act (instinctive judgmetns, e.g., outer perception); b) from *feelings* (including the will) in accordance with an innate tendency to believe that which serves the nourishment of a predominant

feeling c) from *habit*, by which something already held to be true from any motive is always believed in the future more easily and confidently if other forces do not counteract.

3. A judgment can also originate from a joint effect of insight together with one or several of the last named motives, e.g., derived through evident inferring from feeling-judgments.

PART TWO: OF THE TESTING OF COGNITION

SECTION ONE: TESTING IMMEDIATE COGNITION

CHAPTER ONE: TESTING IMMEDIATE *A POSTERIORI* COGNITION

Immediate experiential judgments are in general provided by every perception or by the distinct memory of one. But not every judgment of this sort is an evident judgment, a cognition. Rather, in this regard one must keep apart: *inner* perception, i.e., the judgment which immediately affirms one's own momentary psychical states, *outer* perception, i.e., the judgment which immediately affirms contents of sensation, though not *as* sensed, but rather as independent of consciousness, and *memory* judgments, i.e., immediate affirmations of memory images, whether they concern physical or psychical objects.

§ 13. Inner Perception

We cannot doubt that the momentary psychical states of which we are conscious are true (actual), and indeed as they appear to us. This evidence is explained by the fact that the perceptual act and the perceived are here only two sides of one state. Deceptions are here possible only insofar as the perceived is falsely interpreted, classified, etc. or assertions of memory or of outer perception confused with those of inner perceptions.

§ 14. Outer Perception

Every outer perception is, by virtue of the concept thereof (see above), a deception. The presentations of space, of one's own and other bodies develop with psychological necessity from the sensations and are, once again with psychological necessity, taken as true, but without evidence (§ 12, 2.a). There can however be something true in this, as soon as "external thing" is understood not as the sensory content itself, but as its cause. But in this case the cognition of the external world is no longer immediate, but rather only to be obtained by inferences as far as these in fact extend. Deceptions in this manner are in general grounded by the fact that the same effect can have different causes; individually they originate partly from purely objective circumstances (e.g., broken rudder), partly from the nature of the sensory organs (e.g., perspectives), partly from central causes (hallucinations), partly from merely false interpretation of correctly sensed relations.

§ 15. Memory

What is true of this is analogous to outer perception. Memory can itself be deceptive about one's own psychical states, for what it provides, after all, is not these themselves, but only reproductions of them for whose faithfulness there is no immediate guarantee. The trust is, once again, at first a merely instinctive one and can be raised to the status of cognition only mediately in that we infer from the present memory image to earlier external and internal events as causes of it. The deceptions of memory are usually based in unusual vivacity of phantasy presentations.

CHAPTER TWO: TESTING IMMEDIATELY *A PRIORI* COGNITION

§ 16. Axioms

1. The fact that there is immediately *a priori* cognition is shown by examples such as: either there is a God or not. And since every matter is equally well suited to such a judgment, there are even infinitely many axioms in this sense. But they can be reduced to a finite number of general schemata (axioms in the narrower sense):

a) Law of noncontradiction: "a cannot both be and not be". Equivalent with this: "a is not not-a" (see § 7 regarding negative concepts); and identical with this: "a is a" (§ 11 ad 1).

b) Law of the excluded middle: "Either a is or it is not". This affirmative axiom (cf. § 8, 4) cannot be brought together with the negative one (a) into a unitary judgment, but certainly into a unitary formula: "Of opposite judgments, one is true and one is false".

Remark. Leibniz' law: "Every event and every assertion must have a sufficient reason" is in its second part a prescription, not an axiom, in the first part a metaphysical law which can perhaps be proved *a priori*, though it is not immediately evident.

c) Moreover, from every valid simple inference an axiom can be drawn, e.g., "if both ab and a/b are, then a is not" (cf. § 10, 4). The number and the formulation of these axioms of inference have however not yet been established. (But they may not be regarded, say, as tacit premises. Otherwise *regressus in infinitum*.)

2. The sceptic can dispute the axioms only in words, for without them his own claims and inferences would also be invalid. The extreme empiricist overlooks the fact that induction, too, is an inference and there is already
at least one axiom given in every inference.

3. The numerous principles of the philosophy of "common sense", also Kant's "synthetic principles *a priori*" are partly analytic (reducible to the law of noncontradiction), partly *a posteriori*, partly not even correct. There is moreover no transition from *a posteriori* judgments to *a priori* ones, from synthetic to analytic judgments if the matter is left unchanged, but only a change in the meaning of the names, due to which the same sentence no longer expresses the same judgment.

§ 17. Pseudoaxioms

Besides theoretical errors concerning axioms, there are innumerable pseudoaxioms, i.e., apparently obvious sentences which - partly expressed, partly as hidden maxims of inference - play a harmful role in actual thinking. Included in the expressed ones are sentences in which a disputed feature is co-thought already in the S. (Hence seemingly *a priori* deductions from experiential laws.) Included in the hidden pseudoaxioms are especially sentences about the possible and the impossible, such as: "What is conceivable is possible, what is inconceivable is impossible" (double concept of the possible, § 9, 8), "What can be thought together can exist together, what can be thought apart, can exist apart; what cannot be thought together etc." (There comes into consideration here, besides the concept of possibility, also the subjective compulsion through habitual association as well as the ability to abstract.) Cf. Mill, *System of Logic*, V.iii.

SECTION TWO: TESTING MEDIATE COGNITION

CHAPTER ONE: ARISTOTELIAN-SCHOLASTIC DOCTRINE OF INFERENCE

§ 18. Classification of Inferences

Inferences are divided into those from one premise (immediate ones) and from several premises (mediate ones). The former include conversion and contraposition (§ 11, 3), subalternation (ib., 2) and others. The mediate inferences are divided into 2 classes: syllogism (from the general to the particular) and induction (vice-versa), to which nowadays analogy is usually added (from the particular to the particular). Syllogisms are divided into simple and complex ones, depending on whether they have 2 or more premises, the simple ones again into categorical, hypothetical, disjunctive and mixed ones, in accordance with the nature of the premises.

§ 19. Rules of Simple Categorical Syllogisms

The two premises have as S and P 3 terms, hence a common one (*terminus medius*), and this is omitted in the conclusion. Of the two others the one which becomes S in the conclusion is called *terminus minor*, the one which becomes P *terminus major*; accordingly also the premises *propositio major* and *minor*.

Regarding the position which S and P of the conclusion take in the premises, there are 4 figures of inference:
M P   P M   M P   P M
S P.
S M   S M   M S   M S

Furthermore, every premise can be one of 4 kinds, a e i o, hence in every figure 16 and altogether 54 modes of inference conceivable.

As general rules these essentially hold good: "Every simple categorical inference may have only 3 terms. At least one premise must be general, at least one affirmative.

From 2 affirmations a negation does not follow. The conclusion always follows the weaker (negative, particular) premise".

Special rules for the particular figures: In the second figure only negative, in the third only particular, in the fourth no affirmative conclusions.

It is herewith already given that not all thinkable modes can be valid, but only a determinate number in each figure. The 19 valid ones in the mnemonic verses: Barbara, Celarent, etc. Moreover, Venn diagrams serve as a means of testing in recent times.

§ 20. The Remaining Inferences

1. Among the simple inferences certain mixed forms, besides the categorical ones, are especially pointed out: the hypothetical-categorical ones (modus ponens and tollens), the inferences of exclusion, and the dilemma.

2. Among the complex ones are marked off those in which, instead of drawing the inference, one immediately adds to two premises others and joins the P of the final one with the S of the first or vice-versa: chain-inference or sorites (Aristotelian-Goclenian) in contrast with the chain of inferences.

3. Enthymeme means an inference in which a premise must be supplemented in thought, epichereme one in which still the proof of one premise is inserted into the premise.

4. Induction is usually conceived as syllogism of the third figure with a general conclusion (Überweg):

M_1 and M_2 and M_3 ... are P
Every S is P
M_1 and M_2 and M_3 ... are P

One distinguishes complete and incomplete induction, depending on whether the entire extension from S is summed up in the premises.

CHAPTER TWO

§ 21. Critique

The determinations concerning conversion, etc. suffer from already mentioned defects (§ 11 ad 2 and 3). The division into syllogism, induction, analogy is not sharp; the latter two are still again considered as forms of syllogism, and included among the syllogisms are again inferences from the general to the general (Barbara). The inferences with existential premises are left out of consideration. The rules for the categorical inferences are in large part false as a consequence of the incorrect differentiation a e i o. The justification of so-called incomplete induction seems incomprehensible, after general conclusions in the third figure are forbidden. Moreover, exaggerated specialization (modes) makes the old syllogistic logic practically unusable.

CHAPTER THREE: ESSENTIALS OF A REFORMED DOCTRINE OF INFERENCE

§ 22. General Rules

1. Simple inferences are those which cannot be dissolved into others. These are based on the relations of equivalence, inclusion, or entailment (§ 10, 2-4). They can nonetheless have several premises (example given there in 4). They are correct if the inference and the premises are correct. The inference is correct if it is axiomatically evident when uttered as a unitary judgment (cf. § 16, 1 c). What is primarily to be asked in testing the premises is whether they are likewise immediately evident or mere definitions (§ 8, 2). If neither is the case, an inquiry into their justification must be made, where again the correctness of the inference and of the premises comes into consideration until one arrives at those statements which are self-evident or aleady earlier cognized as true.

2. Complex inferences can be tested by dissolving them into simple ones. But it almost always suffices to see to it a) that no name is taken ambiguously (fallacies), b) that the conclusion is not already in a premise (circular reasoning, especially in longer inferential chains), c) that a premise is not left unexpressed (which easily leads to *petitio principii*, arbitrary presupposition of the main point).

Remark. The so-called simple categorical inferences are in truth already complex. For example:

No M is P = -MP
Every S is M = -S/M   expressed in accordance with
No S is P = -SP   § 11 ad 1

Analysis:
From the first premise follows: -MPS
From the second premise follows: -S/MP according to § 10, 3
Hence: -SP   according to
                                                        the formula:
                                                        -ab
                                          -a/b   -a (§ 10,4).

Instead of analysis, also simple derived rules (Brentano, *Psychologie* I, 303), according to which there are only two modes: eee and iei.

§ 23. Probability Inferences

If we cannot judge about a matter as such, we can nonetheless frequently subsume it under a series of cases of which we know that one is true, but not which one. If the number of these cases is a determinate one, N, and we do not know more about the one than we do about the other, the probability of the matter in question = 1/N. But there can also be several (n) cases corresponding to that matter (an even number in the case of a die); the probability is then = n/N. It is thus designated as the ratio of the "favorable" to the "possible" cases or chances; what is meant by possible cases is the ones concerning which we find ourselves equally ignorant after considering all moments which come into play, including their causes.

The concept of probability, in either its more determinate or less determinate form, is applicable under these presuppositions to matters of every type, not only to future facts, but also to present and past facts, not only to facts, but also to laws (contra Lotze).

For the sake of easier discernment in more complicated cases the following principles (whose application turns the determination of probability into an inference) are especially of service:

1. The probability that several assumptions (facts, laws) which are independent of each other are jointly true is the product of the probability of all assumptions taken one by one. (According to this principle auxiliary hypotheses, the spread of testimonial reports, academic scepticism, probability of a conclusion can be judged.)

2. If a fact or a law can be derived from different presuppositions, the probability of each one is a fraction whose numerator is the probability with which the given follows from this presupposition, and whose denominator is the sum of the corresponding probabilities of the remaining presuppositions ($p/p + p1 + p2 ...$). If the presuppositions are in themselves not equally probable, then p is the product from the probability of these presuppositions into the probability with which the given follows from it; analogously p1, p2. If not all possible presuppositions are considered, there arises a "relative" probability. If infinite presuppositions are possible, or also: if we do not know whether finitely or infinitely many are possible, then the pobability for each one becomes infinitely small. If p is finite, however small it might be, while p1, p2 ... are infinitely small, the probability for p will be = 1 (physical certainty, § 9, 7).

Resulting from this principle together with the first is especially the probability of a law on the basis of repeated observations (§ 24) and the probability of a common cause in the case of so-called co-incidences. In the latter case the probability of accident, i.e., of special causes for every single event, decreases geometrically as the number of co-incidences grows (external world, history, common cause of all things).

3. If two or several species of events are observed in large number, the relation of their chances can be equated with that of the number of the relevant events, and more particularly the precision with which the one relation corresponds to the other grows proportionally with the square root of the entire number of observed cases. This "law of great numbers" is the basis of the so-called *a posteriori* determination of probability. Even in matters which seem inaccessible to mathematical estimation it is in this way possible to obtain a probability in numbers by gradually increasing observations.

In addition, the general truths which are put forward in these rules (rapid decrease of complex probability, principles of estimating hypotheses, significance of preceding cases), even wherever definite numbers cannot at first be established, retain their value for the testing of combinations of thoughts from which probability judgments are derived.

§ 24. Deceptions about Probability

Application of the principles always presupposes that all data which can be discerned according to the circumstances (more specifically also regarding the causes) are discerned. Most mistakes in the estimation of probability itself are due to oversights or underestimations of cases of either the favorable or the unfavorable kind (most frequently the latter), for they have for some reason impressed themselves less on our attention and memory. Herein lies the origin of much superstition. No logical operation is more easily damaged by bias, affect, instinctive assent (§ 12). The last mentioned drive allows that which has only finite probability to appear a thousand times as certain.

§ 25. Inductive Inferences

If we hereby mean inferences from facts to laws, it is, in accordance with the foregoing, no longer difficult to state their logical structure.

1. *Most general form.*

If a series of similar facts are observed under certain similar circumstances (death of an organism in the case of air deprivation), two assumptions are possible: either there is a law or not. If previous experiences do not already provide clues, both assumptions have in themselves the probability 1/2. But according to the first one the agreement of the cases is at once understandable, while according to the second one it has a probability which decreases geometrically as the number of cases increases; from this the corresponding probability for there being a law results according to § 24, 2. Besides the number of cases, however, other things also come into consideration, such as their nature, the degree of agreement, and other circumstances, so that sometimes the probability of a law can already become extraordinarily large in the case of a small amount of observations. It must still be kept in mind that the law is at first related to the very special circumstances of the observations and a restriction in the number of the circumstances which are adopted in the utterance of the law is justified under changed circumstances only by earlier experiences or successive series of observations under changed circumstances.

The form of the inference is therefore the following:

"(1) +A, A1, A2 ... (Series of the facts in agreement)

(2) Casual co-incidence has the probability p.

There is therefore a law with the probability $p1 = 1 - p$."

The second premise is, as a consequence of the *a priori* (because mathematically) evident principles of probability, itself an *a priori* judgment. There follows an experiential law from facts only by mediation of *a priori* laws.

2. Besides this most general form there are two special forms of induction, one of them for causal laws, the other for laws of substance (i.e., those in which a certain property is ascribed to a class of things). Both are abbreviated procedures in that they presuppose a premise as already demonstrated by the most general form.

a) Causal form: "The cause a has in one case the effect b.

Like causes have like effects.

Therefore, every a has an effect b".

By what is meant here by "cause a" is the *entire* complex of the conditions from which b arises. A repetition of the observations is in this case only needed in order to make sure that non of these conditions is overlooked. If, however, this is certain, then the law follows at once from the single case in that the second premise is demonstrated by induction according to the general form and now once and for all tacitly used as a basis.

b) Form of stubstance: "A substance a has in one case the property b.

Properties of this category are species features.

Therefore, all substances of the species a have the property b".

E.g., if the compound weight or the melting point in a piece of pure gold was determined, we at once infer the law that these features belong to all gold, after we have long ago found out by induction according to the general form that compound weight and melting point is common to all bodies which belong to the same natural kind (§ 7, 2; 6, 1b). Such a second premise is however given to us with sufficient certainty only in the case of structureless substances. In the case of organisms there is hardly any category of properties that could be designated with full certainty as a general feature of a class. Inferences of the mentioned form therefore have here only a correspondingly smaller reliability.

PART THREE: OF THE DISCOVERY OF COGNITION (DOCTRINE OF METHOD)

SECTION ONE: CLASSIFICATION AND DEFINITION

These operations accompany every investigation from beginning to end.

§ 26. Classification

1. By this we mean the statement of the species of a genus (§ 7, 2). Since almost all generic concepts are made up of several features, it is possible for the purpose of division to take now this, now that feature as basic (reason for division). The goal of a division can be threefold: a) practical, b) theoretical, and more particularly a) support of memory (including pe-eminently the "artificial" classifications which must be based on a feature as conspicuous as possible), β) initiating or concluding investigations (including the "natural" classifications which are based on substantial features).

2. Let the basis of division be *essential*, i.e., let it in each case correspond to the goal of classification. This alone can also be the sense of demanding *unity* and *constancy* in the continuation the classification; but it cannot be demanded that the reason for division be always one single simple feature; nor that the same category of features be used for the subdivisions as for the main division. *Acuteness* is an obvious requirement insofar as a species may not already contain another one, but not in the sense that each one is precisely delimited. The latter requirement, just like that of *completeness* too, must be satisfied only insofar as the material permits. (Cf. natural classification of the animal realm.)

§ 27. Definition (and Terminology)

1. Definition is the explanation of a name by one or several others. It can be done a) by naming the *parts* of the relevant presentation, especially the logical parts (in the latter case species definition, based on division); b) by stating the circumstances under which the relevant object can be *perceived* or composed or abstracted from perceptions (ostensive definition; then also the genetic definitions which exhibit the object in its origin); c) by merely stating distinct or familiar *names* (purely verbal definition); d) by a bunch of *examples* or by characteristic *properties*. The examples are to be chosen

from classes which differ as much as possible so that the common element is all the more easily seen.

(Often a distinction is made between *real* and *nominal* definition in that the real definition reveals the possibility or reality of the object, in addition to the meaning, of the name. But this demonstration does not belong to the task of a definition.)

2. General rule: The definiens must be more distinct than the definiendum, must summon the same presentation, that is to say, into consciousness in a more complete way. The ordinary rules (not too narrow, not too broad; no abundance; no *idem per idem*; no fallacy; statement of the most proximate genus and specific difference; only essential features) are partly contained in the one above, partly valid only for certain types of definition.

3. All expressions which are not distinct via themselves or via the context are to be defined (for which reason an "or ..." often suffices). The most general concepts can, after all, be defined only in the ways b) - d).

4. Scientific terminology has to be linked up as much as possible with the vocabulary on hand and linguistic usage. Only where the necessary change of linguistic usage would almost completely have to rob an expression of its ordinary meaning, are new terms expedient. (See Mill, *System of Logic*, IV.iii-vi.)

SECTION TWO: QUESTIONS AND HYPOTHESES

§ 28. Questions

For the preliminary orientation concerning the problem of an area a collection of the opposing views is expedient (Aristotle's "aporiai"). In a traditional problem, however, there is usually still a plurality of questions. Thus further: isolate and simplify questions as much as possible. In connection with this, make them precise by means of definitions. Then begin with the easiest and simplest question. (Often mutual dependence between questions and whole areas. Course of scientific investigation much more varied in form than according to Comte.)

§ 29. Hypotheses

1. Hypothesis = preliminary assumption (of a law or a fact). Of service for discovery are a) collection, ordering, and supplementation of material (Bacon's "instances"), b) enumeration, as complete as possible, of the conditions which the hypothesis must satisfy, c) most attentive analysis of concrete cases and comparison of different classes of cases. In the working together of this analyzing and combining activity the essence of investigation consists. Among the aids of hypothesis formation, *analogies* are of the greatest significance.

2. If several hypotheses compete, the order of discussion is conditioned by the preliminary degree of probability and the ease of decision.

3. Hypotheses which, by the nature of the matter, can never be demonstrated with certainty or even just finite probability, indeed even hypotheses which are surely false (fictions), can nonetheless be of use as illustration of an abstract thought or as basis and guide for deductions whose results are then checked. In the misjudgment of this character, however, they have also often become harmful. It is a positivistic exaggeration that *every* hypothesis possesses only the value of a guide for the examination of facts.

(Difference between hypothesis and *theory*: in the former the assumption itself is in question, whereas in the latter a principle which is as such conceded is applied to a certain area of phenomena.)

PART THREE: CONDUCTING PROOFS

§ 30. Direct Proof by Means of Observation and Experiment

1. Observation consists in the attentive perception of given phenomena and their relations; experiment in the production of observed phenomena. The latter has the advantage of making available to observation, under decisive conditions, the phenomena decisive for the investigation, and of making familiar, by means of introducing the simplest changes possible, the most elementary causes and the most general laws.

2. For a good observation the following is necessary: a) distinction of the content of perception from the presentations and judgments associated with it, b) removal of errors immanent to the content of perception, and more particularly a) the *constant* errors attached to the organization, the standpoint, and the possible instrument of the

observer which are eliminated by changing the observer and the mentioned circumstances, β) the *changeable* errors which arise in every observation, which are eliminated by increasing the observations under like circumstances and computing averages.

3. The most important cases whereby direct observation or experiment are decisive concern *causal relations*; and the most important maxims by which one here proceeds are the following (cf. Mill):

1) Between the phenomena a and b there is probably a causal relation if they frequently occur together or fail to occur together under otherwise different circumstances, but especially if they exclusively occur together or fail to occur together, and most probable if both are the case (method of agreement).

2) If b follows a under otherwise equal circumstances, then a is the cause or a part of the cause of b (method of difference). This method is preferrable in service of experiment, whereas the previous one comes more in use for the initiation of an experiment or in such cases where only observation is possible.

3) If a + a is followed by b + b under otherwise equal circumstances and we already know that a is the cause of b, then a is the cause of b (method of residues).

4) If a changes correspondingly with b, one of them depends on the other or both commonly depend on a third thing, or also a on a, b on b, while a and b stand in causal connection (method of variation). This too must often replace the method of difference. By it, moreover, all quantitative determinations concerning the effectiveness of a cause are undertaken. (Previous knowledge of the variety of functional relations of dependence useful.)

What is first discovered by means of all these methods is a factual causal relation between two concrete events; whence there then results at once, according to § 25, 2a, a corresponding law.

In such areas, however, where all events depend on very complicated conditions, as in organic or social life, it is hardly ever possible to reach through direct observation certainty whether a is the complete conditional complex for b or at least belongs to it. Therefore the purely inductive path is here supplemented by the deductive and especially the indirect-deductive method (§ 30 and 31).

§ 30. Direct Proof by Inference (Deductive Method)

A truth can often be derived via inferences from already given ones. The premises which are used to this end are found in affirmative or particular judgments through division, in negative or general ones by analysis of the concepts occurring in them. In both cases it is the subject-concept which is above all to be considered in categorical propositions, and the antecedent in hypothetical ones. Direct deduction is most frequently applied in general judgments. The affirmed truth which is arrived at by analysis can be *a priori* or *a posteriori*, especially also a causal law (deduction of merely empirical causal laws from primary deductions of practicioners).

§ 31. Indirect Proof

Indirect proof (in the broadest sense) does not at once bear upon the proposition to be proved, but rather upon one or several others which stand in such a relation to it that they allow for regressive inferences to it.

1. The proof by *perfect disjunction* gives a classification of the cases which are contained in a proposition and proves each of them singly (also called "perfect induction" and "collective proof"). More simple case: disjunction into opposites.

2. The proof by *exclusion* considers the thesis itself as member of a perfect classification whose other members are demonstrated as false. Most simple case: Falsity of the contradictory (indirect proof in the more narrow sense, deductio ad absurdum, more generally ad falsum).

3. In the proof by *approximation* a proposition which is somehow close to the thesis is proved, then the demonstration adduced that it differs from this proposition by no circumstance which might make a difference for the proof (misuse for sophisms). Here also belongs the proof by *delimitation* which approaches the thesis from two sides.

4. The proof by *derivation with subsequent verification* (briefly also called "deductive method", more precisely "indirect-deductive") draws consequences from the thesis, namely consequences which either co-incide with already affirmed truths or are cognized through observation or experiment as correct. Although the correctness of the proposition is in and of itself not yet herewith guaranteed, since the same consequences can flow also from other presuppositions, its probability can nonetheless be increased by the bunch of correct conclusions and by gradual removal of the competing hypotheses, indeed transformed into certainty. In this way the law of gravity, the most general laws of mechanics, and others are proved. The main instrument of

progress is this method in all the sciences which are concerned with very complex phenomena.

BIBLIOGRAPHY

I. WORKS BY HUSSERL

A. Works published in Husserliana

Volume II. *Die Idee der Phänomenologie. Fünf Vorlesungen.* Edited by Stefan Strasser. The Hague: Martinus Nijhoff, 1963.

Volume III/1. *Ideen zu einer reinen Phänomenologie und phänomenologischen Philosophie. Erstes Buch. Allgemeine Einführung in die reine Phänomenologie.* Edited by Karl Schuhmann. The Hague: Martinus Nijhoff, 1976.

Volume V. *Ideen zu einer reinen Phänomenologie und phänomenologischen Philosophie. Drittes Buch. Die Phänomenologie und die Fundamente der Wissenschaften.* Edited by Marly Biemel. The Hague: Martinus Nijhoff, 1952.

Volume VI. *Die Krisis der europäischen Wissenschaften und die transzendentale Phänomenologie. Eine Einleitung in die phänomenologische Philosophie.* Edited by Walter Biemel. The Hague: Martinus Nijhoff, 1976.

Volume X. *Zur Phänomenologie des inneren Zeitbewußtseins (1893-1917).* Edited by Rudolf Boehm. The Hague: Martinus Nijhoff, 1966.

Volume XII. *Philosophie der Arithmetik. Mit ergänzenden Texten (1890-1901).* Edited by Lothar Eley. The Hague: Martinus Nijhoff, 1970.

Volume XVI. *Ding und Raum. Vorlesungen 1907.* Edited by Ulrich Claesges. The Hague: Martinus Nijhoff, 1973.

Volume XVII. *Formale und transzendentale Logik. Versuch einer Kritik der logischen Vernunft.* Edited by Paul Janssen. The Hague: Martinus Nijhoff, 1974.

Volume XVIII. *Logische Untersuchungen. Erster Band. Prolegomena zur reinen Logik.* Edited by Elmar Holenstein. The Hague: Martinus Nijhoff, 1975.

Volume XIX/1. *Logische Untersuchungen. Zweiter Band, 1. Teil. Untersuchung zur Phänomenologie und Theorie der Erkenntnis.* Edited Ursula Panzer. The Hague: Martinus Nijhoff, 1984.

Volume XIX/2. *Logische Untersuchungen. Zweiter Band, 2. Teil. Untersuchung zur Phänomenologie und Theorie der Erkenntnis.* Edited Ursula Panzer. The Hague: Martinus Nijhoff, 1984.

Volume XXI. *Studien zur Arithmetik und Geometrie. Texte aus dem Nachlass. 1886-1901.* Edited by Ingeborg Strohmeyer. The Hague: Martinus Nijhoff, 1983.

Volume XXII. *Aufsätze und Rezensionen (1890-1910).* Edited by Bernhard Rang. The Hague: Martinus Nijhoff, 1979.

Volume XXIII. *Phantasie, Bildbewußtsein, Erinnerung. Zur Phänomenologie der anschaulichen Vergegenwärtigungen. Texte nach dem Nachlaß (1898-1925).* Edited by Eduard Marbach. The Hague: Martinus Nijhoff, 1980.

Volume XXIV. *Einleitung in die Logik und Erkenntnistheorie. Vorlesungen 1906/07.* Edited by Ullrich Melle. Dordrecht: Kluwer, 1984.

Volume XXV. *Aufsätze und Vorträge (1911-1921).* Edited by Thomas Nenon and Hans Rainer Sepp. Dordrecht: Kluwer, 1987.

Volume XXVI. *Vorlesungen über Bedeutungslehre. Sommersemester 1908.* Edited by Ursula Panzer. Dordrecht: Kluwer, 1987.

Volume XXVIII. *Vorlesungen über Ethik und Wertlehre. 1908-1914.* Edited by Ullrich Melle. Dordrecht: Kluwer, 1988.

Volume XXX. *Logik und allgemeine Wissenschaftslehre. Vorlesungen 1917/18, mit ergänzenden Texten aus der ersten Fassung 1910/11.* Edited by Ursula Panzer. Dordrecht: Kluwer, 1996.

B. Other Published Works

Edmund Husserl. Briefwechsel. Edited by Karl Schuhmann in collaboration with Elisabeth Schuhmann. Dordrecht: Kluwer, 1994.

"Vorwurf einer 'Vorrede' zu den *Logischen Untersuchung*", edited by Eugen Fink, *Tijdschrift voor Philosophie* 1 (1939): 106-133, 319-339.

"Husserls Abhandlung 'Intentionale Gegenstände'. Edition der ursprünglichen Druckfassung", edited by Karl Schuhmann, *Brentano Studien* 3 (1990/91): 137-176.

Erfahrung und Urteil. Untersuchung zur Genealogie der Logik. Edited by Ludwig Landgrebe. Claassen & Goverts: Hamburg, 1948.

Early Writings in the Philosophy of Logic and Arithmetic. Translated by Dallas Willard. Dordrecht: Kluwer, 1994.

C. UNPUBLISHED MATERIALS:[1]

A III 1: "Brentano fasst das Verhältnis von logischer Gattung und Art als Teilverhältnis" (c. 1895).

A VI 26: "Es bedarf der phänomenologischen Reduktion als vollbewusster Herausstellung der reinen psychischen Sphäre" (1927).

F I 20: "Differenzpunkte gegen Brentano" (c. 1900)

F I 27: "Urteilstheorie" (SS 1905).

K I 23: "Aus Vorlesungen über Logik" (1895).

K I 35: Excerpts from Kerry (c. 1893)

---

[1] Besides the following list of unpublished manuscripts, other unpublished materials include the annotations which Husserl had written in his copies of many of the works by other Brentanists, Brentano, and Bolzano listed below.

K I 64: "Aufmerksamkeit" (1898).

K I 66: "Wahrnehmung" (1898).

K I 57: "Folioblätter aus dem Jahr 1893".

K II 4: Excerpts from Stumpf, *Erscheinungen und pyschische Funktionen* and *Zur Einteilung der Wissenschaften* (1907).

K III 33: "Meinongiana" (c. 1902-c. 1910).

Q 8: See under Brentano.

Q 9: See under Brentano.

Q 10: See under Brentano and Marty.

Q 11 1-2: See under Stumpf.

Q 12: See under Stumpf.

Q 13: See under Stumpf.

II. WORKS BY OTHER BRENTANISTS, BRENTANO, AND BOLZANO

Bolzano, Bernard.
Wissenschaftslehre. Versuch einer ausführlichen und größtenteils neuen Darstellung der Logik mit steter Rücksicht auf deren bisherige Bearbeiter. Four Volumes. Sulzbach, J.C. von Seidel, 1837.

Paradoxien des Unendlichen. Hamburg: Felix Meiner, 1975.

Brentano, Franz.
Von der mannigfachen Bedeutung des Seienden nach Aristoteles. Freiburg i.Br.: Herder, 1862.

Die Psychologie des Aristoteles, insbesondere seine Lehre vom Nous Poietikos, nebst einer Beilage über das Wirken des Aristotelischen Gottes. Mainz a.R.: Kirchheim, 1867.

Psychologie vom empirischen Standpunkte I. Duncker & Humblot: Leipzig, 1874.

Ausgewählte psychologische Fragen. Unpublished lecture notes, under signature Q 9 in Husserl Archives, Louvain, 1883.

Metaphysik. Unpublished lecture notes, under signature Q 8 in Husserl Archives, Louvain, 1883/84.

Descriptive Psychologie. Unpublished lecture notes, under signature Q 10 in Husserl Archives, Louvain, 1887/88.

Vom Ursprung sittlicher Erkenntnis. Duncker & Humblot: Leipzig, 1889.

Psychologie vom empirischen Standpunkt II. Edited by Oskar Kraus. Leipzig: Felix Meiner, 1925.

Wahrheit und Evidenz. Edited by Oskar Kraus. Leipzig: Felix Meiner, 1930.

Über die Zukunft der Philosophie. Edited by Oskar Kraus. Leipzig: Felix Meiner, 1929.

Vom Ursprung sittlicher Erkenntnis. Edited by Oskar Kraus. Leipzig: Felix Meiner, 1935.

Deskriptive Psychologie. Edited by Roderick M. Chisholm and Wilhelm Baumgartner. Hamburg: Felix Meiner, 1982.

Briefe an Carl Stumpf 1867-1917. Edited by Peter Goller and Gerhard Oberkofler. Graz: Akademische Druck- und Verlagsanstalt, 1989.

"Briefe Franz Brentanos an Hugo Bergmann", edited by Hugo Bergmann, *Philosophy and Phenomenological Research* 7 (1946/47): 83-158.

Ehrenfels, Christian von.
Über Fühlen und Wollen. Eine psychologische Studie. Vienna: Kaiserliche Akademie der Wissenschaften, 1887.

"Über Gestaltqualitäten", in *Vierteljahrsschrift für wissenschaftliche Philosophie* 14 (1890): 249-347.

"Zur Philosophie der Mathematik", in *Vierteljahrsschrift für wissenschaftliche Philosophie* 15 (1891): 285-347.

"Werth-Theorie und Ethik", *Vierteljahrsschrift für wissenschaftliche Philosophie* 17 (1893): 76-110, 200-266, 321-363, 413-475; 18 (1894): 77-97.

System der Werth-Theorie. Leipzig: O.R. Reisland, 1897/98.

Höfler, Alois.
Logik. In collaboration with Alexius Meinong. Vienna: Tempsky, 1890.

Review of Benno Kerry, *System einer Theorie der Grenzbegriffe*, in *Vierteljahrsschrift für wissenschaftliche Philosophie* 16 (1892): 230-242.

Review of Benno Kerry, "Über Anschauung und ihre psychische Verarbeitung"; Edmund Husserl, *Philosophie der Arithmetik*; Christian von Ehrenfels, "Zur Philosophie der Mathematik", in *Zeitschrift für Psycholgie und Physiologie der Sinnesorgane* 6 (1894): 44-58.

"Die Philosophie des Alois Höfler", in Raymund Schmidt (ed.), *Die Philosophie der Gegenwart in Selbstdarstellungen* II, pp. 121-164.

Kerry, Benno.
"Über Anschauung und ihre psychische Verarbeitung", in *Vierteljahrsschrift für wissenschaftliche Philosophie* 9 (1885): 433-493; (1886) 10, 419-467; 11 (1887): 53-116, 249-307; 13 (1889): 71-124, 392-419; 14 (1890): 317-353; 15 (1891): 127-167.

"Über G. Cantor's Mannigfaltigkeitsuntersuchungen", *Vierteljahrsschrift für wissenschaftliche Philosophie* 9 (1885): 191-232.

System einer Theorie der Grenzbegriffe. Ein Beitrag zur Erkenntnistheorie I.
Edited by G. Kohn. Leipzig and Vienna, 1890.

Marty, Anton.
Gesammelte Schriften. Edited by J. Eisenmeier, A. Kastil, and O. Kraus. Halle a.S.:
Max Niemeyer, 1916-20.

Kritik der Theorien über den Sprachursprung. Würzburg: J.M. Richter, 1875.

"Über das Verhältnis von Grammatik und Logik" in *Symbolae Pragenses.*
Vienna/Prague: Tempsky; Leipzig: G. Freytag, 1893.

"Über subjectlose Sätze und das Verhältnis der Grammatik zur Logik und
Psychologie", *Vierteljahrsschrift für wissenschaftliche Philosophie* 8 (1884): 56-
94, 161-192, 292-340; 18 (1894): 320-356, 421-471; 19 (1895): 19-87, 263-334.

Genetische Psychologie. Unpublished lecture notes, under signature Q 10 in
Husserl Archives, Louvain, 1889.

"Elemente der deskriptiven Psychologie. Zwei Auszüge aus Vorlesungen Anton
Martys", edited by Johann Christian Marek and Barry Smith, *Conceptus* 21 (1987):
49-66.

*Untersuchung zur Grundlegung der allgemeinen Grammatik und
Sprachphilosophie* I. Halle a.S.: Max Niemeyer, 1908.

Meinong, Alexius (ed.).
Untersuchung zur Gegenstandstheorie und Psychologie. Leipzig: Johann Johann
Ambrosius Barth, 1904.

Meinong, Alexius.
Gesamtausgabe. Edited by Rudolf Haller et al. Graz: Akademische Druck- und
Verlagsanstalt, 1968-78.

Hume-Studien I: Zur Geschichte und Kritik des modernen Nominalismus. Vienna:
Kaiserliche Akademie der Wissenschaften, 1877.

Hume-Studien II: Zur Relationstheorie. Vienna: Kaiserliche Akademie der Wissenschaften, 1882.

"Zur erkenntnistheoretischen Würdigung des Gedächtnisses", *Vierteljahrsschrift für wissenschaftliche Philosophie* 10 (1886): 7-33.

"Über Begriff und Eigenschaften der Empfindung", *Vierteljahrsschrift für wissenschaftliche Philosophie* 12 (1888): 324-354, 477-502; 13 (1889): 1-31.

"Zur Psychologie der Komplexionen und Relationen", *Zeitschrift für Psychologie und Physiologie der Sinnesorgane* 2 (1891): 245-264.

Beiträge zur Theorie der psychischen Analyse. Hamburg/Leipzig: Leopold Voss, 1894.

Psychologisch-ethische Untersuchungen zur Werth-Theorie. Graz: Leuscher & Lubensky, 1894.

"Über Gegenstände höherer Ordnung und deren Verhältnis zur inneren Wahrnehmung", *Zeitschrift für Psychologie und Physiologie der Sinnesorgane* 21 (1899): 181-271.

"Abstrahieren und Vergleichen", *Zeitschrift für Psychologie und Physiologie der Sinnesorgane* 24 (1900): 34-82.

Über Annahmen. Leipzig: Johann Ambrosius Barth, 1902.

"Über Gegenstandstheorie". In Alexius Meinong (ed.), *Untersuchung zur Gegenstandstheorie und Psychologie*, pp. 1-50.

"Über die Erfahrungsgrundlagen unseres Wissens", *Abhandlungen zur Didaktik und Philosophie der Naturwissenschaft* 1 (1906): 381-491.

Über die Stellung der Gegenstandstheorie im System der Wissenschaften. Leipzig: R. Voigtländer, 1907.

Philosophenbriefe. Aus der wissenschaftlichen Korrespondenz von Alexius Meinong. Edited by Rudolf Kindinger. Graz: Akademische Druck- und Verlagsanstalt, 1965.

Stumpf, Carl.
Über den psychologischen Ursprung der Raumvorstellung. Leipzig: Hirzel, 1873.

Tonpsychologie. Leipzig: Hirzel, 1883/90.

Psychologie. Unpublished lecture notes (1886/87): under signature Q 11 in Husserl Archives, Louvain.

Psychologie. Diktate vom Winter 1886/87. Unpublished syllabus for psychology: under signature Q 12 in Husserl Archives, Louvain.

Logik. Diktate vom Sommer 1888. Unpublished syllabus for logic: under signature Q 13 in Husserl Archives, Louvain.

Erscheinungen und psychische Funktionen. Berlin: Königliche preußische Akademie der Wissenschaften. 1907.

Zur Einteilung der Wissenschaften. Berlin: Königliche preussische Akademie der Wissenschaften, 1907.

"Zum Gedächtnis Lotzes", *Kantstudien* 22 (1918): 1-26.

"Erinnerungen an Franz Brentano", in Oskar Kraus (ed.), *Franz Brentano*, pp. 87-189.

"Selbstdarstellung", in Schmidt (ed.), *Die Philosophie der Gegenwart in Selbstdarstellungen* V, pp. 205-265.

Erkenntnislehre. Leipzig: Johann Ambrosius Barth, 1939/40.

Twardowski, Kasimir.
Idee und Perzeption. Eine erkenntnistheoretische Untersuchung aus Descartes. Vienna: Konegen, 1892.

Zur Lehre vom Inhalt und Gegenstand der Vorstellungen. Eine psychologische Studie. Vienna: Alfred Hölder, 1894.

Utitz, E.
"Franz Brentano", *Kantstudien* 22 (1918): 217-242.

III. ADDITIONAL RELEVANT LITERATURE

Albertazzi, Liliana et al.
The School of Franz Brentano. Dordrecht: Kluwer, 1996.

Aristotle.
The Complete Works of Aristotle: The Revised Oxford Translation. Edited by Barnes. Princeton, N.J.: Princeton University, 1985.

Bar-Hillel, Y.
"Husserl's Conception of a Purely Logical Grammar", in J.N. Mohanty (ed.), *Readings on Husserl's Logical Investigations*, pp. 128-136.

Baumgartner, Wilhelm.
"Mills und Brentanos Methode der beschreibenden Analyse", *Brentano Studien* 2 (1989): 63-78.

Bell, David.
Husserl. London and New York: Routledge & Kegan Paul, 1990.

"A Brentanian Philosophy of Arithmetic", *Brentano Studien* 2 (1989): 139-144.

Bergmann, Hugo.
Das philosophische Werk Bernard Bolzanos. Halle: Max Niemeyer, 1909.

Bernet, Rudolf.
"Husserls Begriff des Noema", in IJsseling (ed.), *Husserl-Ausgabe und Husserl-Forschung*, pp. 61-80.

Beyer, Christian.
Von Bolzano zu Husserl: Eine Untersuchung über den Ursprung der phänomenologischen Bedeutungslehre. Dordrecht, Kluwer, 1996.

Biemel, Walter.
"Die entscheidenden Phasen der Entfaltung von Husserls Philosophie", *Zeitschrift für philosophische Forschung* 13 (1959): 187-213.

Brück, Maria.
Über das Verhältnis Edmund Husserls zu Franz Brentano, vornehmlich mit Rücksicht auf Brentanos Psychologie. Würzburg: Triltsch, 1933.

Cantor, Georg.
Grundlagen einer allgemeinen Mannigfaltigkeitslehre. Leipzig: B.G. Teubner, 1883

Carr, David.
Interpreting Husserl: Critical and Comparative Studies. Dordrecht: Martinus Nijhoff, 1987.

Cavallin, Jens.
Content and Object: Husserl, Twardowski and Psychologism. Dordrecht: Kluwer, 1997.

Coniglione, Francesco et al. (eds.).
Polish Scientific Philosophy: The Lvov-Warsaw School. Amsterdam: Rodopi, 1993.

Cornelius, Hans.
"Über Verschmelzung und Analyse", *Vierteljahrsschrift für wissenschaftliche Philosophie* 16 (1892): 404-446; 17 (1893): 30-75.

Dauben, Joseph Warren.
Georg Cantor: His Mathematics and Philosophy of the Infinite. Princeton, New Jersey: Princeton University, 1979.

Descartes, René.
"Meditations on First Philosophy", in John Cottingham et al. (trans.), *The Philosophical Writings of Descartes*. Cambridge: Cambridge University, 1984.

Dreyfus, Hubert L. and Hall, Harrison (ed.).
Husserl, Intentionality, and Cognitive Science. Cambridge, Massachussetts: MIT, 1982.

Dummett, Michael.
Frege: Philosophy of Mathematics. London: Duckworth, 1991.

Ursprünge der analytischen Philosophie. Frankfurt: Suhrkamp, 1988.

Eaton, H.O.
The Austrian Philosophy of Value. Norman: University of Oklahoma, 1930.

Eisler, Rudolf.
Philosophen-Lexikon. Leben, Werke und Lehren der Denker. Berlin: Ernst Siegfried Mittler und Sohn, 1912.

Fabian, Reinhard (ed.).
Christian von Ehrenfels: Leben und Werk. Amsterdam: Rodopi, 1986.

Fabian, Reinhard.
"Leben und Wirken von Christian v. Ehrenfels. Ein Beitrag zur intellektuellen Biographie", in Fabian (ed.), *Christian von Ehrenfels*, pp. 1-64.

Frege, Gottlob.
Die Grundlagen der Arithmetik. Eine logisch-mathematische Untersuchung über den Begriff der Zahl. Breslau: Wilhelm Koebner, 1884.

"Über Begriff und Gegenstand", *Vierteljahrsschrift für wissenschaftliche Philosophie* 16 (1892): 192-205.

Findlay, J.N.
"Meinong the Phenomenologist", *Revue Internationale de la Philosophie* 27 (1973): 161-177.

Grossmann, Reinhardt.
Meinong. London: Routledge, 1974.

Haaparanta, Leila (ed.).
Mind, Meaning and Mathematics: Philosophical Views of Husserl and Frege. Dordrecht: Kluwer, 1994.

Haller, Rudolf (ed.).
Jenseits von Sein und Nichtsein. Graz: Akademische Druck-und Verlagsanstalt, 1972.

Haller, Rudolf.
"Franz Brentano, ein Philosoph des Empirismus", *Brentano Studien* 1 (1988): 19-30.

Heidegger, Martin.
Sein und Zeit. Tübingen: Max Niemeyer, 1986[16].

Heinrich, Erich.
Untersuchung zur Lehre vom Begriff. Göttingen: Kaestner, 1910.

Herbart, Johann Friedrich.
Sämtliche Werke. In chronologischer Reihenfolge V-VIII. Edited by Karl Kehrbach. Langesalza: Hermann Beyer & Söhne, 1890/92-93.

Lehrbuch zur Einleitung in die Philosophie. Edited by Wolfhart Henckmann. Hamburg: Felix Meiner, 1993.

Heymans, Gerardus.
Die Gesetze und Elemente des wissenschaftlichen Denkens. Leipzig: Johan Ambrosius Barth, 1905[2].

Hintikka, Jaako.
"Meinong in a Long Perspective", *Grazer Philosophische Studien* 50 (1995): 29-46.

Holenstein, Elmar.
Phänomenologie der Assoziation. Zu Struktur und Funktion eines Grundprinzips der passiven Genesis bei E. Husserl. The Hague: Martinus Nijhoff, 1972.

Hume, David.
A Treatise of Human Nature: Being an Attempt to introduce the experimental Method of Reasoning into Moral Subjects. Edited by L.A. Selby-Bigge. Second edition with text revised and varient readings by P.H. Nidditch. Oxford: Clarendon, 1978.

Enquiries concerning Human Understanding and concerning the Principles of Morals. Edited by L.A. Selby-Bigge. Third edition with text revised and notes by P.H. Nidditch. Oxford: Clarendon, 1975.

IJsseling, Samuel (ed.).
Husserl-Ausgabe und Husserl-Forschung. Dordrecht: Kluwer, 1990.

Jacquette, Dale.
"The Origins of Gegenstandstheorie: Immanent and Transcendent Objects in Brentano, Twardowski, and Meinong", *Brentano-Studien* 3 (1990/91): 177-202.

"Alexius Meinong (1853-1920)", in Liliana Albertazzi et al. (eds.), *The School of Franz Brentano*.

James, William.
Principles of Psychology. New York: Holt, 1890.

Kant Immanuel.
Kritik der reinen Vernunft. Edited by Raymund Schmidt. Hamburg: Felix Meiner, 1956.

Prolegomena zu einer jeden künftigen Metaphysik. Edited by Karl Vorländer. Leipzig: Felix Meiner, 1920.

Kritik der Urteilskraft. Edited by Wilhelm Weischedel. Frankfurt: Suhrkamp, 1978.

Kritik der praktischen Vernunft and *Grundlegung zur Metaphysik der Sitten*. Edited by Wilhelm Weischedel. Frankfurt: Suhrkamp, 1977.

Kastil, Alfred.
Die Philosophie Franz Brentanos. Eine Einführung in seine Lehre. Bern: A. Franke, 1951

Kern, Iso.
Husserl und Kant. Eine Untersuchung über Husserls Verhältnis zu Kant und zum Neukantianismus. The Hague: Martinus Nijhoff, 1964.

Kraus, Oskar.
"Martys Leben und Werke. Eine Skizze", in Anton Marty, *Gesammelte Schriften* I (1918). See above under Marty.

Franz Brentano. Zur Kenntnis seines Lebens und seiner Lehre. Munich: Oskar Beck, 1919.

"Zur Phänomenognosie des Zeitbewußtseins. Aus dem Briefwechsels Franz Brentanos mit Anton Marty, nebst einem Vorlesungsbruchstück über Brentanos Zeitlehre aus dem Jahre 1895, nebst Einleitung und Anmerkungen veröffentlicht", *Archiv für die gesamte Psychologie* 75 (1930): 1-22.

Lange, Friedrich Albert.
Geschichte des Materialismus. Iserlohn/Leipzig: Baedeker, 1866.

Lindenfeld, David F.
The Transformation of Positivism: Alexius Meinong and European Thought, 1880-1920. Berkeley/Los Angeles/London: University of California, 1980.

Locke, John.
An Essay concerning Human Understanding. Edited by Peter H. Nidditch. Oxford: Clarendon, 1975.

Lotze, Hermann.
Logik (System der Philosophie I). Edited by Georg Misch. Leipzig: Felix Meiner, 1912.

Mach, Ernst.
Beiträge zur Analyse der Empfindungen. Jena: Gustav Fischer, 1886.

Erkenntnis und Irrtum. Leipzig: Johann Ambrosius Barth, 1905.

Marek, Johannes.
"Psychognosie - Geognosie: Apriorisches und Emprisches in der deskriptiven Psychologie Brentanos", *Brentano-Studien* 2 (1989): 53-61.

Mauthner, Fritz.
"Selbstdarstellung", in Schmidt (ed.), *Die Philosophie der Gegenwart in*

Selbstdarstellung III, pp. 121-144.

Melle, Ullrich.
"Objektivierende und nicht-objektivierende Akte", in Samuel IJsseling (ed.), *Husserl-Ausgabe und Husserl-Forschung*, pp. 35-49.

Mill, John Stuart.
A System of Logic, Rationative and Inductive. Being a Connected view of the Principles of Evidence and the Methods of Scientific Investigation. London: Longman, Green & Co, 1959. (First published in 1843.)

An Examination of Sir William Hamilton's Philosophy and of the Principal Philosophical Questions discussed in his Writings. London, 1878.[5]

Mohanty, J.N.
"The Development of Husserl's Thought", in Smith and Smith (eds.), *The Cambridge Campanion to Husserl*, pp. 45-77.

Mohanty, J.N. (ed.).
Readings on Edmund Husserl's Logical Investigations. The Hague: Martin Nijhoff, 1977.

Moran, Dermot.
"Brentano's Thesis", *Proceedings of the Aristotelian Society*. Supplementary Volume (1996): 1-27.

Morscher, Edgar.
Das logische An-sich bei Bernard Bolzano. Salzburg: Anton Pustet, 1973.

Mulligan, Kevin (ed.)
Mind, Meaning and Metaphysics: The Philosophy and Theory of Language of Anton Marty. Dordrecht: Martinus Nijhoff, 1990.

Mulligan Kevin.
"Perception", in Smith and Smith (eds.), *The Cambridge Campanion to Husserl*, pp. 168-238.

Mulligan, Kevin, Smith, Barry and Simons, Peter.

"Truth-Makers", *Philosophy and Phenomenological Research* 44 (1984): 287-321.

Münch, Dieter.
Intention und Zeichen. Untersuchung zu Franz Brentano und zu Edmund Husserls Frühwerk. Frankfurt am Main: Suhrkamp, 1993.

Noack, Ludwig.
Philosophie-geschichtliches Lexikon. Historisch-biographisches Handwörterbuch zur Geschichte der Philosophie. Leipzig: Erich Koschny, 1879.

Novak, J. (ed.).
On Masaryk. Amsterdam: Rodopi, 1988.

Peckhaus, Volker.
"Benno Kerry. Beiträge zu seiner Biographie", *History and Philosophy of Logic* 15 (1994): 1-8.

Pester, Reinhardt.
Hermann Lotze - Wege seines Denkens und Forschens. Ein Kapitel deutscher Philosophie- und Wissenschaftsgeschichte im 19. Jahrhundert. Würzburg: Königshausen & Neumann, 1997.

Philipse, Hermann.
"The Concept of Intentionality: Husserl's Development from the Brentano Period to the *Logical Investigations*", *Philosophy Research Archives* 12 (1986/87): 293-328.

Picardi, Eva.
"Kerry und Frege über Begriff und Gegenstand", *History and Philosophy of Logic* 15 (1994): 9-32.

Quine, Willard van Orman.
From a Logical Point of View: Logico-Philosophical Essays. New York: Harper & Row, 1961.

Reinach, Adolf.
Sämtliche Werke. Textkritische Ausgabe in 2 Bänden. Edited by Karl Schuhmann and Barry Smith. Munich: Philosophia, 1989.

Rollinger, R.D.
"Husserl and Brentano on Imagination", *Archiv für Geschichte der Philosophie* 75 (1993): 195-210.

Meinong and Husserl on Abstraction and Universals: From Hume Studies I to Logical Investigations II. Amsterdam: Rodopi, 1993.

"Meinong on Perception: Two Questions concerning Propositional Seeing", *Grazer Philosophische Studien* 50 (1995): 445-455.

"Meinong and Husserl on Assumptions", *Axiomathes* 7 (1996): 89-102.

Santambrogio, Marco.
"Meinongian Theories of Generality", *Nous* 24 (1990): 550-567.

Schapp, W.
Beiträge zur Phänomenologie der Wahrnehmung. Göttingen: Kaestner, 1910;[1] Erlangen: Philosophische Akademie, 1925.[2]

Scharwath, Alfred G.
Tradition, Aufbau und Fortbildung der Tugendlehre Franz Brentanos innerhalb seines gesamten philosophischen Schaffens. Meisenheim am Glan: Anton Hain, 1967.

Schermann, Hans.
Meinong und Husserl. Eine vergleichende Studie. Unpublished Ph.D. dissertation. University of Louvain, 1970.

"Husserls II. logische Untersuchung und Meinongs Hume-Studien I", in Rudolf Haller (ed.), *Jenseits von Sein und Nichtsein*.

Schlick, Moritz.
Philosophische Logik. Edited by Bernd Philippi. Frankfurt a.M.: Suhrkamp, 1986.

Schmidt, Raymund (ed.).
Die Philosophie der Gegenwart in Selbstdarstellungen I-V Leipzig: Felix Meiner, 1921-24.

Schopenhauer, Arthur.
Über die vierfache Wurzel des Satzes vom zureichenden Grunde. Zürich: Diogenes, 1977.

Schuhmann, Karl.
Husserl-Chronik. Denk- und Lebensweg Edmund Husserls. The Hague: Martinus Nijhoff, 1977.

"Husserl and Masaryk", in J. Novak (ed.), *On Masaryk*, pp. 129-156.

"Malvine Husserls 'Skizze eines Lebensbildes von E. Husserl'", *Husserl Studies* 5 (1988): 105-126.

"Husserl and Twardowski", in Francesco Coniglione et al. (eds.): *Polish Scientific Philosophy: The Lvov-Warsaw School*, pp. 41-58.

"Carl Stumpf (1848-1936)" in L. Albertazzi et al. (eds.), *The School of Franz Brentano.*

"Intentionalität und intentionaler Gegenstand beim frühen Husserl", *Phänomenologische Forschungen* 24/25 (1991): 46-75.

"Der Wertbegriff beim frühen Meinong", *Grazer Philosophische Studien* 50 (1995): 521-535.

Searle, John.
Intentionality: An Essay in the Philosophy of Mind. Cambridge: Cambridge University, 1983.

Sigwart, Christian.
Logik I & II. Tübingen: J.C.B. Mohr (Paul Siebeck), 1873/78[1], 1889/93[2], 1904.[3]

Simons, Peter.
"Mathematik als Wissenschaft der Gestalten", in Reinhard Fabian (ed.), *Christian von Ehrenfels*, pp. 112-135.

"Meinong's Theory of Sense and Reference", *Grazer Philosophische Studien* 50 (1995): 171-186.

Smith, Barry.
"Ontologische Aspekte der Husserlschen Phänomenologie", *Husserl Studies* 3 (1986): 115-130.

Austrian Philosophy: The Legacy of Franz Brentano. Chicago: Open Court, 1994.

"Husserl's Theory of Meaning and Reference", in L. Haaparanta (ed.), *Mind, Meaning and Mathematics*.

Smith, Barry (ed.).
Parts and Moments: Studies in Logic and Formal Ontology. Munich: Philosophia, 1988.

Smith, Barry and Smith, D.W. (eds.).
The Cambridge Companion to Husserl. Cambridge: Cambridge University, 1995.

Spiegelberg, Herbert.
The Phenomenological Movement. Dordrecht: Kluwer, 1982.

The Context of the Phenomenological Movement. The Hague: Martinus Nijhoff, 1981.

Srzednicki, Jan.
Franz Brentano's Analysis of Truth. The Hague: Martinus Nijhoff, 1965.

Stock, M. and Stock, W.G.
Psychologie und Philosophie der Grazer Schule. Amsterdam: Rodopi, 1992.

Willard, Dallas.
Logic and the Objectivity of Knowledge: A Study in Husserl's Early Philosophy. Athens, Ohio: Ohio University, 1984.

Wittgenstein, Ludwig.
Werkausgabe in 8 Bänden. Edited by Joachim Schulte. Frankfurt a.M.: Suhrkamp, 1984.

Wolenski, Jan.
Logic and Philosophy in the Lvov-Warsaw School. Dordrecht: Reidel, 1989.

Wundt, Wilhelm.
Physiologische Psychologie. Leipzig: Wilhelm Engelmann, 1874.

Ziegenfuss, Werner and Jung, Gertrud.
Philosophen-Lexikon. Handwörterbuch der Philosophie nach Personen. Berlin: Walter de Gruyter, 1950.

Zimmermann, Robert.
Philosophische Propädeutik. Vienna: Braumüller, 1853,[1] 1860,[2] 1867[3].

Zindler, Konrad.
Beiträge zur Theorie der mathematischen Erkenntnis. Vienna: Kaiserliche Akademie der Wissenschaften, 1889.

INDEX OF NAMES

Note - Husserl and other philosophers whose names appear in chapter headings are not listed in this index for obvious reasons. Nor is there any indication of occurrences of names in either the preface or the bibliography.

Albertazzi, Liliana 85, 158
Aquinas, Thomas 84
Aristotle 5, 13, 14, 26, 72, 115, 118, 125, 127, 156, 247, 300, 333
Augustine 30
Baumgartner, Wilhelm 22
Bell, David 1
Bergmann, Hugo 19, 20, 71, 72, 75, 90, 210
Bernet, Rudolf 115
Beyer, Christian 95
Biemel, Walter 9
Blaustein, Leopold 139
Böck, Ernst 21
Brentano, Christian 13
Brentano, Lujo 13
Brück, Maria 3
Cantor, Georg 86, 125, 132 f.
Cavallin, Jens 3
Cornelius, Hans 169 f., 178, 212
Dauben, Joseph Warren 125
Daubert, Johannes 20, 46, 147
Deetjen, Carl 210
Descartes, René 34, 35, 129, 139
Dummett, Michael 111, 127, 128
Ehrenfels, Christian von 2, 4, 5, 27, 108, 126, 156, 156, 178, 242, 244, 249

Fabian, Reinhard 4, 155, 156, 178
Fechner, Gustav 5, 293
Fichte, J.G. 80, 129, 209
Findlay, J.N. 3
Fink, Eugen 9, 81, 87
Fischer, Alois 187
Frege, Gottlob 5, 44, 134, 136
Galileo 19
Grossmann, Reinhardt 194
Haller, Rudolf 3, 35, 127, 155, 157, 191
Hegel, G.W.F. 14, 36, 38, 129
Heidegger, Martin 8, 48, 211
Heinrich, E. 187
Helmholtz, Ludwig von 36
Herbart, Johannes 28, 95, 129, 172, 234, 287, 295
Heymans, Gerardus 46
Hillebrand, Franz 22
Hintikka, Jaako 164
Höfler, Aois 2, 4, 73, 126 f., 140, 144, 156, 157, 202
Holenstein, Elmar 3
Hume, David 5, 17, 23, 39, 48, 115, 120, 129, 156, 300
Ingarden, Roman 139
Jacquette, Dale 158
James, William 30, 31, 88, 122, 211 ff.

Kant, Immanuel 14, 29, 36, 39, 40, 66, 70 ff., 80, 114, 129, 177, 209, 234, 300, 320, 324
Kastil, Alfred 13, 210
Katkov, Georg 21
Kern, Iso 14
Kraus, Oskar 4, 29, 38
Lange, Friedrich Albert 23
Leibniz, Gottfried Wilhelm 70 ff., 129, 300, 324
Lindenfeld, David F. 157
Locke, John 115, 129, 300
Lotze, Rudolf Hermann 2, 9, 44, 81 f., 84, 86, 118, 207, 209
Mach, Ernst 150, 206 f.
Marek, Johannes 35
Masaryk, Thomas 2, 3, 15, 16, 87
Mauthner, Fritz 69
Mehmel, Gottlieb Ernst August 80 f.
Melle, Ullrich 63, 66
Mill, James 5, 171
Mill, John Stuart 5, 85, 115, 159, 171, 207, 212, 240, 331
Mohanty, J.N. 8
Morscher, Edgar 75
Müller, Johannes 300
Münch, Dieter 3
Natorp, Paul 20
Noack, Ludwig 80
Paulsen, Friedrich 15 f.
Peckhaus, Volker 125
Philipse, Herman 3
Picardi, Eva 127
Plato 84
Quine, Willard van Orman 43
Rollinger, Robin D. 3, 8, 81, 131, 144, 159

Runge, Carl 16
Ryle, Gilbert 59, 191
Santambrogio, Marco 144
Schapp, W. 120
Schelling, F.W.J. 126, 209
Schermann, Hans 3
Schlick, Moritz 46
Schmidkunz, Hans 22, 85
Schopenhauer, Arthur 162
Schuhmann, Karl 11, 70, 90, 139, 151
Searle, John 6
Sigwart, Christian 92, 129, 157, 228, 238
Simons, Peter 126, 191
Smith, Barry 1, 2, 90, 104, 108, 111, 139, 178, 222, 223
Spencer, Herbert 38
Spiegelberg, Herbert 1, 8
Steinschneider, Malvina 18
Strawson, P.F. 58
Trendelenburg, F.A. 13
Vogt, Theodor 16
Weber, E.H. 5
Weierstrass, Carl 15 f.
Willard, Dallas 3
Windelband, Wilhelm 34
Wittgenstein, Ludwig 58, 112, 128, 222
Wolenski, Jan 139
Wundt, Wilhelm 5, 245
Ziegenfuss, Werner 80
Zimmermann, Robert 16, 69-73, 139
Zindler, Konrad 159

Phaenomenologica

110. J. Patočka: *Le monde naturel et le mouvement de l'existence humaine.* 1988
ISBN 90-247-3577-7
111. K.-H. Lembeck: *Gegenstand Geschichte.* Geschichtswissenschaft in Husserls Phänomenologie. 1988 ISBN 90-247-3635-8
112. J.K. Cooper-Wiele: *The Totalizing Act.* Key to Husserl's Early Philosophy. 1989
ISBN 0-7923-0077-7
113. S. Valdinoci: *Le principe d'existence.* Un devenir psychiatrique de la phénoménologie. 1989 ISBN 0-7923-0125-0
114. D. Lohmar: *Phänomenologie der Mathematik.* 1989 ISBN 0-7923-0187-0
115. S. IJsseling (Hrsgb.): *Husserl-Ausgabe und Husserl-Forschung.* 1990
ISBN 0-7923-0372-5
116. R. Cobb-Stevens: *Husserl and Analytic Philosophy.* 1990 ISBN 0-7923-0467-5
117. R. Klockenbusch: *Husserl und Cohn.* Widerspruch, Reflexion und Telos in Phänomenologie und Dialektik. 1989 ISBN 0-7923-0515-9
118. S. Vaitkus: *How is Society Possible?* Intersubjectivity and the Fiduciary Attitude as Problems of the Social Group in Mead, Gurwitsch, and Schutz. 1991
ISBN 0-7923-0820-4
119. C. Macann: *Presence and Coincidence.* The Transformation of Transcendental into Ontological Phenomenology. 1991 ISBN 0-7923-0923-5
120. G. Shpet: *Appearance and Sense.* Phenomenology as the Fundamental Science and Its Problems. Translated from Russian by Th. Nemeth. 1991 ISBN 0-7923-1098-5
121. B. Stevens: *L'apprentissage des signes.* Lecture de Paul Ricœur. 1991
ISBN 0-7923-1244-9
122. G. Soffer: *Husserl and the Question of Relativism.* 1991 ISBN 0-7923-1291-0
123. G. Römpp: *Husserls Phänomenologie der Intersubjektivität.* Und Ihre Bedeutung für eine Theorie intersubjektiver Objektivität und die Konzeption einer phänomenologischen Philosophie. 1991 ISBN 0-7923-1361-5
124. S. Strasser: *Welt im Widerspruch.* Gedanken zu einer Phänomenologie als ethischer Fundamentalphilosophie. 1991 ISBN Hb: 0-7923-1404-2; Pb: 0-7923-1551-0
125. R. P. Buckley: *Husserl, Heidegger and the Crisis of Philosophical Responsibility.* 1992 ISBN 0-7923-1633-9
126. J. G. Hart: *The Person and the Common Life.* Studies in a Husserlian Social Ethics. 1992 ISBN 0-7923-1724-6
127. P. van Tongeren, P. Sars, C. Bremmers and K. Boey (eds.): *Eros and Eris.* Contributions to a Hermeneutical Phenomenology. Liber Amicorum for Adriaan Peperzak. 1992 ISBN 0-7923-1917-6
128. Nam-In Lee: *Edmund Husserls Phänomenologie der Instinkte.* 1993
ISBN 0-7923-2041-7
129. P. Burke and J. Van der Veken (eds.): *Merleau-Ponty in Contemporary Perspective.* 1993 ISBN 0-7923-2142-1
130. G. Haefliger: *Über Existenz: Die Ontologie Roman Ingardens.* 1994
ISBN 0-7923-2227-4
131. J. Lampert: *Synthesis and Backward Reference in Husserl's Logical Investigations.* 1995 ISBN 0-7923-3105-2
132. J.M. DuBois: *Judgment and Sachverhalt.* An Introduction to Adolf Reinach's Phenomenological Realism. 1995 ISBN 0-7923-3519-8

Phaenomenologica

133. B.E. Babich (ed.): *From Phenomenology to Thought, Errancy, and Desire*. Essays in Honor of William J. Richardson, S.J. 1995   ISBN 0-7923-3567-8
134. M. Dupuis: *Pronoms et visages. Lecture d'Emmanuel Levinas.* 1996
    ISBN 0-7923-3655-0; Pb 0-7923-3994-0
135. D. Zahavi: *Husserl und die transzendentale Intersubjektivität*. Eine Antwort auf die sprachpragmatische Kritik. 1996   ISBN 0-7923-3713-1
136. A. Schutz: *Collected Papers, IV*. Edited with preface and notes by H. Wagner and G. Psathas, in collaboration with F. Kersten. 1996   ISBN 0-7923-3760-3
137. P. Kontos: *D'une phénoménologie de la perception chez Heidegger.* 1996
    ISBN 0-7923-3776-X
138. F. Kuster: *Wege der Verantwortung*. Husserls Phänomenologie als Gang durch die Faktizität. 1996   ISBN 0-7923-3916-9
139. C. Beyer: *Von Bolzano zu Husserl*. Eine Untersuchung über den Ursprung der phänomenologischen Bedeutungslehre. 1996   ISBN 0-7923-4050-7
140. J. Dodd: *Idealism and Corporeity*. An Essay on the Problem of the Body in Husserl's Phenomenology. 1997   ISBN 0-7923-4400-6
141. E. Kelly: *Structure and Diversity*. Studies in the Phenomenological Philosophy of Max Scheler. 1997   ISBN 0-7923-4492-8
142. J. Cavallin: *Content and Object*. Husserl, Twardowski and Psychologism. 1997
    ISBN 0-7923-4734-X
143. H.P. Steeves: *Founding Community*. A Phenomenological-Ethical Inquiry. 1997
    ISBN 0-7923-4798-6
144. M. Sawicki: *Body, Text, and Science*. The Literacy of Investigative Practices and the Phenomenology of Edith Stein. 1997   ISBN 0-7923-4759-5
145. O.K. Wiegand: *Interpretationen der Modallogik*. Ein Beitrag zur phänomenologischen Wissenschaftstheorie. 1998   ISBN 0-7923-4809-5
146. P. Marrati-Guénoun: *La genèse et la trace*. Derrida lecteur de Husserl et Heidegger. 1998   ISBN 0-7923-4969-5
147. D. Lohmar: *Erfahrung und kategoriales Denken*. 1998   ISBN 0-7923-5117-7
148. N. Depraz and D. Zahavi (eds.): *Alterity and Facticity*. New Perspectives on Husserl. 1998   ISBN 0-7923-5187-8
149. E. Øverenget: *Seeing the Self*. Heidegger on Subjectivity. 1998   ISBN 0-7923-5219-X

Previous volumes are still available

Further information about *Phenomenology* publications are available on request

Kluwer Academic Publishers – Dordrecht / Boston / London